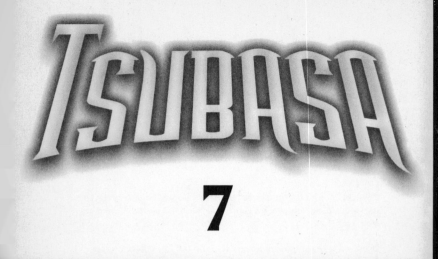

7

CLAMP

TRANSLATED AND ADAPTED BY
William Flanagan

LETTERED BY
Dana Hayward

BALLANTINE BOOKS · NEW YORK

Tsubasa, Volume 7 is a work of fiction. Names, characters, places, and incidents are the products of the author's imagination or are used fictitiously. Any resemblance to actual events, locales, or persons, living or dead, is entirely coincidental.

2005 Del Rey® Trade Paperback Edition

Published in the United States by Del Rey Books, an imprint of The Random House Publishing Group, a division of Random House, Inc., New York.

DEL REY is a registered trademark and the Del Rey colophon is a trademark of Random House, Inc.

First published in serialization and subsequently published in book form by Kodansha Ltd. Tokyo in 2004.

ISBN 0-345-47797-9

Printed in the United States of America

www.delreymanga.com

9 8 7 6 5

Lettered by Dana Hayward

Contents

Tsubasa crosses over with *xxxHOLiC*. Although it isn't necessary to read *xxxHOLiC* to understand the events in *Tsubasa*, you'll get to see the same events from different perspectives if you read both!

Honorifics Explained

Throughout the Del Rey Manga books, you will find Japanese honorifics left intact in the translations. For those not familiar with how the Japanese use honorifics and, more important, how they differ from American honorifics, we present this brief overview.

Politeness has always been a critical facet of Japanese culture. Ever since the feudal era, when Japan was a highly stratified society, use of honorifics — which can be defined as polite speech that indicates relationship or status — has played an essential role in the Japanese language. When addressing someone in Japanese, an honorific usually takes the form of a suffix attached to one's name (example: "Asuna-san"), or as a title at the end of one's name or in place of the name itself (example: "Negi-sensei," or simply "Sensei!").

Honorifics can be expressions of respect or endearment. In the context of manga and anime, honorifics give insight into the nature of the relationship between characters. Many translations into English leave out these important honorifics, and therefore distort the "feel" of the original Japanese. Because Japanese honorifics contain nuances that English honorifics lack, it is our policy at Del Rey not to translate them. Here, instead, is a guide to some of the honorifics you may encounter in Del Rey Manga.

-san: This is the most common honorific, and is equivalent to Mr., Miss, Ms., Mrs., etc. It is the all-purpose honorific and can be used in any situation where politeness is required.

-sama: This is one level higher than "-san." It is used to confer great respect.

-dono: This comes from the word "tono," which means "lord." It is an even higher level than "-sama" and confers utmost respect.

-kun: This suffix is used at the end of boys' names to express familiarity or endearment. It is also sometimes used by men among friends, or when addressing someone younger or of a lower station.

-chan: This is used to express endearment, mostly toward girls. It is also used for little boys, pets, and even among lovers. It gives a sense of childish cuteness.

Bozu: This is an informal way to refer to a boy, similar to the English term "kid" or "squirt."

Sempai/senpai: This title suggests that the addressee is one's senior in a group or organization. It is most often used in a school setting, where underclassmen refer to their upperclassmen as "sempai." It can also be used in the workplace, such as when a newer employee addresses an employee who has seniority in the company.

Kohai: This is the opposite of "sempai," and is used toward underclassmen in school or newcomers in the workplace. It connotes that the addressee is of lower station.

Sensei: Literally meaning "one who has come before," this title is used for teachers, doctors, or masters of any profession or art.

-[blank]: Usually forgotten in these lists, but perhaps the most significant difference between Japanese and English. The lack of honorific means that the speaker has permission to address the person in a very intimate way. Usually, only family, spouses, or very close friends have this kind of permission. Known as *yobisute*, it can be gratifying when someone who has earned the intimacy starts to call one by one's name without an honorific. But when that intimacy hasn't been earned, it can also be very insulting.

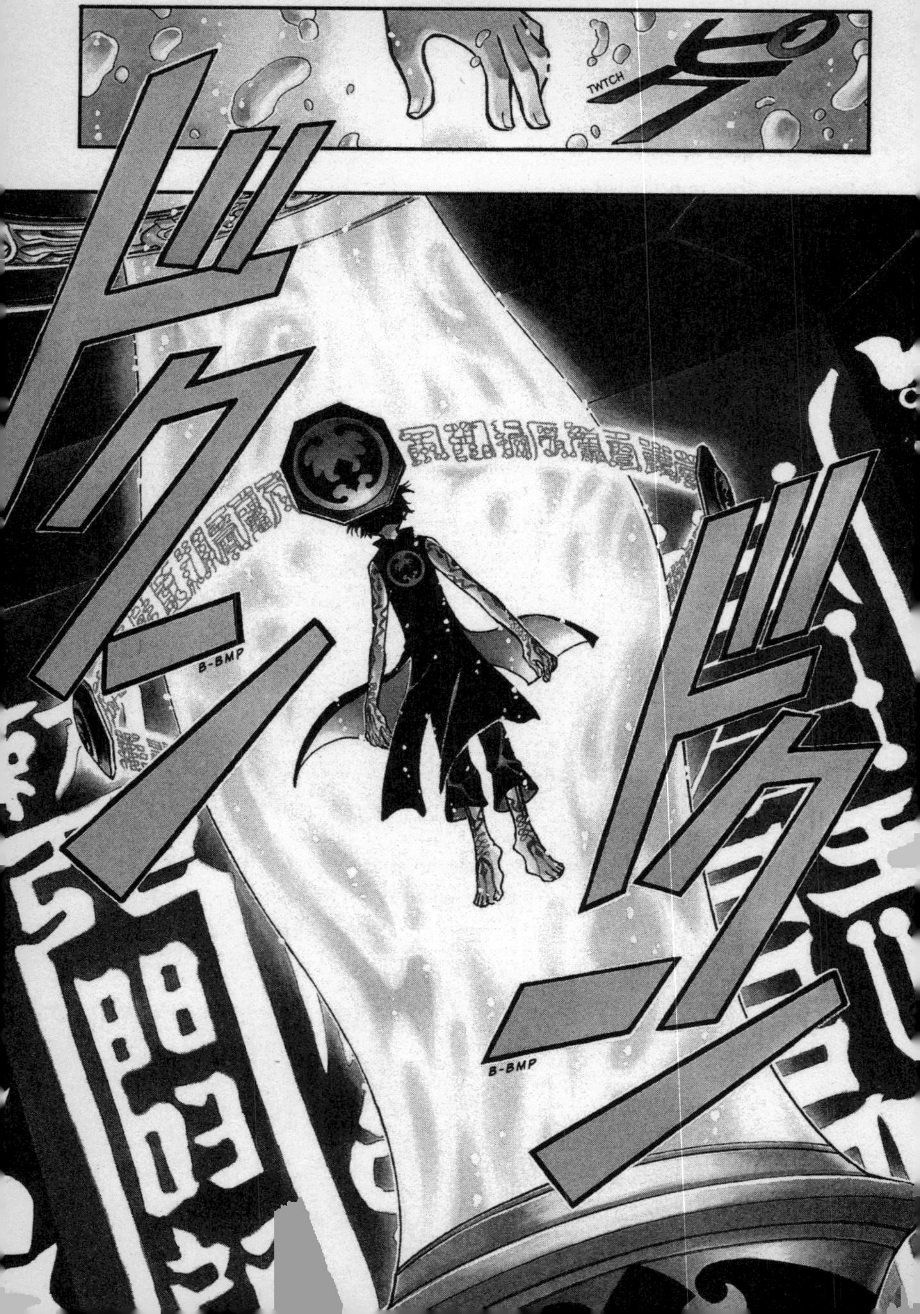
TWITCH
B-BMP
B-BMP

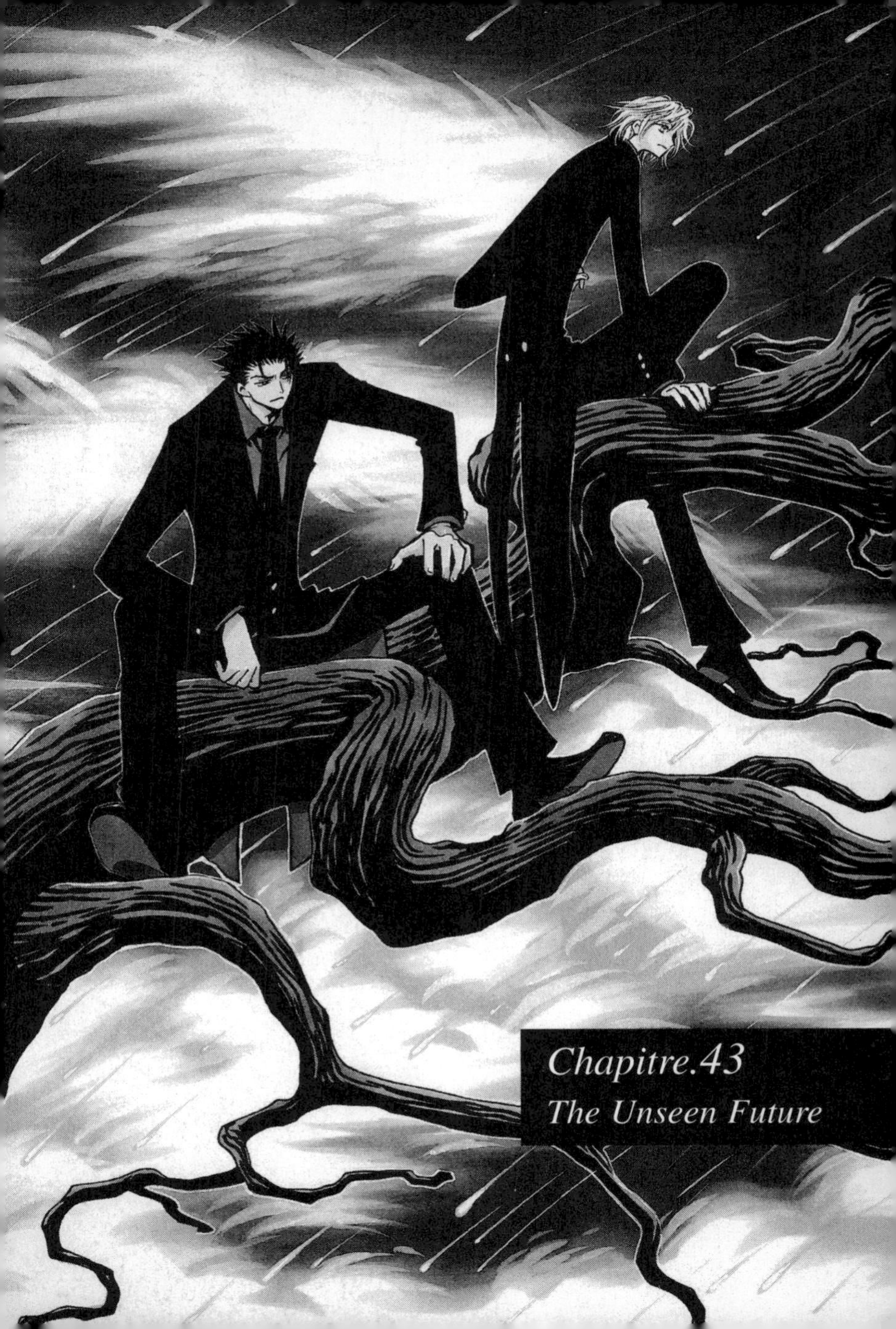
Chapitre.43
The Unseen Future

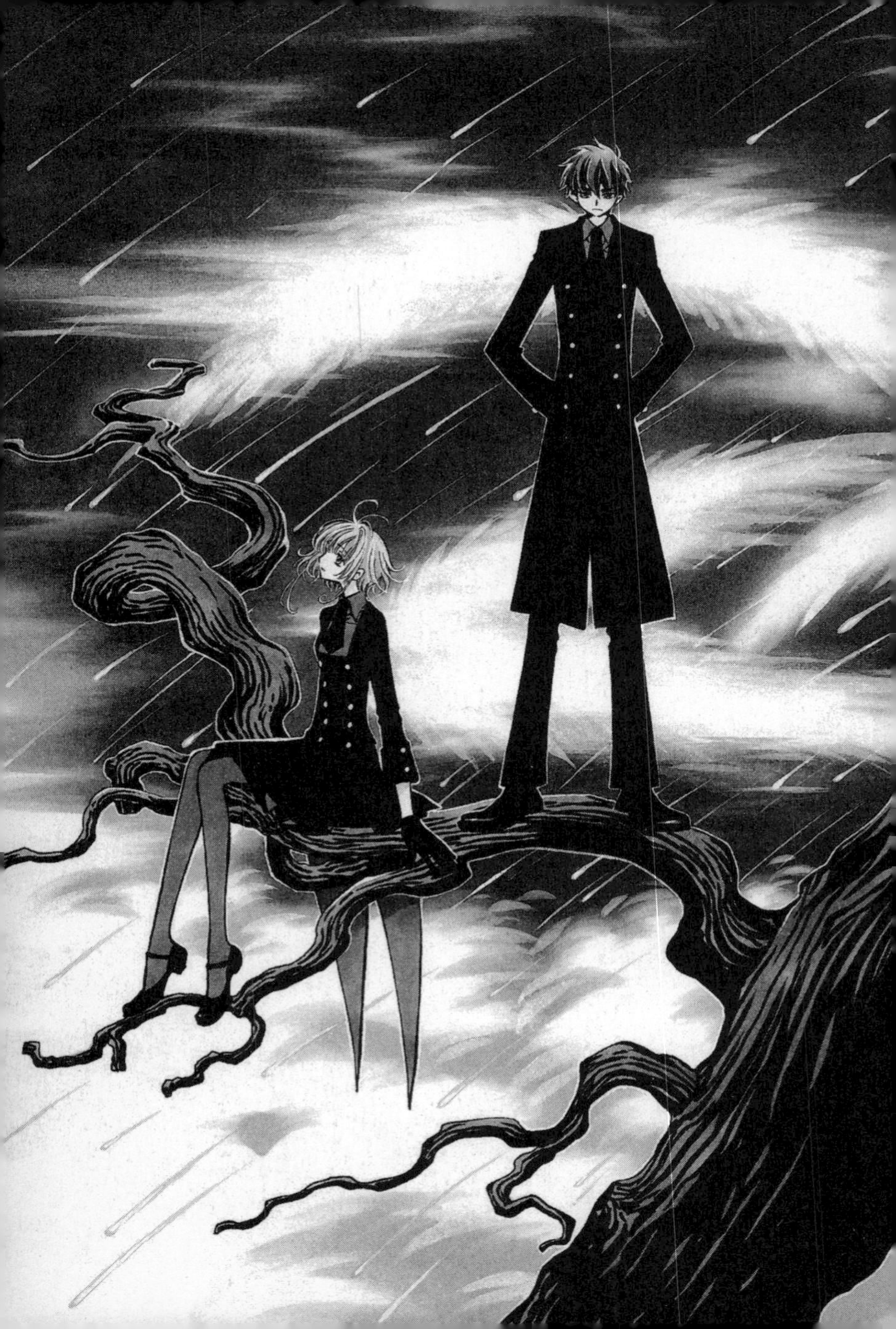

ツバサ

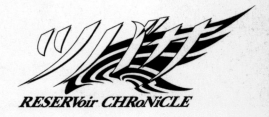

RESERVoir CHRoNiCLE

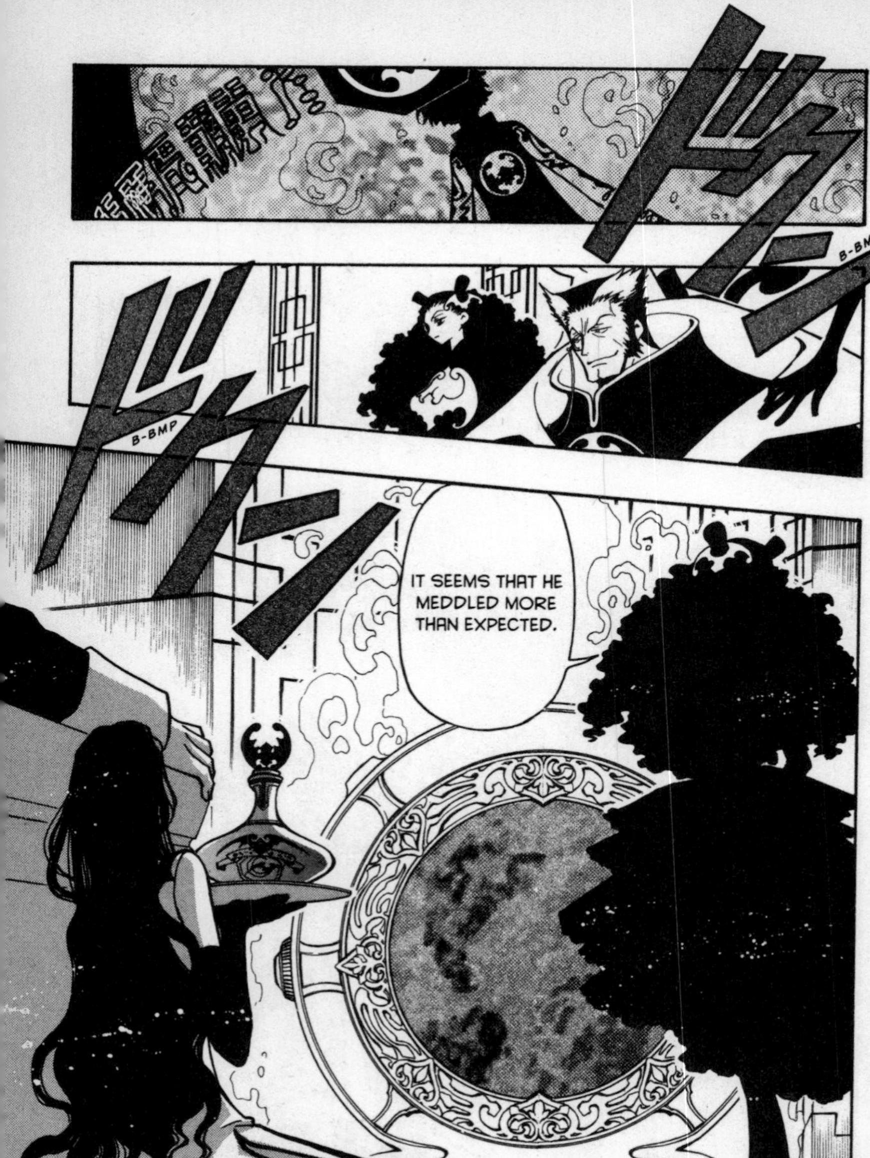
B-BMP
B-BMP
IT SEEMS THAT HE MEDDLED MORE THAN EXPECTED.

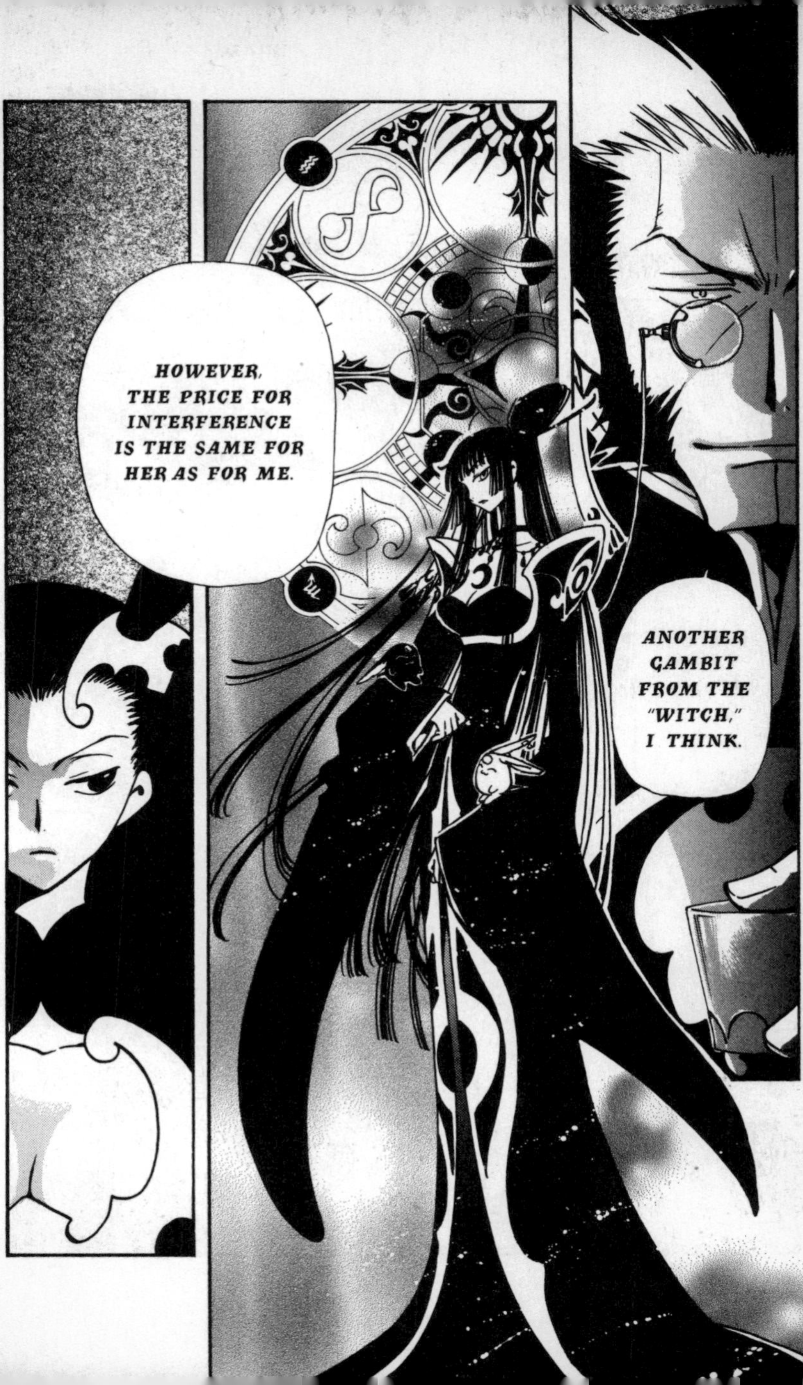
ANOTHER GAMBIT FROM THE "WITCH," I THINK.
HOWEVER, THE PRICE FOR INTERFERENCE IS THE SAME FOR HER AS FOR ME.

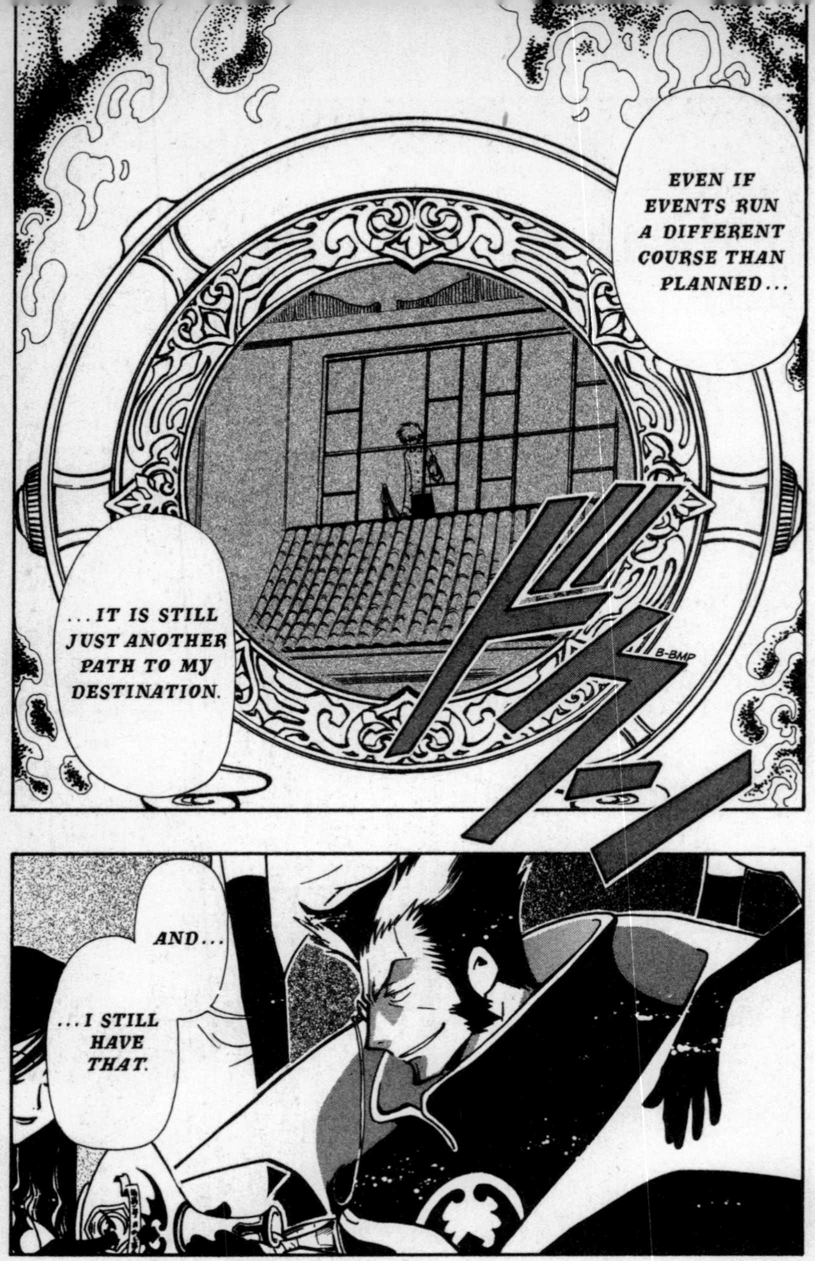
EVEN IF EVENTS RUN A DIFFERENT COURSE THAN PLANNED...
...IT IS STILL JUST ANOTHER PATH TO MY DESTINATION.
B-BMP
AND...
...I STILL HAVE THAT.

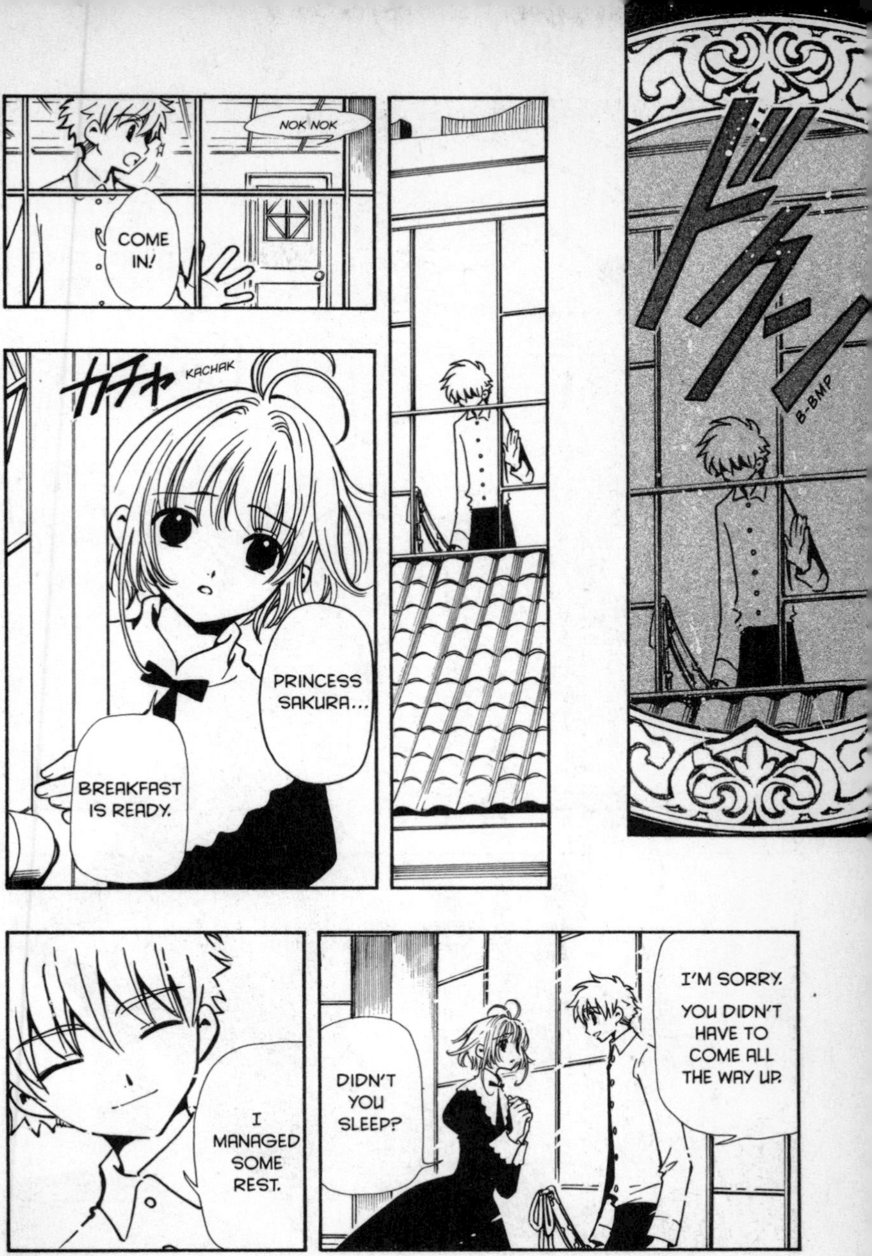
ドクン
B-BMP
NOK NOK
COME IN!
カチャ
KACHAK
PRINCESS SAKURA...
BREAKFAST IS READY.
I'M SORRY.
YOU DIDN'T HAVE TO COME ALL THE WAY UP.
DIDN'T YOU SLEEP?
I MANAGED SOME REST.

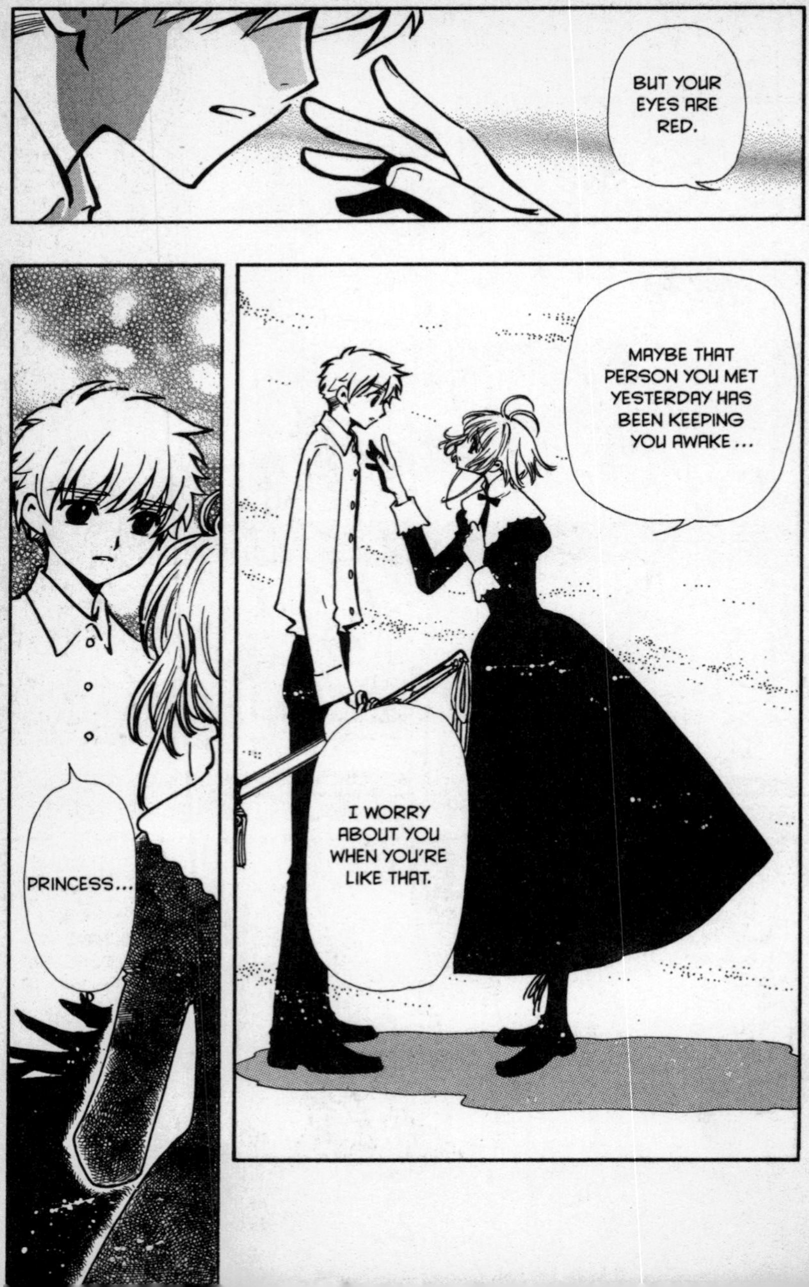
BUT YOUR EYES ARE RED.
MAYBE THAT PERSON YOU MET YESTERDAY HAS BEEN KEEPING YOU AWAKE...
I WORRY ABOUT YOU WHEN YOU'RE LIKE THAT.
PRINCESS...

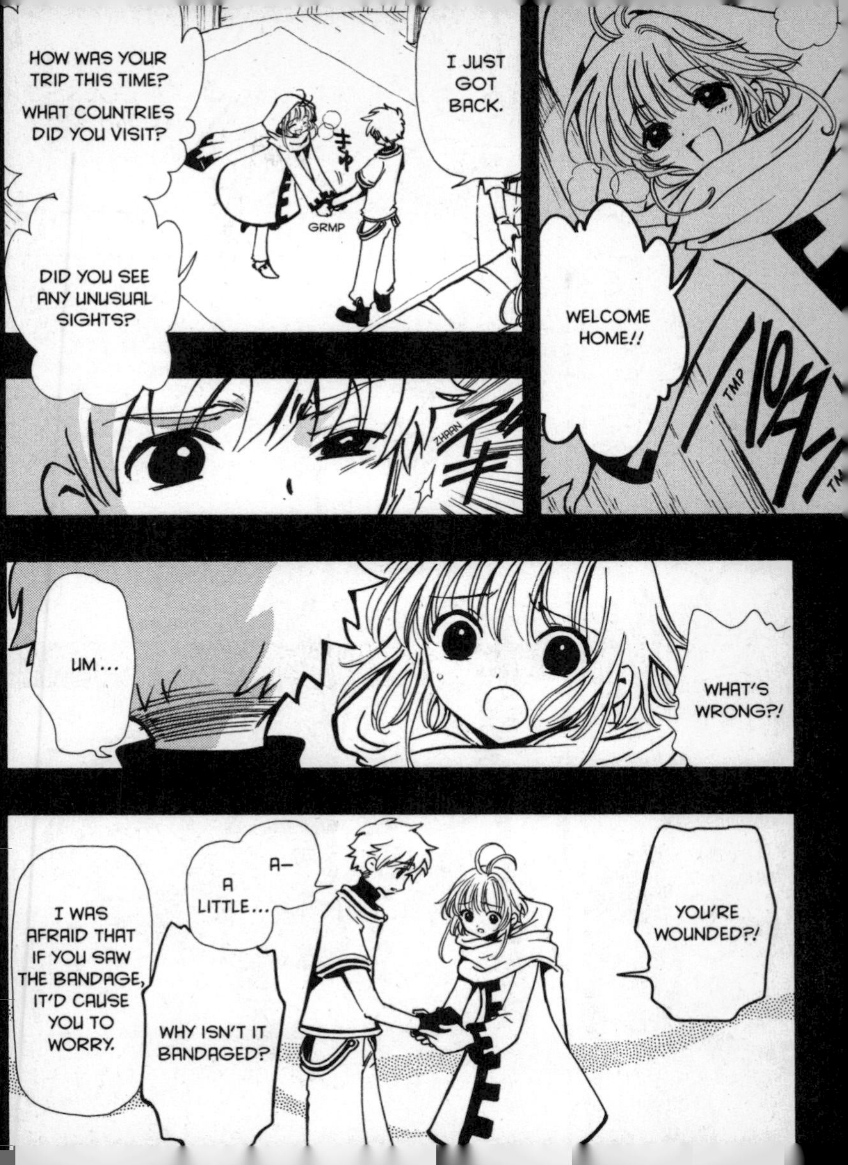
WELCOME HOME!!
TMP
TMP
I JUST GOT BACK.
HOW WAS YOUR TRIP THIS TIME? WHAT COUNTRIES DID YOU VISIT?
GRMP
DID YOU SEE ANY UNUSUAL SIGHTS?
ZHAAN
WHAT'S WRONG?!
UM...
YOU'RE WOUNDED?!
A— A LITTLE...
WHY ISN'T IT BANDAGED?
I WAS AFRAID THAT IF YOU SAW THE BANDAGE, IT'D CAUSE YOU TO WORRY.

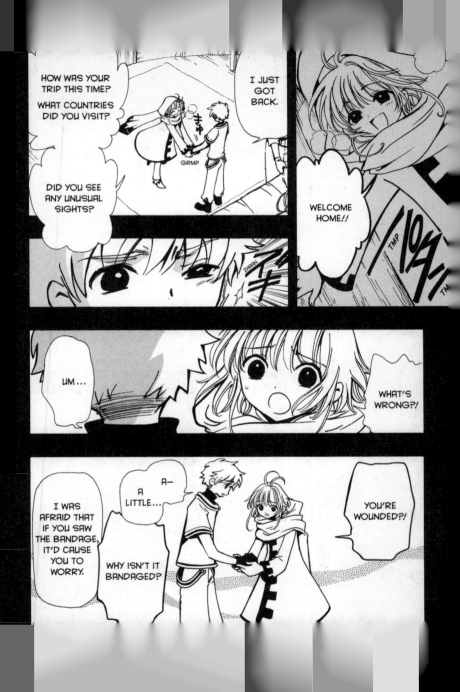

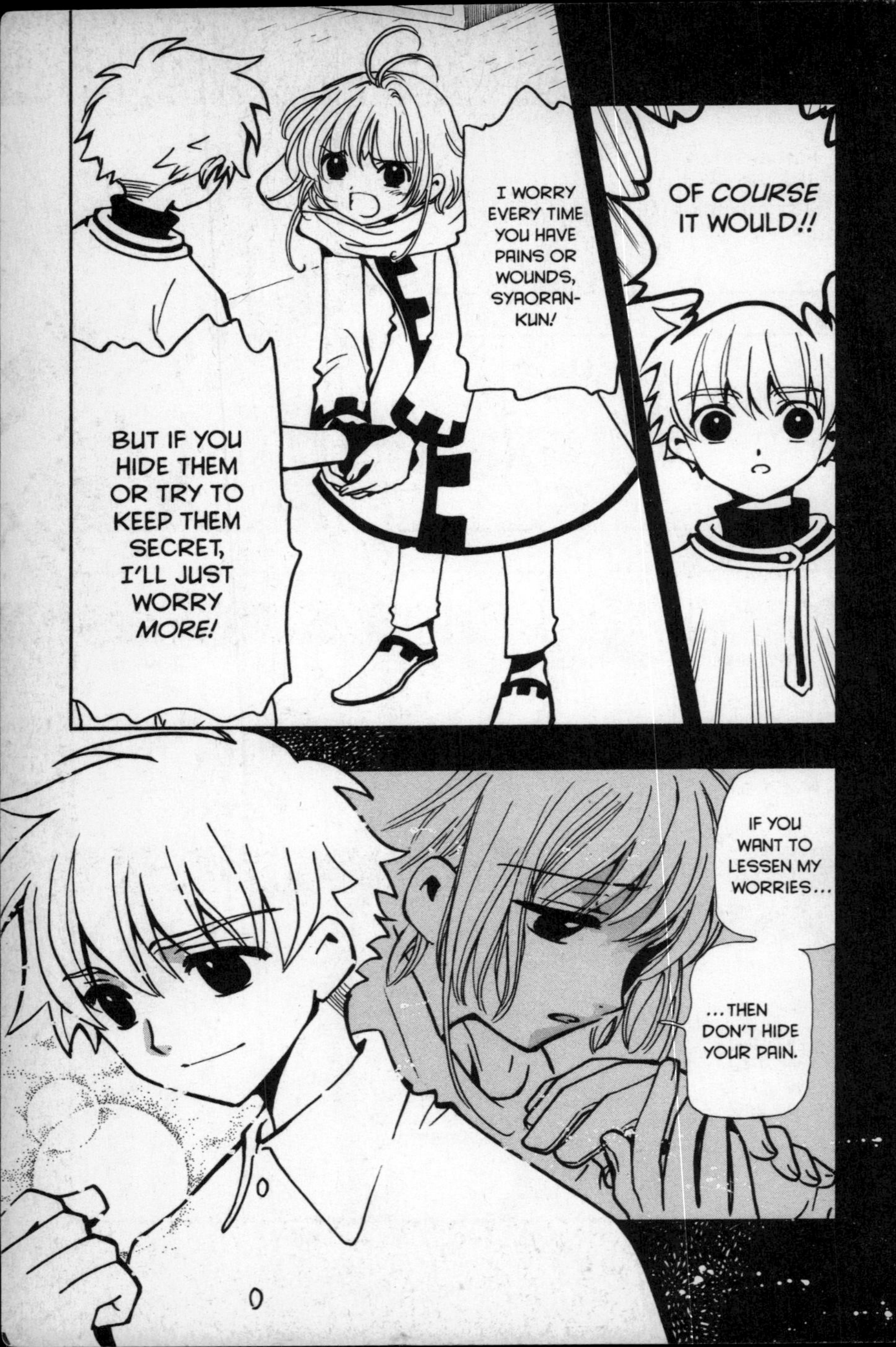
OF *COURSE* IT WOULD!!
I WORRY EVERY TIME YOU HAVE PAINS OR WOUNDS, SYAORAN-KUN!
BUT IF YOU HIDE THEM OR TRY TO KEEP THEM SECRET, I'LL JUST WORRY *MORE!*
IF YOU WANT TO LESSEN MY WORRIES...
...THEN DON'T HIDE YOUR PAIN.

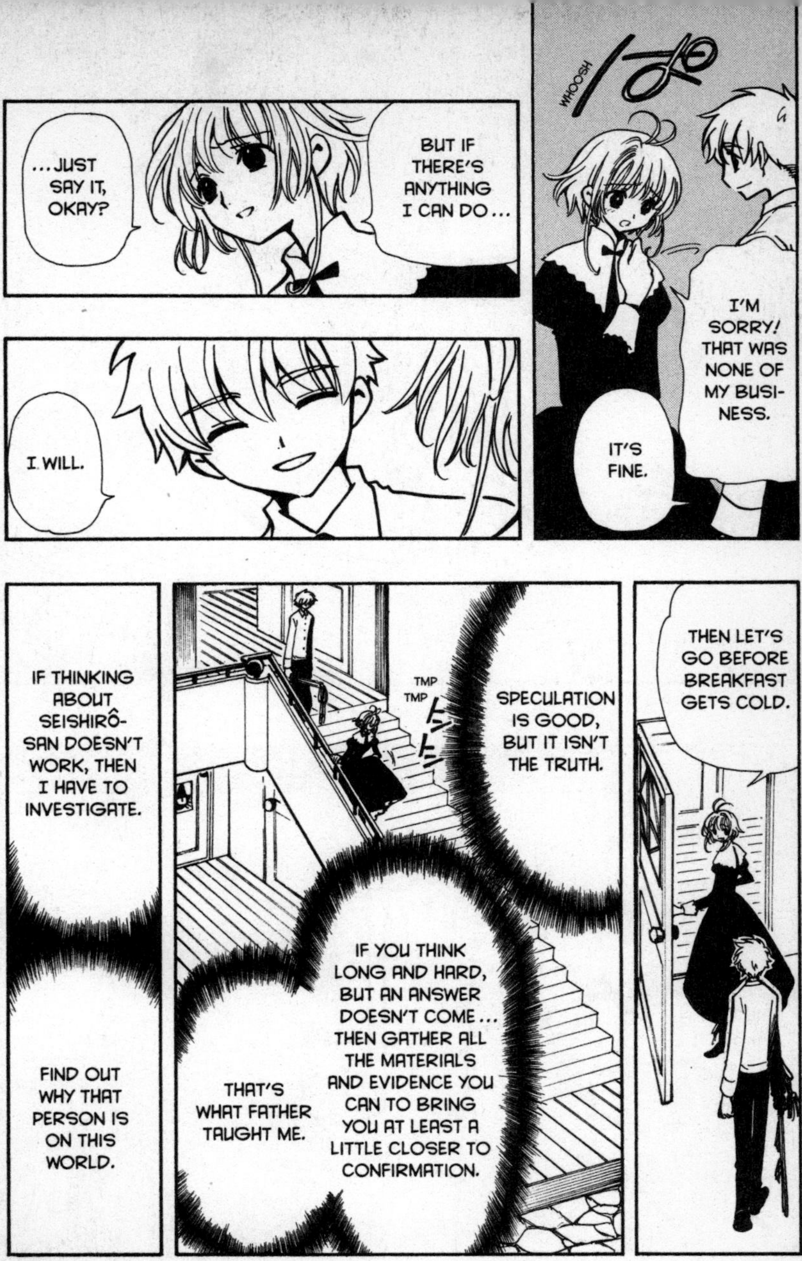
WHOOSH
I'M SORRY! THAT WAS NONE OF MY BUSINESS.
IT'S FINE.
BUT IF THERE'S ANYTHING I CAN DO...
...JUST SAY IT, OKAY?
I WILL.
THEN LET'S GO BEFORE BREAKFAST GETS COLD.
TMP TMP
SPECULATION IS GOOD, BUT IT ISN'T THE TRUTH.
IF YOU THINK LONG AND HARD, BUT AN ANSWER DOESN'T COME... THEN GATHER ALL THE MATERIALS AND EVIDENCE YOU CAN TO BRING YOU AT LEAST A LITTLE CLOSER TO CONFIRMATION.
THAT'S WHAT FATHER TAUGHT ME.
IF THINKING ABOUT SEISHIRÔ-SAN DOESN'T WORK, THEN I HAVE TO INVESTIGATE.
FIND OUT WHY THAT PERSON IS ON THIS WORLD.

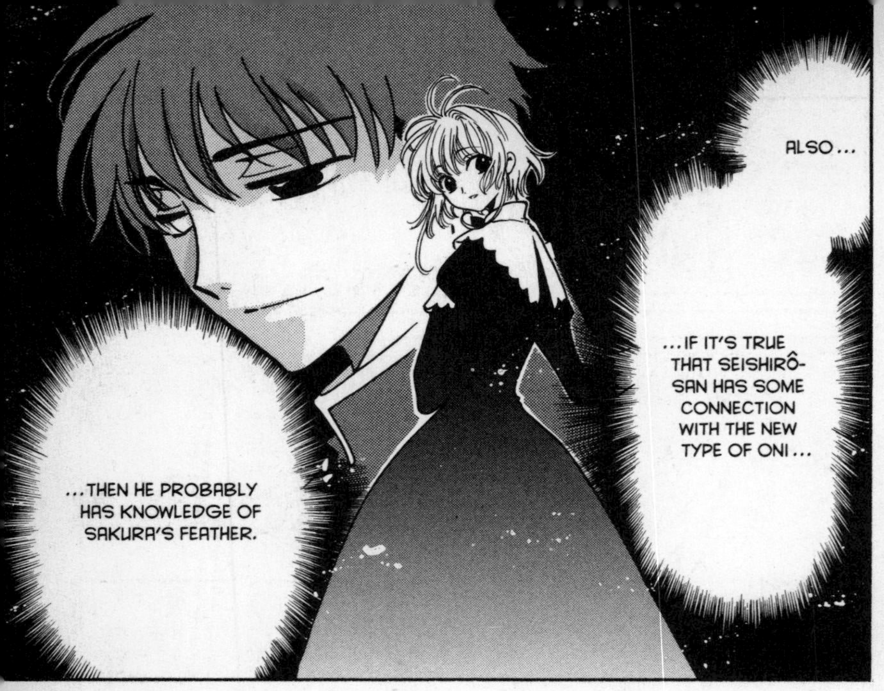
ALSO...
...IF IT'S TRUE THAT SEISHIRÔ-SAN HAS SOME CONNECTION WITH THE NEW TYPE OF ONI...
...THEN HE PROBABLY HAS KNOWLEDGE OF SAKURA'S FEATHER.

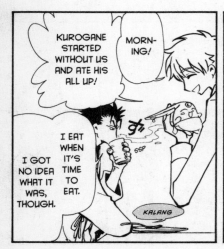

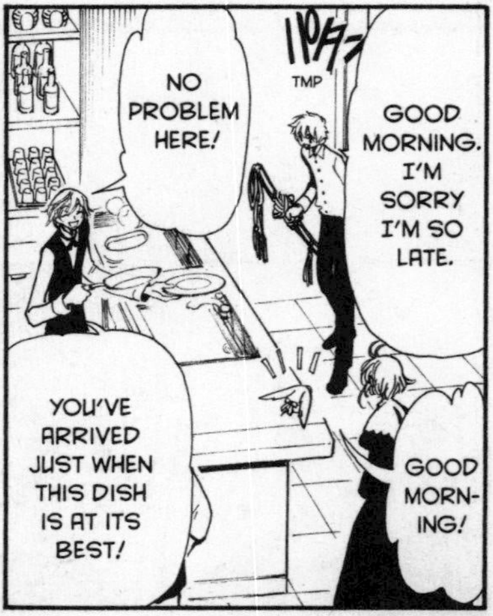
TMP
GOOD MORNING. I'M SORRY I'M SO LATE.
NO PROBLEM HERE!
GOOD MORNING!
YOU'VE ARRIVED JUST WHEN THIS DISH IS AT ITS BEST!

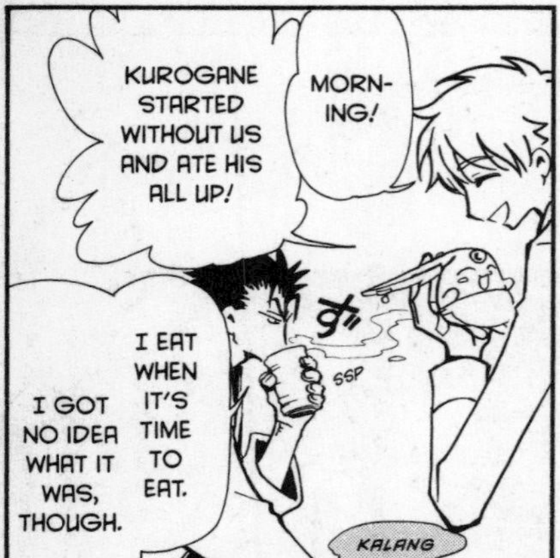
MORNING!
KUROGANE STARTED WITHOUT US AND ATE HIS ALL UP!
I EAT WHEN IT'S TIME TO EAT.
SSP
I GOT NO IDEA WHAT IT WAS, THOUGH.
KALANG

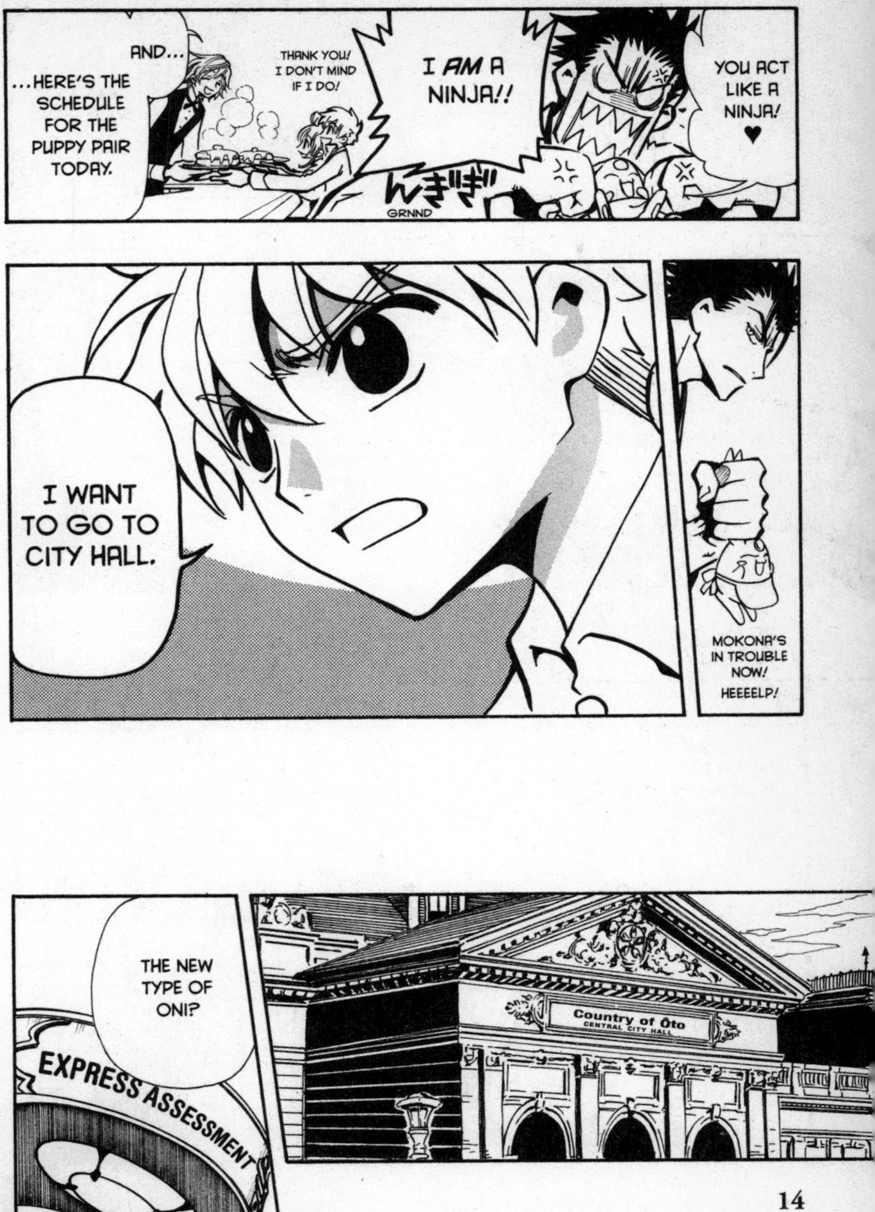
YOU ACT LIKE A NINJA! ♥
I AM A NINJA!!
んぎぎ
GRNND
THANK YOU! I DON'T MIND IF I DO!
AND...
...HERE'S THE SCHEDULE FOR THE PUPPY PAIR TODAY.
MOKONA'S IN TROUBLE NOW!
HEEEELP!
I WANT TO GO TO CITY HALL.
Country of Ôto
CENTRAL CITY HALL
THE NEW TYPE OF ONI?
EXPRESS ASSESSMENT

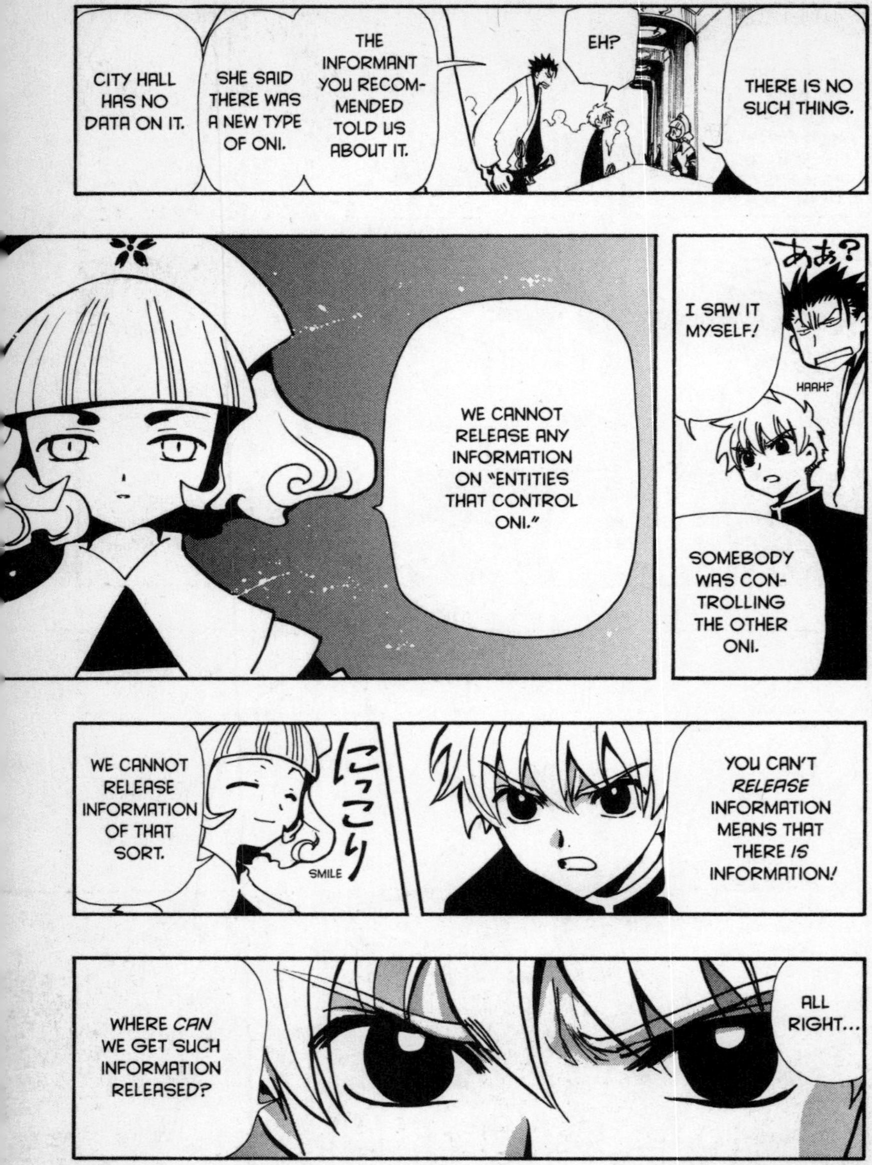
THERE IS NO SUCH THING.
EH?
THE INFORMANT YOU RECOMMENDED TOLD US ABOUT IT.
SHE SAID THERE WAS A NEW TYPE OF ONI.
CITY HALL HAS NO DATA ON IT.
ああ？
HAAH?
I SAW IT MYSELF!
SOMEBODY WAS CONTROLLING THE OTHER ONI.
WE CANNOT RELEASE ANY INFORMATION ON "ENTITIES THAT CONTROL ONI."
YOU CAN'T *RELEASE* INFORMATION MEANS THAT THERE *IS* INFORMATION!
にっこり
SMILE
WE CANNOT RELEASE INFORMATION OF THAT SORT.
ALL RIGHT...
WHERE *CAN* WE GET SUCH INFORMATION RELEASED?

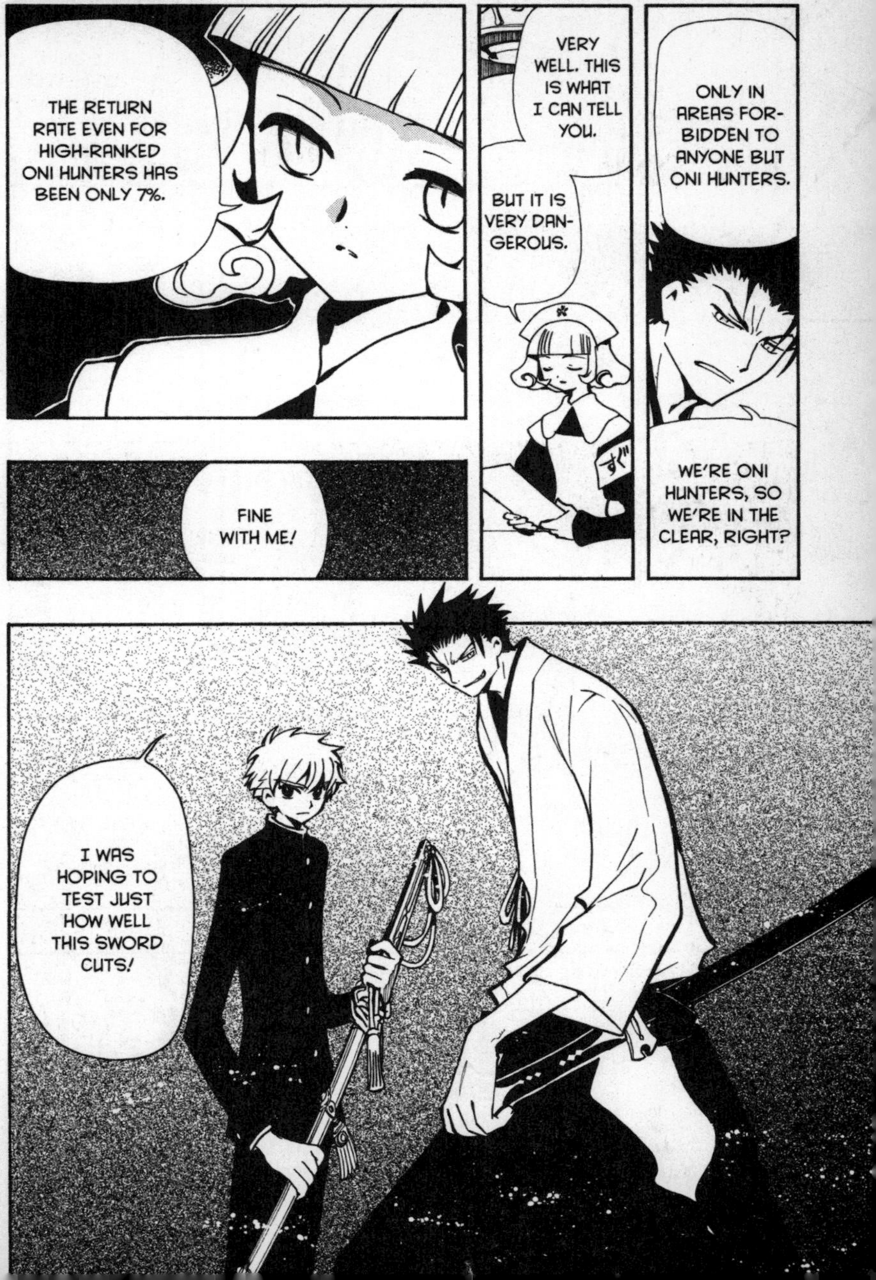
ONLY IN AREAS FOR-BIDDEN TO ANYONE BUT ONI HUNTERS.
WE'RE ONI HUNTERS, SO WE'RE IN THE CLEAR, RIGHT?
VERY WELL. THIS IS WHAT I CAN TELL YOU.
BUT IT IS VERY DAN-GEROUS.
THE RETURN RATE EVEN FOR HIGH-RANKED ONI HUNTERS HAS BEEN ONLY 7%.
FINE WITH ME!
I WAS HOPING TO TEST JUST HOW WELL THIS SWORD CUTS!

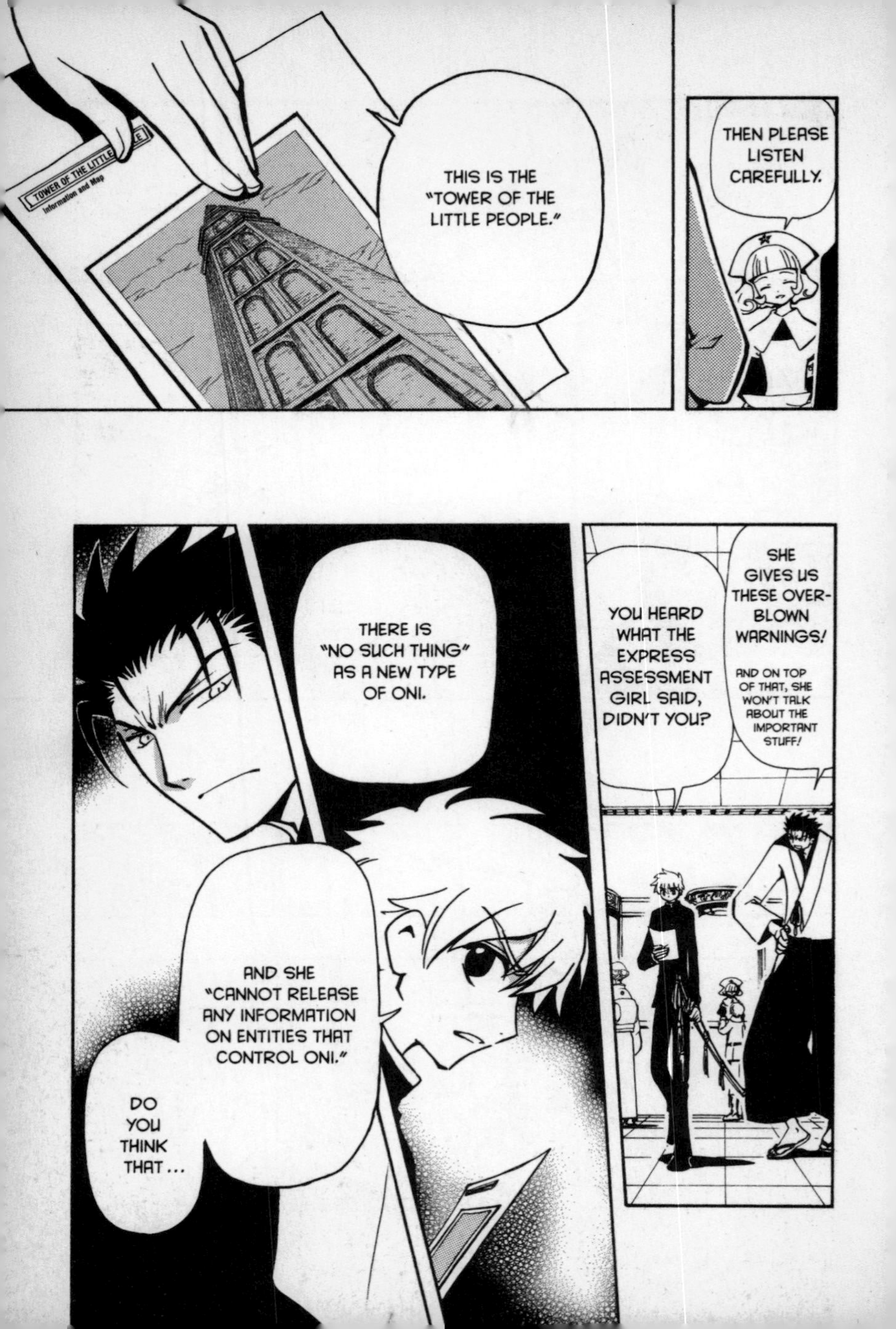
THEN PLEASE LISTEN CAREFULLY.
TOWER OF THE LITTLE
Information and Map
THIS IS THE "TOWER OF THE LITTLE PEOPLE."
SHE GIVES US THESE OVER-BLOWN WARNINGS!
AND ON TOP OF THAT, SHE WON'T TALK ABOUT THE IMPORTANT STUFF!
YOU HEARD WHAT THE EXPRESS ASSESSMENT GIRL SAID, DIDN'T YOU?
THERE IS "NO SUCH THING" AS A NEW TYPE OF ONI.
AND SHE "CANNOT RELEASE ANY INFORMATION ON ENTITIES THAT CONTROL ONI."
DO YOU THINK THAT...

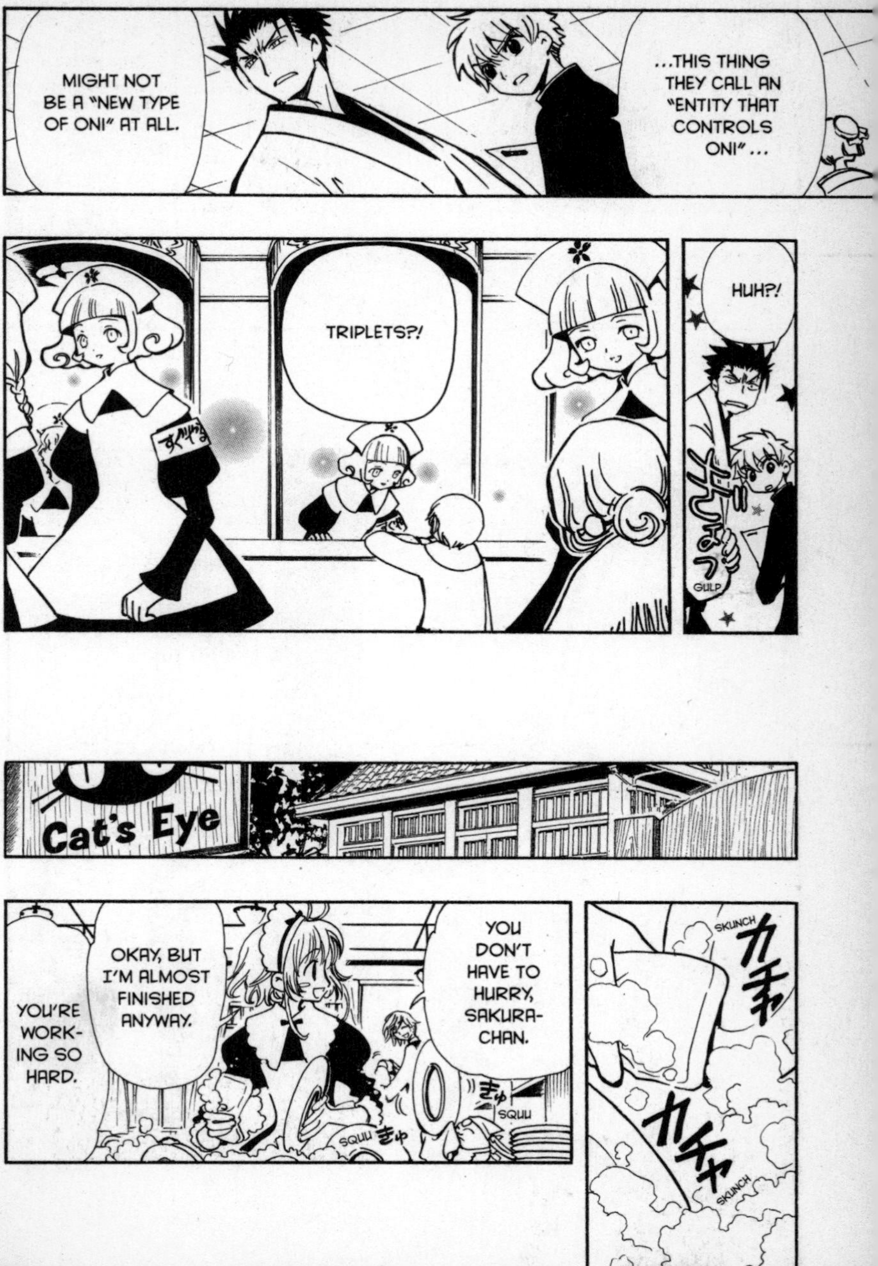
...THIS THING THEY CALL AN "ENTITY THAT CONTROLS ONI"...
MIGHT NOT BE A "NEW TYPE OF ONI" AT ALL.
HUH?!
GULP
TRIPLETS?!
Cat's Eye
SKUNCH
カチャ
SKUNCH
YOU DON'T HAVE TO HURRY, SAKURA-CHAN.
OKAY, BUT I'M ALMOST FINISHED ANYWAY.
YOU'RE WORKING SO HARD.
SQUU
SQUU

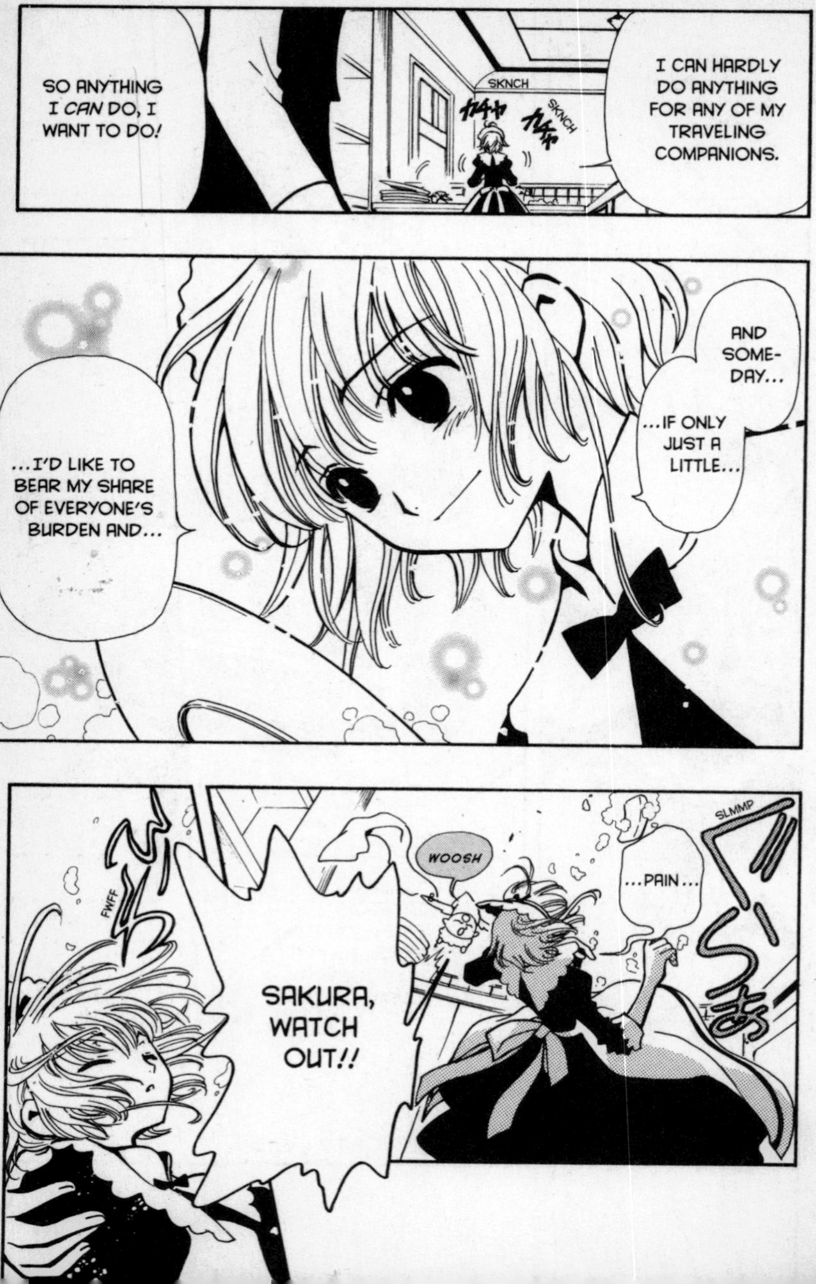
I CAN HARDLY DO ANYTHING FOR ANY OF MY TRAVELING COMPANIONS.
SKNCH
SKNCH
SO ANYTHING I *CAN* DO, I WANT TO DO!
AND SOME-DAY...
...IF ONLY JUST A LITTLE...
...I'D LIKE TO BEAR MY SHARE OF EVERYONE'S BURDEN AND...
SLMMP
...PAIN...
WOOSH
SAKURA, WATCH OUT!!
FWFF

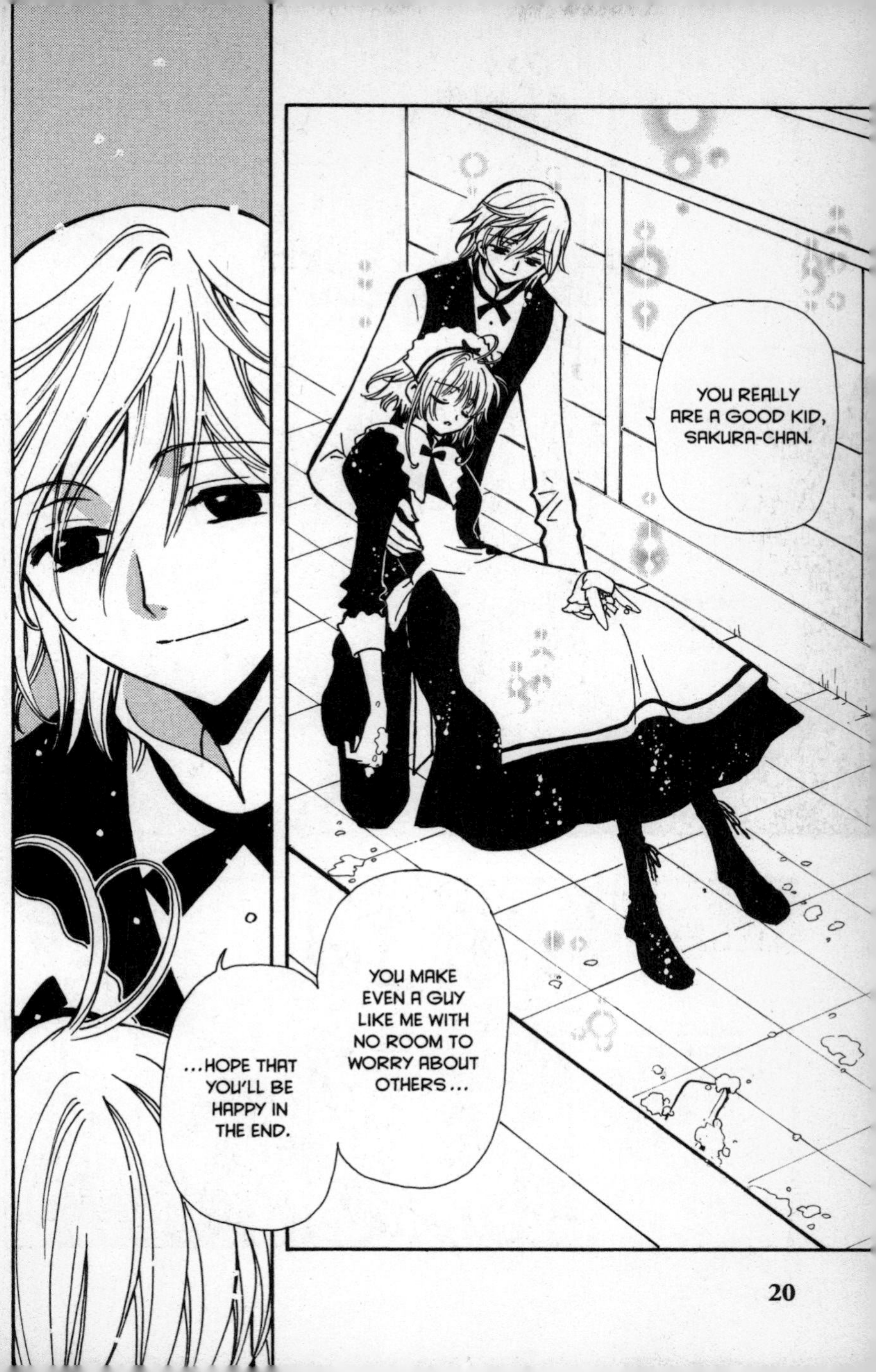
YOU REALLY ARE A GOOD KID, SAKURA-CHAN.
YOU MAKE EVEN A GUY LIKE ME WITH NO ROOM TO WORRY ABOUT OTHERS...
...HOPE THAT YOU'LL BE HAPPY IN THE END.

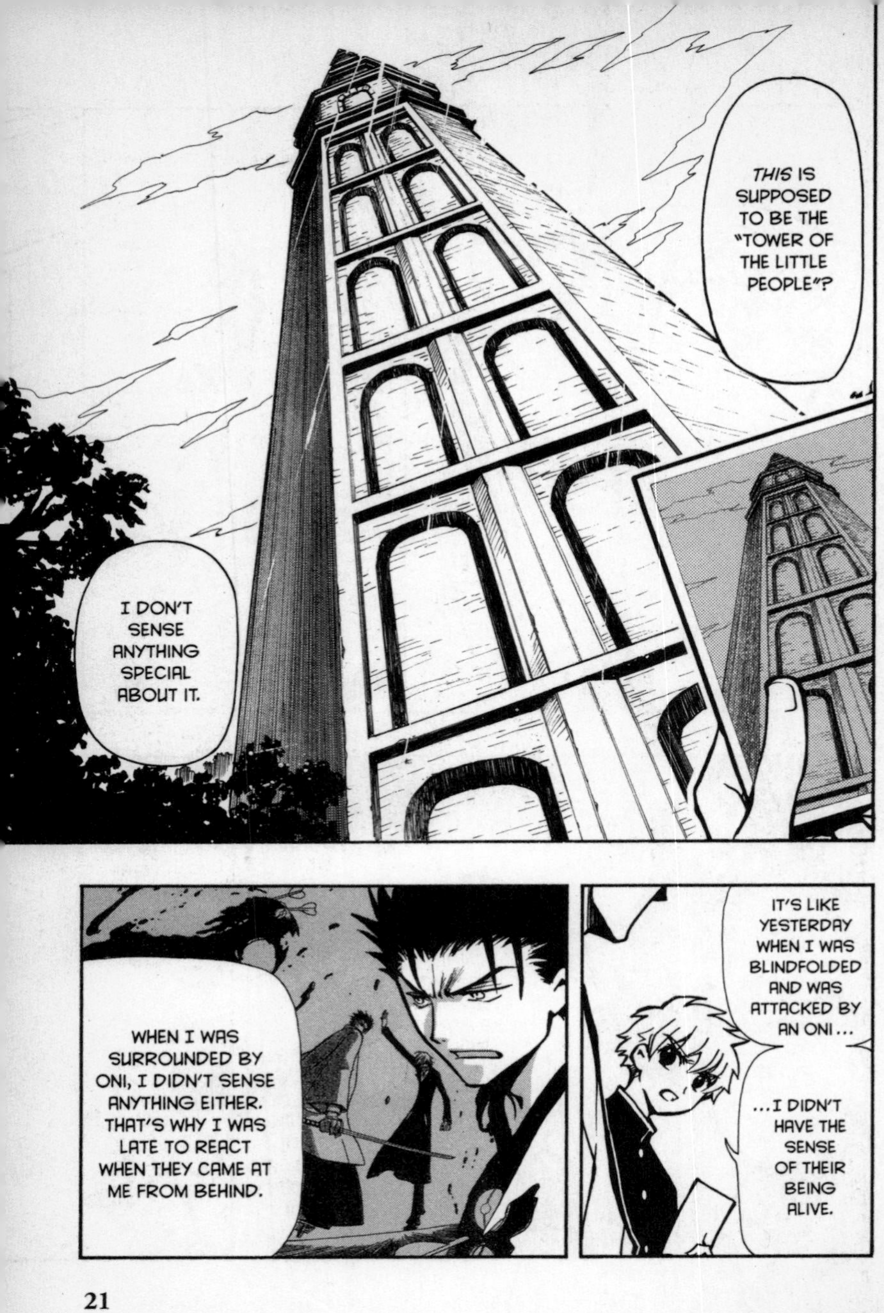
THIS IS SUPPOSED TO BE THE "TOWER OF THE LITTLE PEOPLE"?
I DON'T SENSE ANYTHING SPECIAL ABOUT IT.
IT'S LIKE YESTERDAY WHEN I WAS BLINDFOLDED AND WAS ATTACKED BY AN ONI...
...I DIDN'T HAVE THE SENSE OF THEIR BEING ALIVE.
WHEN I WAS SURROUNDED BY ONI, I DIDN'T SENSE ANYTHING EITHER. THAT'S WHY I WAS LATE TO REACT WHEN THEY CAME AT ME FROM BEHIND.

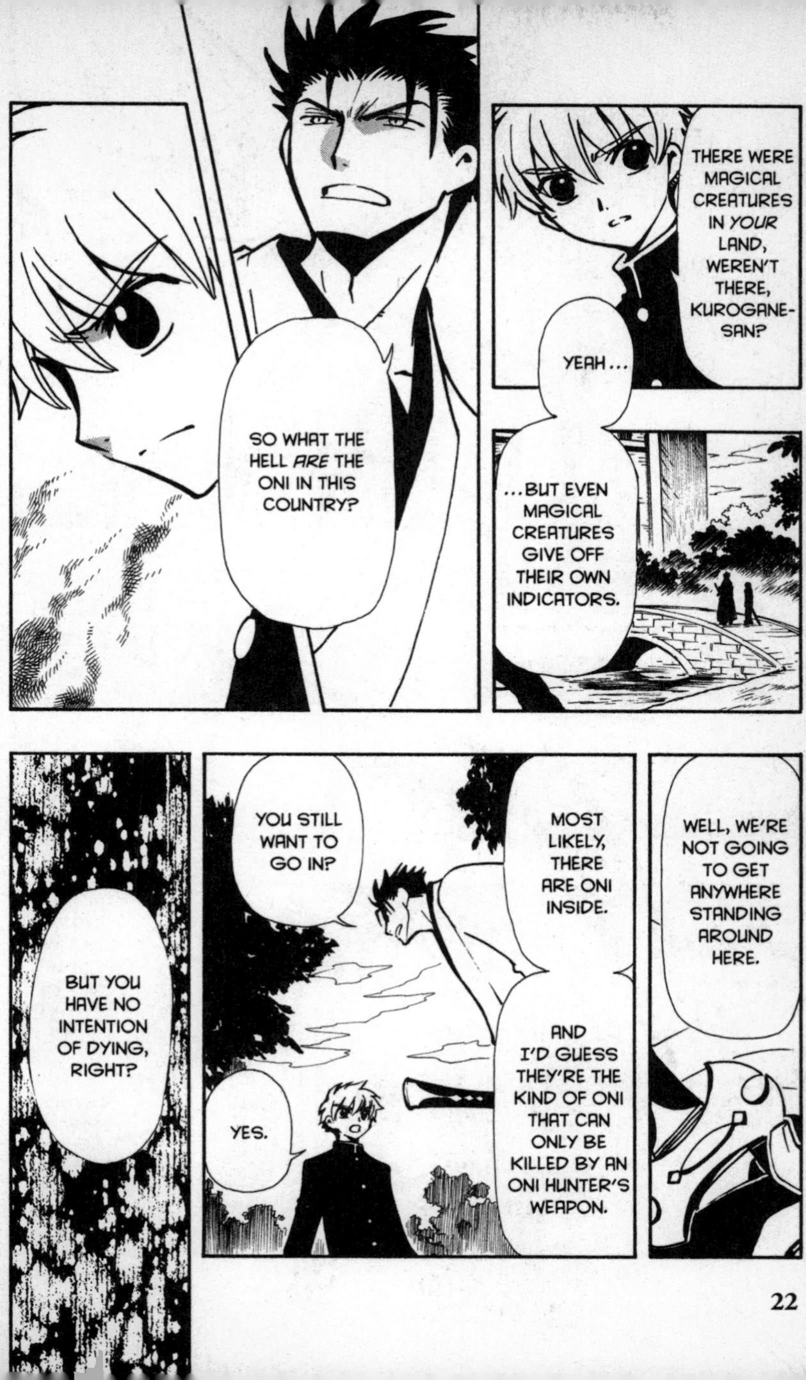
THERE WERE MAGICAL CREATURES IN *YOUR* LAND, WEREN'T THERE, KUROGANE-SAN?
YEAH...
...BUT EVEN MAGICAL CREATURES GIVE OFF THEIR OWN INDICATORS.
SO WHAT THE HELL *ARE* THE ONI IN THIS COUNTRY?
WELL, WE'RE NOT GOING TO GET ANYWHERE STANDING AROUND HERE.
MOST LIKELY, THERE ARE ONI INSIDE.
AND I'D GUESS THEY'RE THE KIND OF ONI THAT CAN ONLY BE KILLED BY AN ONI HUNTER'S WEAPON.
YOU STILL WANT TO GO IN?
YES.
BUT YOU HAVE NO INTENTION OF DYING, RIGHT?

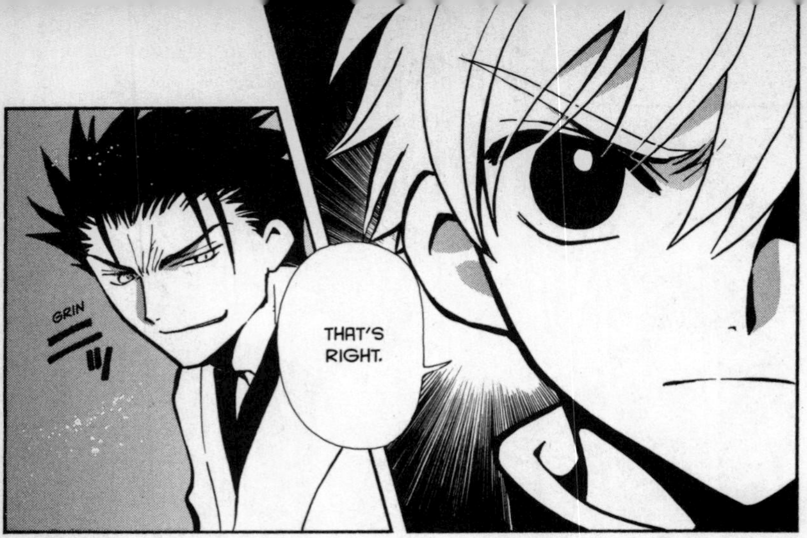
THAT'S RIGHT.
GRIN
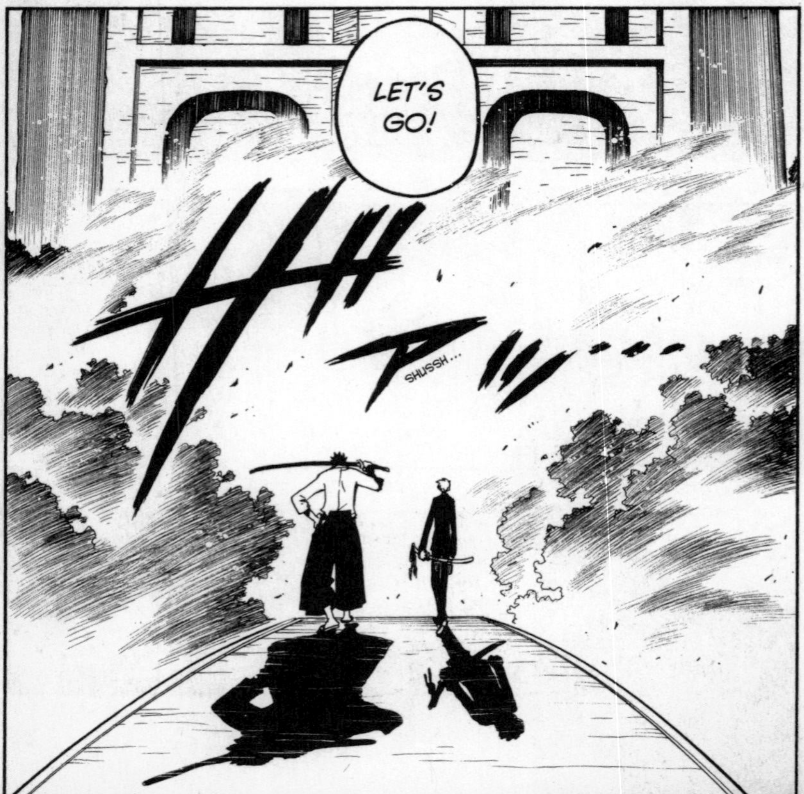
LET'S GO!
SHUSSH...

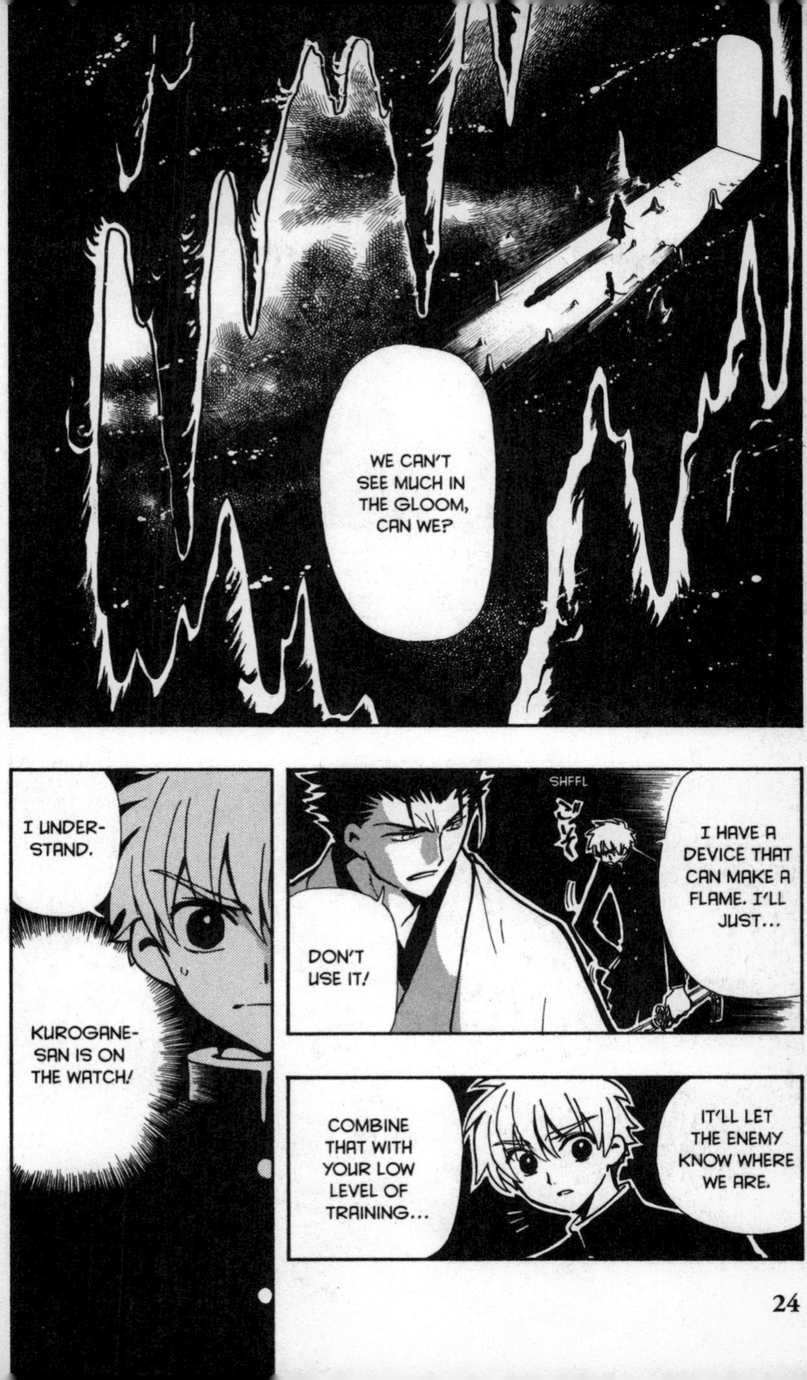

WE CAN'T SEE MUCH IN THE GLOOM, CAN WE?
SHFFL
I HAVE A DEVICE THAT CAN MAKE A FLAME. I'LL JUST...
DON'T USE IT!
IT'LL LET THE ENEMY KNOW WHERE WE ARE.
COMBINE THAT WITH YOUR LOW LEVEL OF TRAINING...
I UNDER-STAND.
KUROGANE-SAN IS ON THE WATCH!

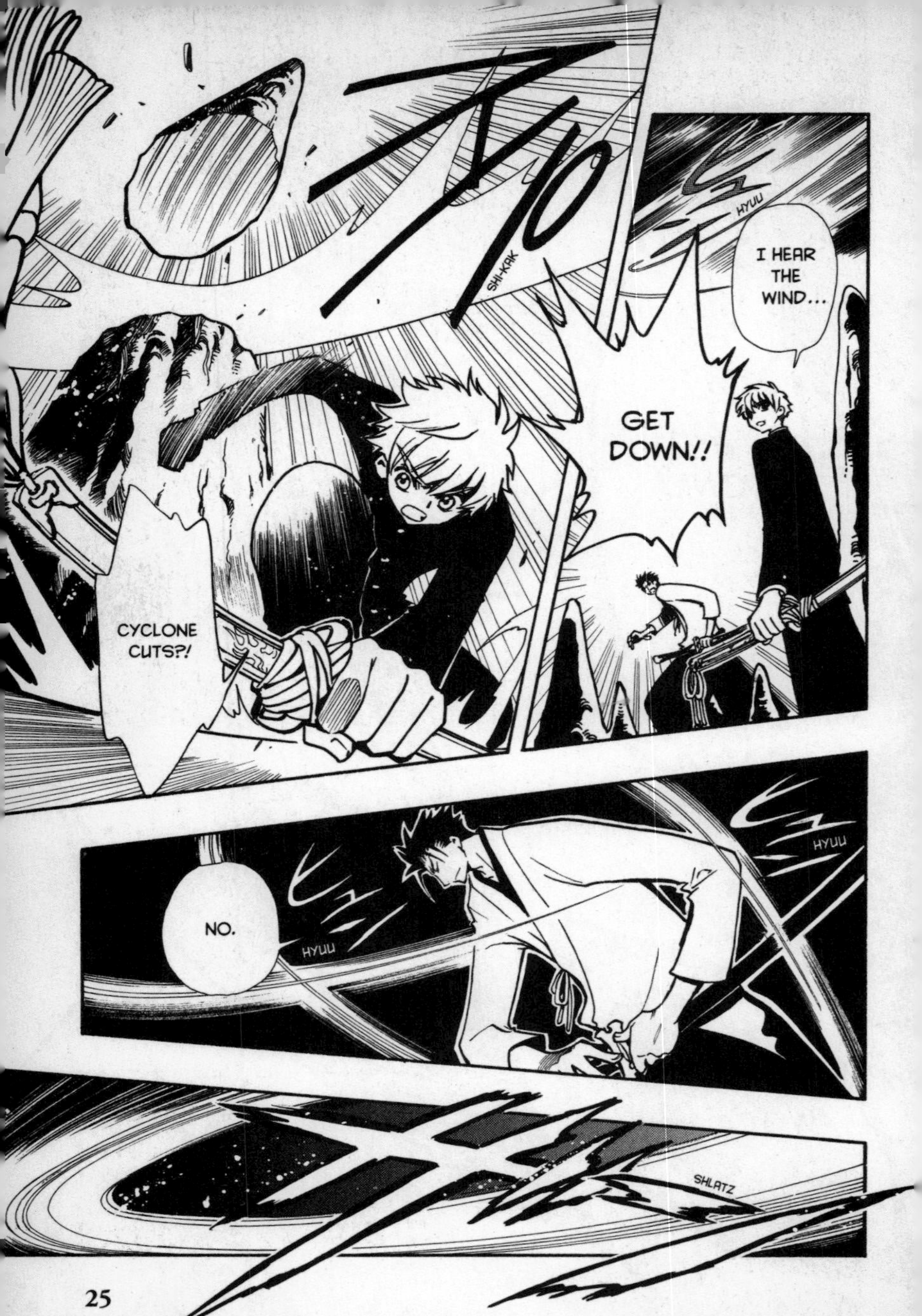
HYUU
I HEAR THE WIND...
SHI-KAK
GET DOWN!!
CYCLONE CUTS?!
HYUU
NO.
HYUU
SHLATZ

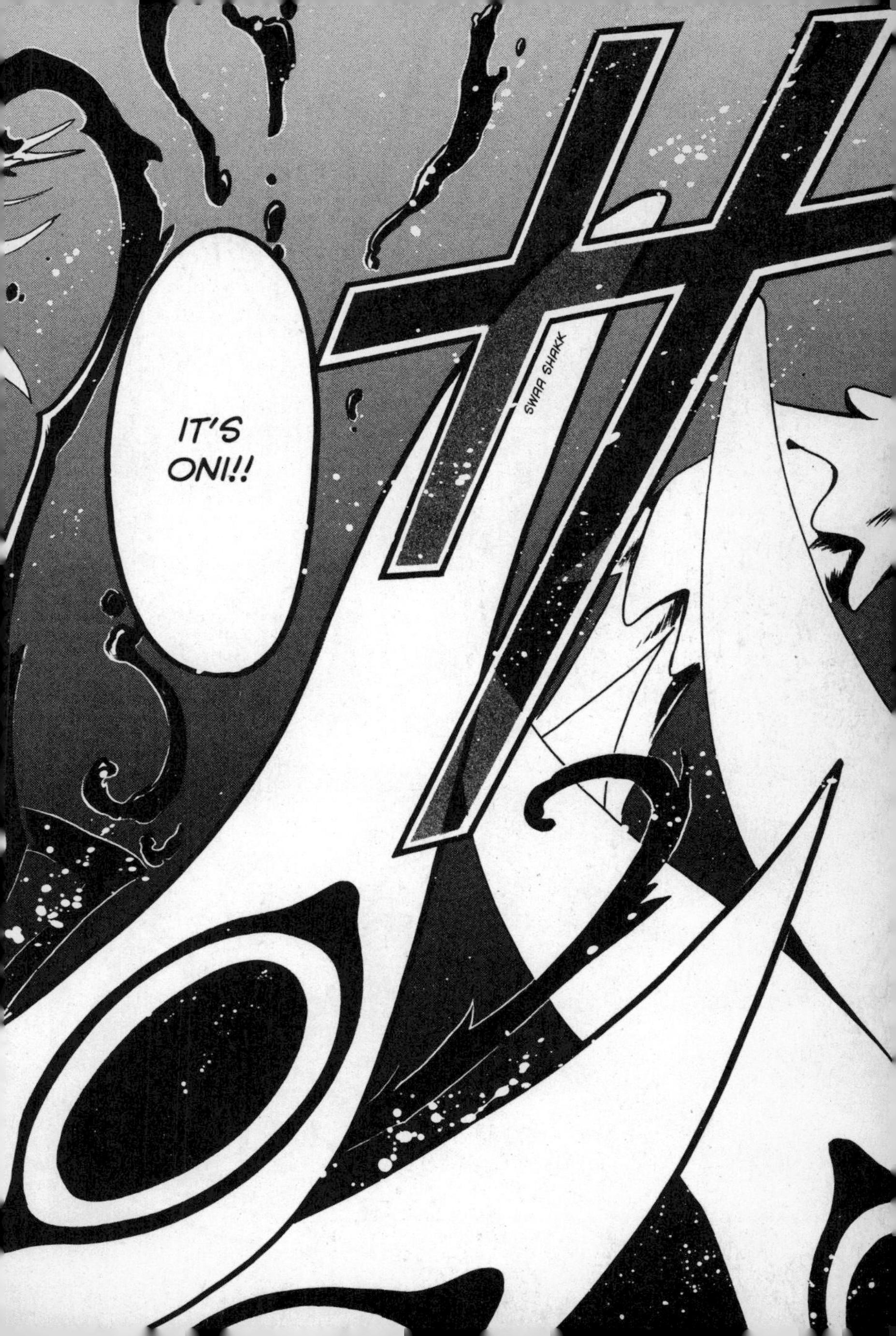
IT'S ONI!!
SWAA SHAKK

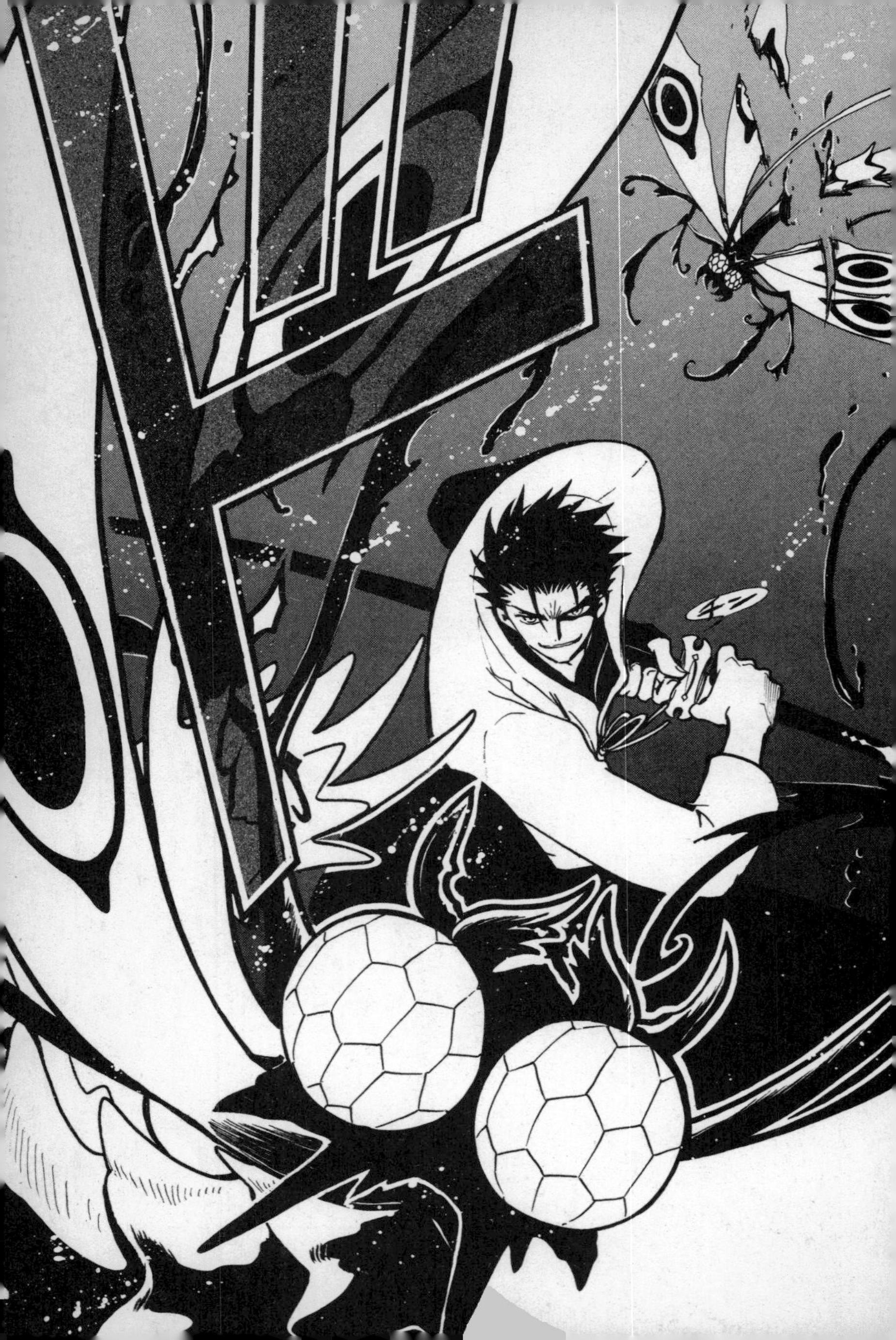

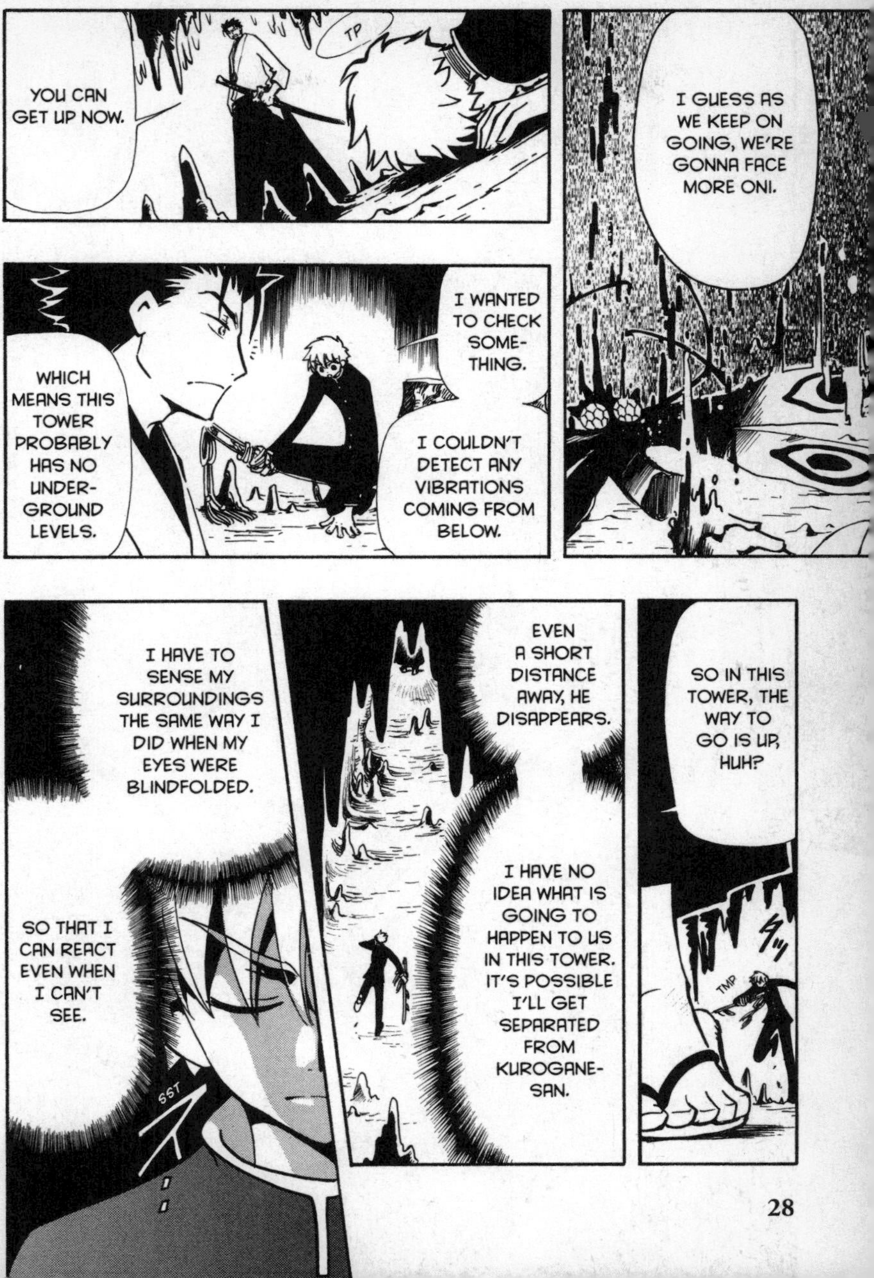
I GUESS AS WE KEEP ON GOING, WE'RE GONNA FACE MORE ONI.
TP
YOU CAN GET UP NOW.
I WANTED TO CHECK SOME-THING.
I COULDN'T DETECT ANY VIBRATIONS COMING FROM BELOW.
WHICH MEANS THIS TOWER PROBABLY HAS NO UNDER-GROUND LEVELS.
SO IN THIS TOWER, THE WAY TO GO IS UP, HUH?
TMP
EVEN A SHORT DISTANCE AWAY, HE DISAPPEARS.
I HAVE NO IDEA WHAT IS GOING TO HAPPEN TO US IN THIS TOWER. IT'S POSSIBLE I'LL GET SEPARATED FROM KUROGANE-SAN.
I HAVE TO SENSE MY SURROUNDINGS THE SAME WAY I DID WHEN MY EYES WERE BLINDFOLDED.
SO THAT I CAN REACT EVEN WHEN I CAN'T SEE.
SST

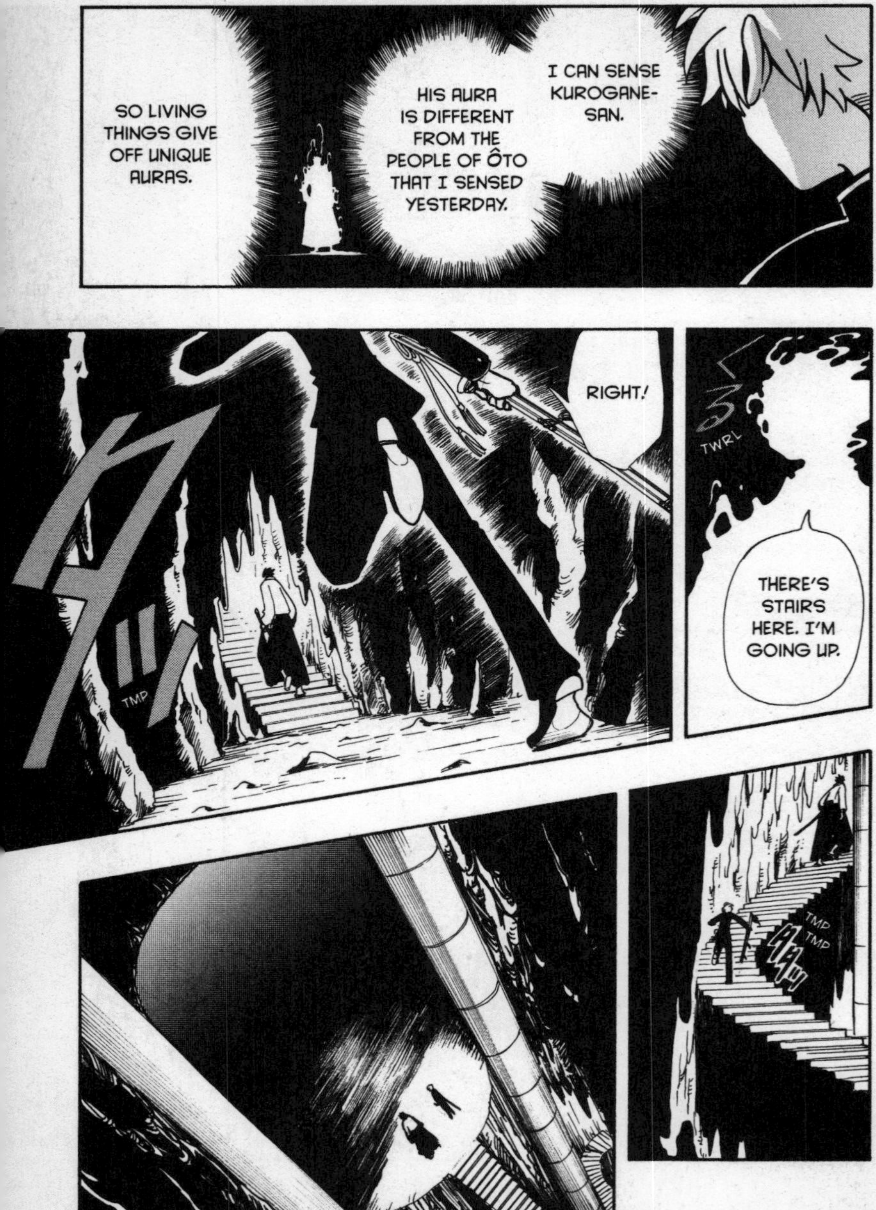
I CAN SENSE KUROGANE-SAN.
HIS AURA IS DIFFERENT FROM THE PEOPLE OF ÔTO THAT I SENSED YESTERDAY.
SO LIVING THINGS GIVE OFF UNIQUE AURAS.
TWRL
THERE'S STAIRS HERE. I'M GOING UP.
RIGHT!
TMP
TMP
TMP

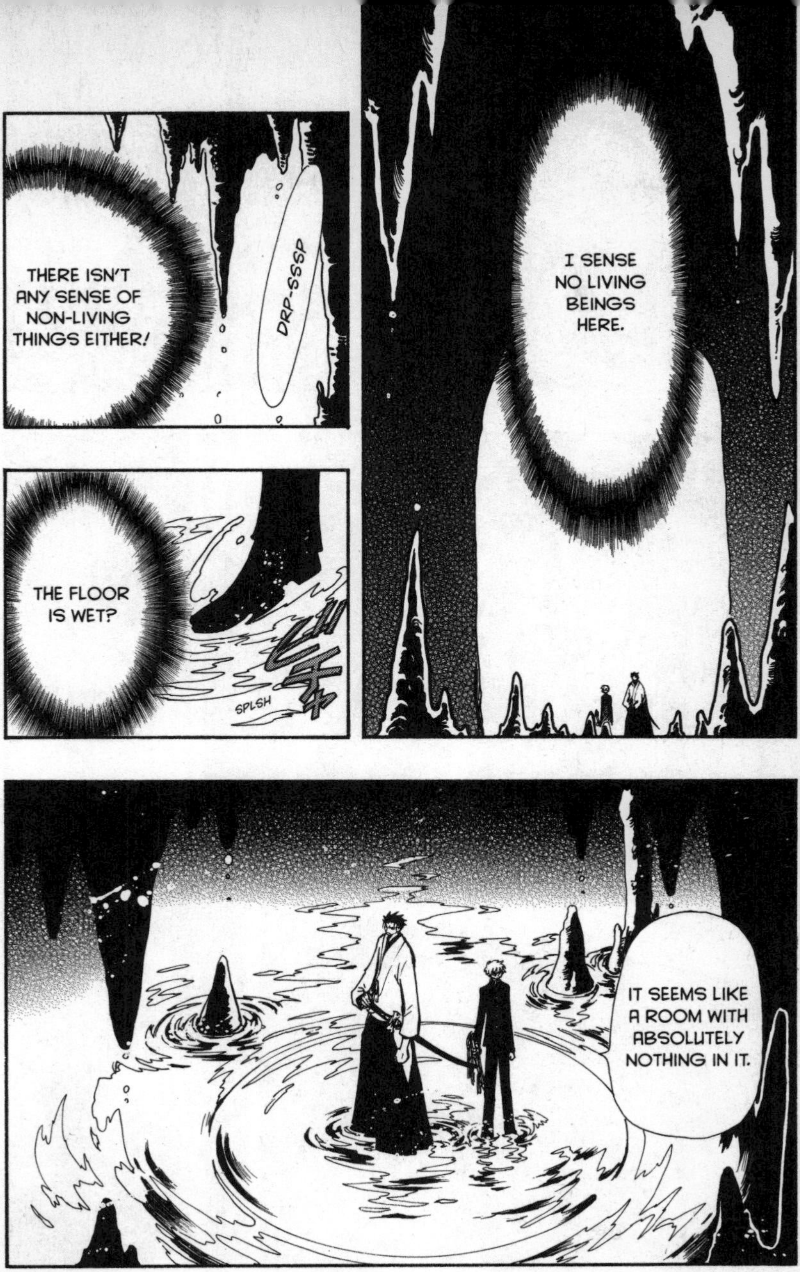
I SENSE NO LIVING BEINGS HERE.
THERE ISN'T ANY SENSE OF NON-LIVING THINGS EITHER!
DRP-SSSP
THE FLOOR IS WET?
SPLSH
IT SEEMS LIKE A ROOM WITH ABSOLUTELY NOTHING IN IT.

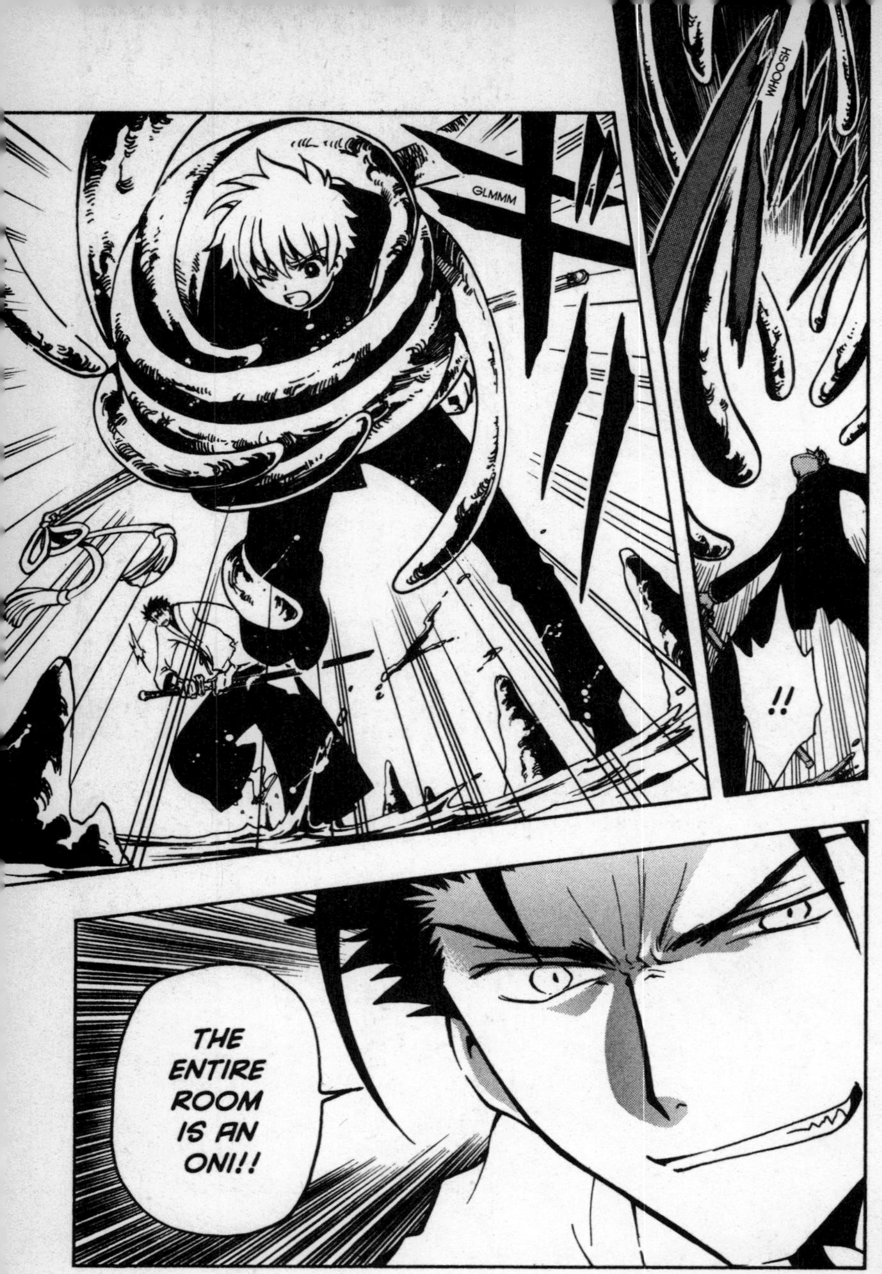
WHOOSH
!!
GLMMM
THE ENTIRE ROOM IS AN ONI!!

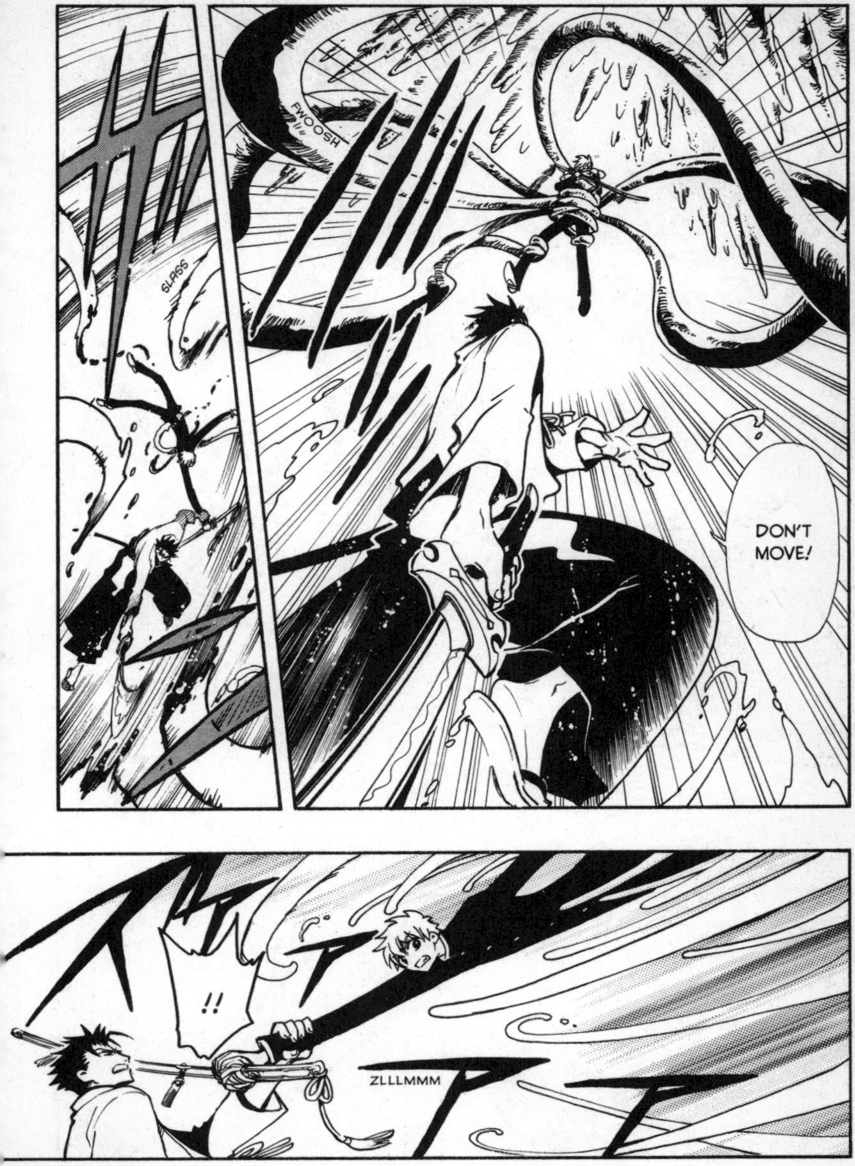
FWOOSH
DON'T MOVE!
SLASS
!!
ZLLLMMM

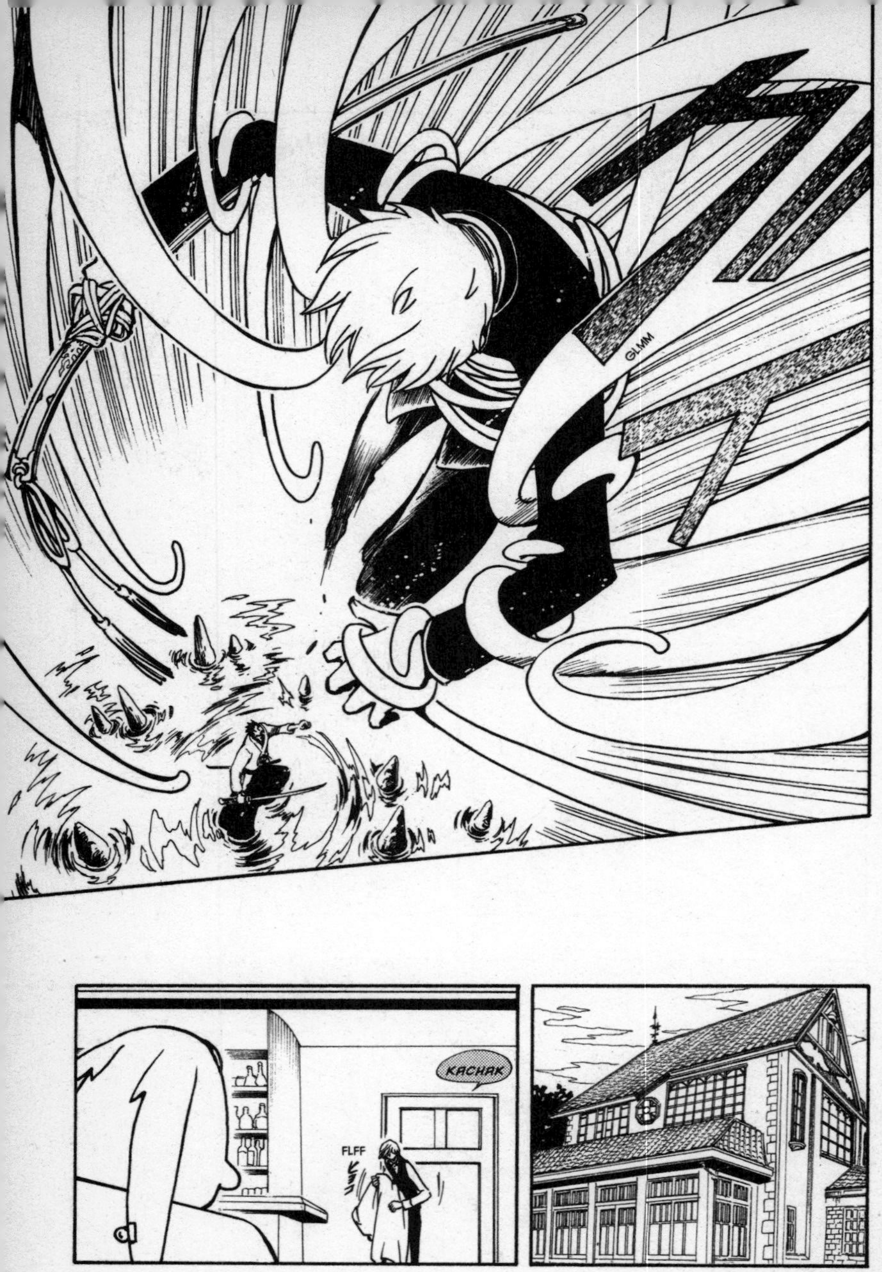
GLMM
KACHAK
FLFF

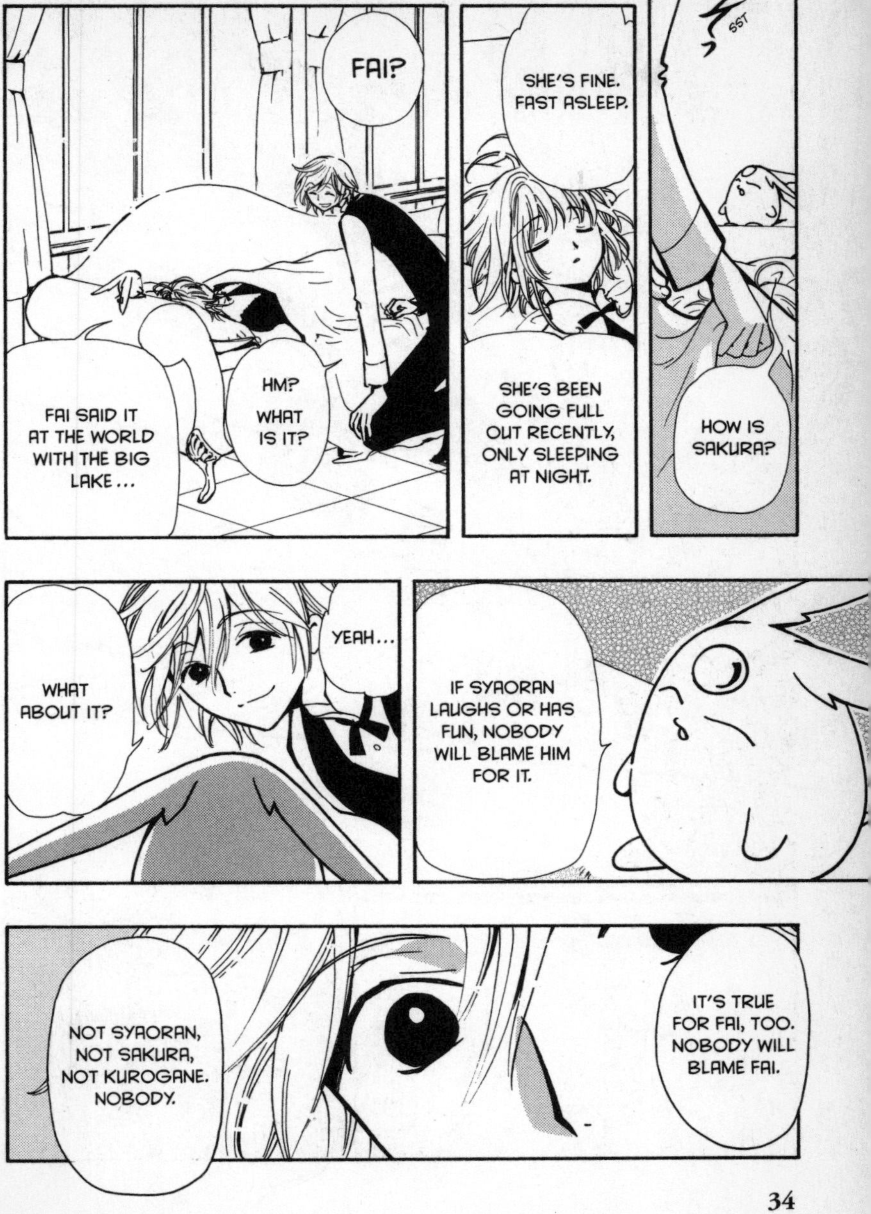
SST
HOW IS SAKURA?
SHE'S FINE. FAST ASLEEP.
SHE'S BEEN GOING FULL OUT RECENTLY, ONLY SLEEPING AT NIGHT.
FAI?
HM? WHAT IS IT?
FAI SAID IT AT THE WORLD WITH THE BIG LAKE...
IF SYAORAN LAUGHS OR HAS FUN, NOBODY WILL BLAME HIM FOR IT.
YEAH...
WHAT ABOUT IT?
IT'S TRUE FOR FAI, TOO. NOBODY WILL BLAME FAI.
NOT SYAORAN, NOT SAKURA, NOT KUROGANE. NOBODY.

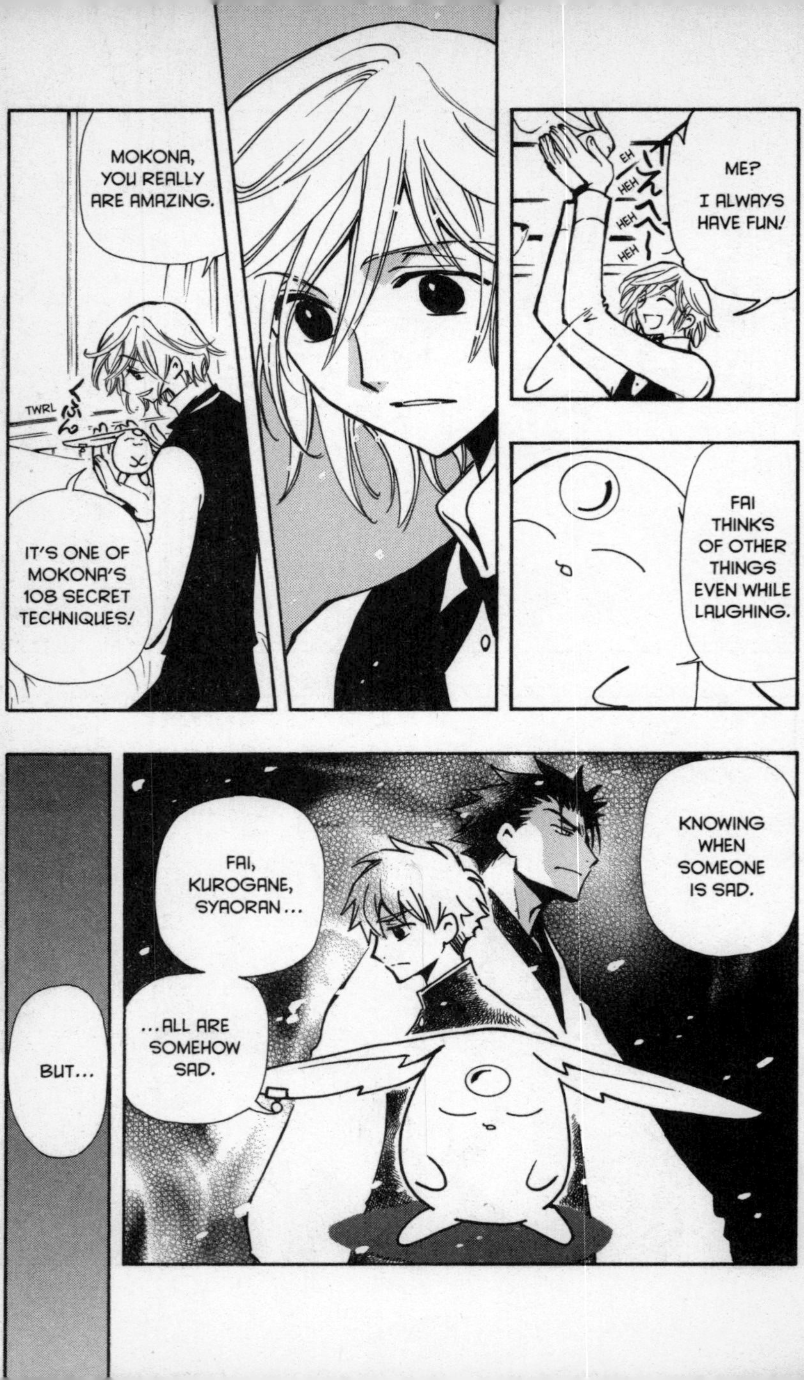
EH HEH HEH HEH
ME? I ALWAYS HAVE FUN!
FAI THINKS OF OTHER THINGS EVEN WHILE LAUGHING.
MOKONA, YOU REALLY ARE AMAZING.
TWRL
IT'S ONE OF MOKONA'S 108 SECRET TECHNIQUES!
KNOWING WHEN SOMEONE IS SAD.
FAI, KUROGANE, SYAORAN...
...ALL ARE SOMEHOW SAD.
BUT...

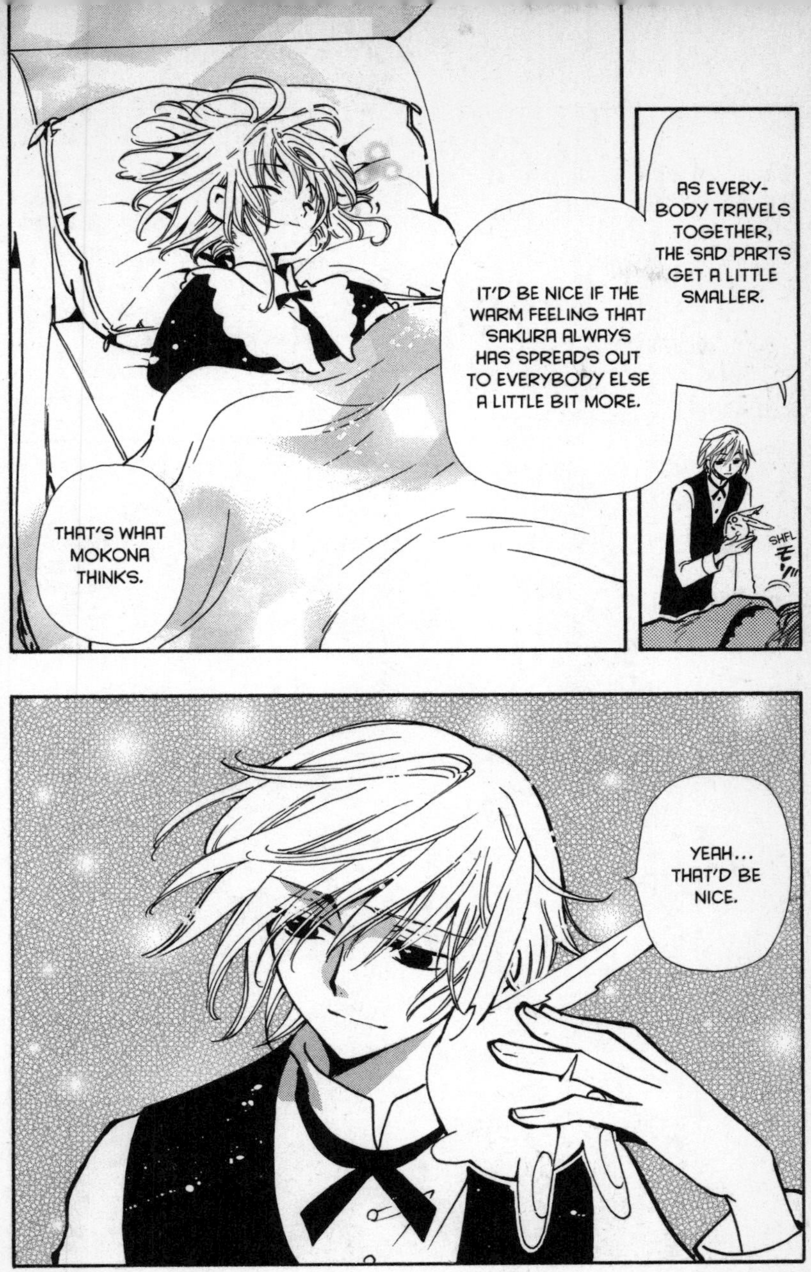
AS EVERY-BODY TRAVELS TOGETHER, THE SAD PARTS GET A LITTLE SMALLER.
IT'D BE NICE IF THE WARM FEELING THAT SAKURA ALWAYS HAS SPREADS OUT TO EVERYBODY ELSE A LITTLE BIT MORE.
THAT'S WHAT MOKONA THINKS.
SHFL
YEAH... THAT'D BE NICE.

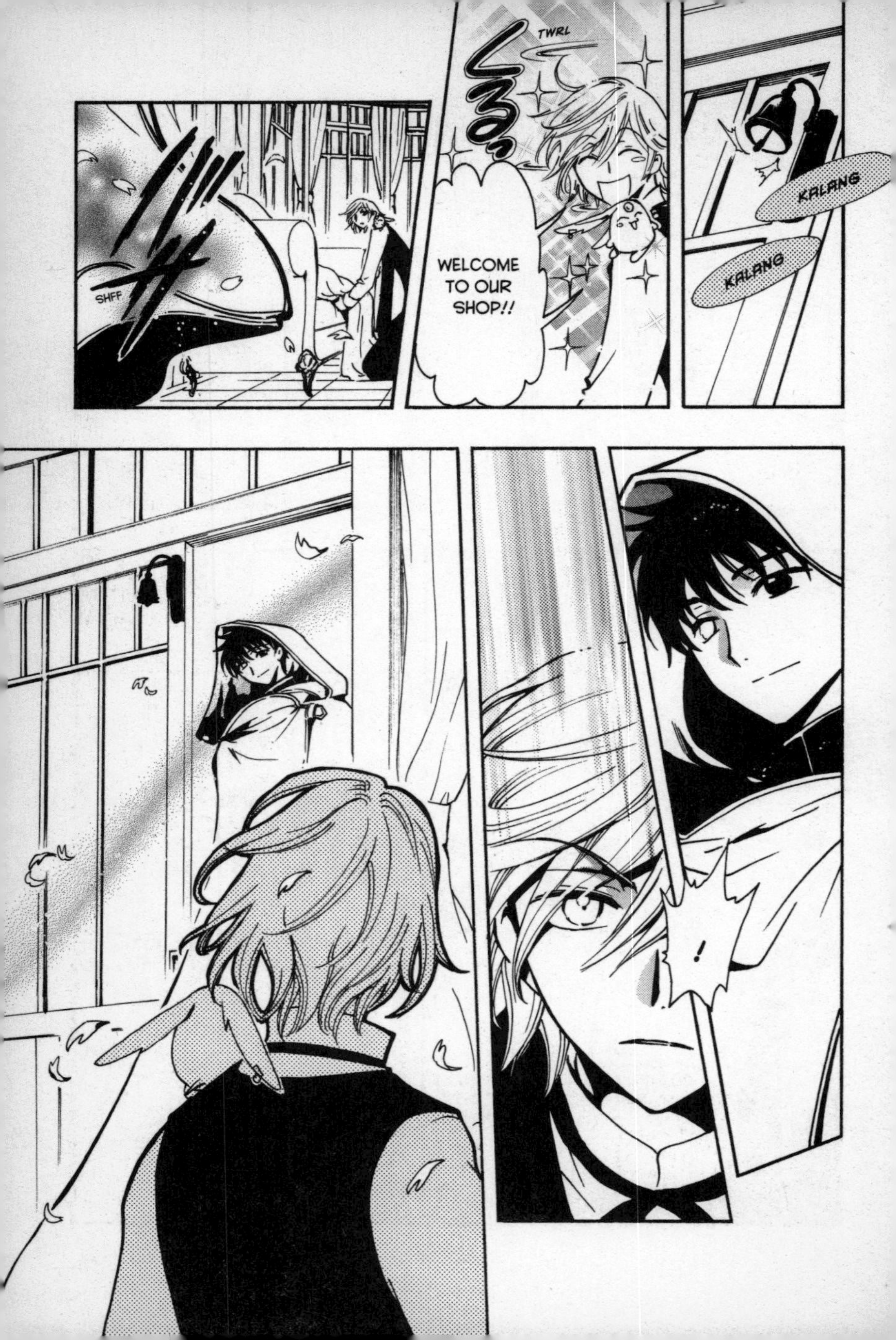
KALANG
KALANG
TWRL
WELCOME TO OUR SHOP!!
SHFF
!

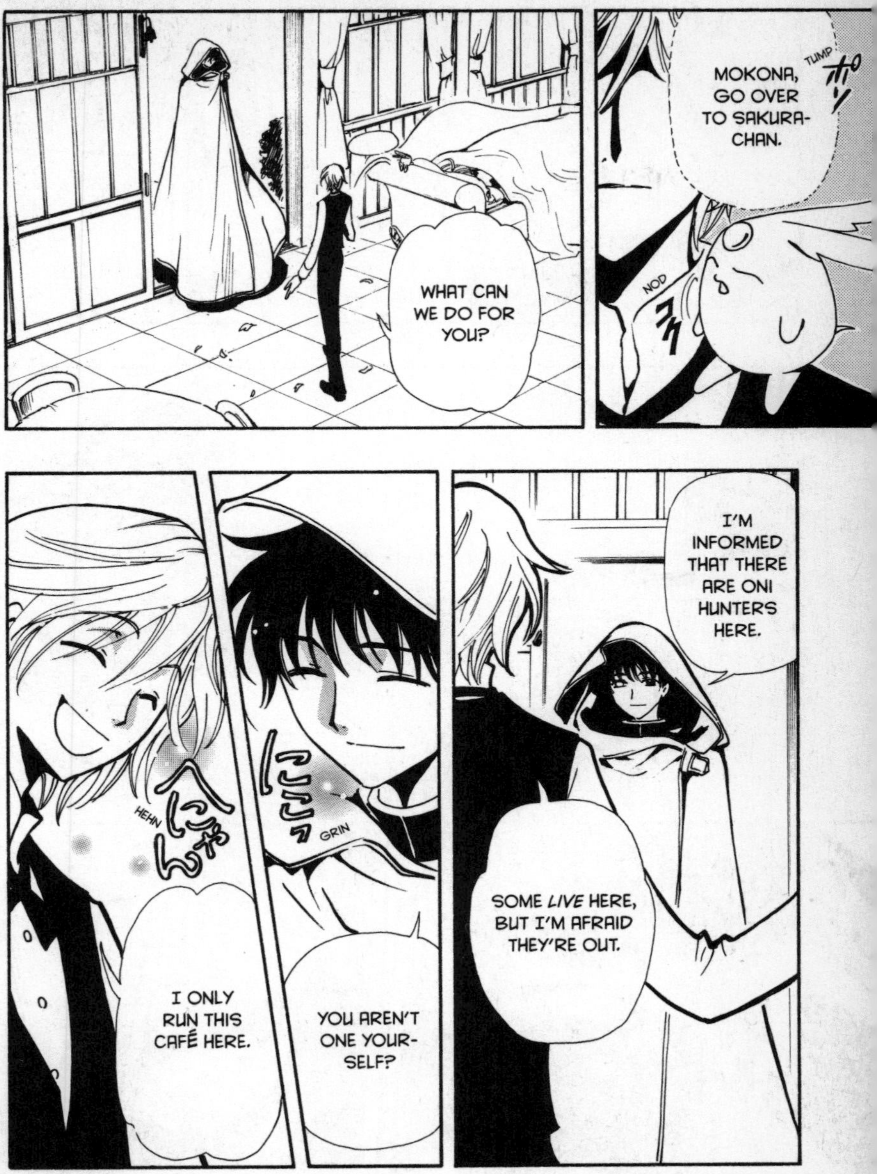
MOKONA, GO OVER TO SAKURA-CHAN.
TUMP
NOD
WHAT CAN WE DO FOR YOU?
I'M INFORMED THAT THERE ARE ONI HUNTERS HERE.
SOME *LIVE* HERE, BUT I'M AFRAID THEY'RE OUT.
GRIN
YOU AREN'T ONE YOUR-SELF?
HEHN
I ONLY RUN THIS CAFÉ HERE.

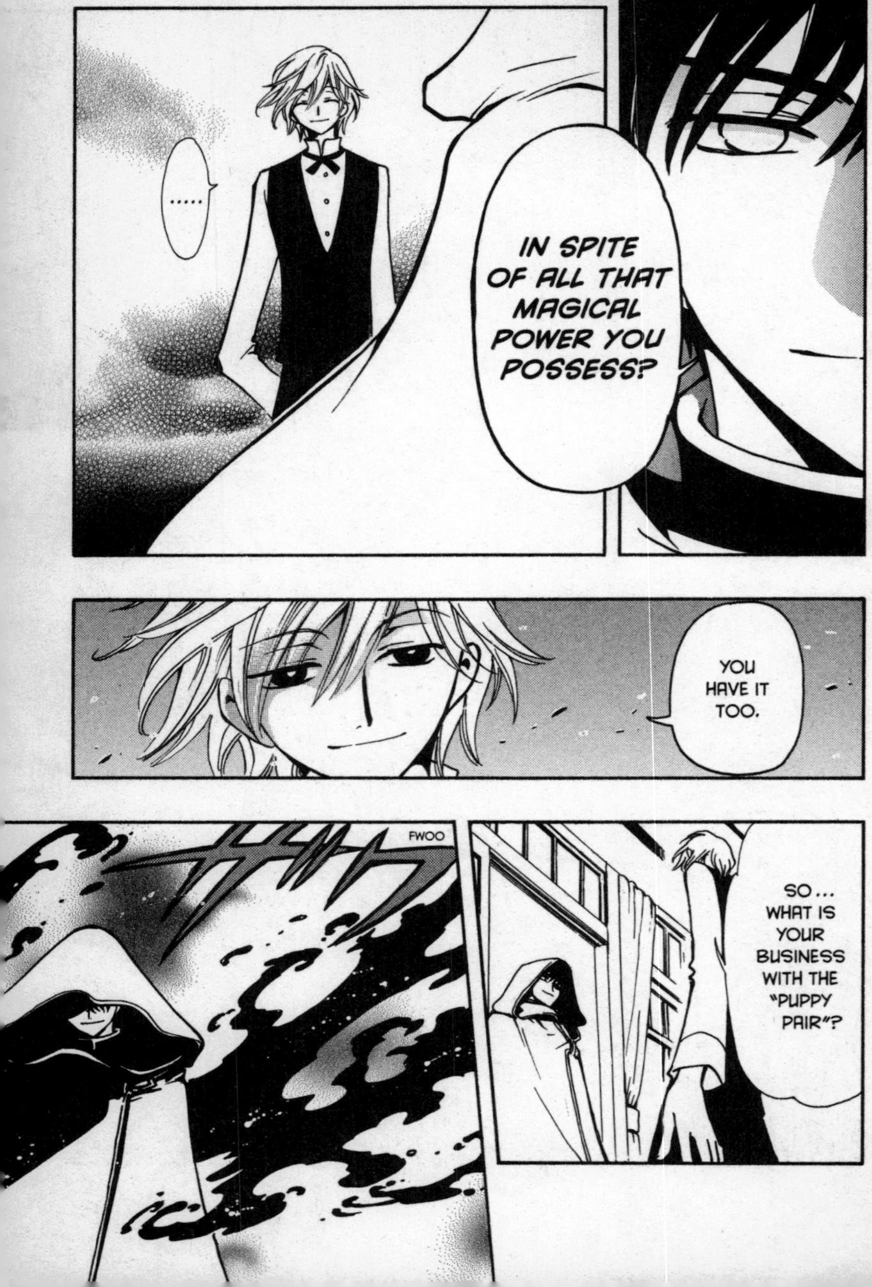
IN SPITE OF ALL THAT MAGICAL POWER YOU POSSESS?
......
YOU HAVE IT TOO.
SO... WHAT IS YOUR BUSINESS WITH THE "PUPPY PAIR"?
FWOO

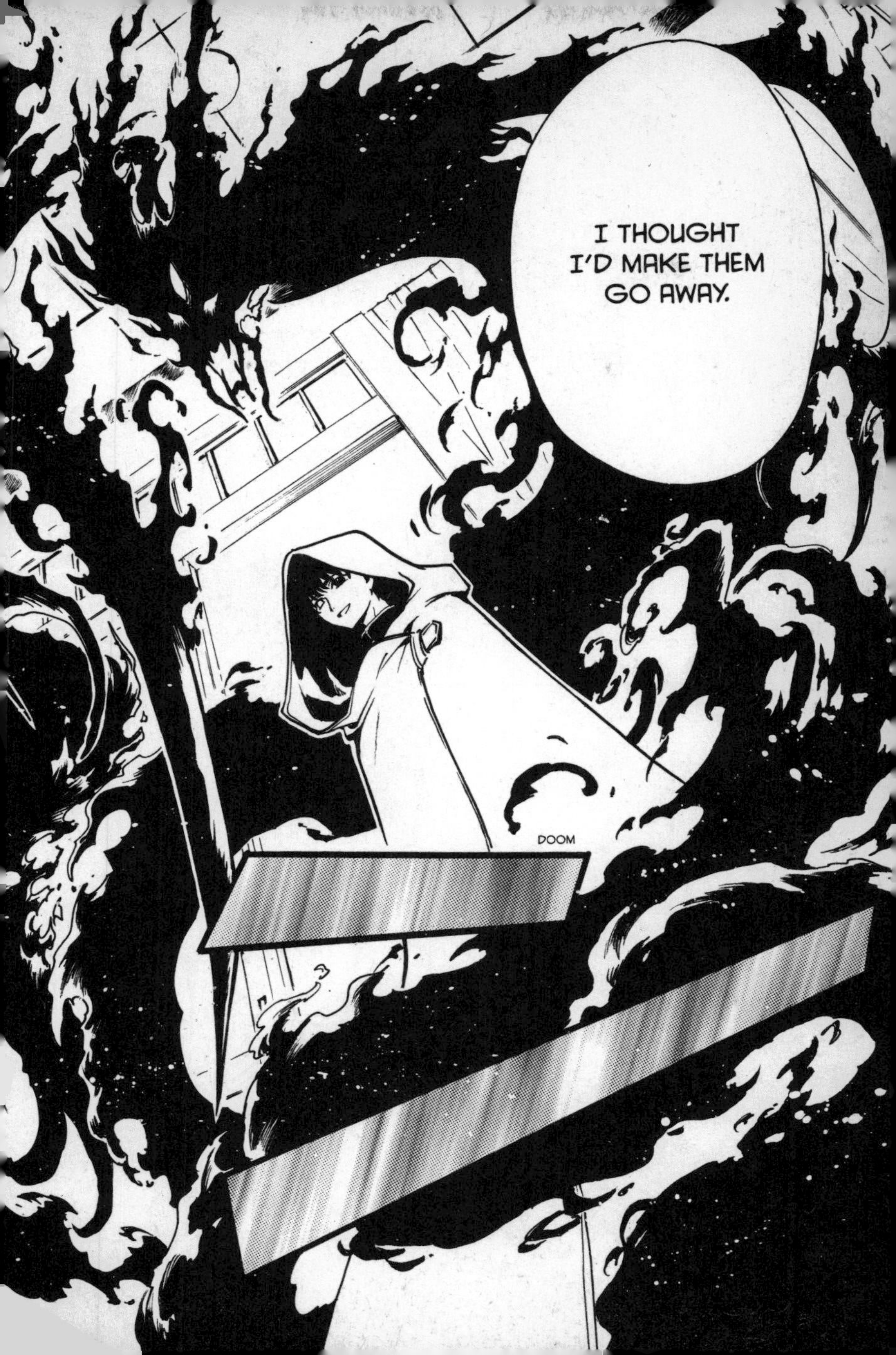
I THOUGHT I'D MAKE THEM GO AWAY.
DOOM

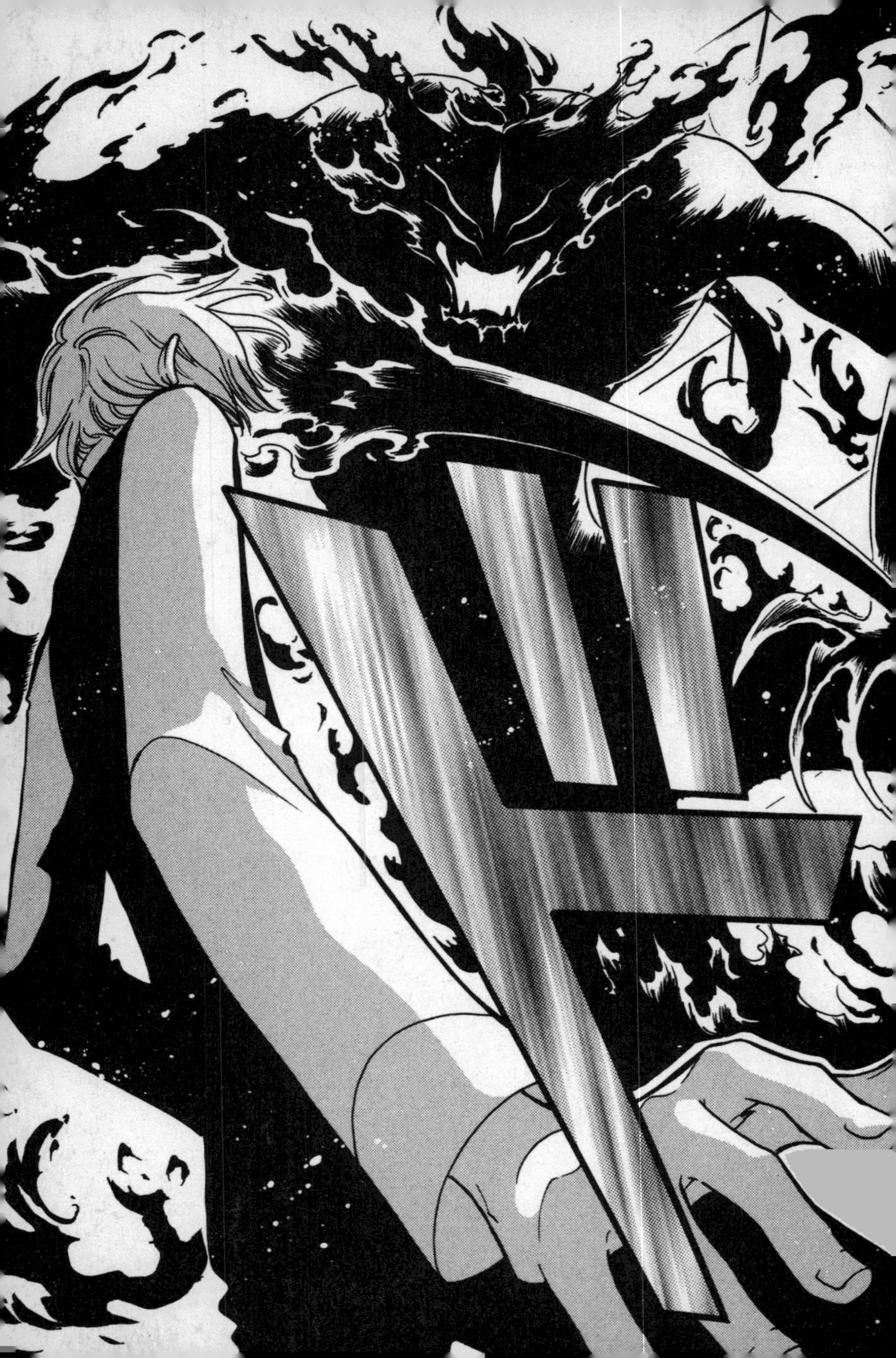

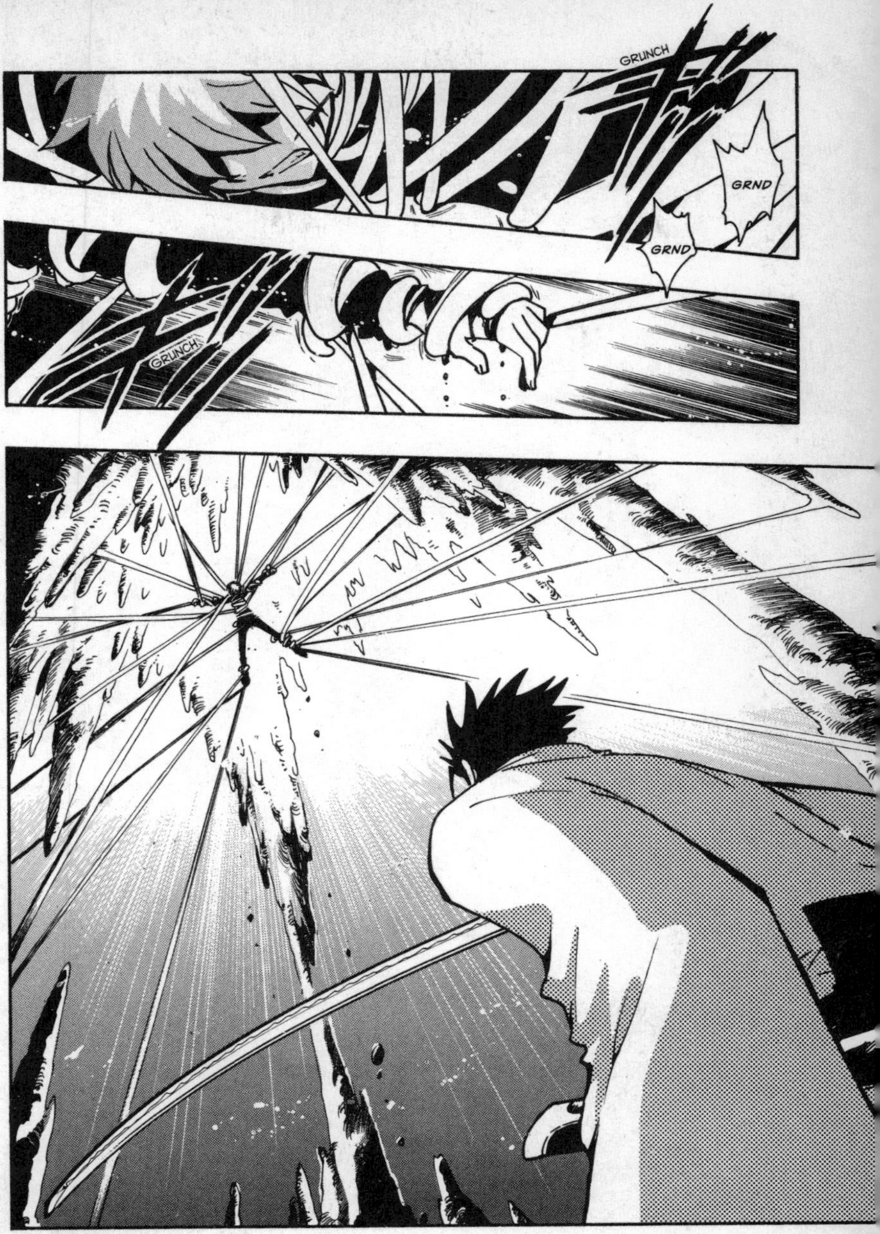
GRUNCH
GRND
GRND
GRUNCH

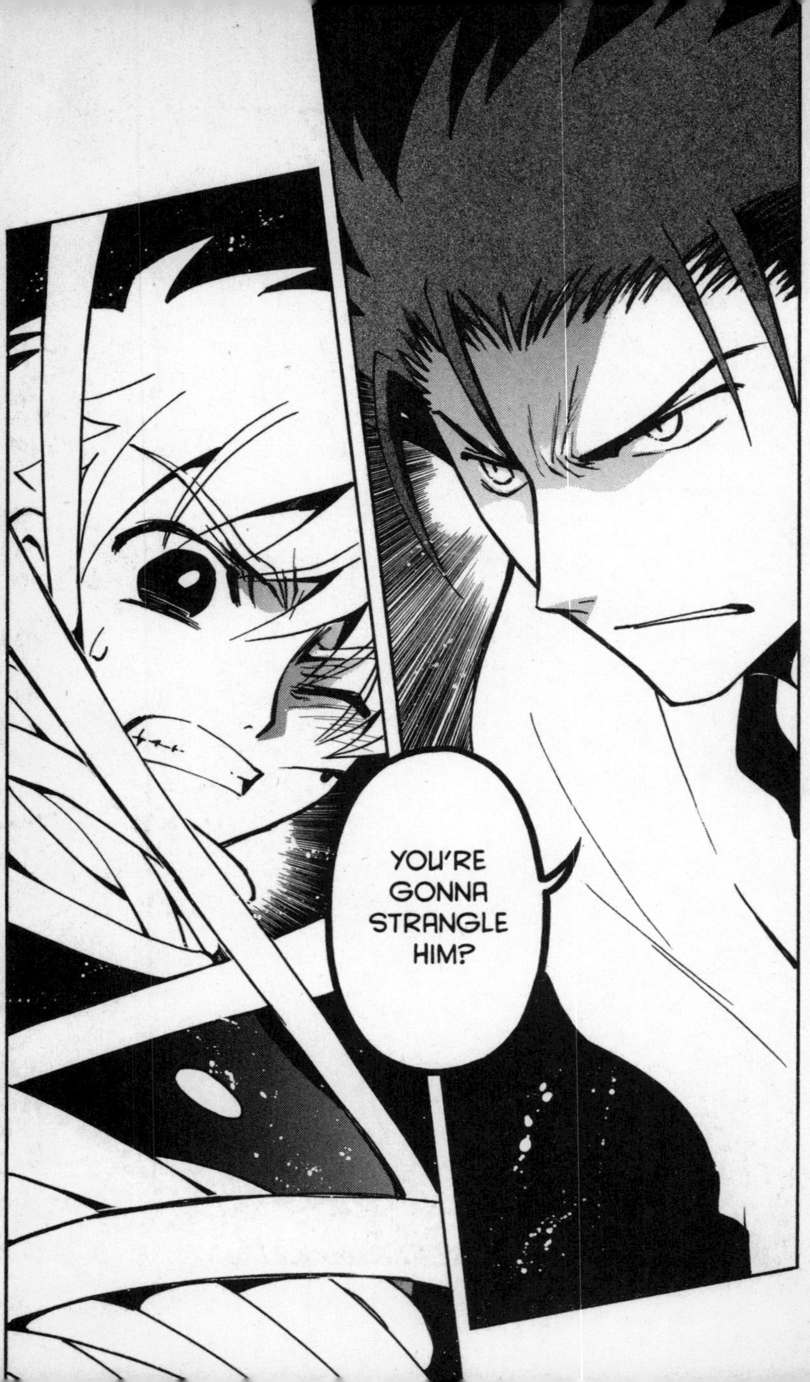
YOU'RE GONNA STRANGLE HIM?

ツバサ

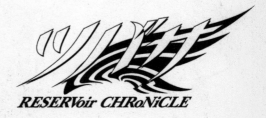

RESERVoir CHRoNiCLE

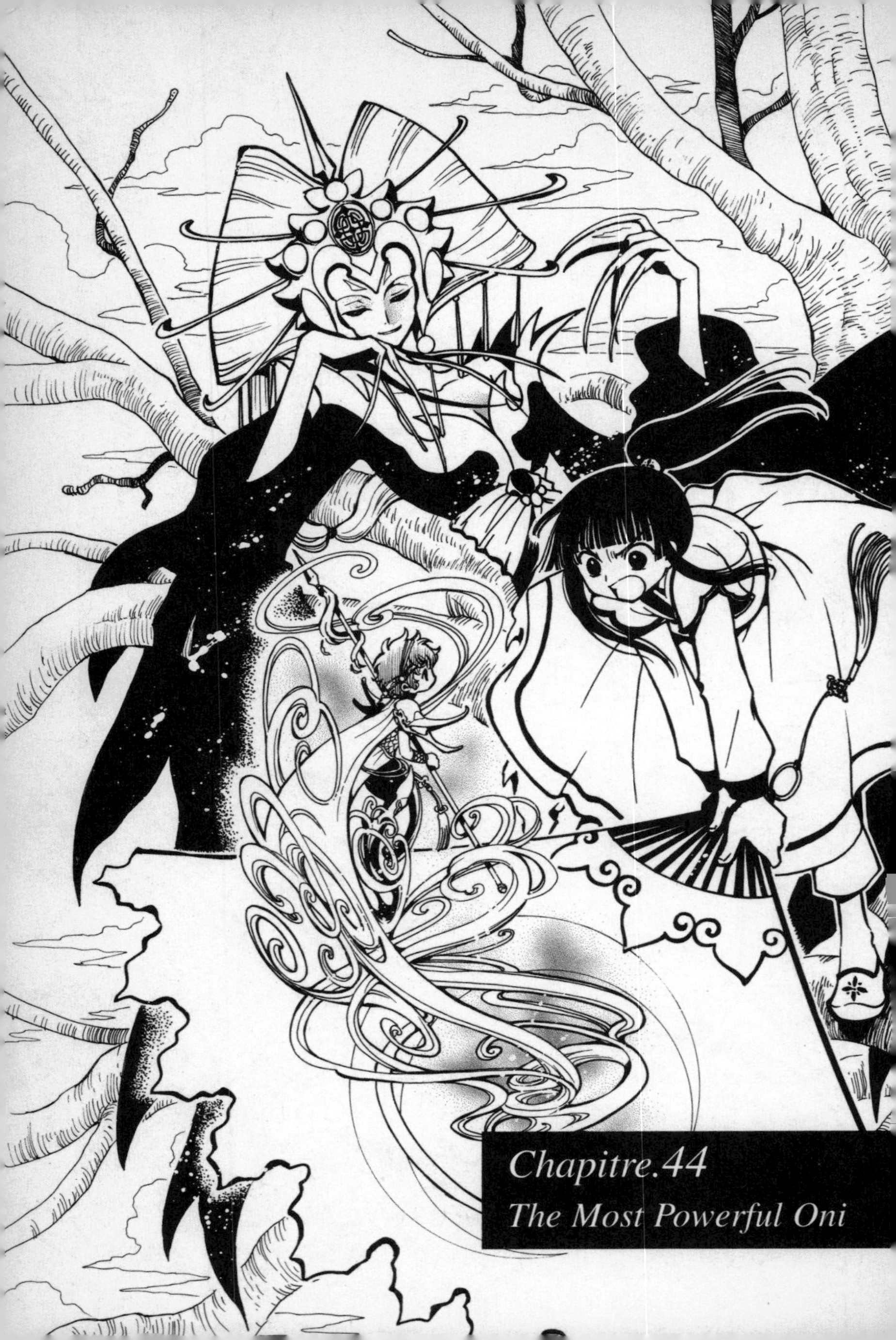

Chapitre.44

The Most Powerful Oni

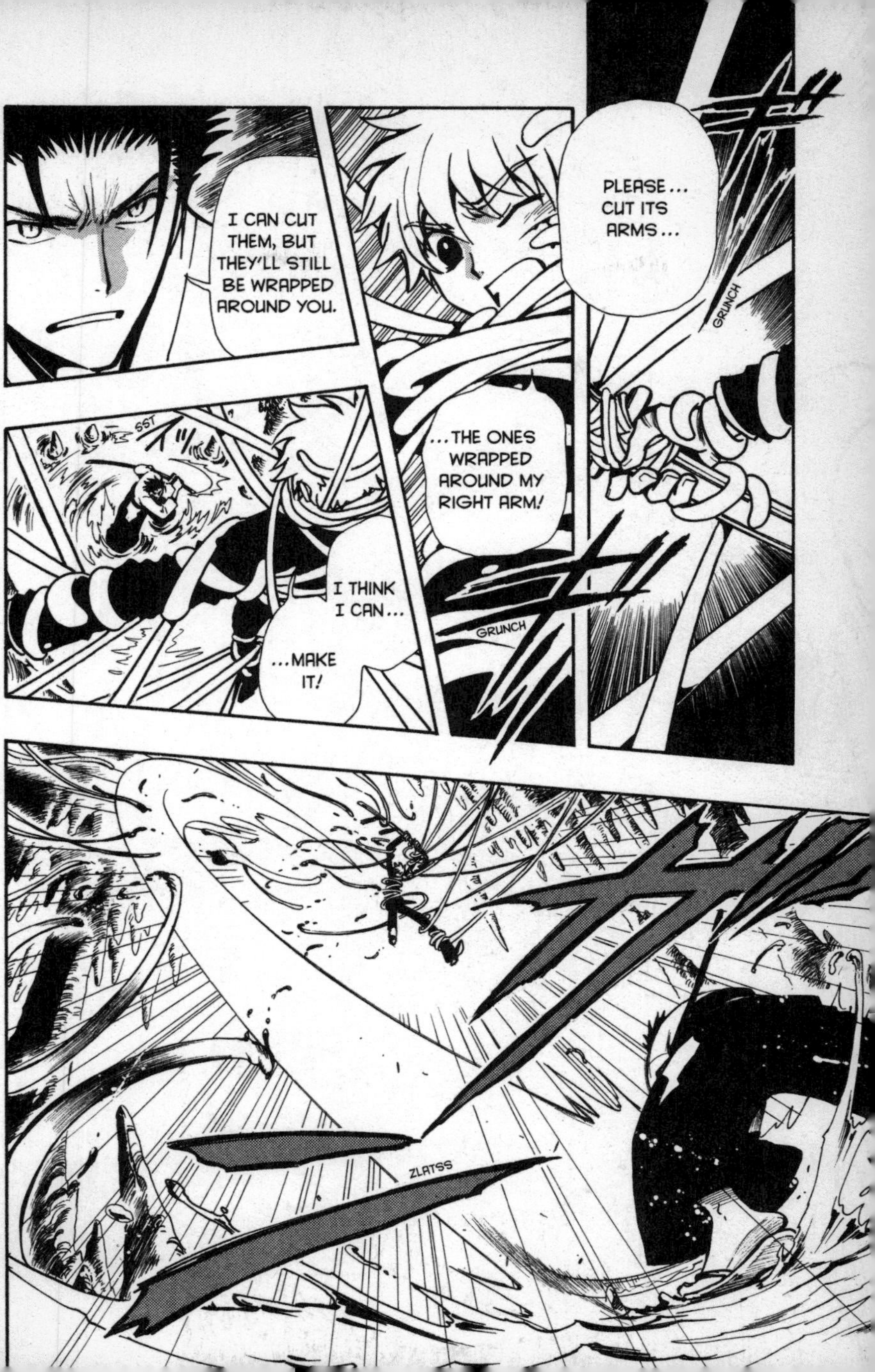
PLEASE... CUT ITS ARMS...
GRUNCH
...THE ONES WRAPPED AROUND MY RIGHT ARM!
GRUNCH
I CAN CUT THEM, BUT THEY'LL STILL BE WRAPPED AROUND YOU.
SST
I THINK I CAN...
...MAKE IT!
ZLATSS

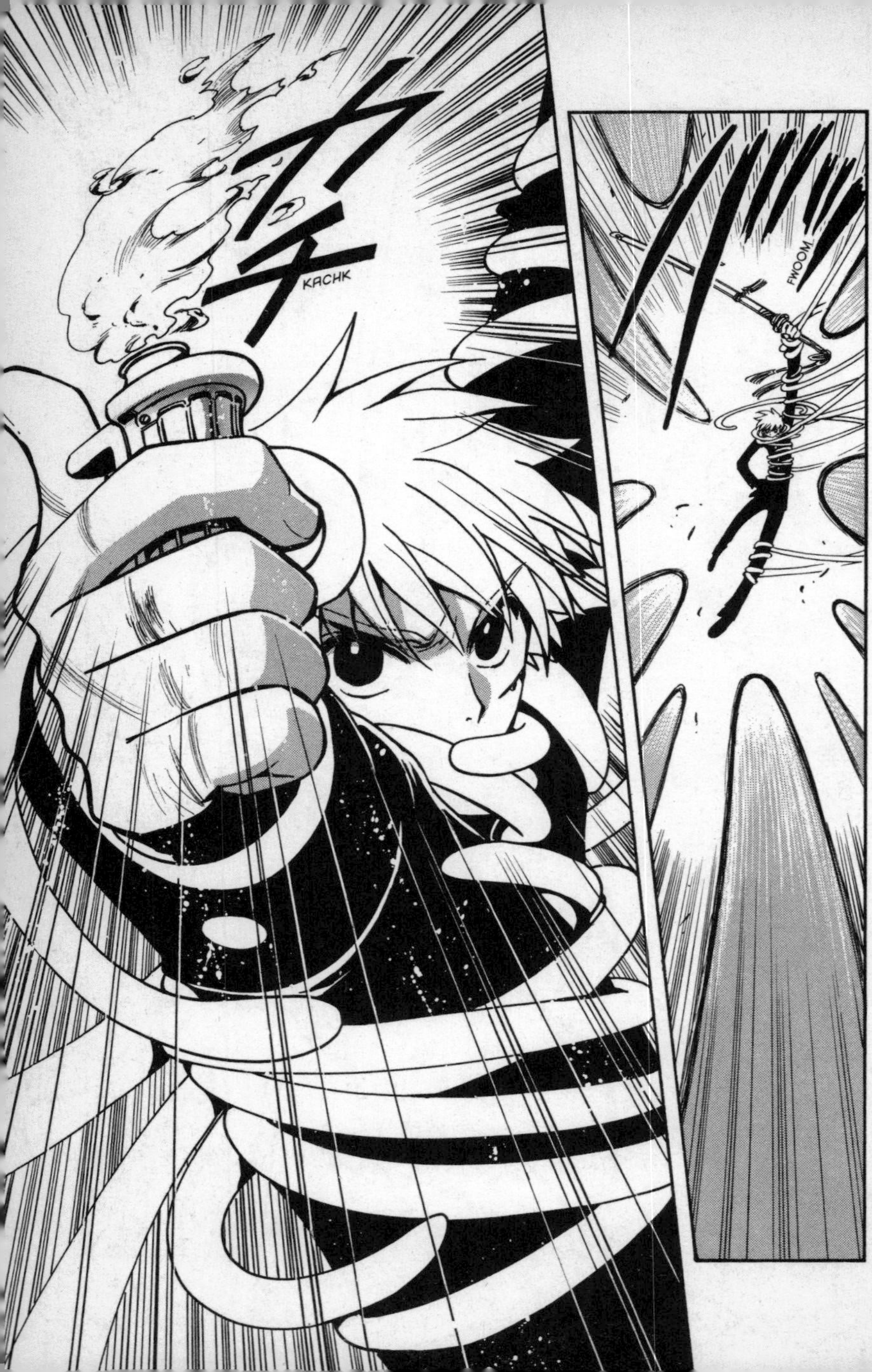
FWOOM
カチ
KACHK

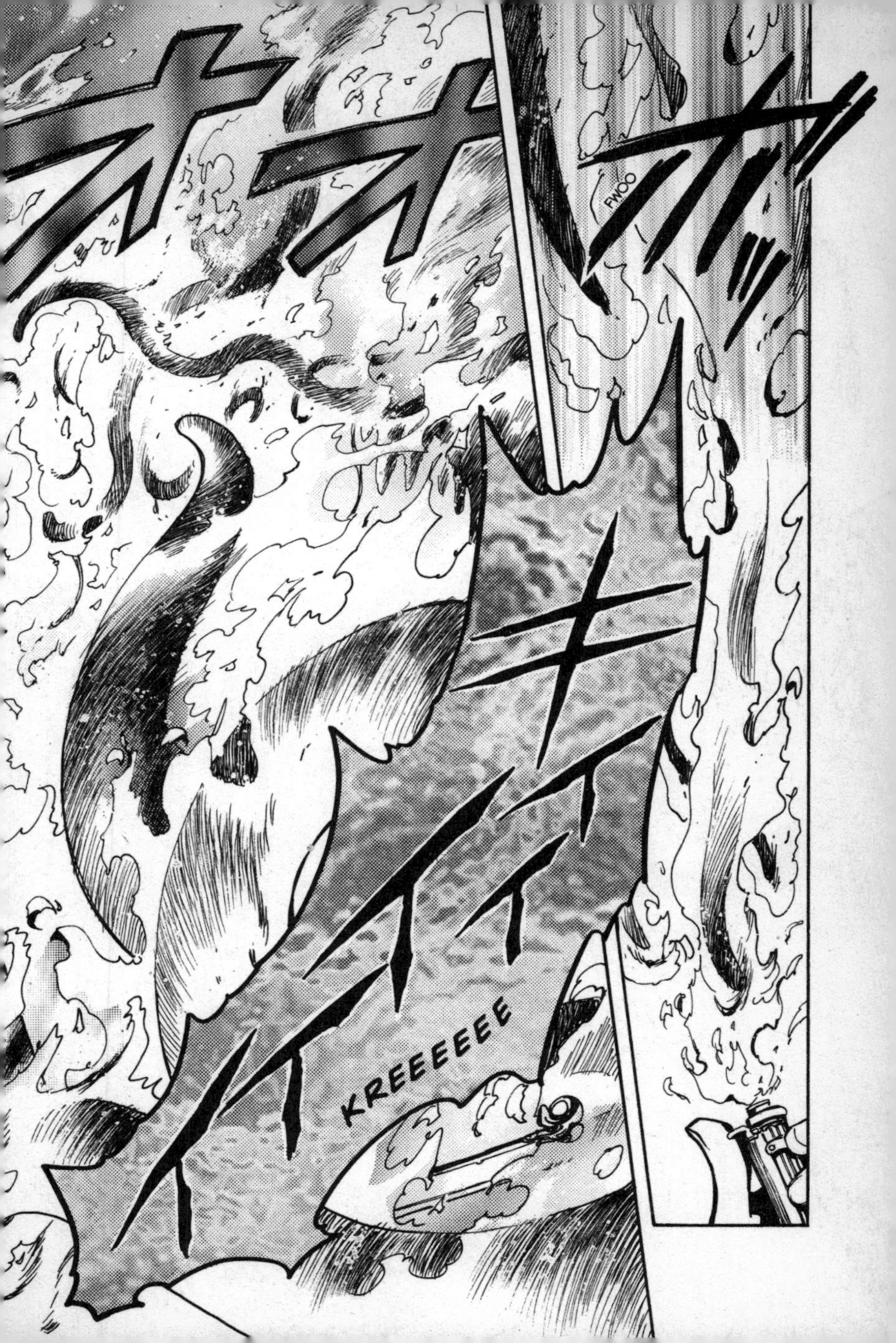

FWOO
KREEEEEEE

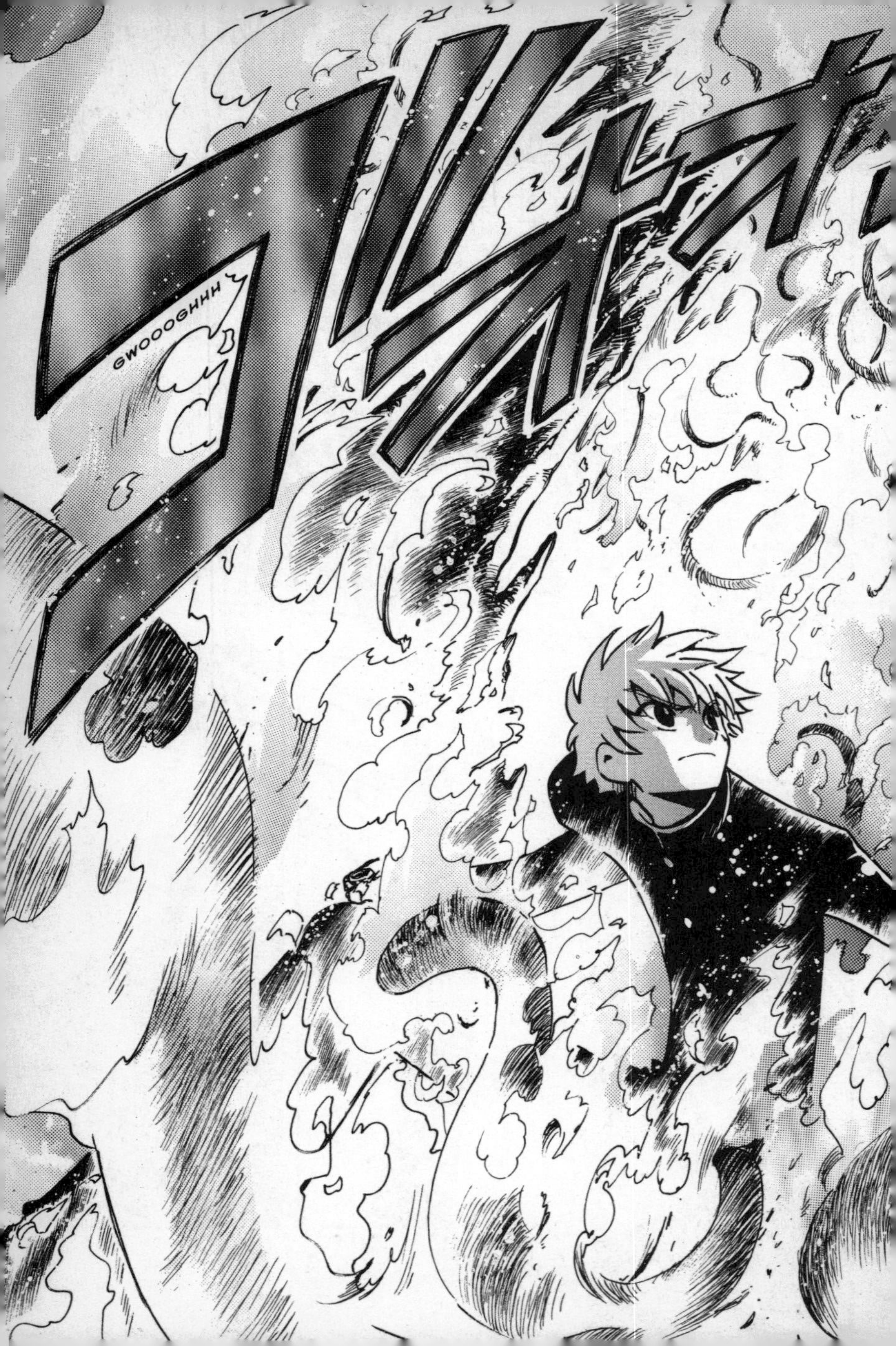
GWOOOGHHH

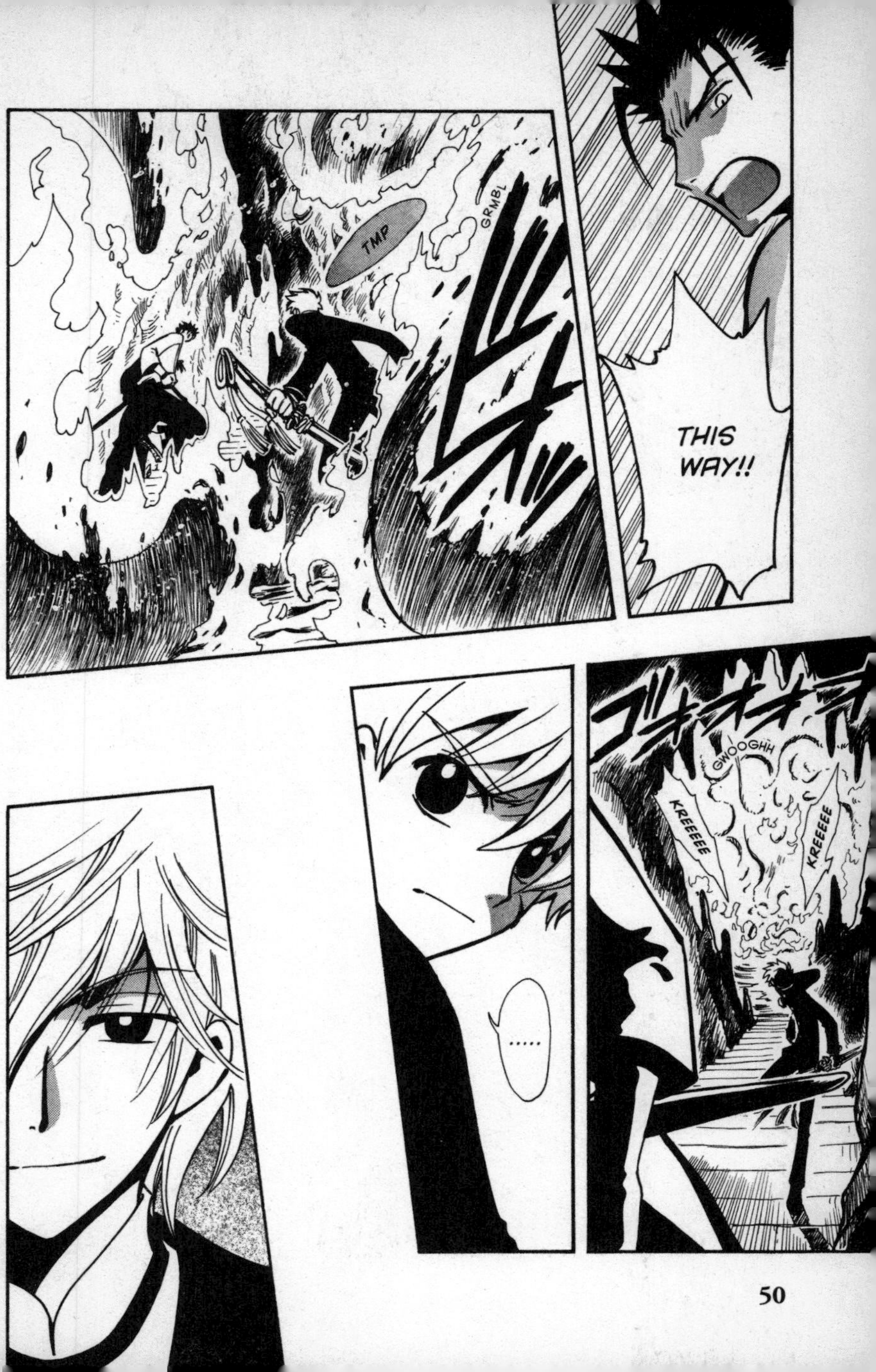
THIS WAY!!
GRMBL
TMP
GWOOGHH
KREEEEEE
KREEEEE
......

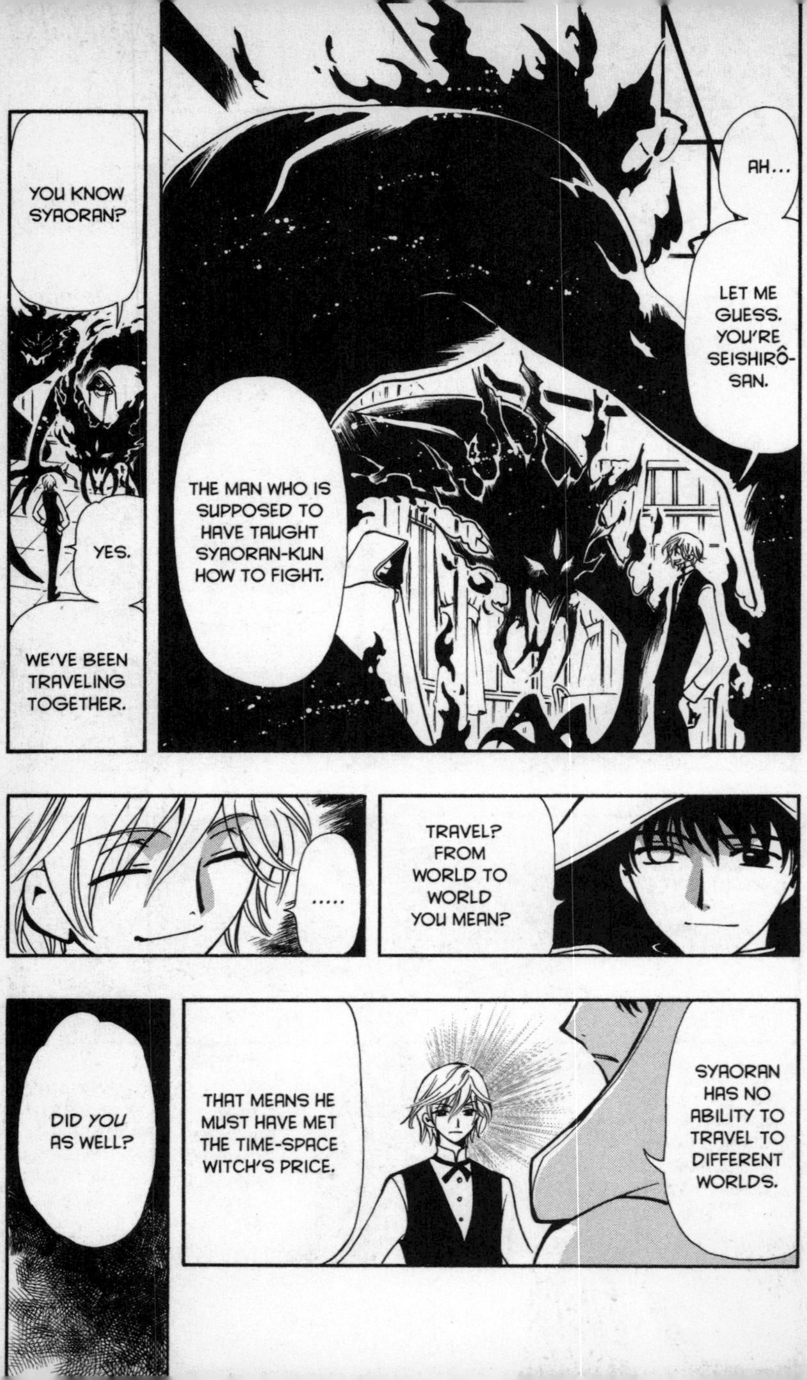
AH...
LET ME GUESS. YOU'RE SEISHIRÔ-SAN.
THE MAN WHO IS SUPPOSED TO HAVE TAUGHT SYAORAN-KUN HOW TO FIGHT.
YOU KNOW SYAORAN?
YES.
WE'VE BEEN TRAVELING TOGETHER.
TRAVEL? FROM WORLD TO WORLD YOU MEAN?
.....
SYAORAN HAS NO ABILITY TO TRAVEL TO DIFFERENT WORLDS.
THAT MEANS HE MUST HAVE MET THE TIME-SPACE WITCH'S PRICE.
DID *YOU* AS WELL?

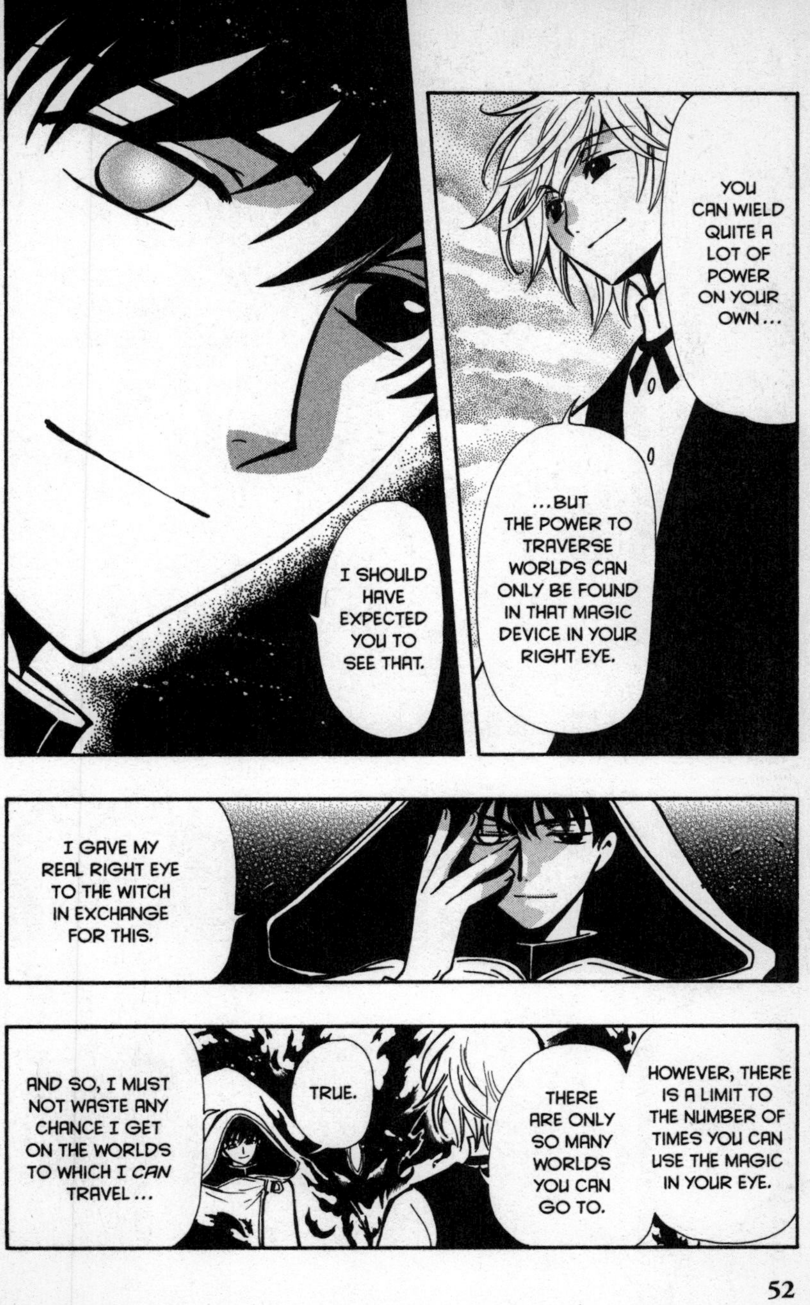
YOU CAN WIELD QUITE A LOT OF POWER ON YOUR OWN...
...BUT THE POWER TO TRAVERSE WORLDS CAN ONLY BE FOUND IN THAT MAGIC DEVICE IN YOUR RIGHT EYE.
I SHOULD HAVE EXPECTED YOU TO SEE THAT.
I GAVE MY REAL RIGHT EYE TO THE WITCH IN EXCHANGE FOR THIS.
HOWEVER, THERE IS A LIMIT TO THE NUMBER OF TIMES YOU CAN USE THE MAGIC IN YOUR EYE.
THERE ARE ONLY SO MANY WORLDS YOU CAN GO TO.
TRUE.
AND SO, I MUST NOT WASTE ANY CHANCE I GET ON THE WORLDS TO WHICH I *CAN* TRAVEL...

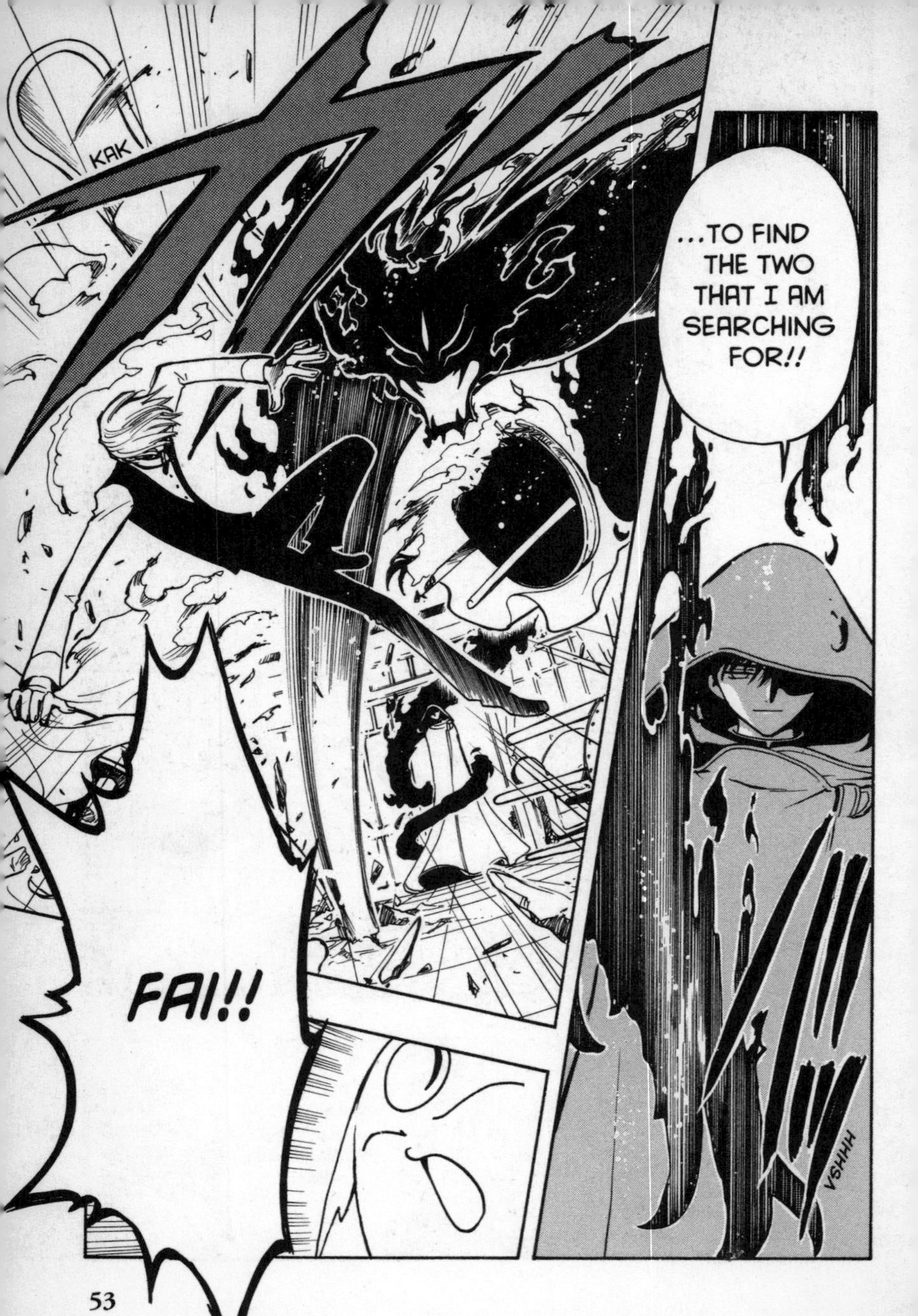
...TO FIND THE TWO THAT I AM SEARCHING FOR!!
VSHHH
KAK
FAI!!

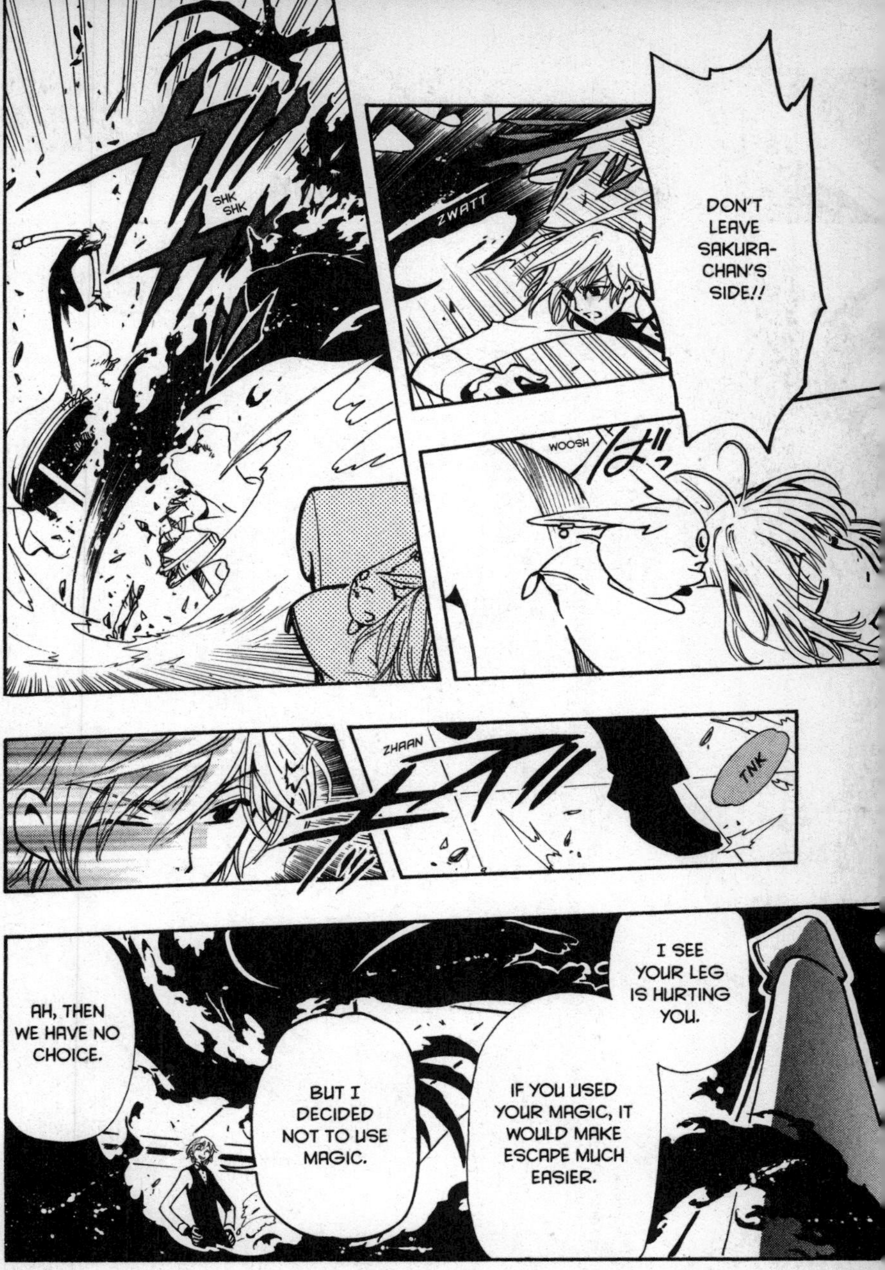
ZWATT
DON'T LEAVE SAKURA-CHAN'S SIDE!!
WOOSH
ばっ
SHK SHK
TNK
ZHAAN
I SEE YOUR LEG IS HURTING YOU.
IF YOU USED YOUR MAGIC, IT WOULD MAKE ESCAPE MUCH EASIER.
BUT I DECIDED NOT TO USE MAGIC.
AH, THEN WE HAVE NO CHOICE.

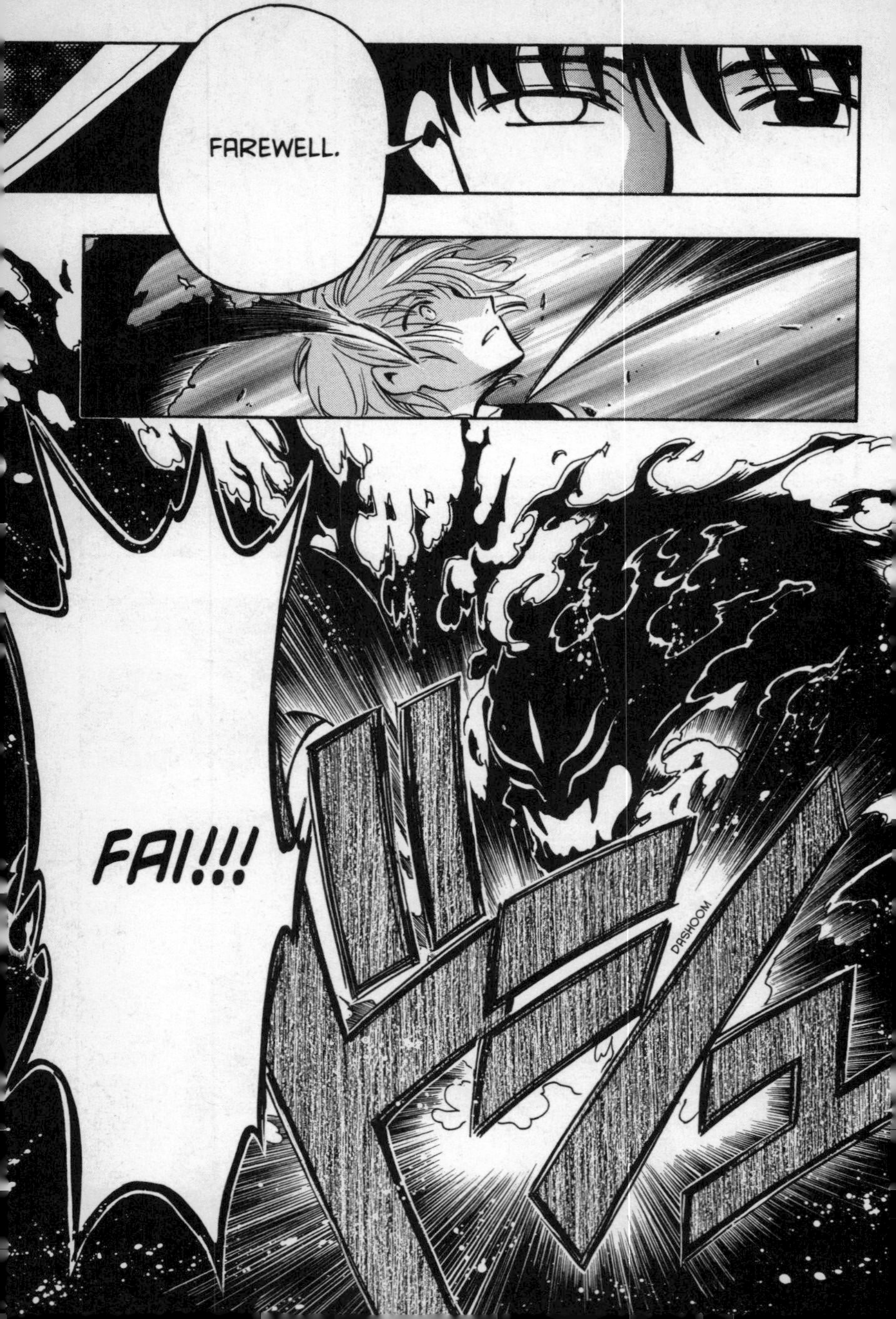
FAREWELL.
DASHOOM
FAI!!!

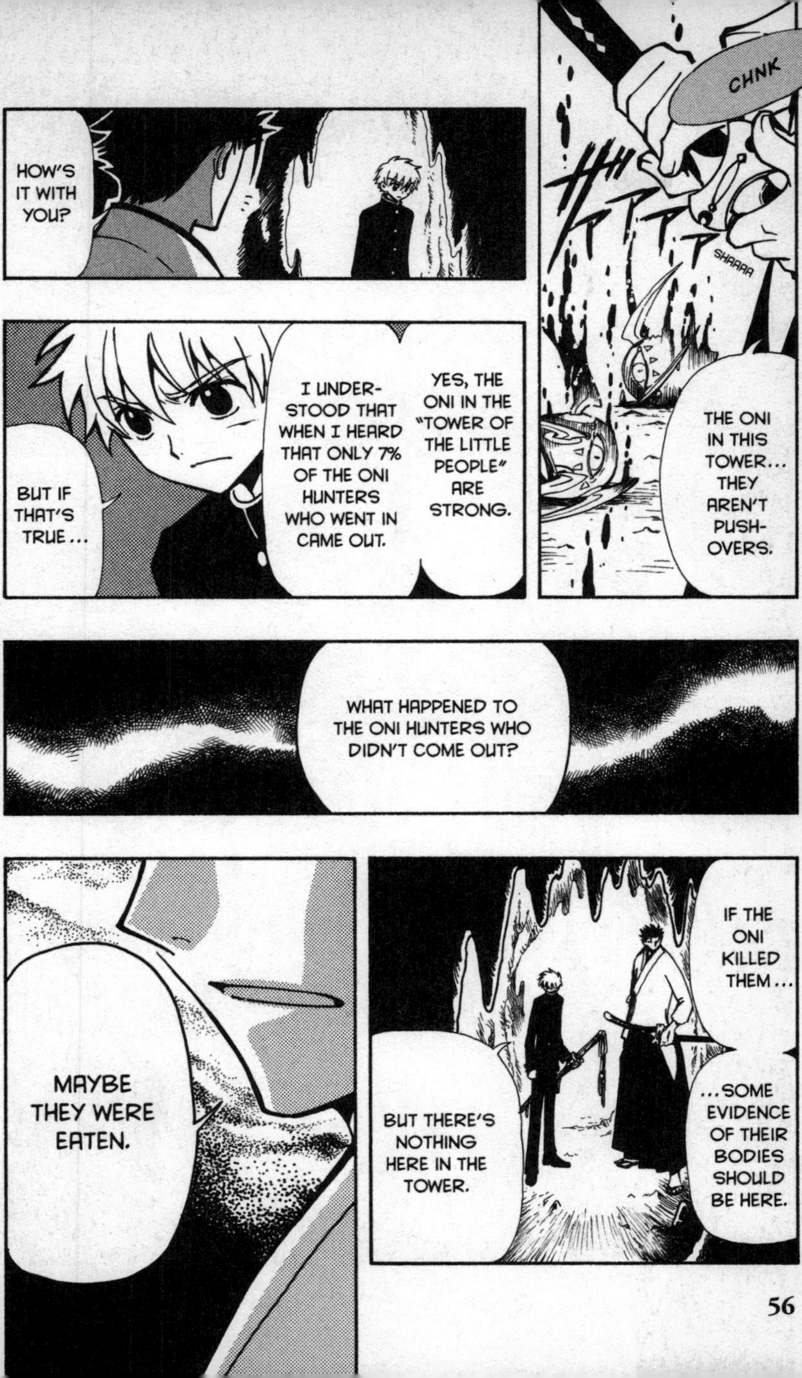
CHNK
SHAAAA
THE ONI IN THIS TOWER... THEY AREN'T PUSHOVERS.
HOW'S IT WITH YOU?
YES, THE ONI IN THE "TOWER OF THE LITTLE PEOPLE" ARE STRONG.
I UNDERSTOOD THAT WHEN I HEARD THAT ONLY 7% OF THE ONI HUNTERS WHO WENT IN CAME OUT.
BUT IF THAT'S TRUE...
WHAT HAPPENED TO THE ONI HUNTERS WHO DIDN'T COME OUT?
IF THE ONI KILLED THEM...
...SOME EVIDENCE OF THEIR BODIES SHOULD BE HERE.
BUT THERE'S NOTHING HERE IN THE TOWER.
MAYBE THEY WERE EATEN.

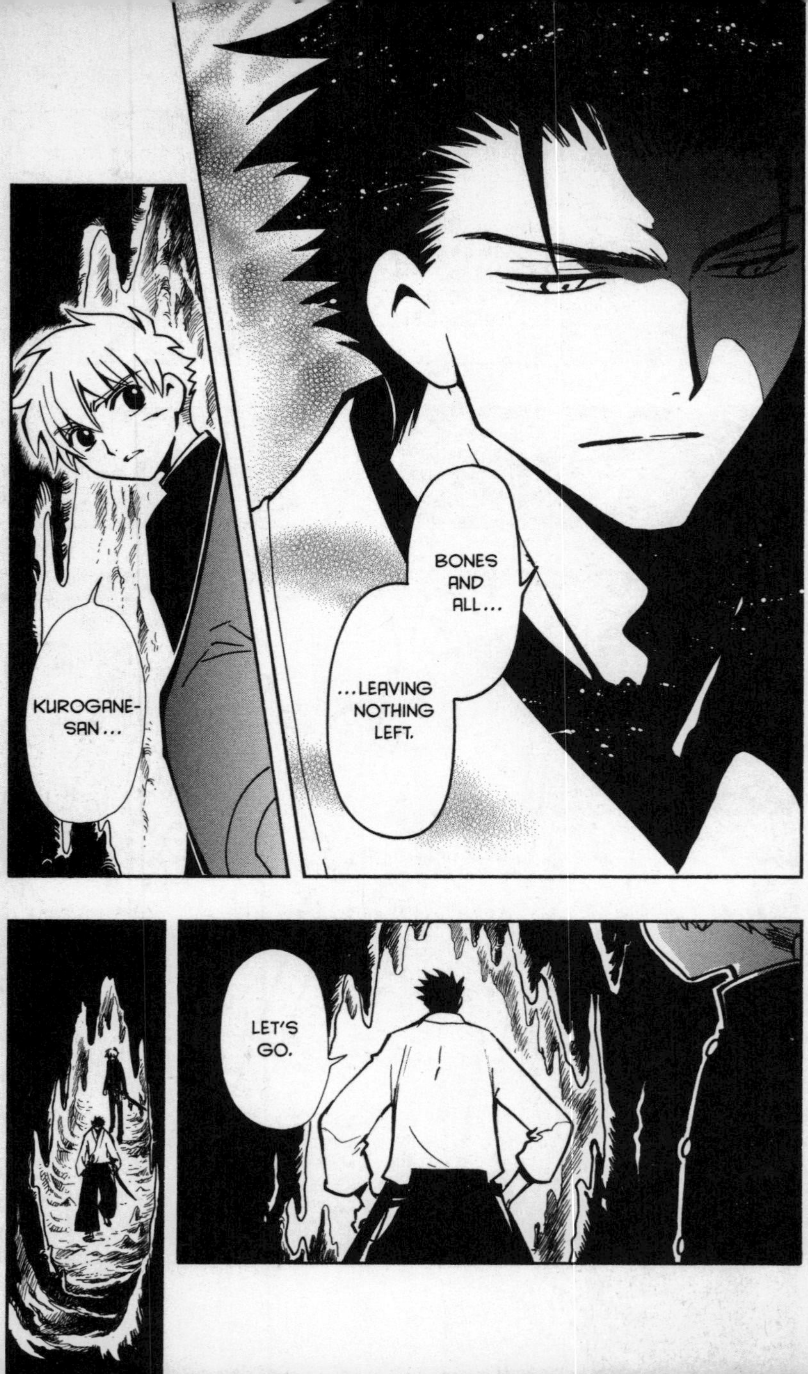
BONES AND ALL...
...LEAVING NOTHING LEFT.
KUROGANE-SAN...
LET'S GO.

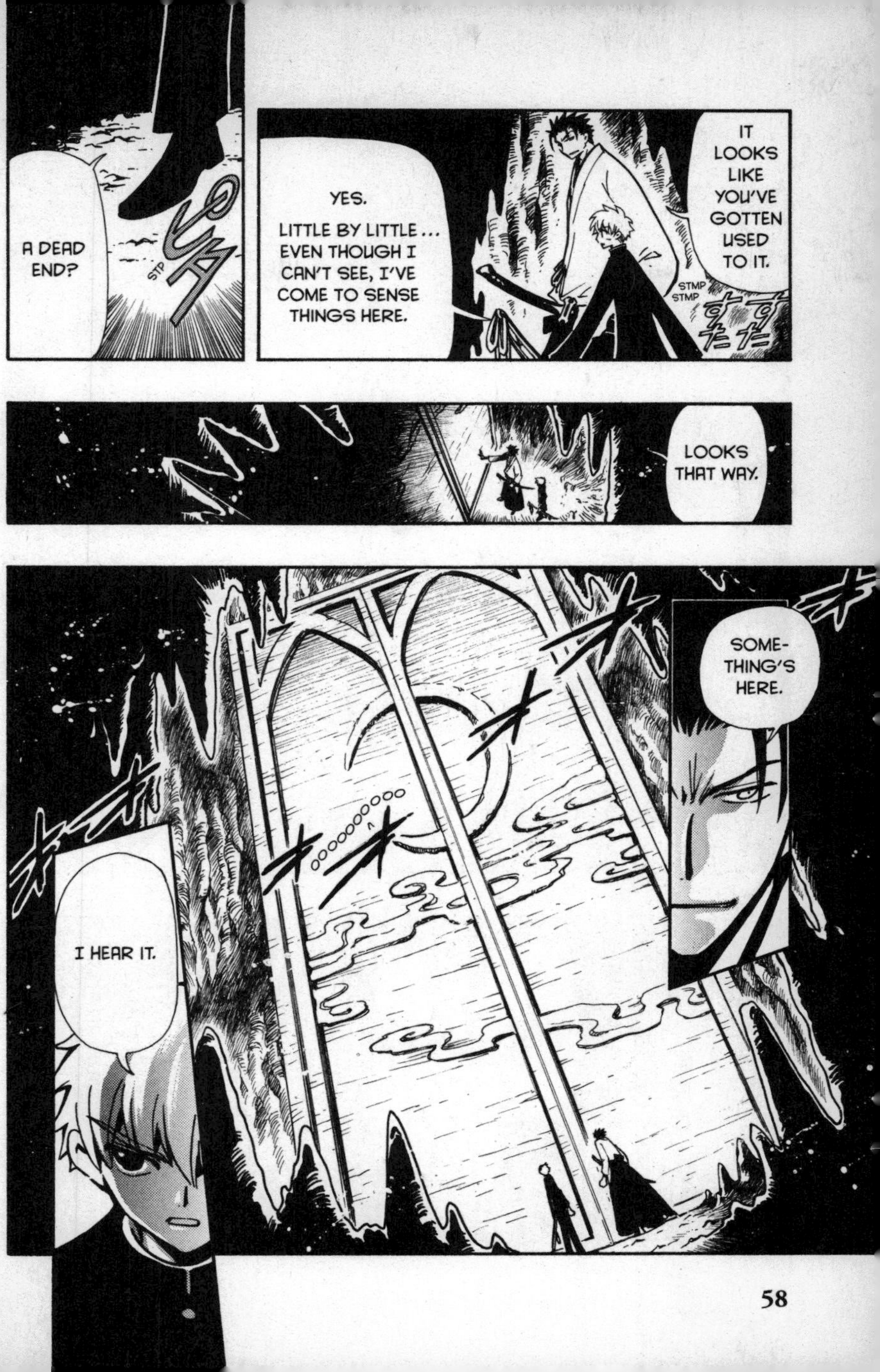
IT LOOKS LIKE YOU'VE GOTTEN USED TO IT.
STMP STMP
YES.
LITTLE BY LITTLE … EVEN THOUGH I CAN'T SEE, I'VE COME TO SENSE THINGS HERE.
STP
A DEAD END?
LOOKS THAT WAY.
SOME-THING'S HERE.
I HEAR IT.

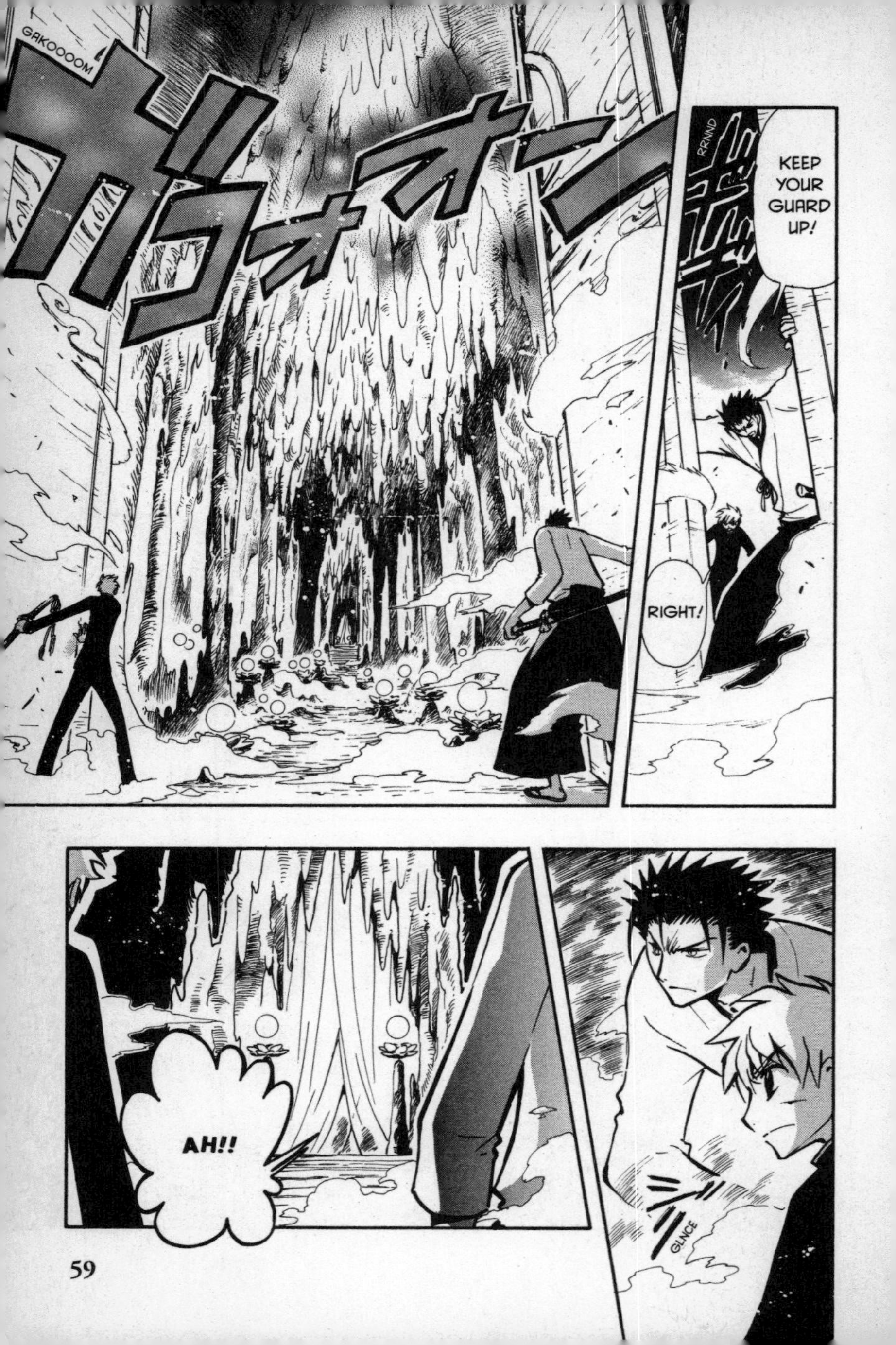
RRNND
KEEP YOUR GUARD UP!
RIGHT!
GAKOOOOM
GLNCE
AH!!

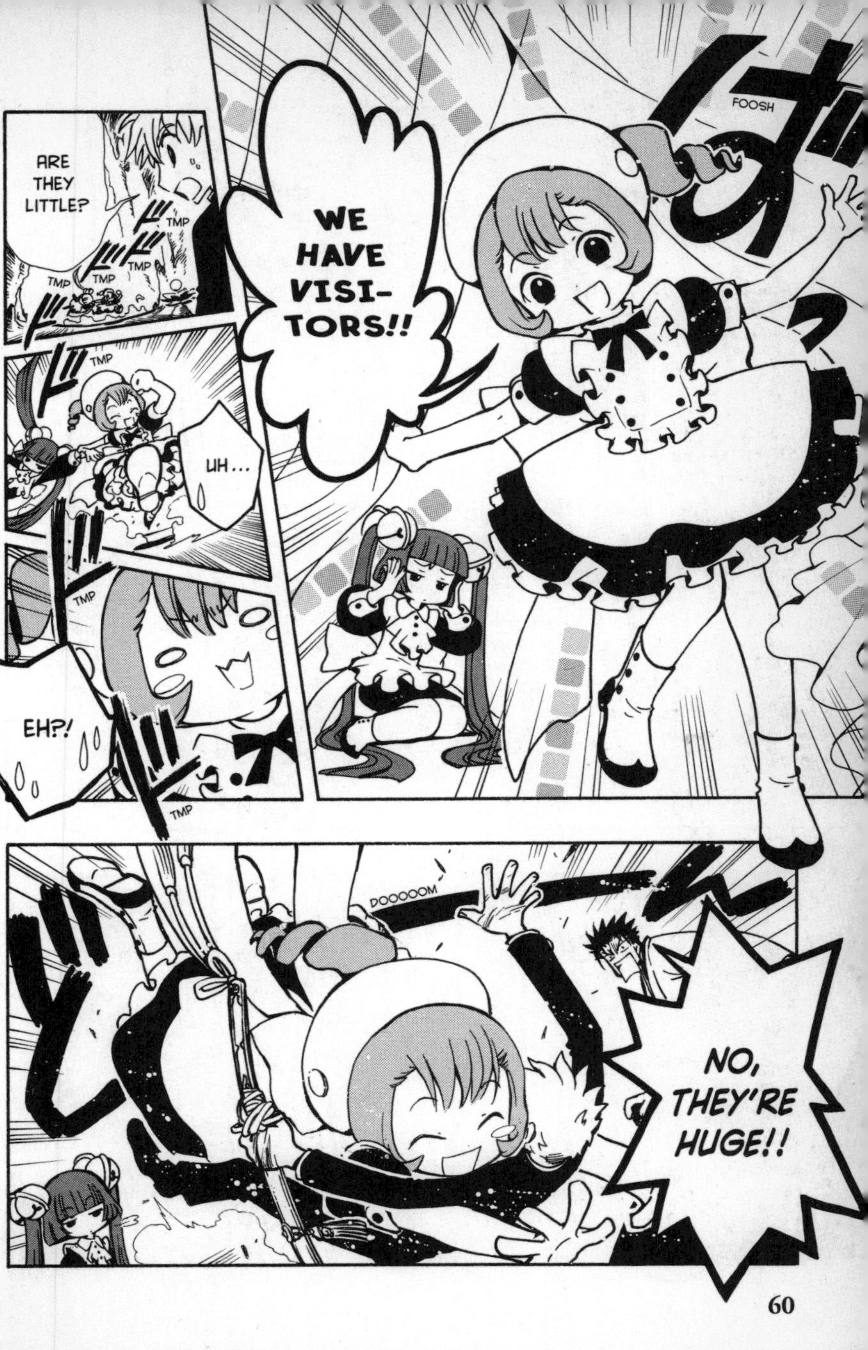
FOOSH
WE HAVE VISITORS!!
ARE THEY LITTLE?
TMP
TMP
TMP
TMP
TMP
UH...
TMP
EH?!
TMP
DOOOOOM
NO, THEY'RE HUGE!!

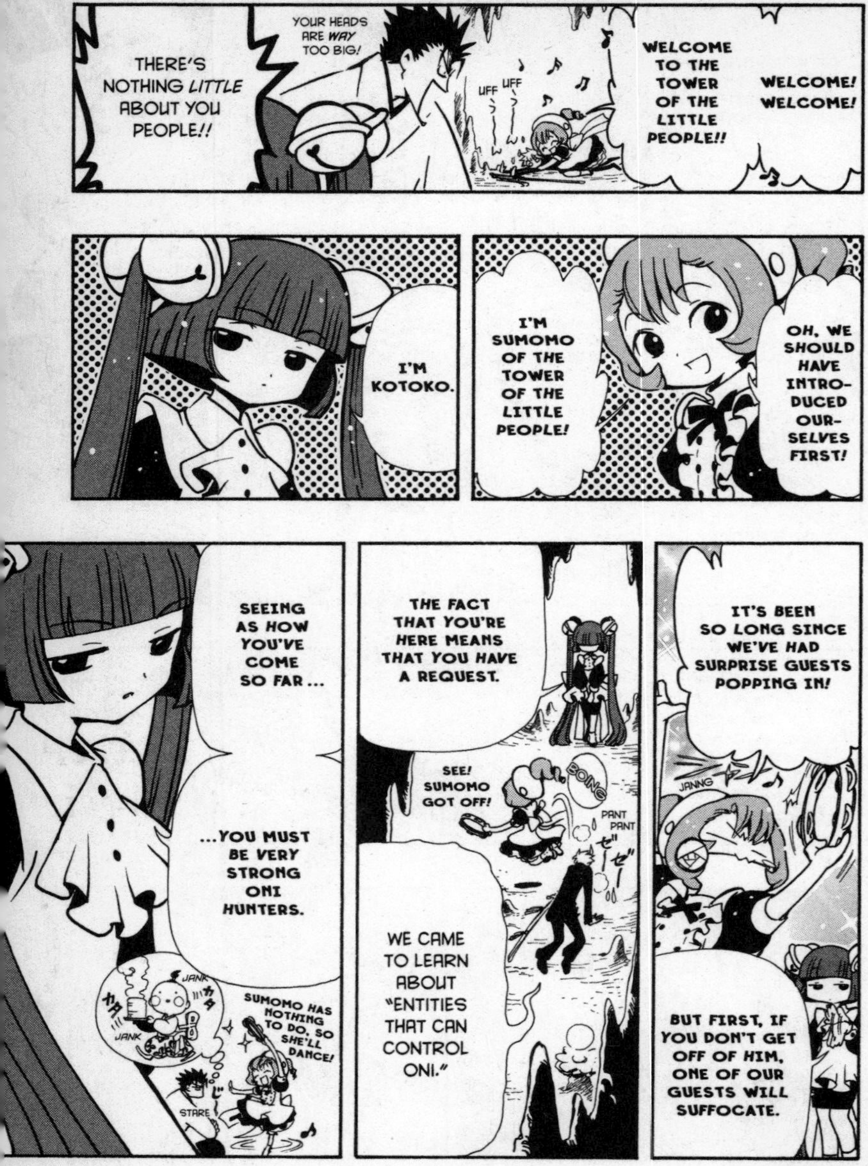
WELCOME! WELCOME!
WELCOME TO THE TOWER OF THE LITTLE PEOPLE!!
UFF UFF
YOUR HEADS ARE WAY TOO BIG!
THERE'S NOTHING LITTLE ABOUT YOU PEOPLE!!
OH, WE SHOULD HAVE INTRODUCED OURSELVES FIRST!
I'M SUMOMO OF THE TOWER OF THE LITTLE PEOPLE!
I'M KOTOKO.
IT'S BEEN SO LONG SINCE WE'VE HAD SURPRISE GUESTS POPPING IN!
JANNG
BUT FIRST, IF YOU DON'T GET OFF OF HIM, ONE OF OUR GUESTS WILL SUFFOCATE.
THE FACT THAT YOU'RE HERE MEANS THAT YOU HAVE A REQUEST.
SEE! SUMOMO GOT OFF!
BOING
PANT PANT
WE CAME TO LEARN ABOUT "ENTITIES THAT CAN CONTROL ONI."
SEEING AS HOW YOU'VE COME SO FAR...
...YOU MUST BE VERY STRONG ONI HUNTERS.
SUMOMO HAS NOTHING TO DO, SO SHE'LL DANCE!
JANK
JANK
STARE

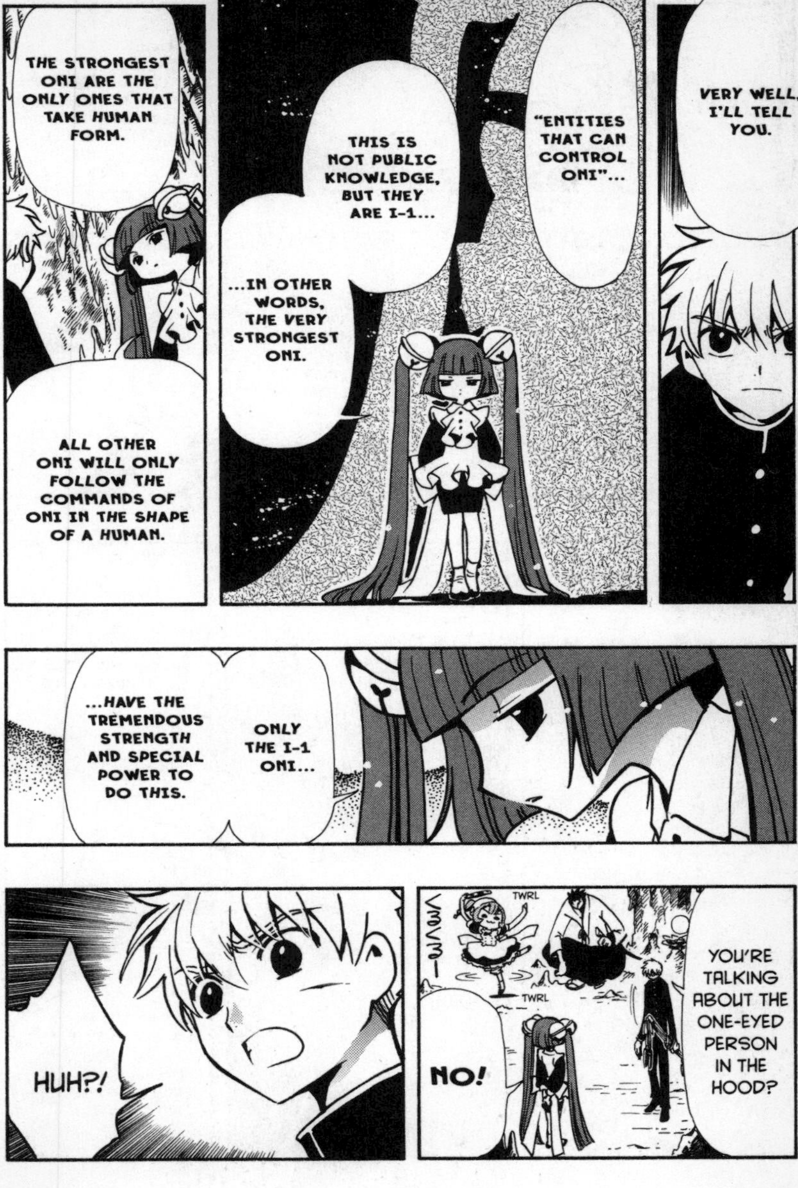
VERY WELL, I'LL TELL YOU.
"ENTITIES THAT CAN CONTROL ONI"...
THIS IS NOT PUBLIC KNOWLEDGE, BUT THEY ARE I-1...
...IN OTHER WORDS, THE VERY STRONGEST ONI.
THE STRONGEST ONI ARE THE ONLY ONES THAT TAKE HUMAN FORM.
ALL OTHER ONI WILL ONLY FOLLOW THE COMMANDS OF ONI IN THE SHAPE OF A HUMAN.
ONLY THE I-1 ONI...
...HAVE THE TREMENDOUS STRENGTH AND SPECIAL POWER TO DO THIS.
YOU'RE TALKING ABOUT THE ONE-EYED PERSON IN THE HOOD?
TWRL
TWRL
NO!
HUH?!

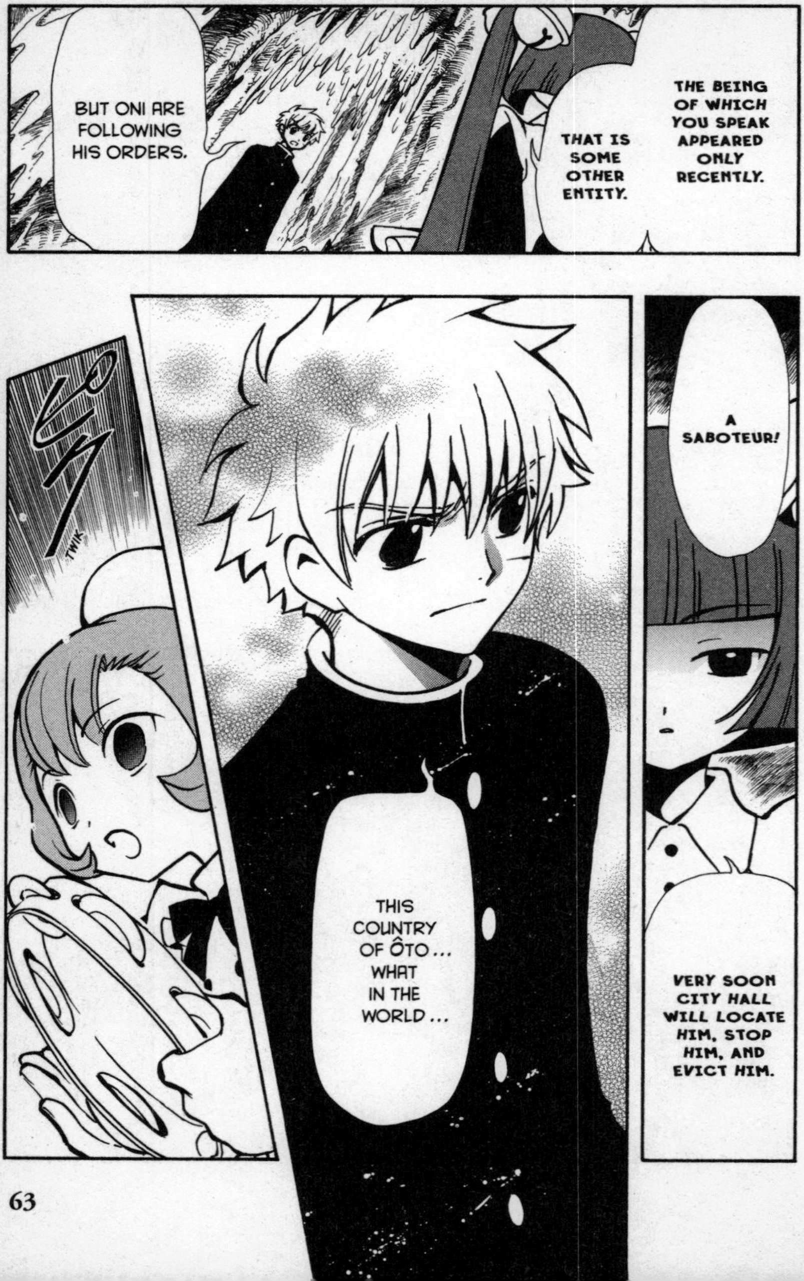
THE BEING OF WHICH YOU SPEAK APPEARED ONLY RECENTLY.
THAT IS SOME OTHER ENTITY.
BUT ONI ARE FOLLOWING HIS ORDERS.
A SABOTEUR!
VERY SOON CITY HALL WILL LOCATE HIM, STOP HIM, AND EVICT HIM.
THIS COUNTRY OF ÔTO... WHAT IN THE WORLD...
TWIK

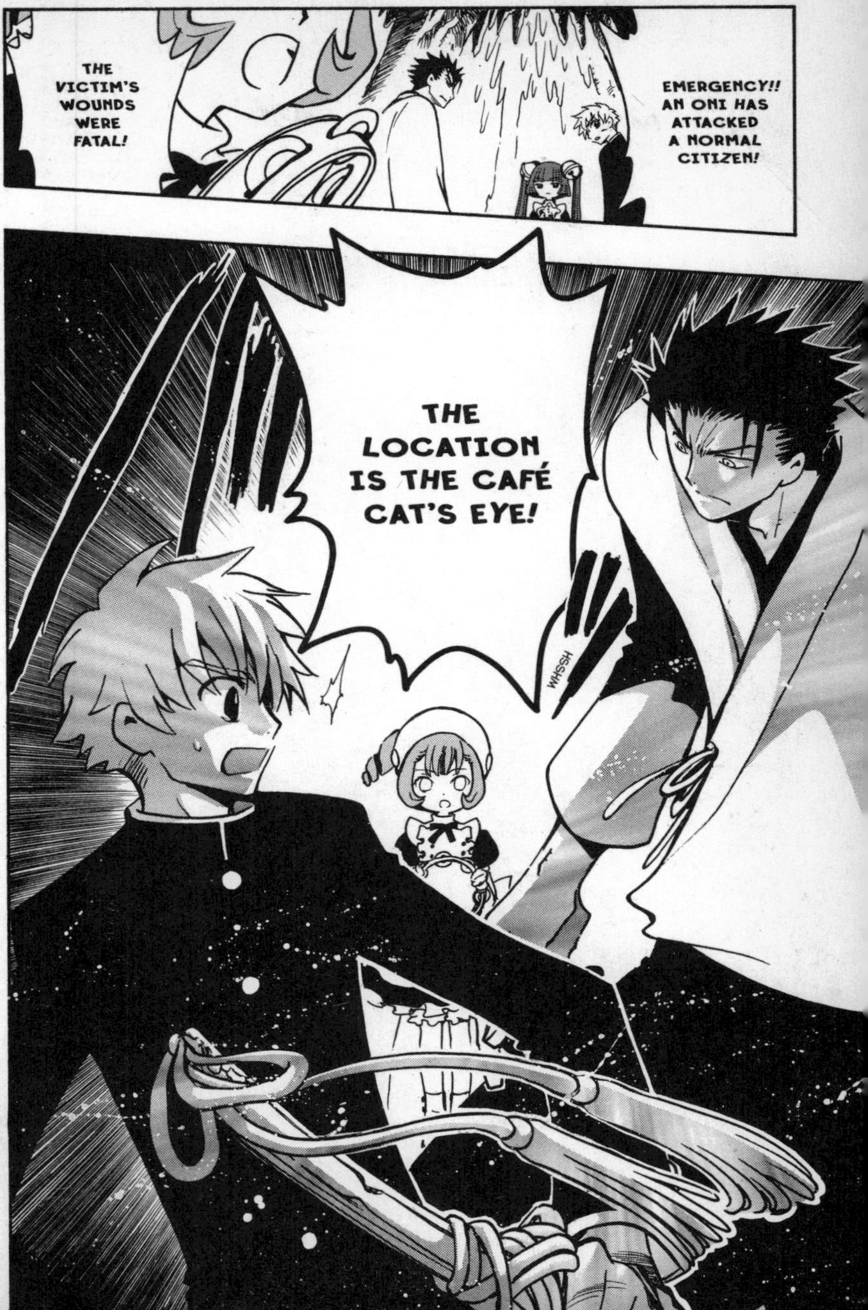
EMERGENCY!! AN ONI HAS ATTACKED A NORMAL CITIZEN!
THE VICTIM'S WOUNDS WERE FATAL!
THE LOCATION IS THE CAFÉ CAT'S EYE!
WHSSH

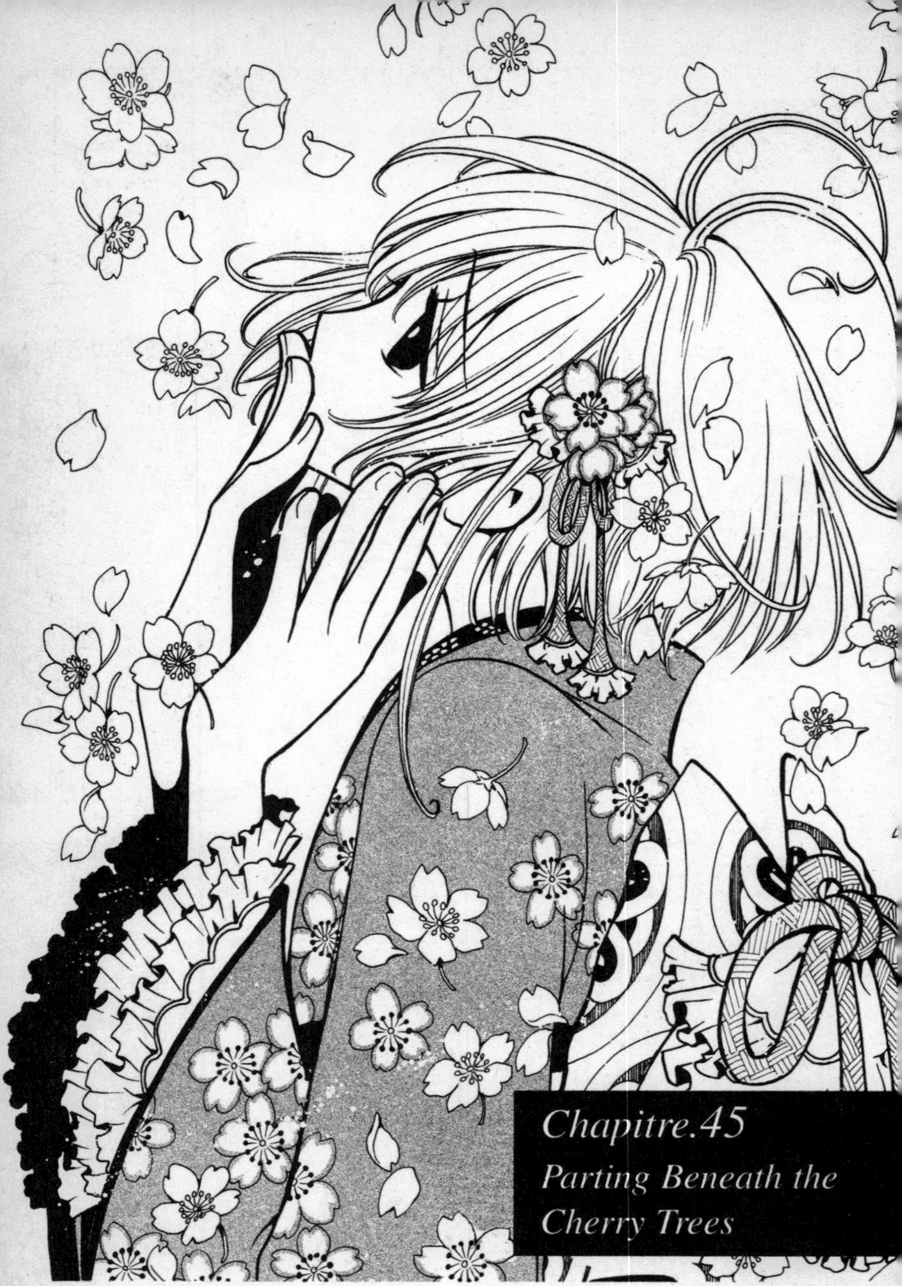

Chapitre.45
Parting Beneath the Cherry Trees

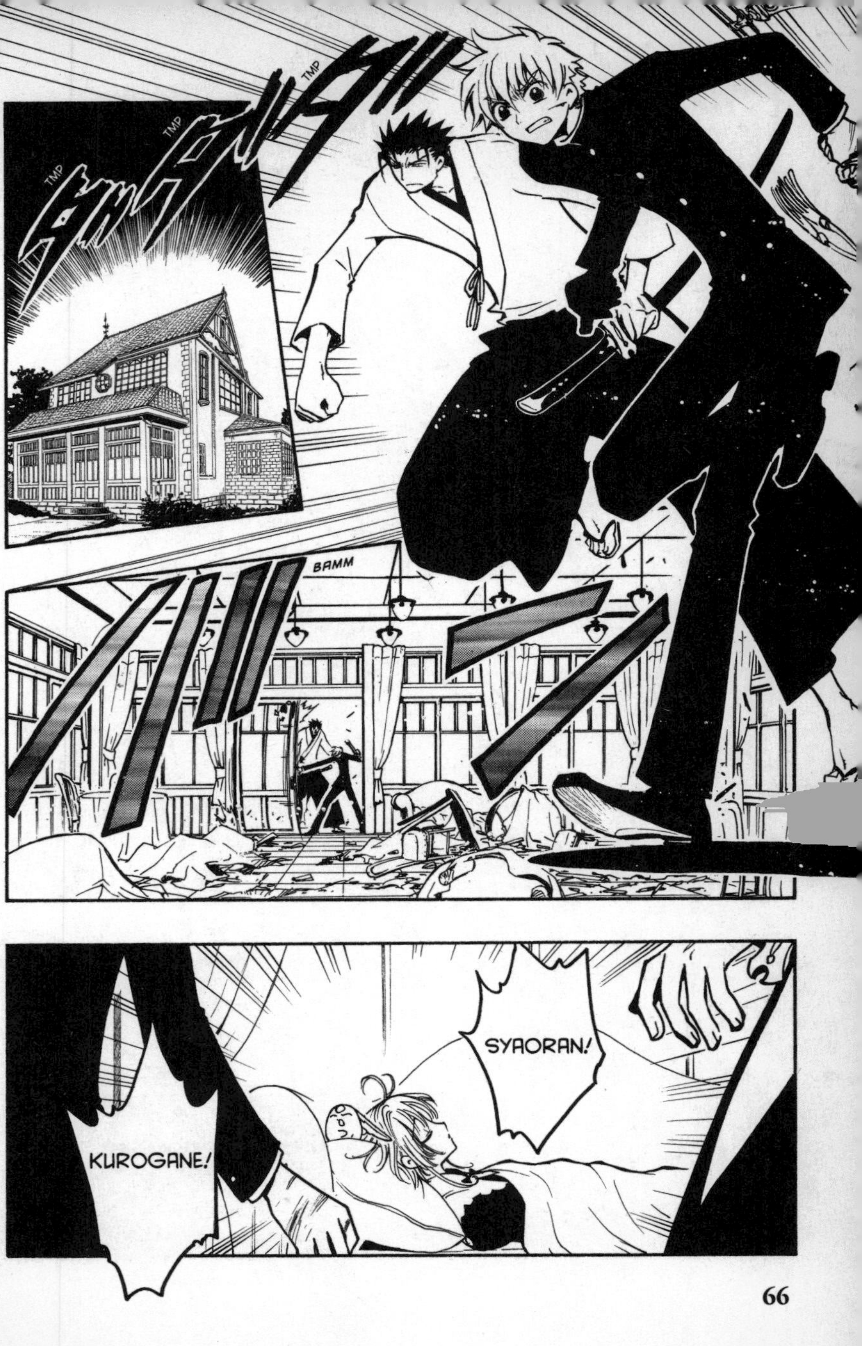
TMP
TMP
TMP
BAMM
SYAORAN!
KUROGANE!

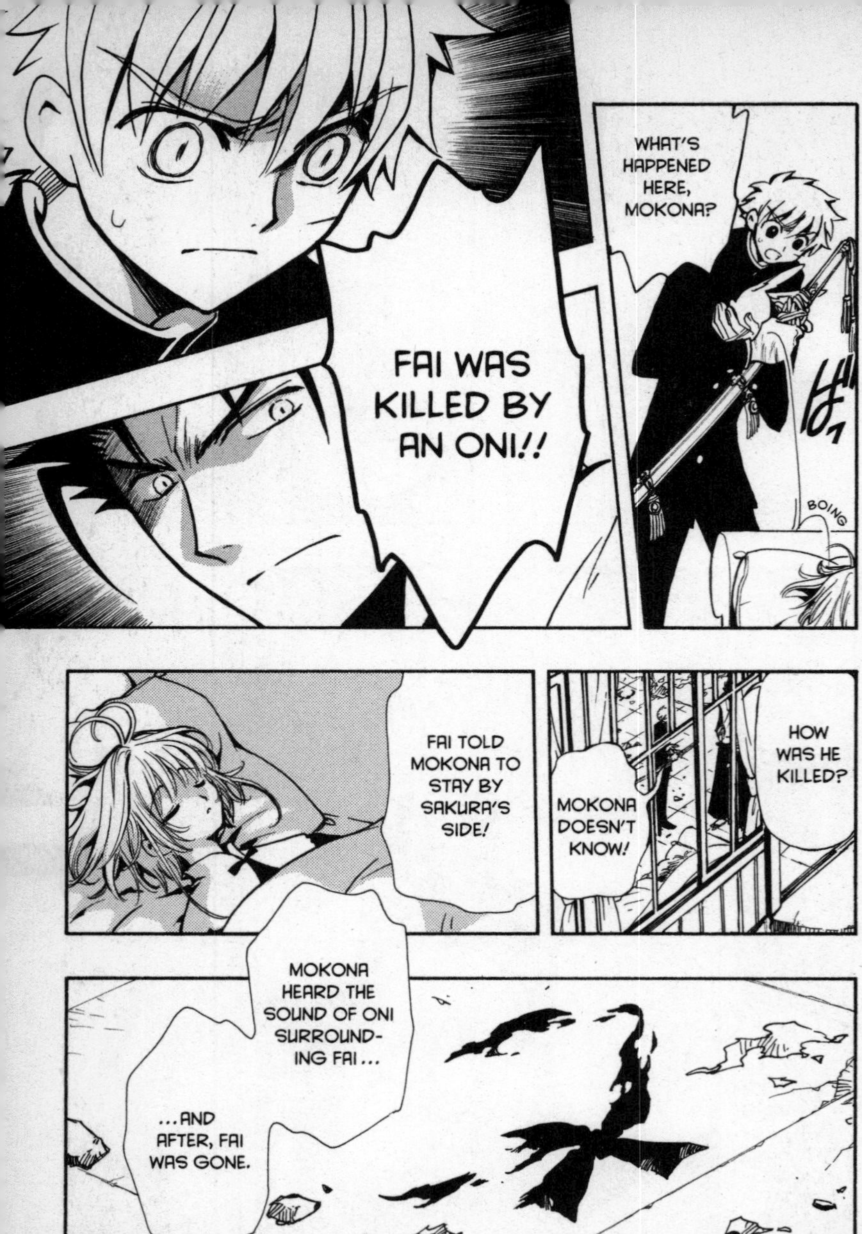
WHAT'S HAPPENED HERE, MOKONA?
BOING
FAI WAS KILLED BY AN ONI!!
HOW WAS HE KILLED?
MOKONA DOESN'T KNOW!
FAI TOLD MOKONA TO STAY BY SAKURA'S SIDE!
MOKONA HEARD THE SOUND OF ONI SURROUND-ING FAI...
...AND AFTER, FAI WAS GONE.

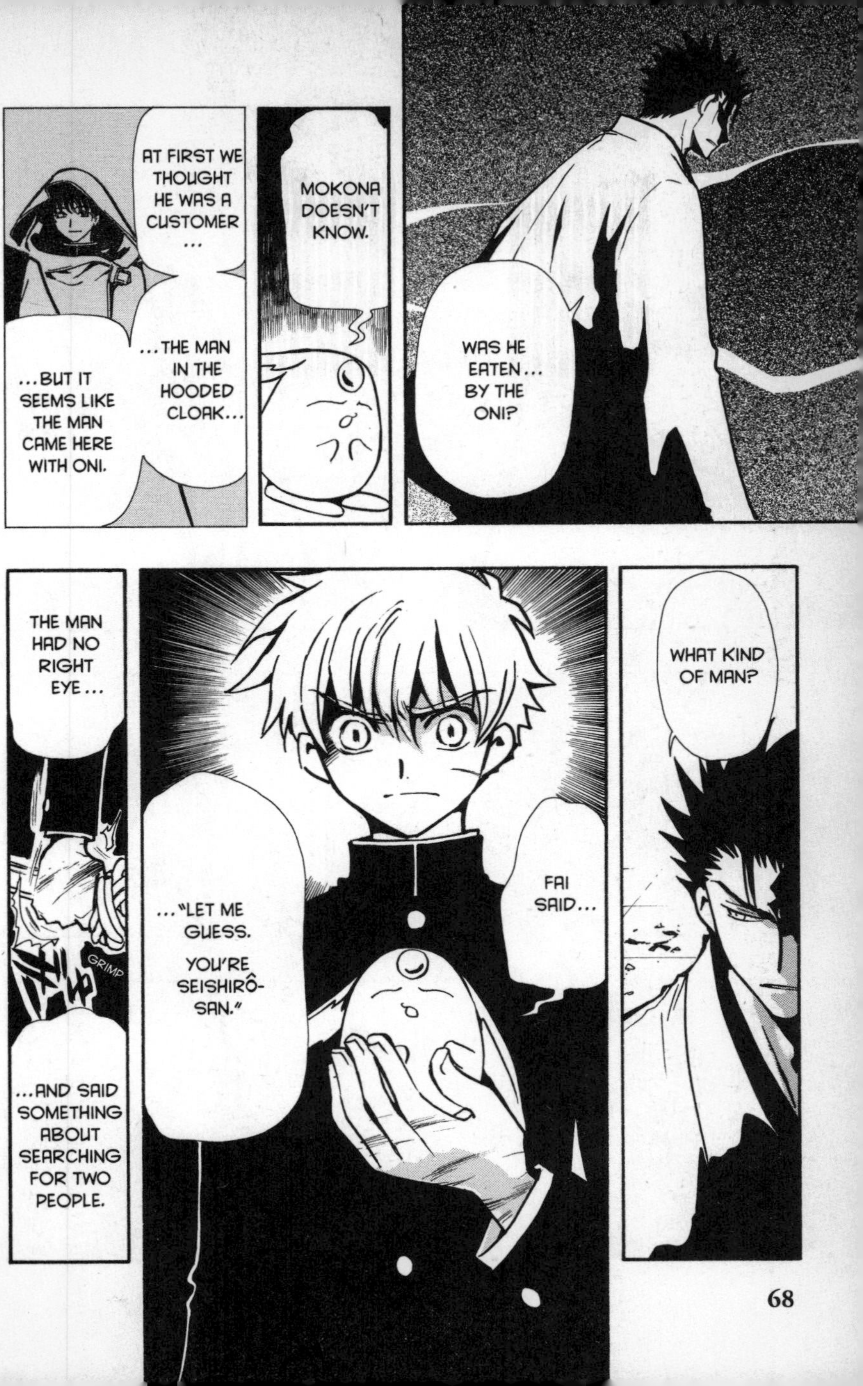
WAS HE EATEN... BY THE ONI?
MOKONA DOESN'T KNOW.
AT FIRST WE THOUGHT HE WAS A CUSTOMER ...
...THE MAN IN THE HOODED CLOAK...
...BUT IT SEEMS LIKE THE MAN CAME HERE WITH ONI.
WHAT KIND OF MAN?
FAI SAID...
..."LET ME GUESS. YOU'RE SEISHIRÔ-SAN."
THE MAN HAD NO RIGHT EYE...
GRIMP
...AND SAID SOMETHING ABOUT SEARCHING FOR TWO PEOPLE.

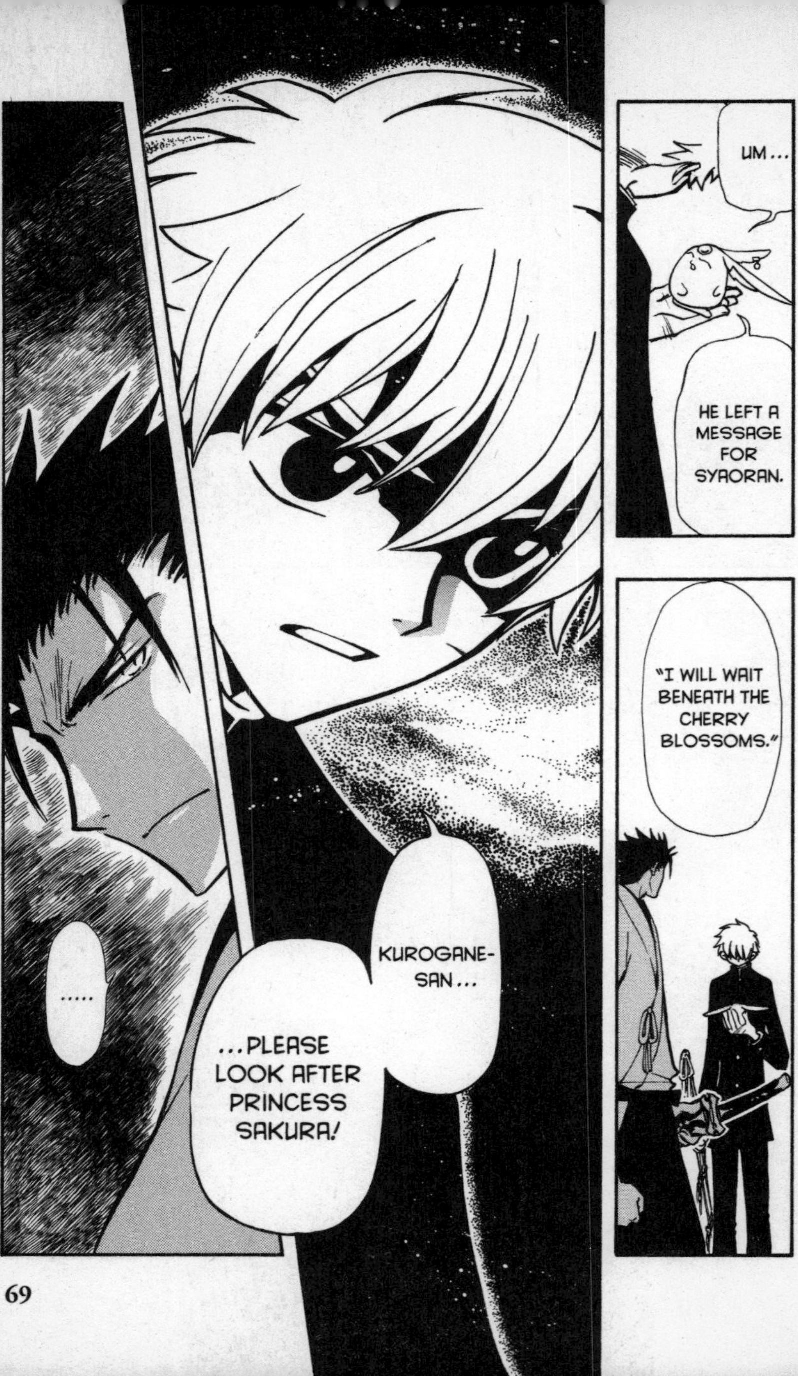
UM...
HE LEFT A MESSAGE FOR SYAORAN.
"I WILL WAIT BENEATH THE CHERRY BLOSSOMS."
KUROGANE-SAN...
...PLEASE LOOK AFTER PRINCESS SAKURA!
.....

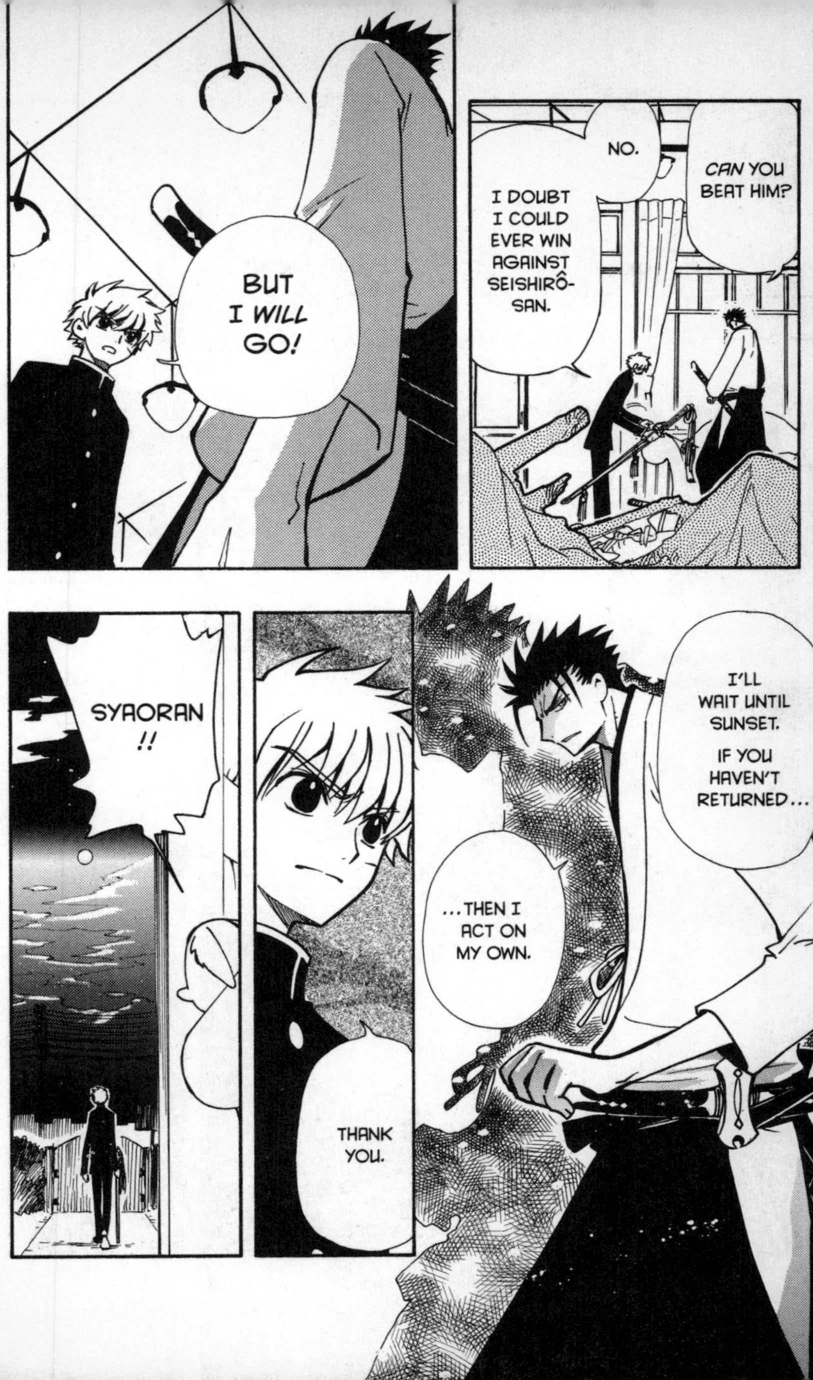
CAN YOU BEAT HIM?
NO.
I DOUBT I COULD EVER WIN AGAINST SEISHIRÔ-SAN.
BUT I WILL GO!
I'LL WAIT UNTIL SUNSET.
IF YOU HAVEN'T RETURNED...
...THEN I ACT ON MY OWN.
THANK YOU.
SYAORAN !!

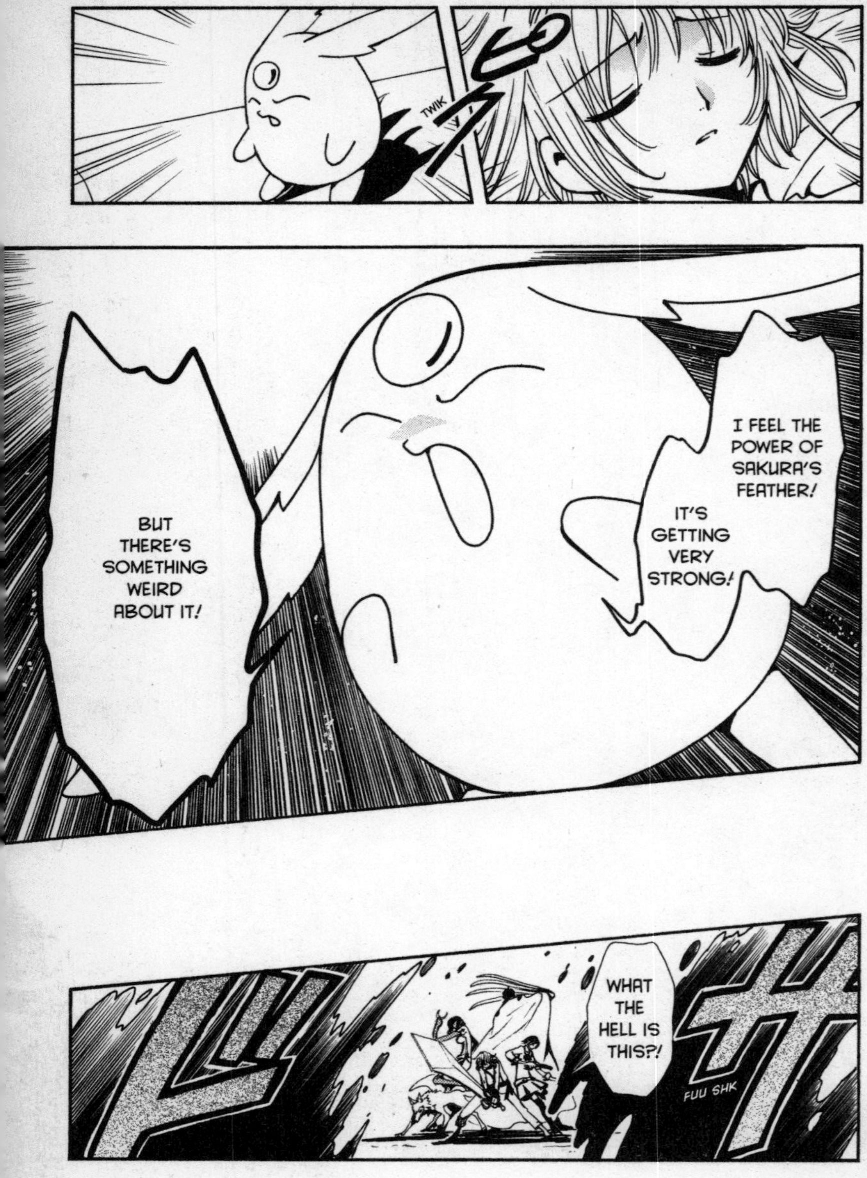
TWIK
I FEEL THE POWER OF SAKURA'S FEATHER!
IT'S GETTING VERY STRONG!
BUT THERE'S SOMETHING WEIRD ABOUT IT!
FUU SHK
WHAT THE HELL IS THIS?!

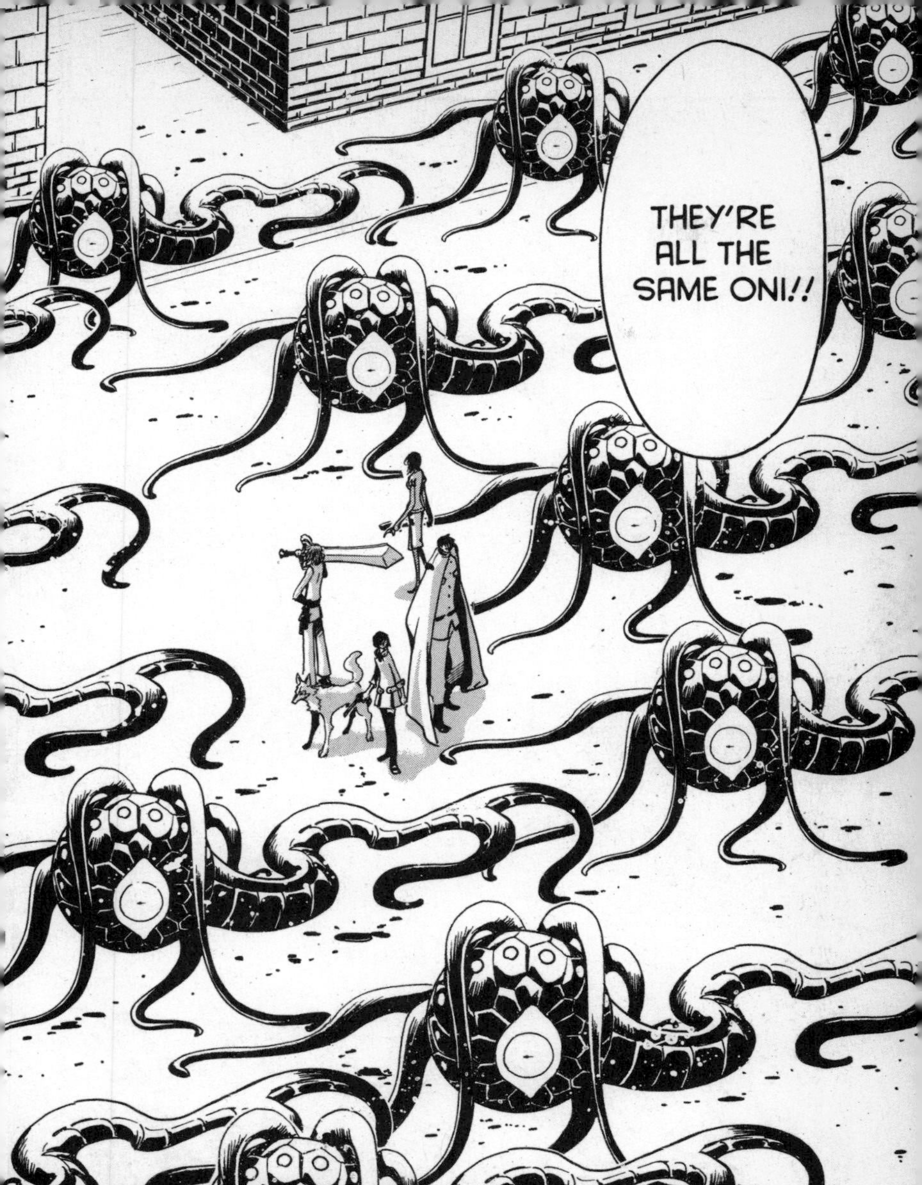
THEY'RE ALL THE SAME ONI!!

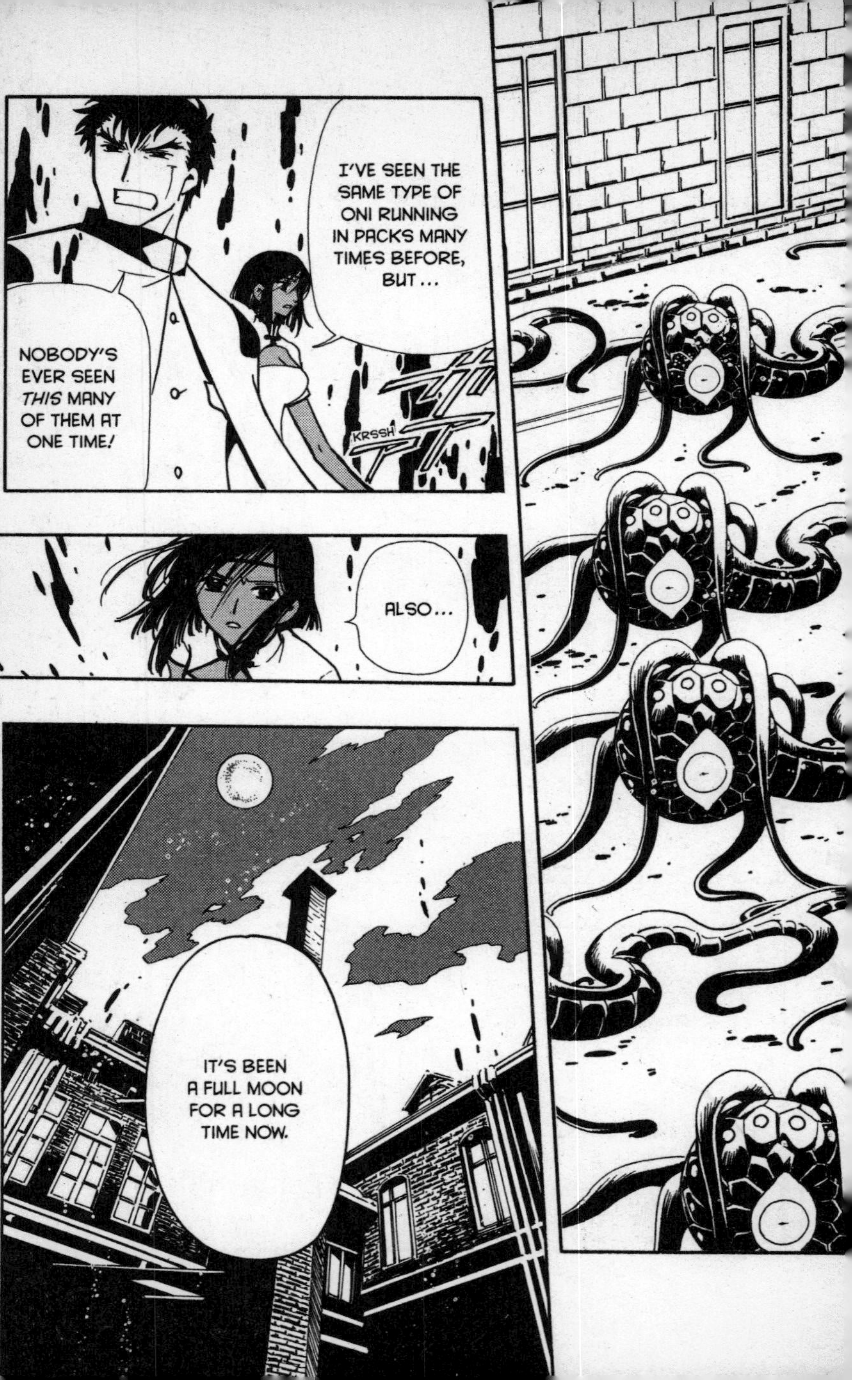
I'VE SEEN THE SAME TYPE OF ONI RUNNING IN PACKS MANY TIMES BEFORE, BUT ...
NOBODY'S EVER SEEN *THIS* MANY OF THEM AT ONE TIME!
KRSSH
ALSO...
IT'S BEEN A FULL MOON FOR A LONG TIME NOW.

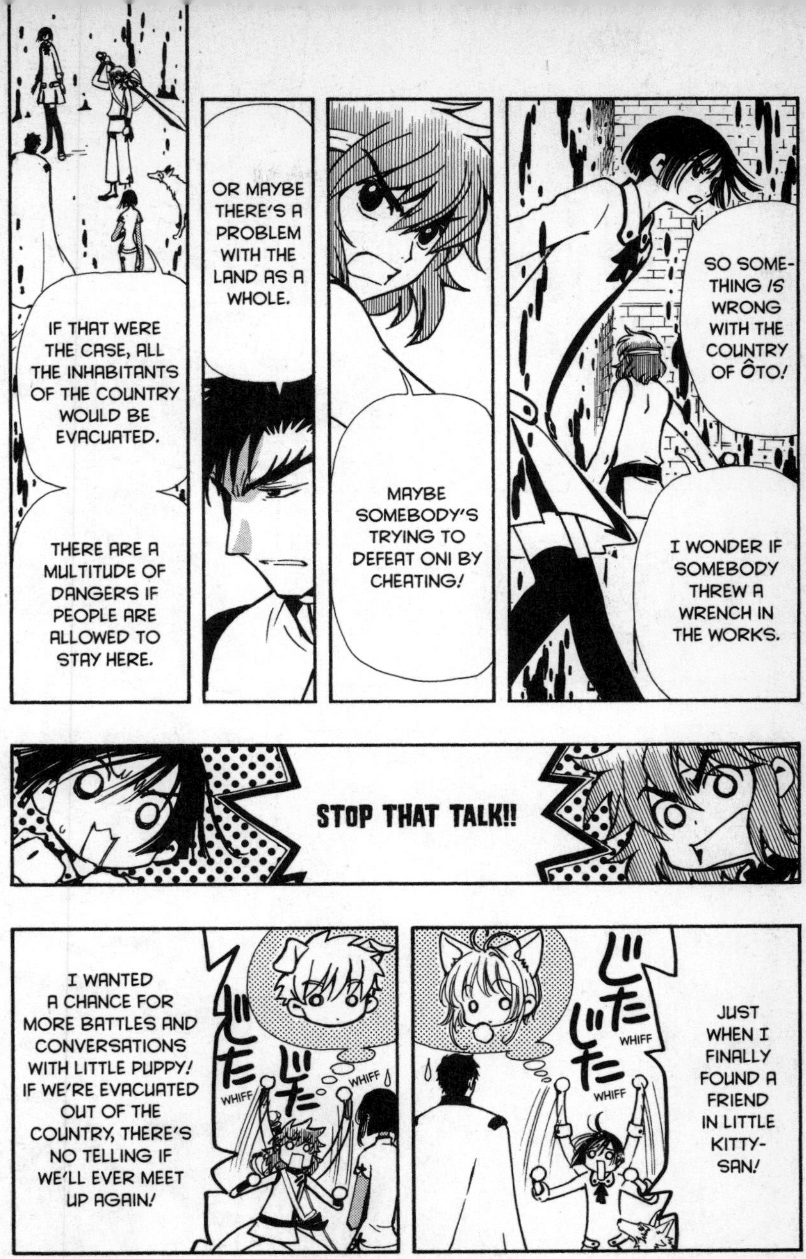
SO SOMETHING *IS* WRONG WITH THE COUNTRY OF ÔTO!
I WONDER IF SOMEBODY THREW A WRENCH IN THE WORKS.
MAYBE SOMEBODY'S TRYING TO DEFEAT ONI BY CHEATING!
OR MAYBE THERE'S A PROBLEM WITH THE LAND AS A WHOLE.
IF THAT WERE THE CASE, ALL THE INHABITANTS OF THE COUNTRY WOULD BE EVACUATED.
THERE ARE A MULTITUDE OF DANGERS IF PEOPLE ARE ALLOWED TO STAY HERE.
STOP THAT TALK!!
じた
じた
WHIFF
WHIFF
JUST WHEN I FINALLY FOUND A FRIEND IN LITTLE KITTY-SAN!
じた
じた
WHIFF
WHIFF
I WANTED A CHANCE FOR MORE BATTLES AND CONVERSATIONS WITH LITTLE PUPPY! IF WE'RE EVACUATED OUT OF THE COUNTRY, THERE'S NO TELLING IF WE'LL EVER MEET UP AGAIN!

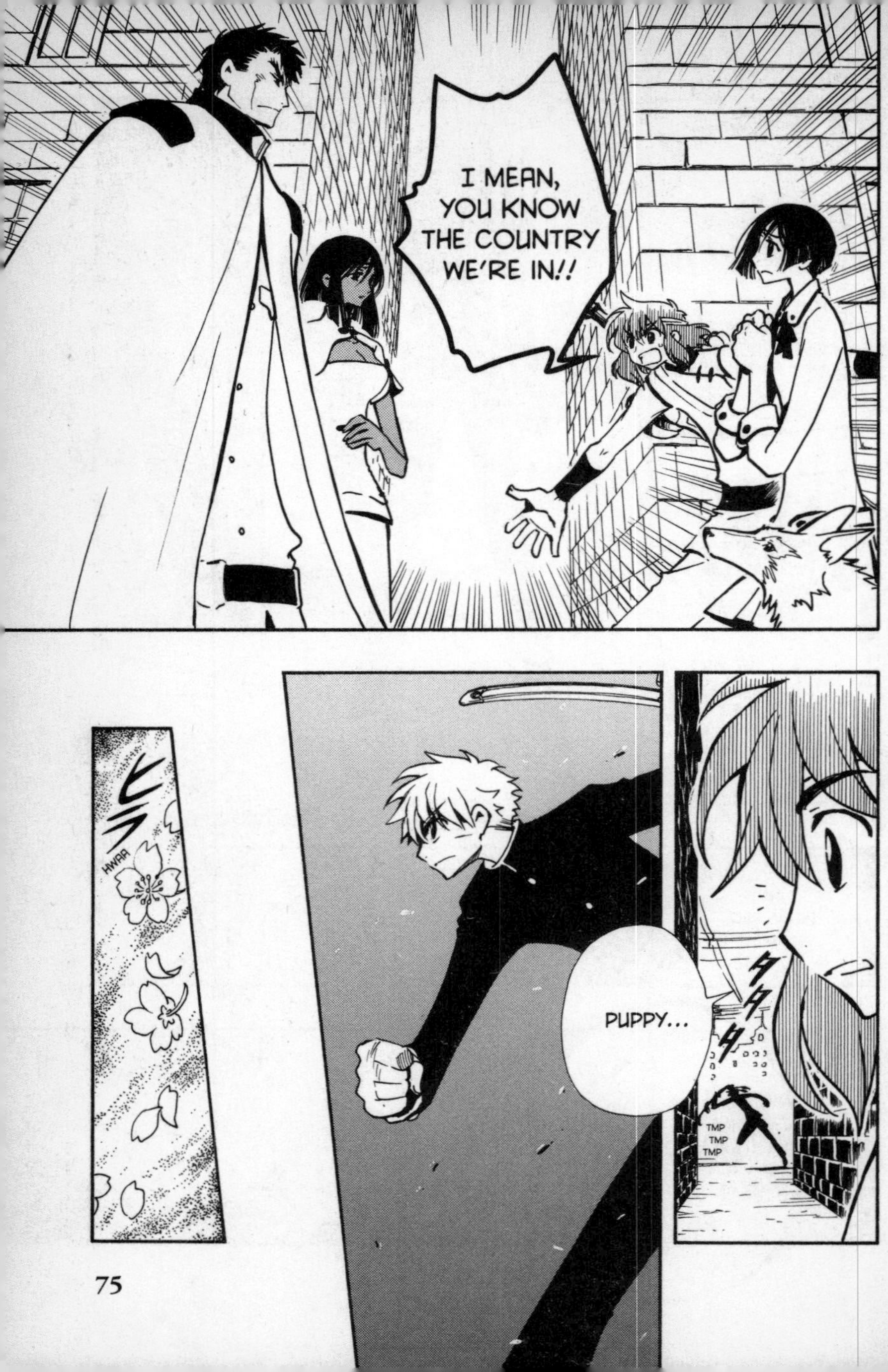
I MEAN, YOU KNOW THE COUNTRY WE'RE IN!!
TMP TMP TMP
PUPPY...
HWAA

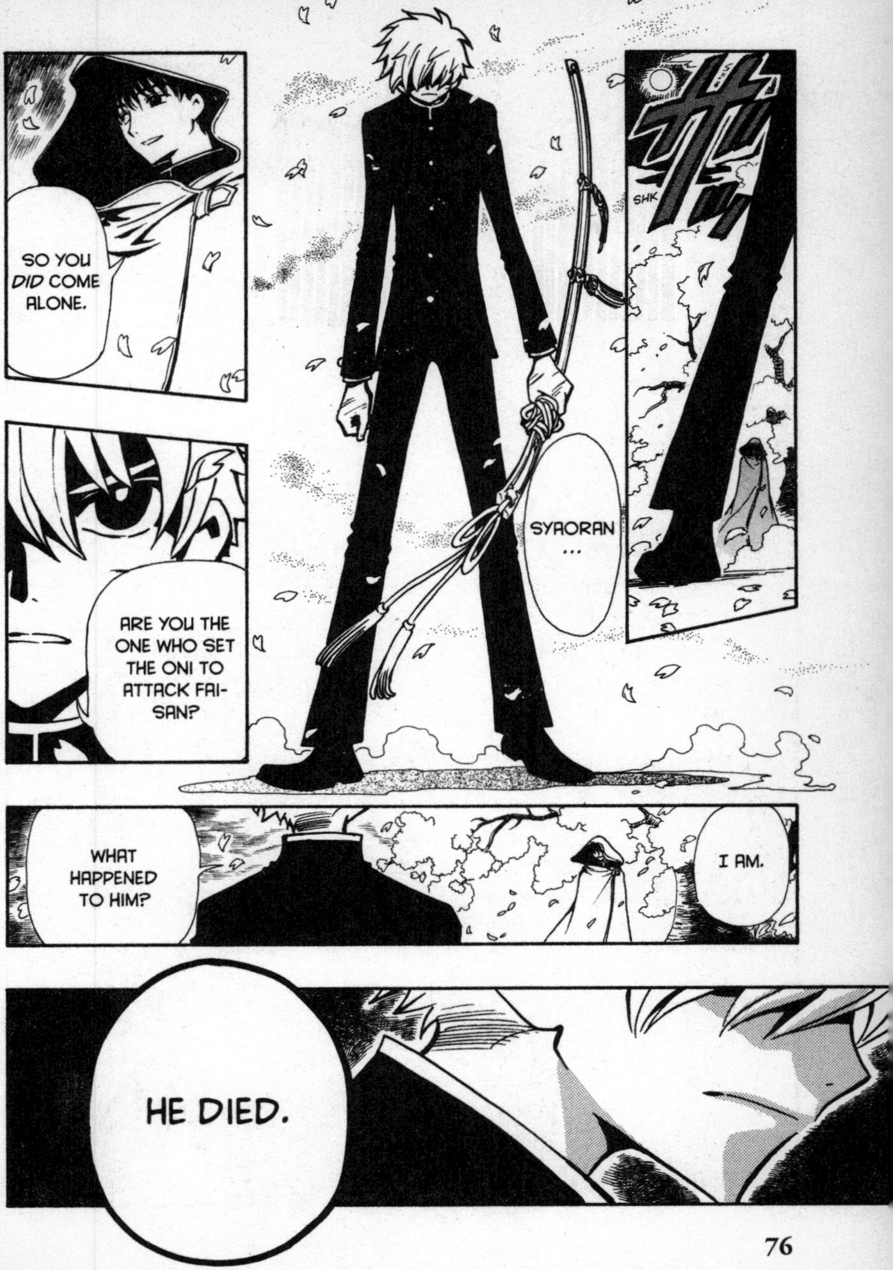
SHK
SYAORAN ...
SO YOU *DID* COME ALONE.
ARE YOU THE ONE WHO SET THE ONI TO ATTACK FAI-SAN?
I AM.
WHAT HAPPENED TO HIM?
HE DIED.

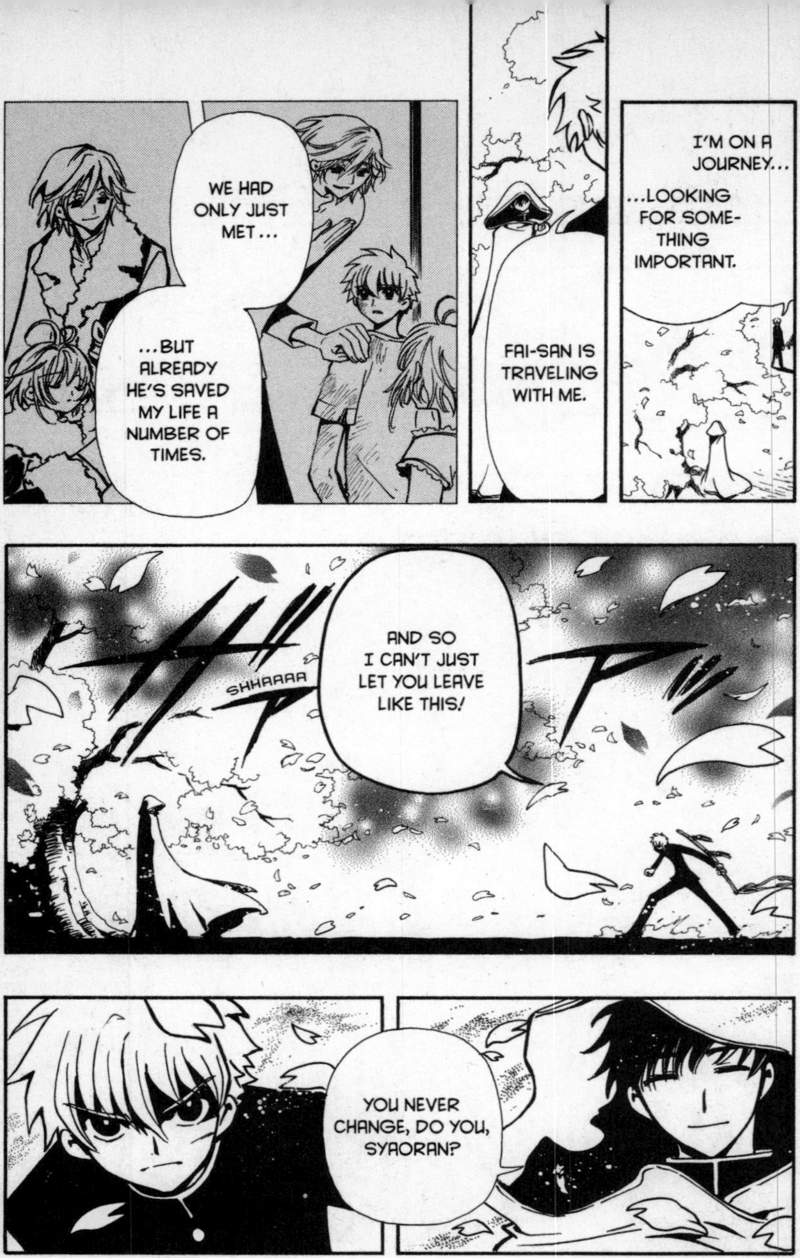
I'M ON A JOURNEY...
...LOOKING FOR SOME-THING IMPORTANT.
FAI-SAN IS TRAVELING WITH ME.
WE HAD ONLY JUST MET...
...BUT ALREADY HE'S SAVED MY LIFE A NUMBER OF TIMES.
AND SO I CAN'T JUST LET YOU LEAVE LIKE THIS!
SHHAAAA
YOU NEVER CHANGE, DO YOU, SYAORAN?

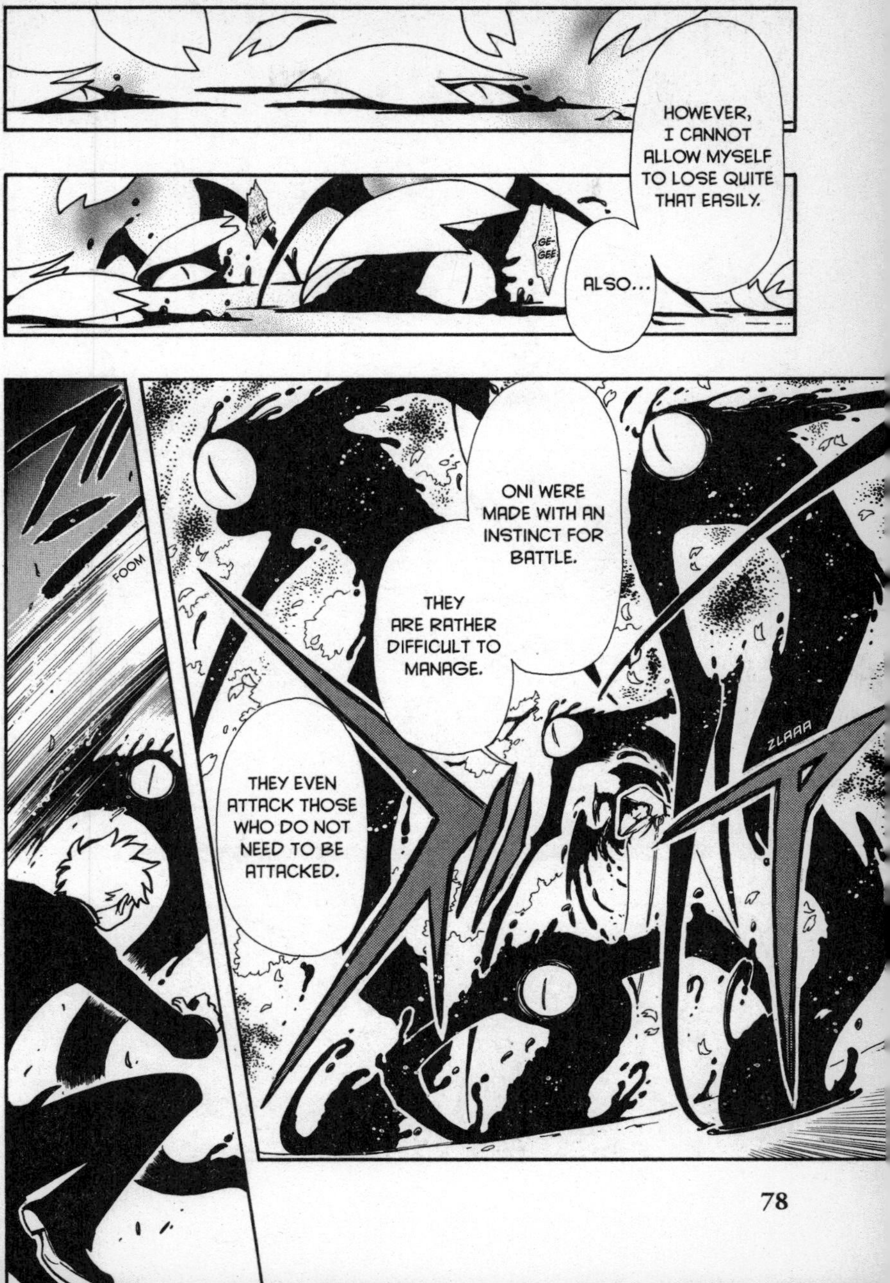
HOWEVER, I CANNOT ALLOW MYSELF TO LOSE QUITE THAT EASILY.
ALSO...
GE-GEE
KEE
ONI WERE MADE WITH AN INSTINCT FOR BATTLE.
THEY ARE RATHER DIFFICULT TO MANAGE.
ZLAAA
THEY EVEN ATTACK THOSE WHO DO NOT NEED TO BE ATTACKED.
FOOM

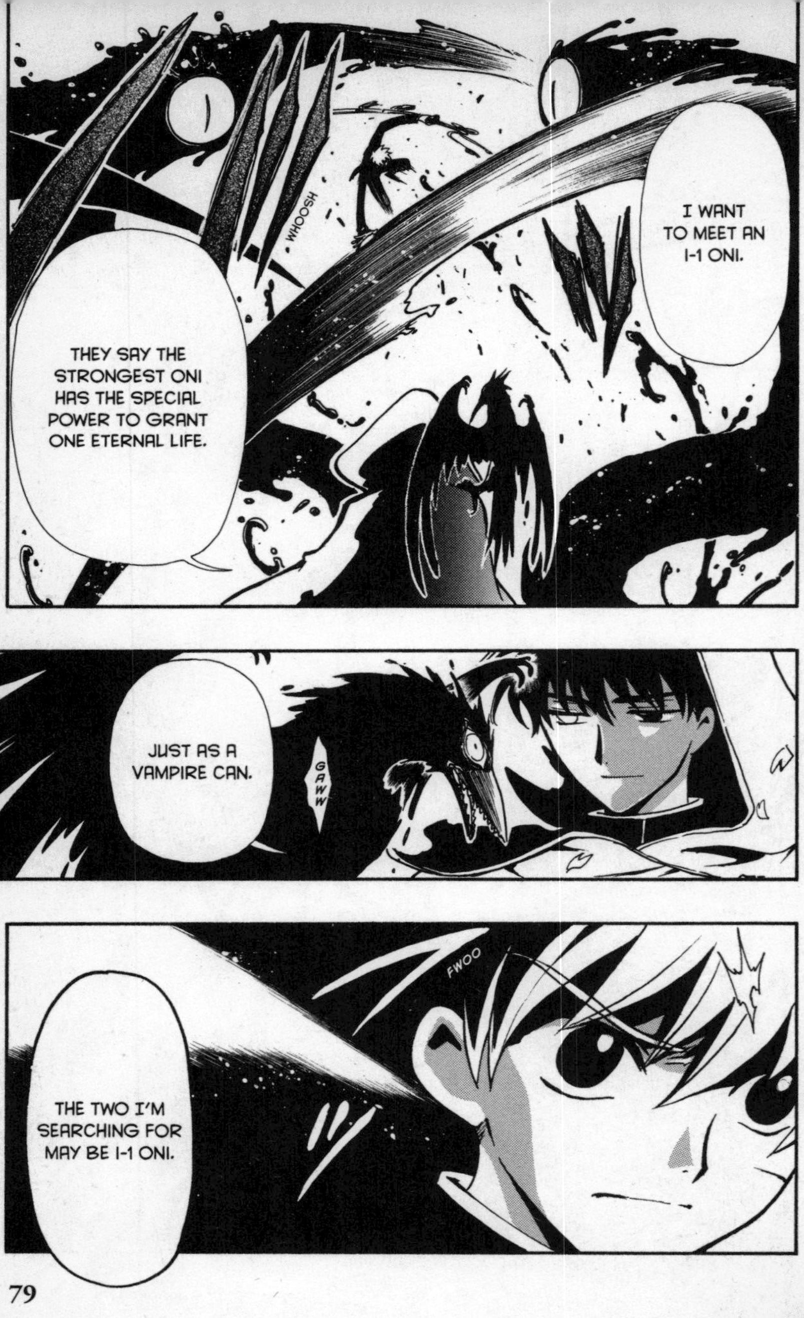
I WANT TO MEET AN I-1 ONI.
WHOOSH
THEY SAY THE STRONGEST ONI HAS THE SPECIAL POWER TO GRANT ONE ETERNAL LIFE.
GAWW
JUST AS A VAMPIRE CAN.
FWOO
THE TWO I'M SEARCHING FOR MAY BE I-1 ONI.

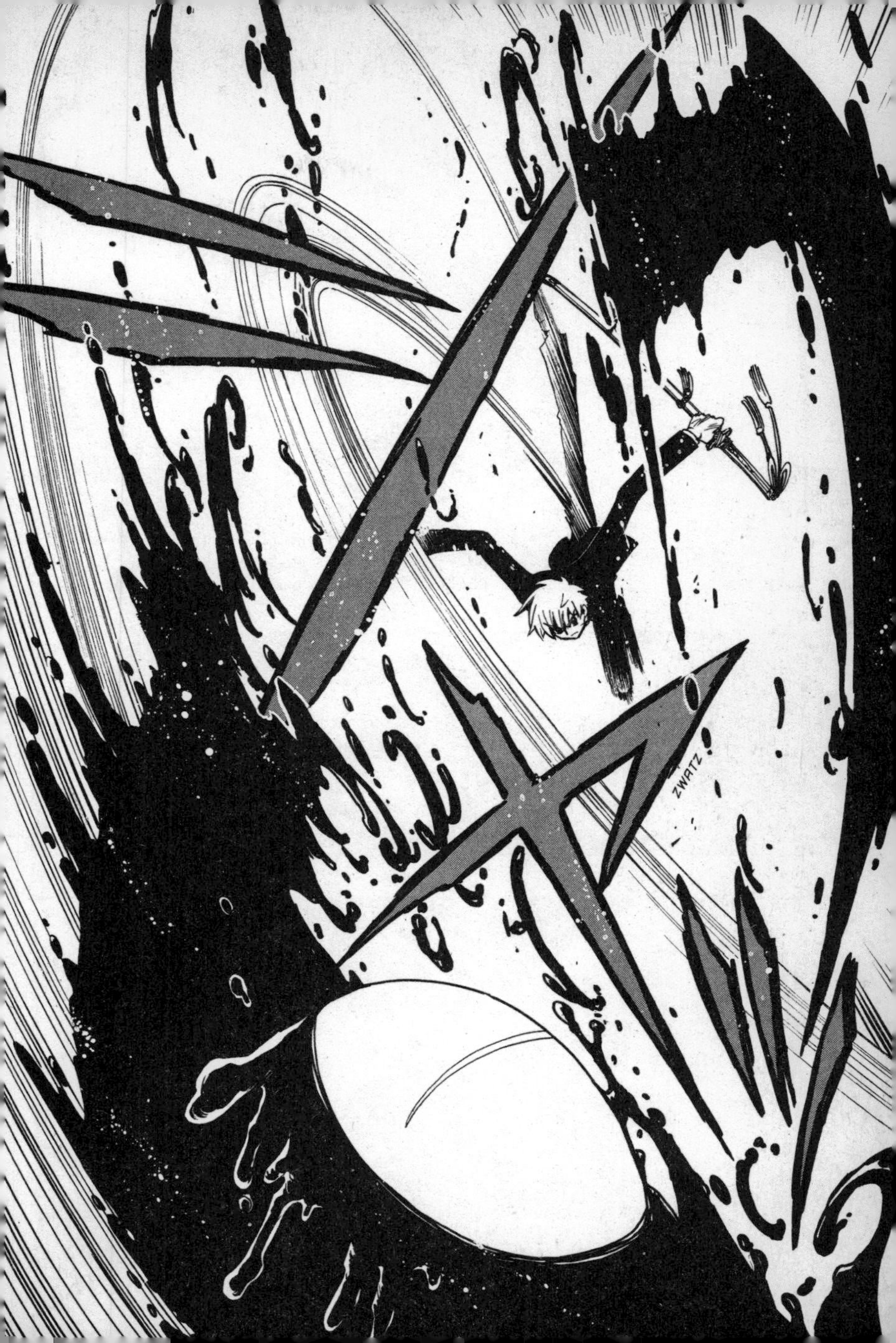
ZWATZ

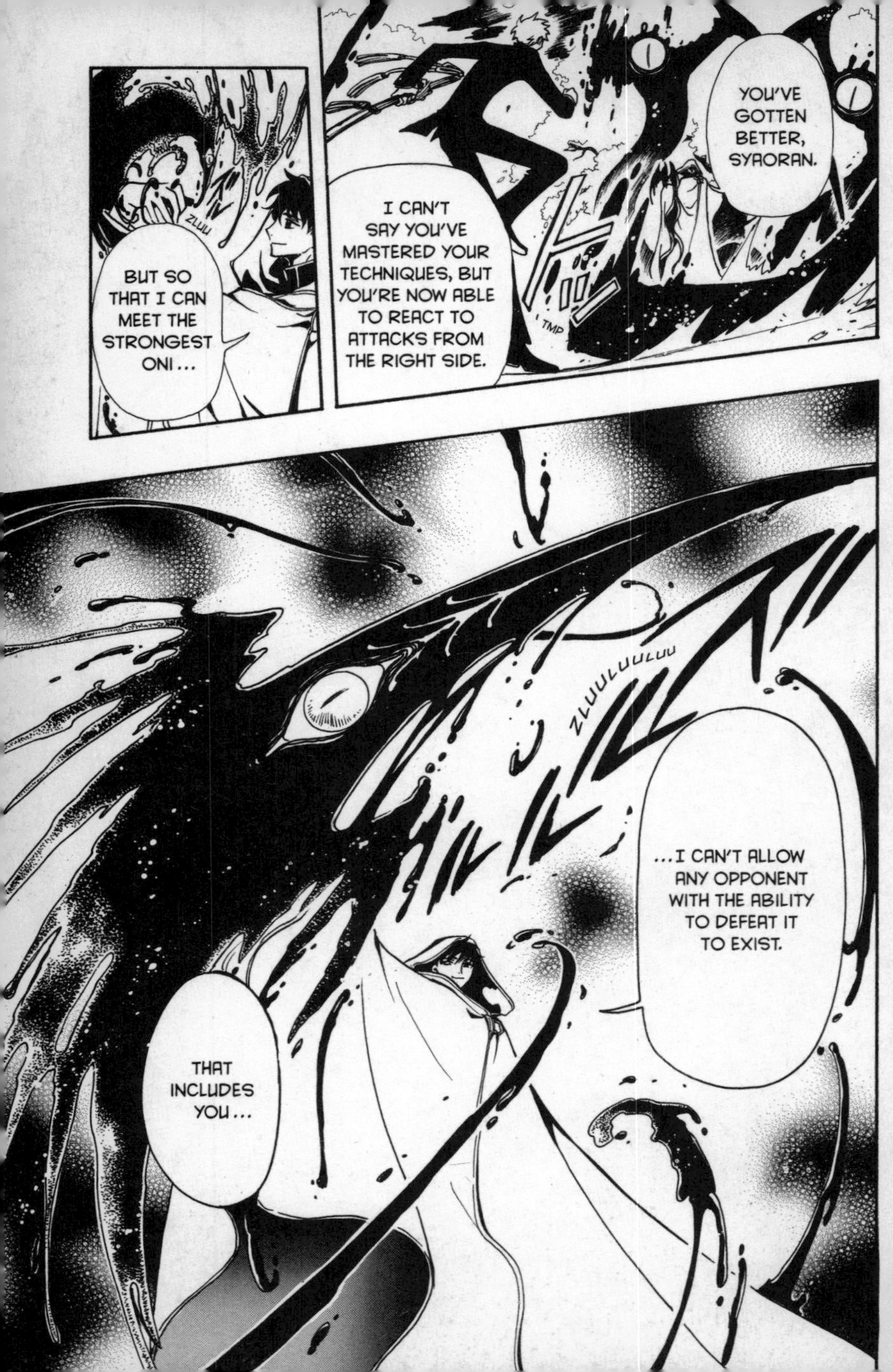
YOU'VE GOTTEN BETTER, SYAORAN.
I CAN'T SAY YOU'VE MASTERED YOUR TECHNIQUES, BUT YOU'RE NOW ABLE TO REACT TO ATTACKS FROM THE RIGHT SIDE.
TMP
ZLUU
BUT SO THAT I CAN MEET THE STRONGEST ONI...
ZLUULUULUU
...I CAN'T ALLOW ANY OPPONENT WITH THE ABILITY TO DEFEAT IT TO EXIST.
THAT INCLUDES YOU...

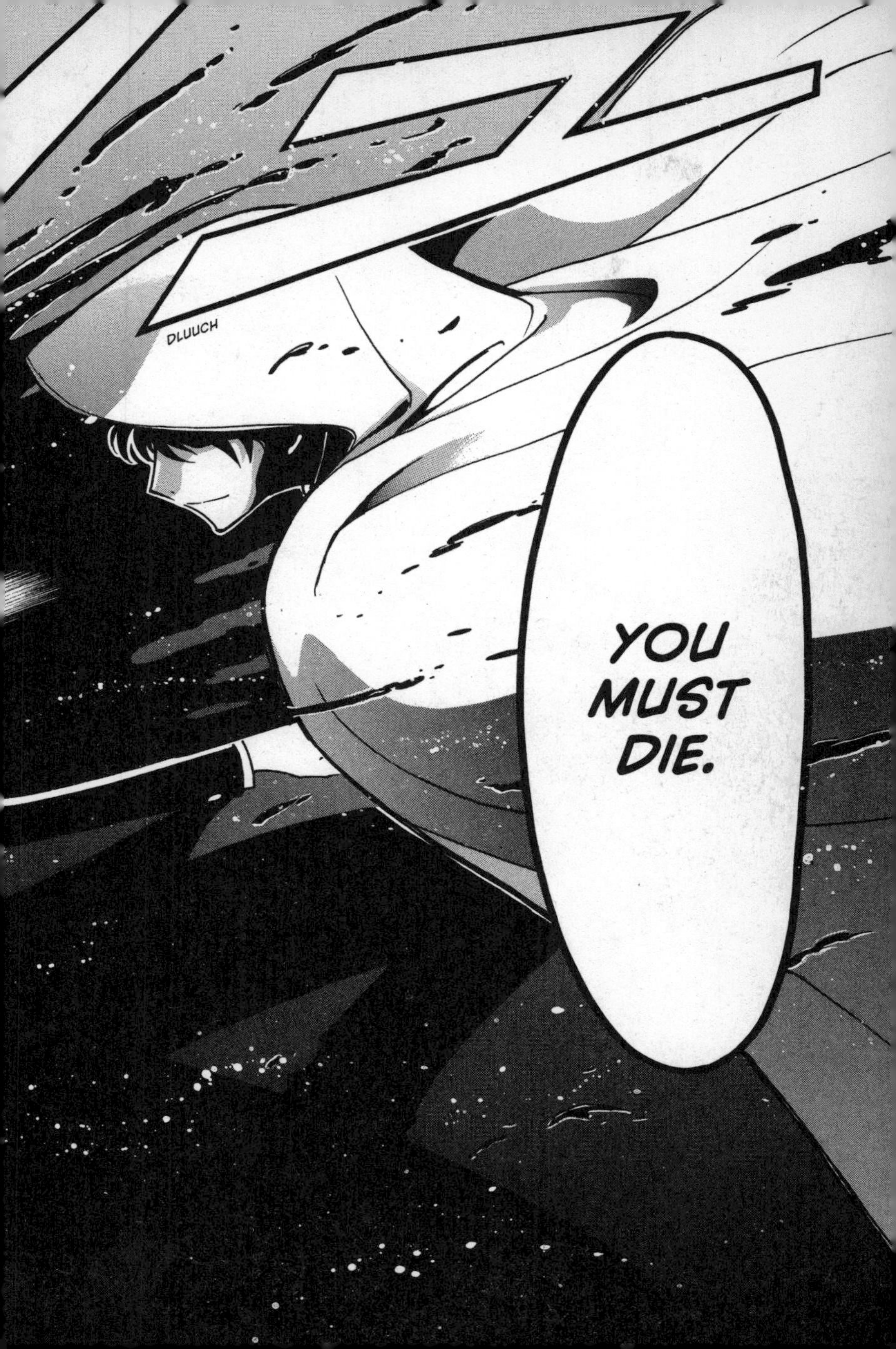

YOU MUST DIE.
DLUUCH

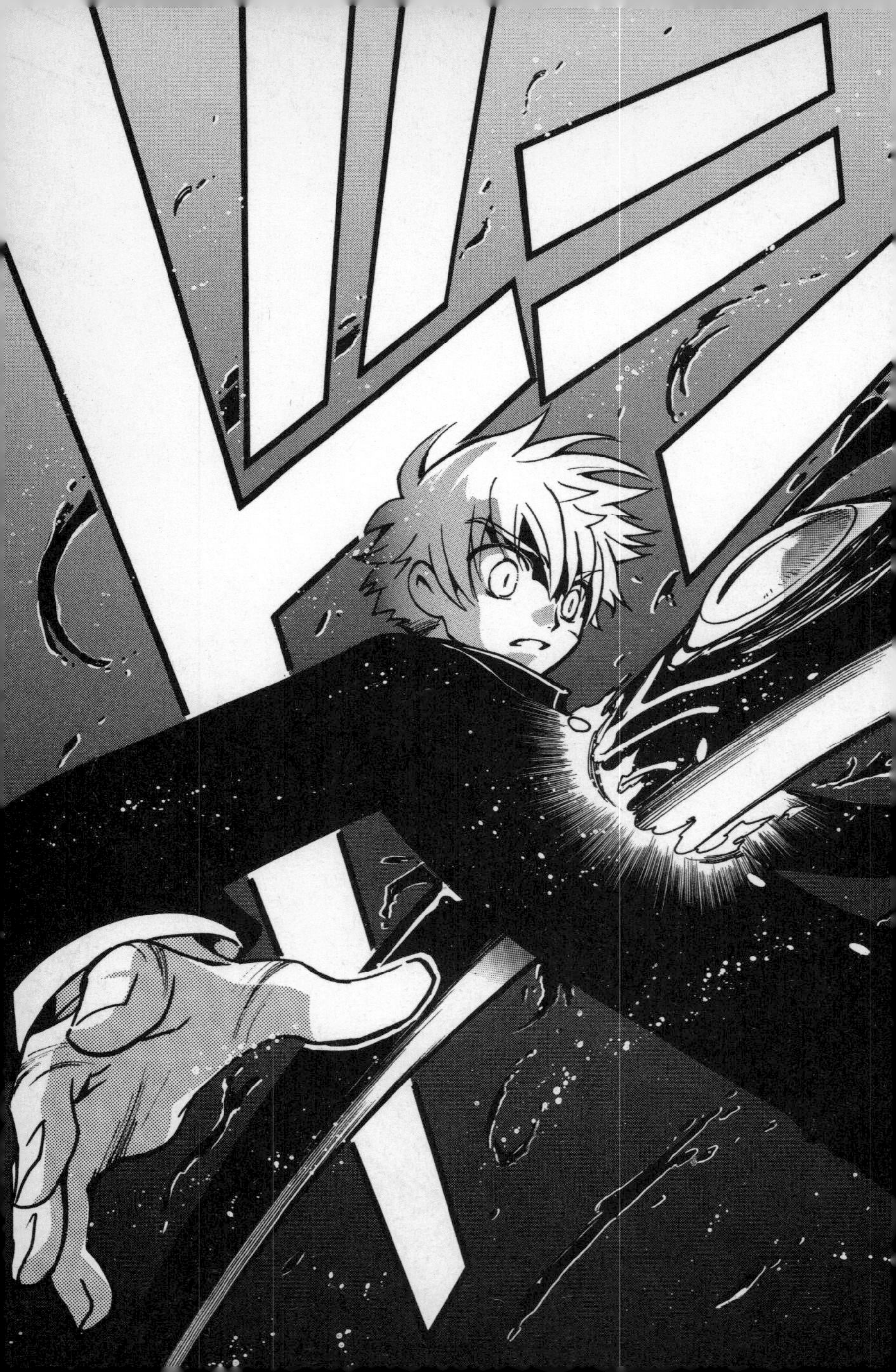

ツバサ

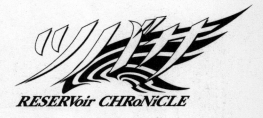

RESERVoir CHRoNiCLE

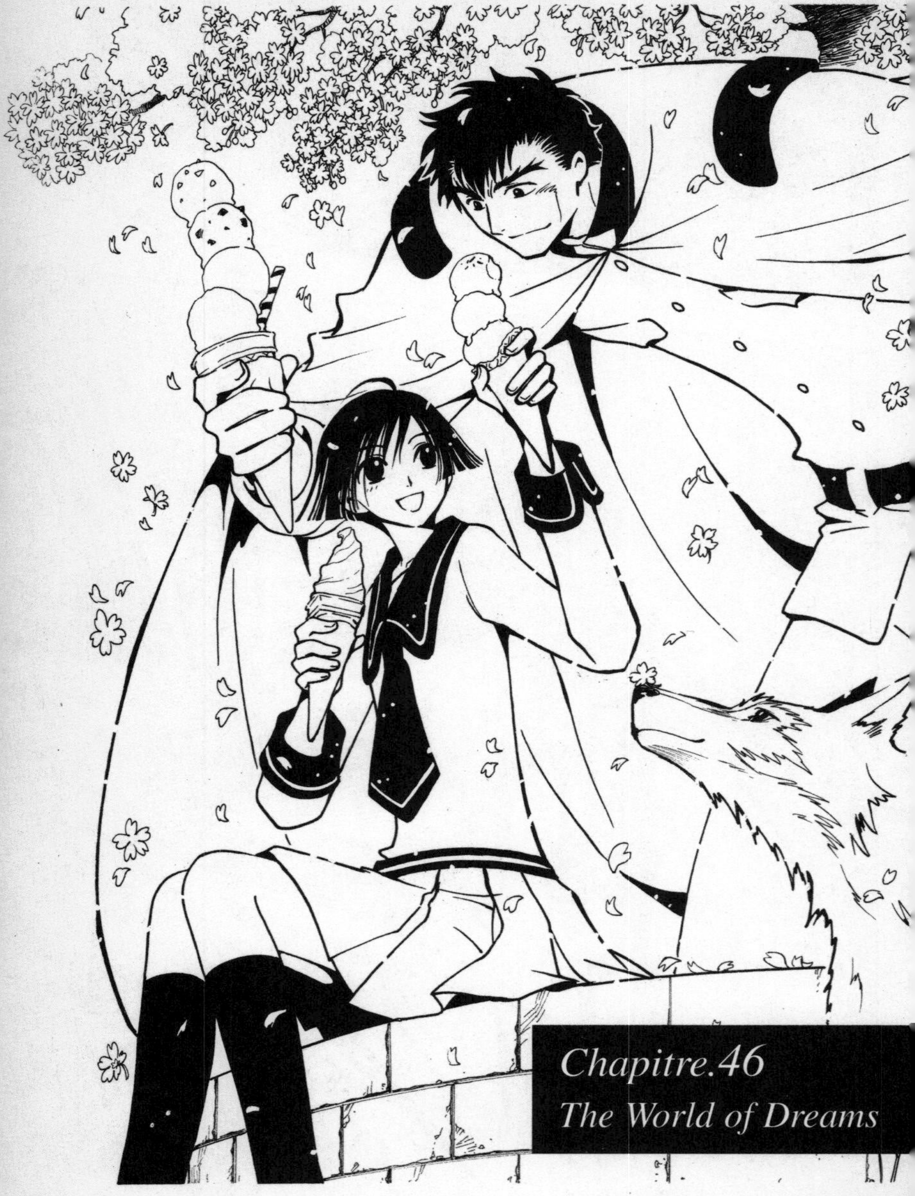

Chapitre.46
The World of Dreams

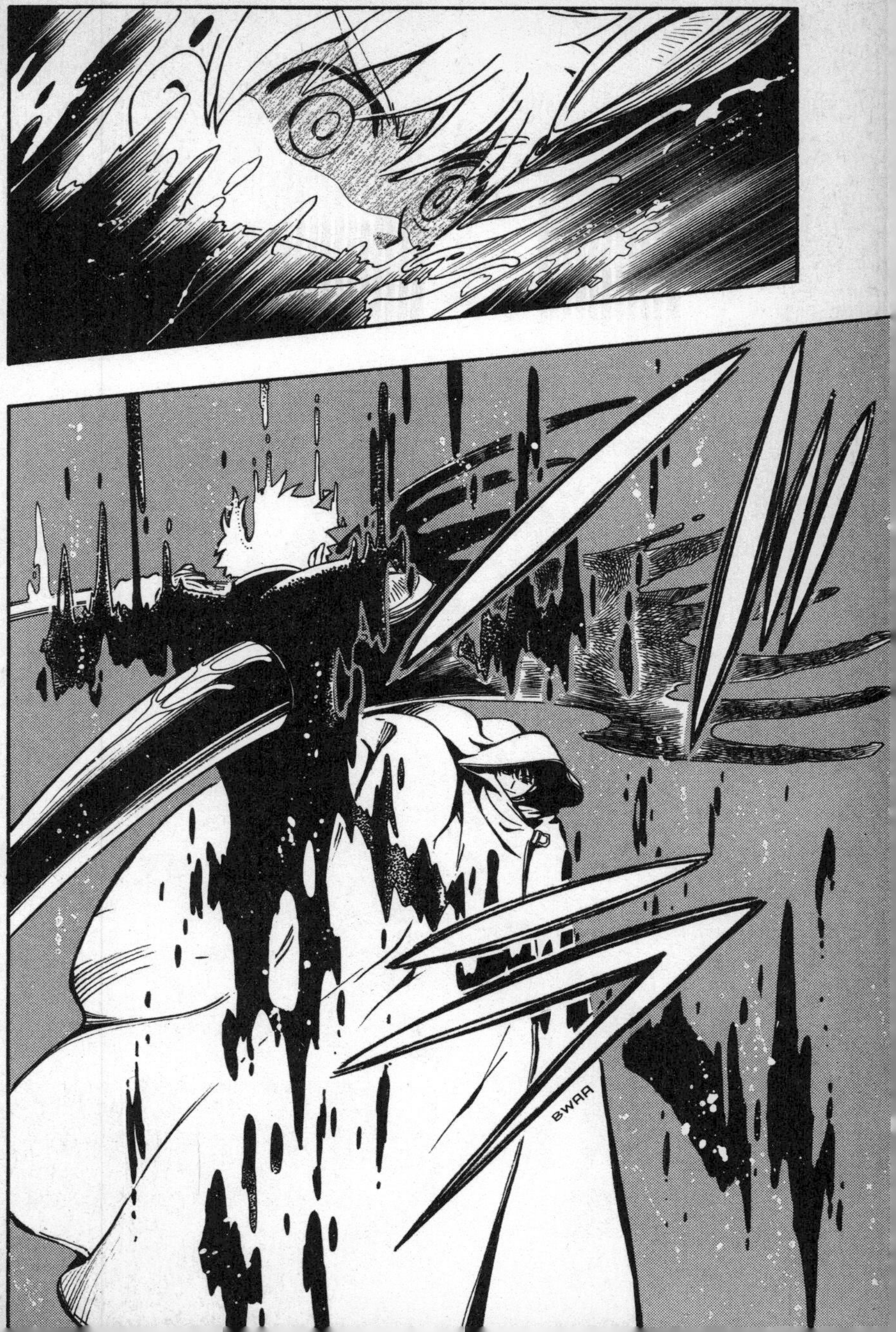
BWAA

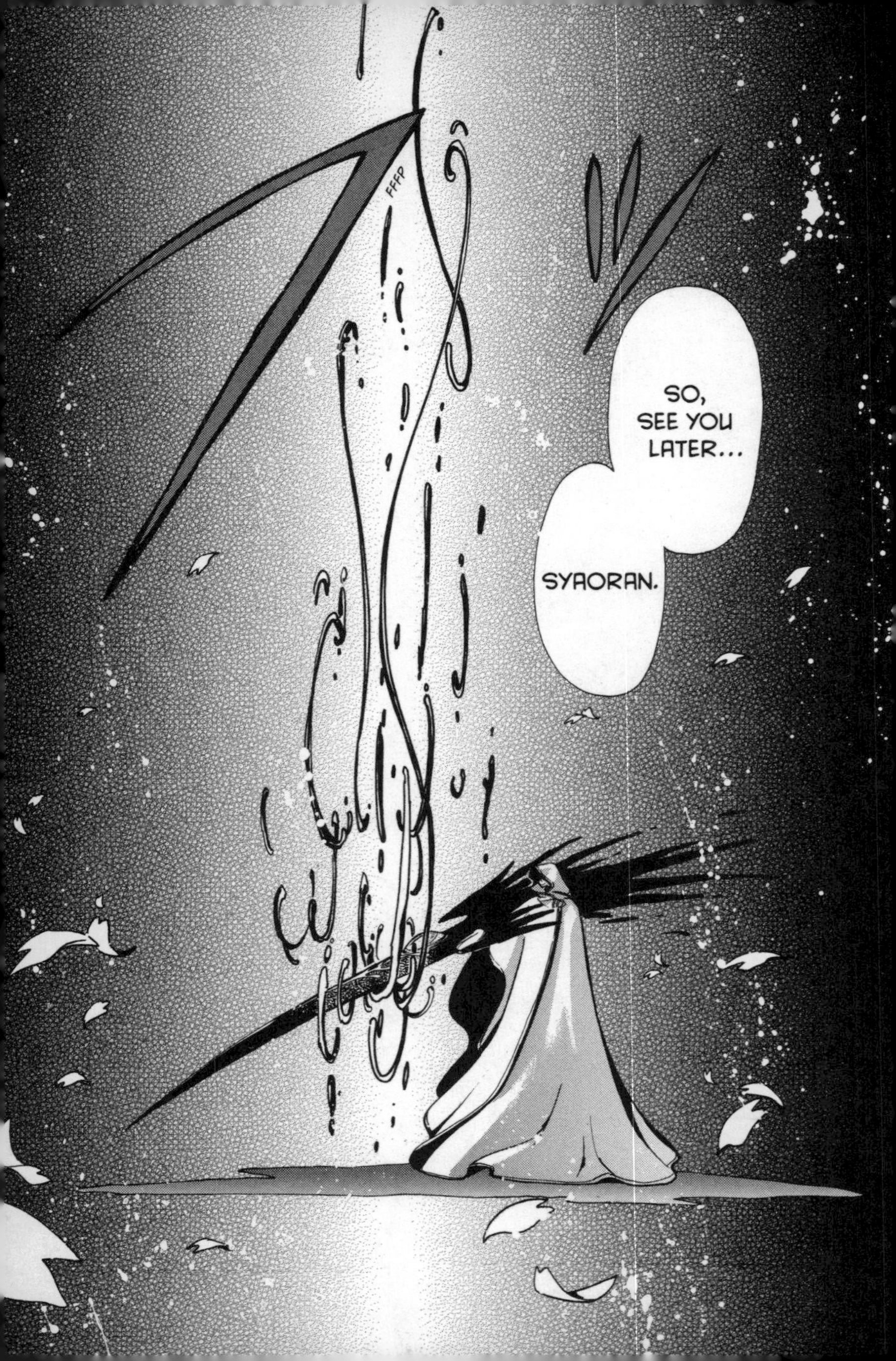
FFFP
SO, SEE YOU LATER...
SYAORAN.

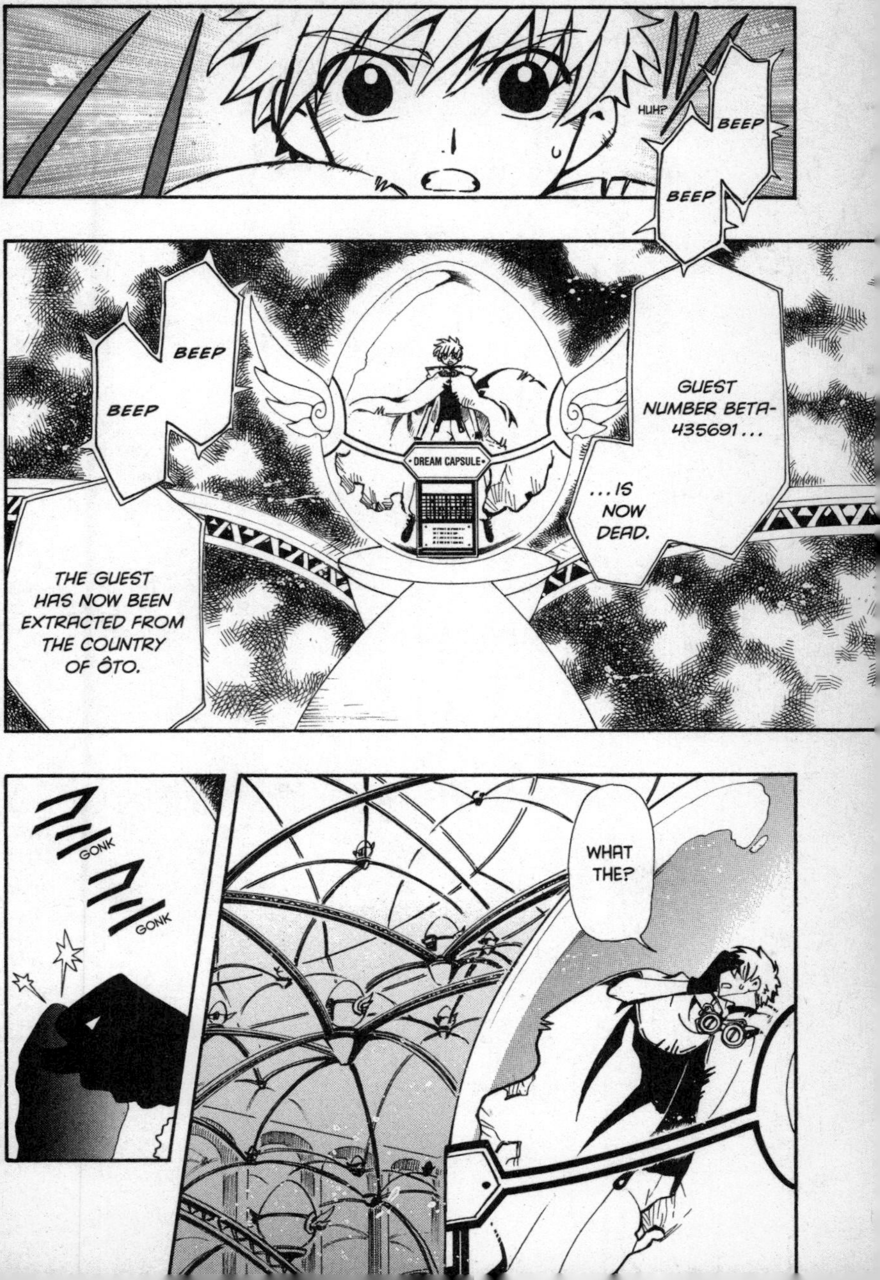
BEEP
BEEP
HUH?
GUEST NUMBER BETA-435691...
...IS NOW DEAD.
BEEP
BEEP
DREAM CAPSULE
THE GUEST HAS NOW BEEN EXTRACTED FROM THE COUNTRY OF ÔTO.
WHAT THE?
GONK
GONK

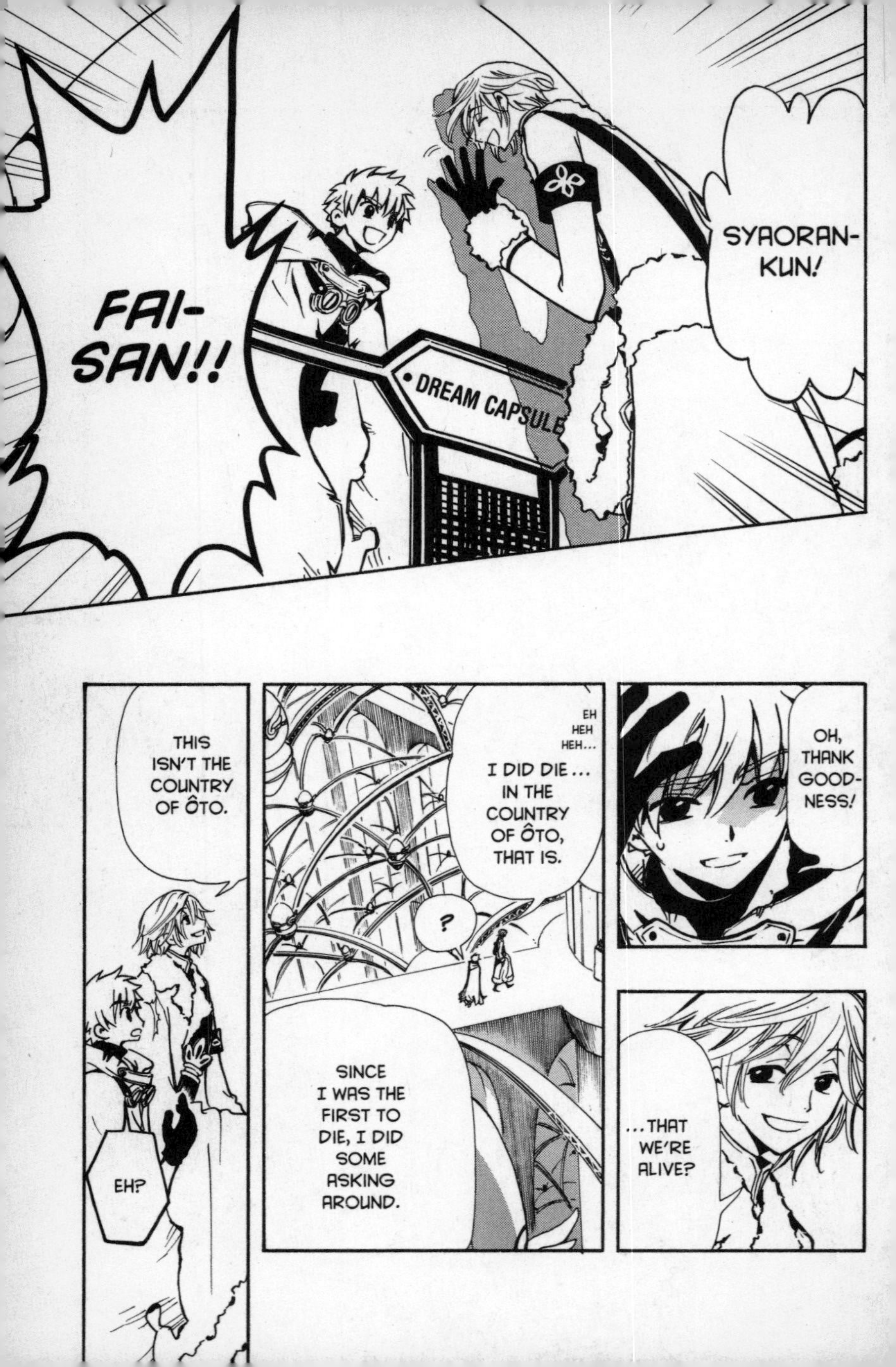
SYAORAN-KUN!
FAI-SAN!!
DREAM CAPSULE
OH, THANK GOODNESS!
...THAT WE'RE ALIVE?
EH HEH HEH...
I DID DIE... IN THE COUNTRY OF ÔTO, THAT IS.
?
SINCE I WAS THE FIRST TO DIE, I DID SOME ASKING AROUND.
THIS ISN'T THE COUNTRY OF ÔTO.
EH?

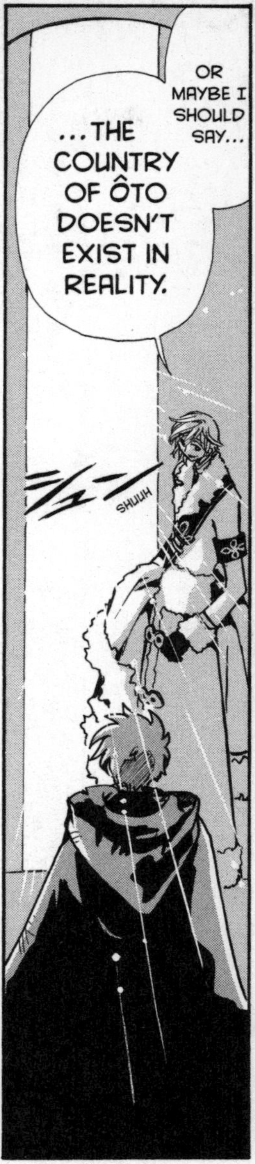
OR MAYBE I SHOULD SAY...
...THE COUNTRY OF ÔTO DOESN'T EXIST IN REALITY.
SHUUH
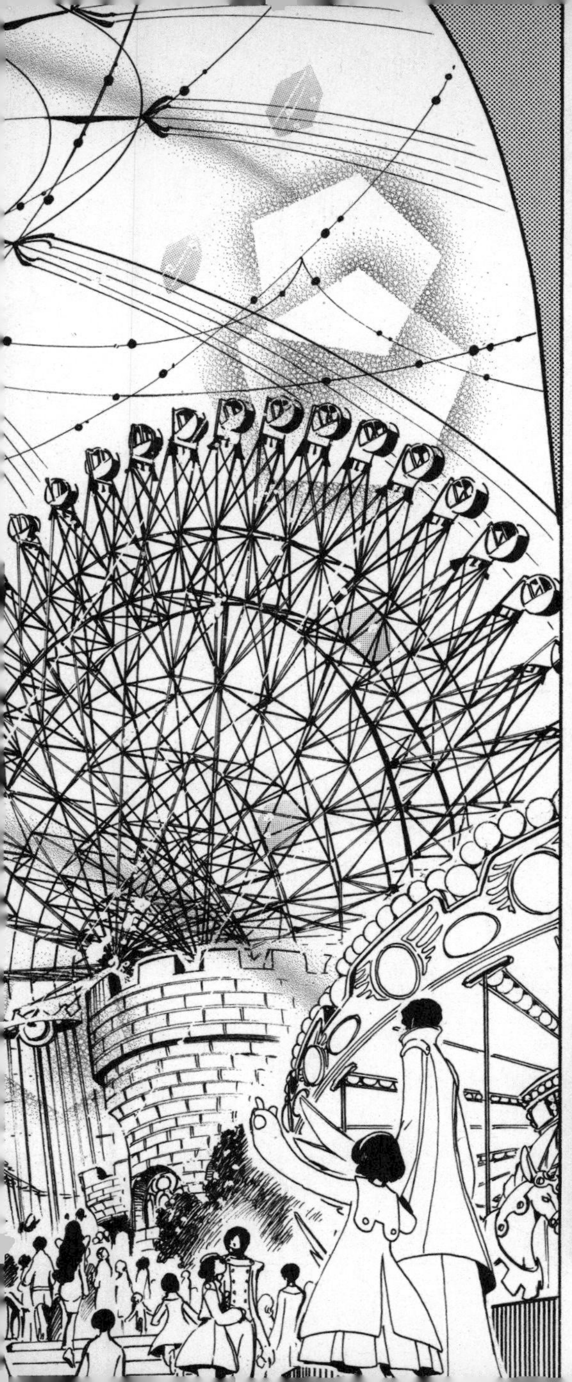

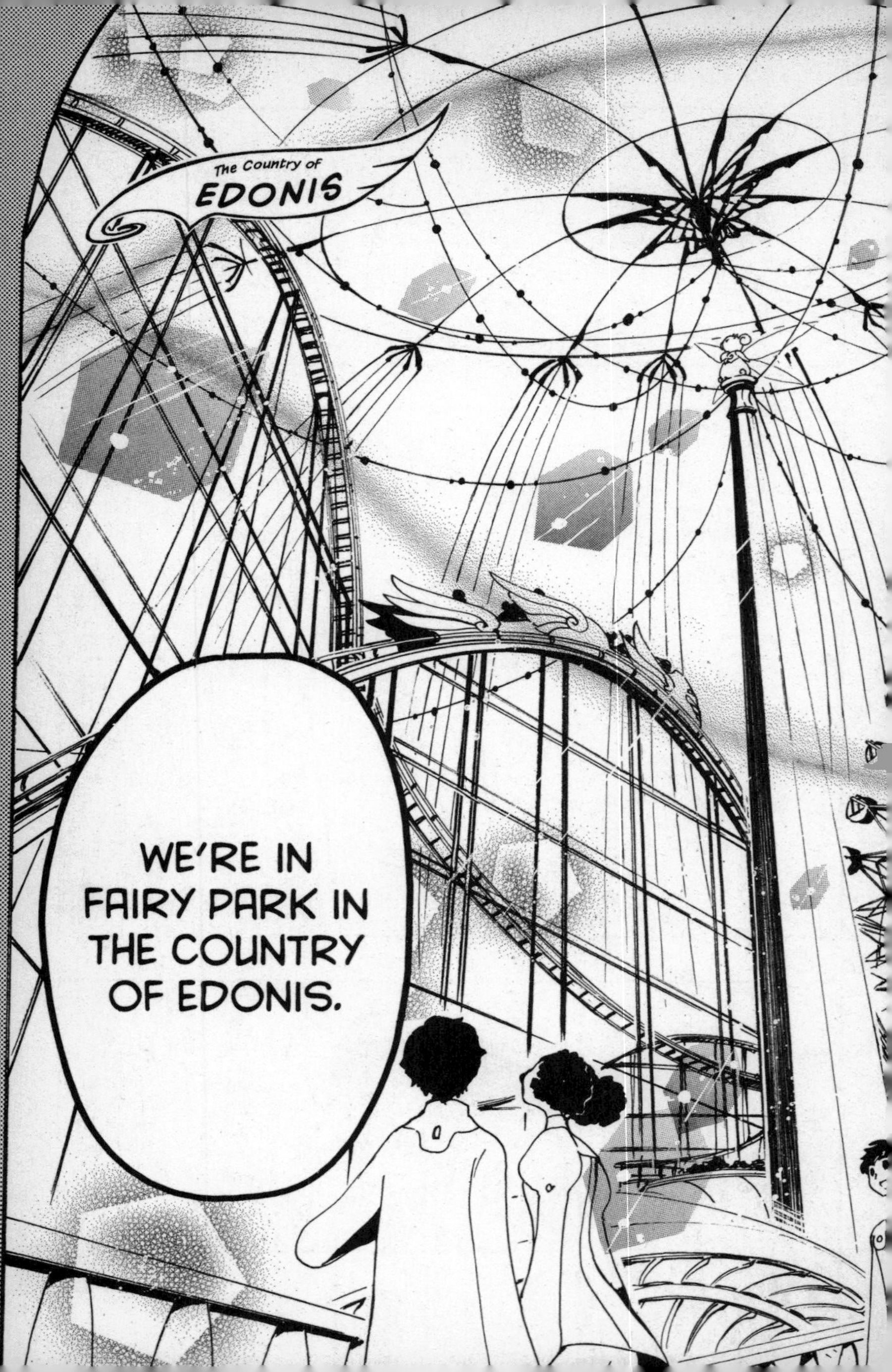
The Country of
EDONIS
WE'RE IN FAIRY PARK IN THE COUNTRY OF EDONIS.

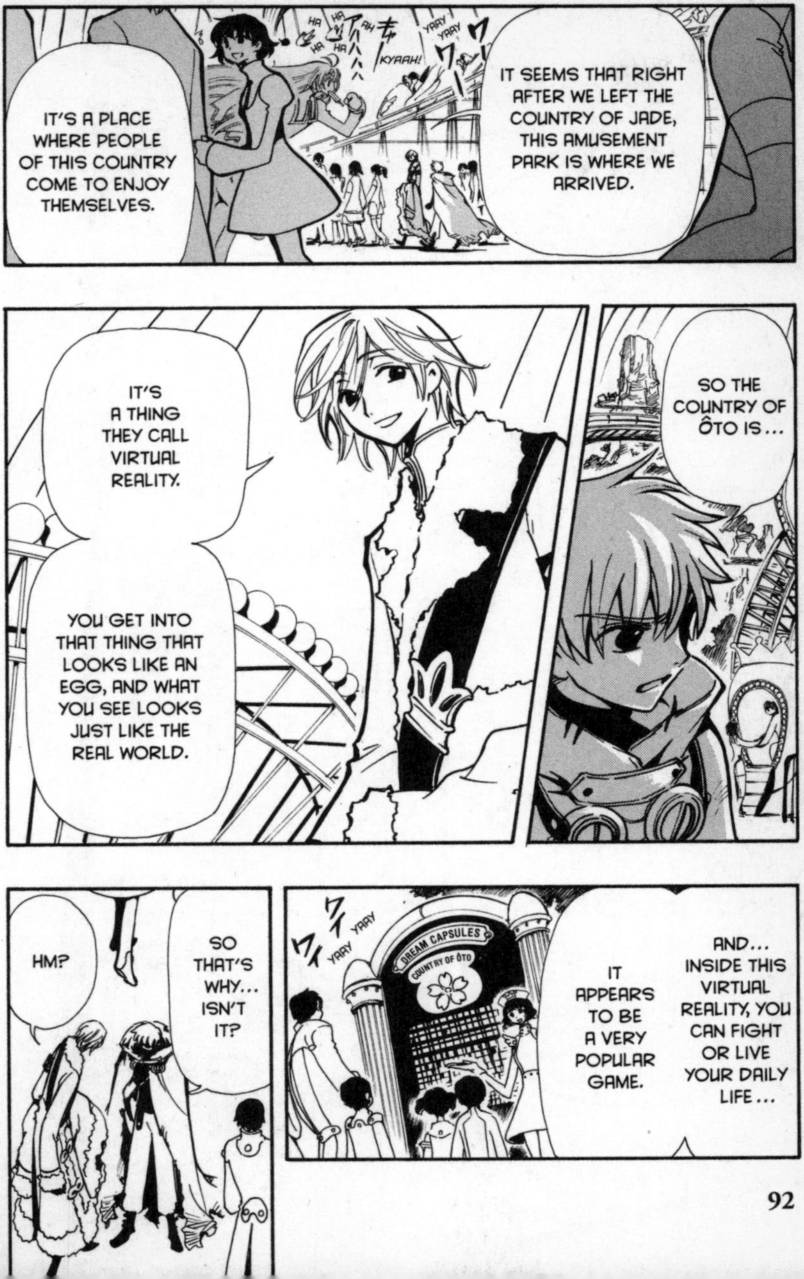
YAAY YAAY
KYAAH!
HA HA HA HA
IT SEEMS THAT RIGHT AFTER WE LEFT THE COUNTRY OF JADE, THIS AMUSEMENT PARK IS WHERE WE ARRIVED.
IT'S A PLACE WHERE PEOPLE OF THIS COUNTRY COME TO ENJOY THEMSELVES.
SO THE COUNTRY OF ÔTO IS...
IT'S A THING THEY CALL VIRTUAL REALITY.
YOU GET INTO THAT THING THAT LOOKS LIKE AN EGG, AND WHAT YOU SEE LOOKS JUST LIKE THE REAL WORLD.
AND... INSIDE THIS VIRTUAL REALITY, YOU CAN FIGHT OR LIVE YOUR DAILY LIFE...
IT APPEARS TO BE A VERY POPULAR GAME.
DREAM CAPSULES
COUNTRY OF ÔTO
YAAY YAAY
SO THAT'S WHY... ISN'T IT?
HM?

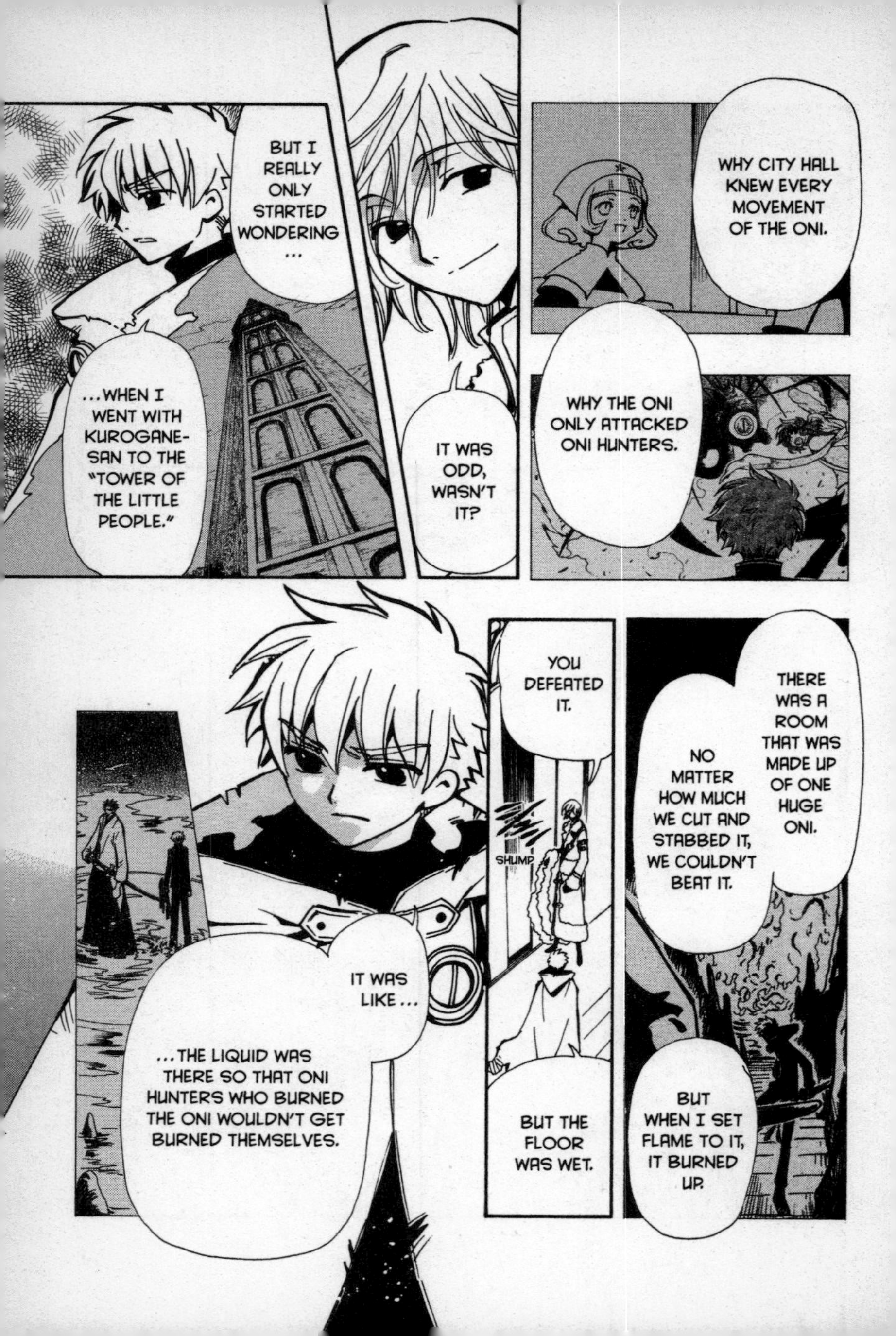
WHY CITY HALL KNEW EVERY MOVEMENT OF THE ONI.
WHY THE ONI ONLY ATTACKED ONI HUNTERS.
IT WAS ODD, WASN'T IT?
BUT I REALLY ONLY STARTED WONDERING ...
...WHEN I WENT WITH KUROGANE-SAN TO THE "TOWER OF THE LITTLE PEOPLE."
THERE WAS A ROOM THAT WAS MADE UP OF ONE HUGE ONI.
NO MATTER HOW MUCH WE CUT AND STABBED IT, WE COULDN'T BEAT IT.
BUT WHEN I SET FLAME TO IT, IT BURNED UP.
YOU DEFEATED IT.
SHUMP
BUT THE FLOOR WAS WET.
IT WAS LIKE...
...THE LIQUID WAS THERE SO THAT ONI HUNTERS WHO BURNED THE ONI WOULDN'T GET BURNED THEMSELVES.

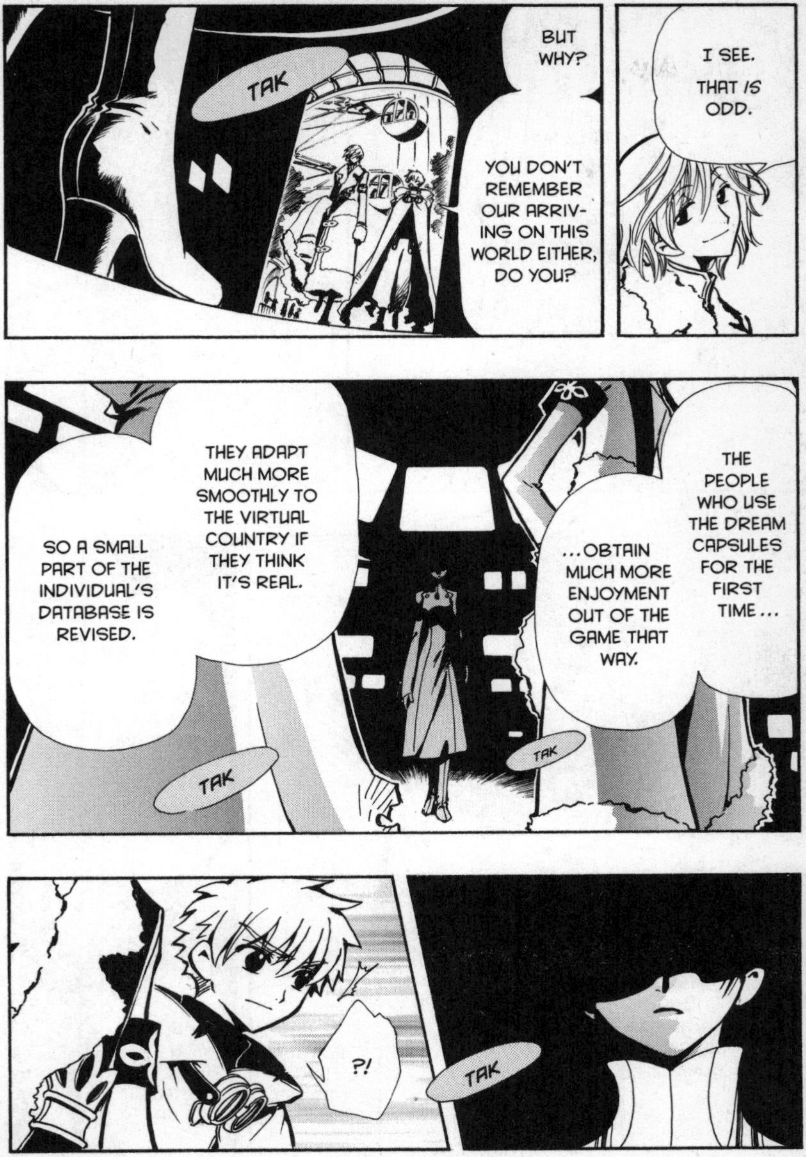
I SEE. THAT IS ODD.
BUT WHY?
TAK
YOU DON'T REMEMBER OUR ARRIV-ING ON THIS WORLD EITHER, DO YOU?
THE PEOPLE WHO USE THE DREAM CAPSULES FOR THE FIRST TIME...
...OBTAIN MUCH MORE ENJOYMENT OUT OF THE GAME THAT WAY.
THEY ADAPT MUCH MORE SMOOTHLY TO THE VIRTUAL COUNTRY IF THEY THINK IT'S REAL.
SO A SMALL PART OF THE INDIVIDUAL'S DATABASE IS REVISED.
TAK
TAK
TAK
?!

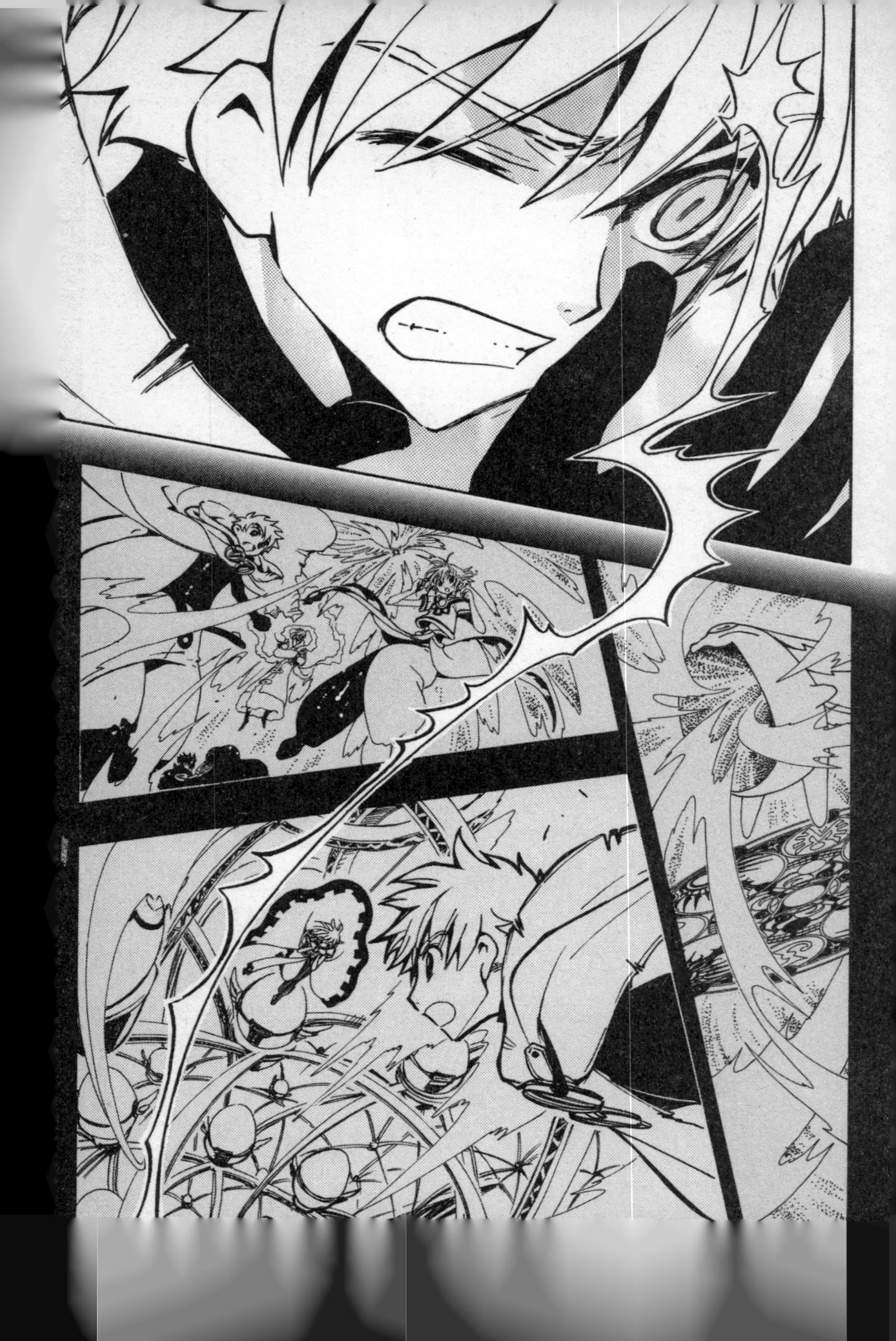

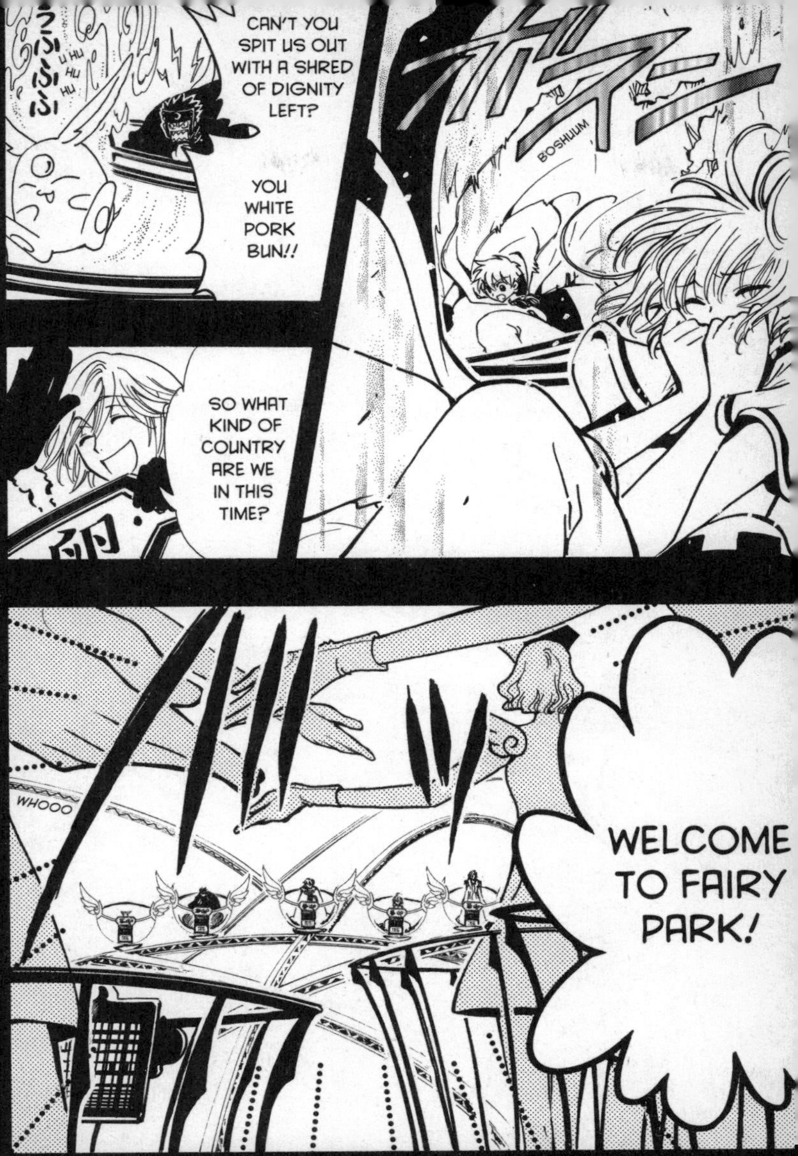
BOSHUUM
うふふふ
U HU HU HU
CAN'T YOU SPIT US OUT WITH A SHRED OF DIGNITY LEFT?
YOU WHITE PORK BUN!!
SO WHAT KIND OF COUNTRY ARE WE IN THIS TIME?
WELCOME TO FAIRY PARK!
WHOOO

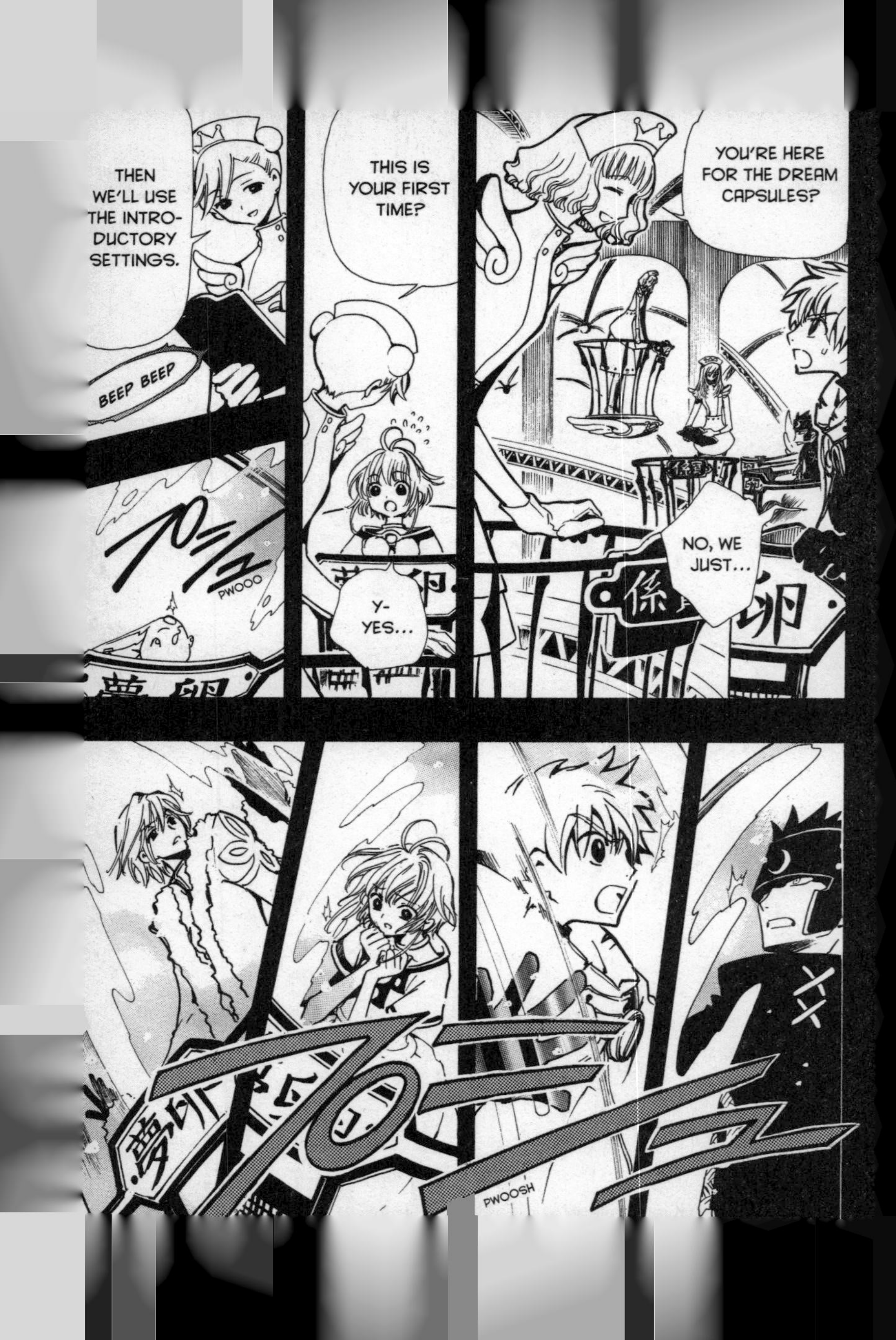
YOU'RE HERE FOR THE DREAM CAPSULES?
NO, WE JUST...
THIS IS YOUR FIRST TIME?
Y-YES...
THEN WE'LL USE THE INTRO-DUCTORY SETTINGS.
BEEP BEEP
PWOOO
PWOOSH

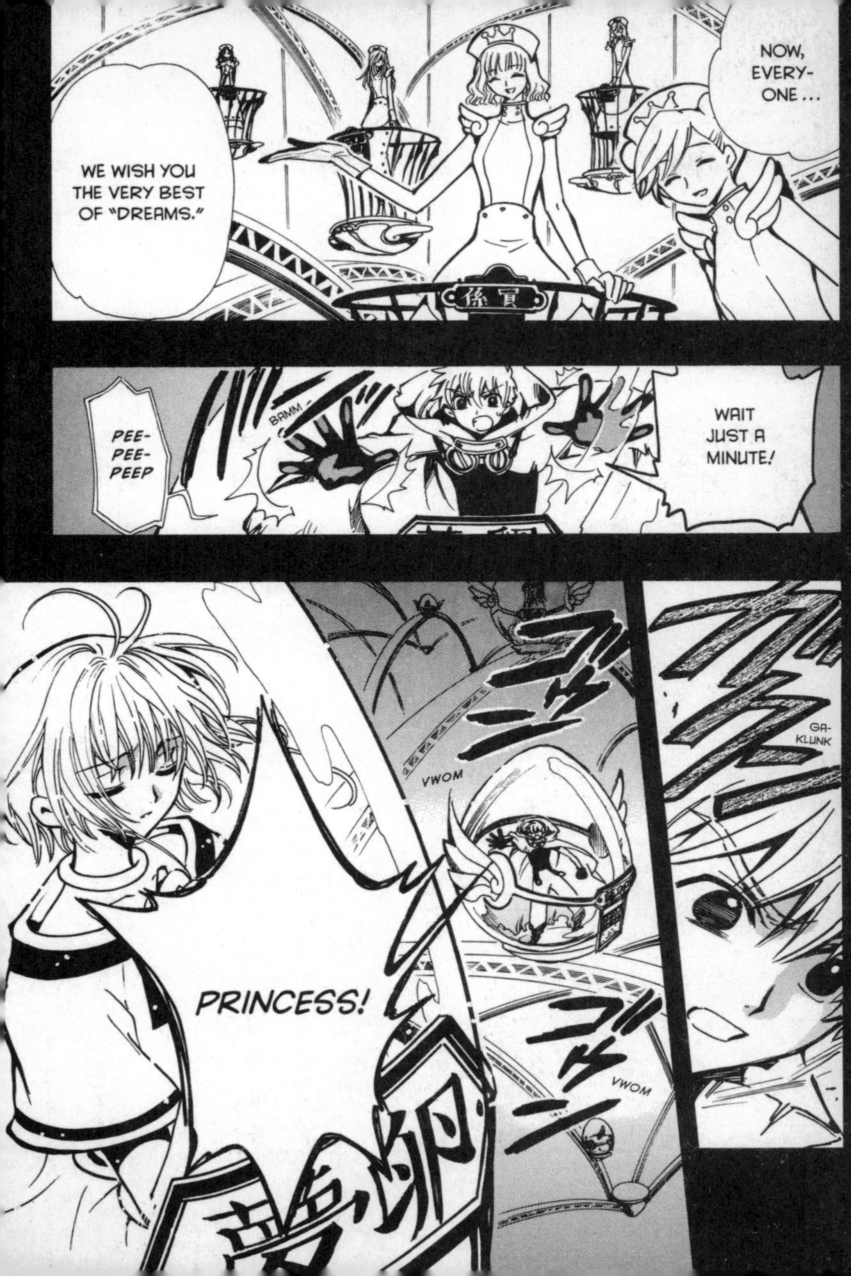
NOW, EVERY- ONE . . .
WE WISH YOU THE VERY BEST OF "DREAMS."
WAIT JUST A MINUTE!
BAMM
PEE- PEE- PEEP
GA- KLUNK
VWOM
VWOM
PRINCESS!

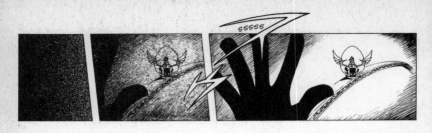

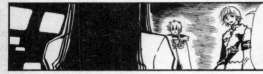

I REMEMBER!!

IN OTHER WORDS, YOU ARRANGED FOR US TO THINK THAT THE COUNTRY WAS ACTUALLY REALITY.

AND THAT'S WHY WE FORGOT ABOUT THE AMUSEMENT PARK WHILE IN ÔTO.

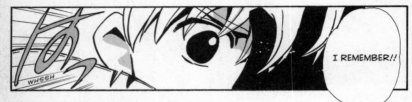

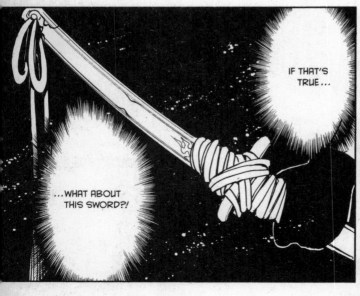

IF THAT'S TRUE...

...WHAT ABOUT THIS SWORD?!

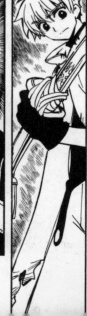

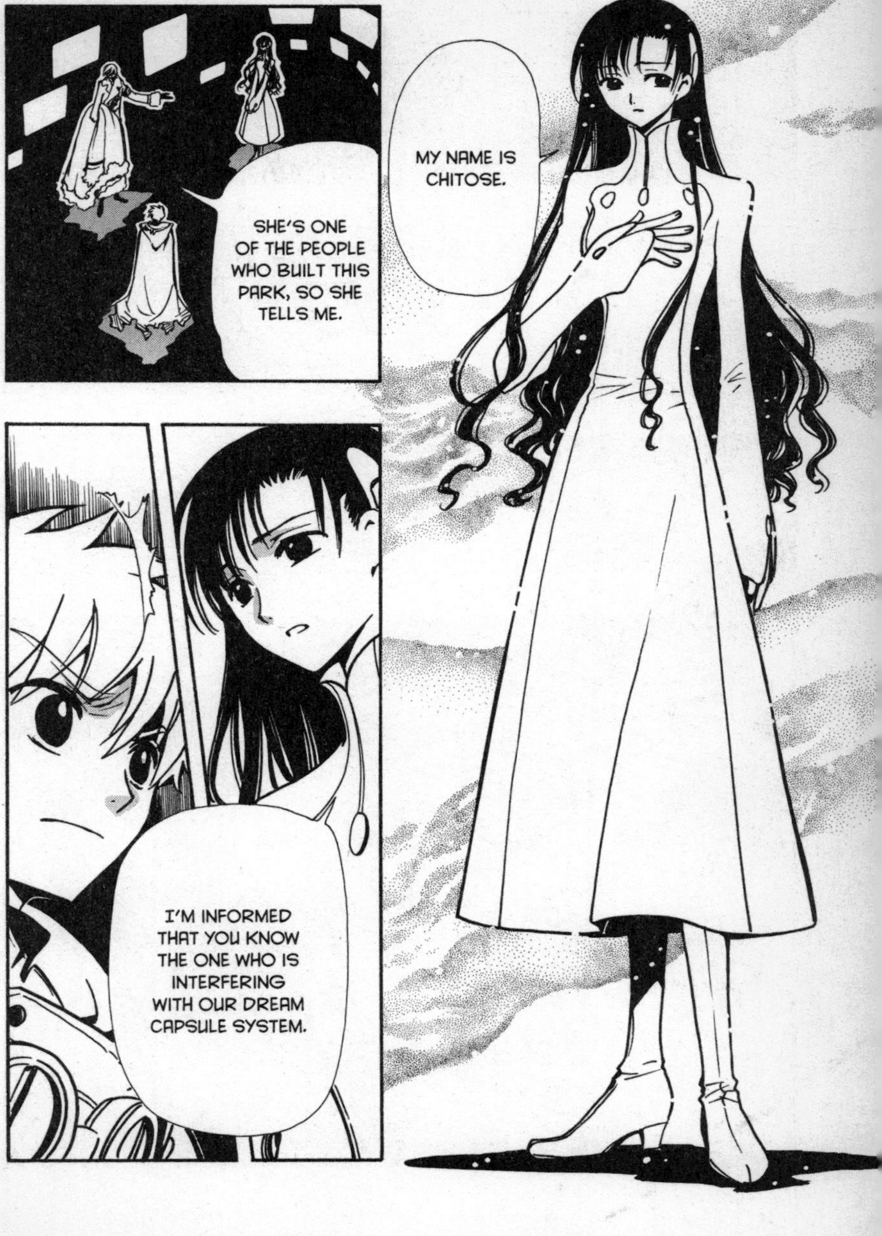
MY NAME IS CHITOSE.
SHE'S ONE OF THE PEOPLE WHO BUILT THIS PARK, SO SHE TELLS ME.
I'M INFORMED THAT YOU KNOW THE ONE WHO IS INTERFERING WITH OUR DREAM CAPSULE SYSTEM.

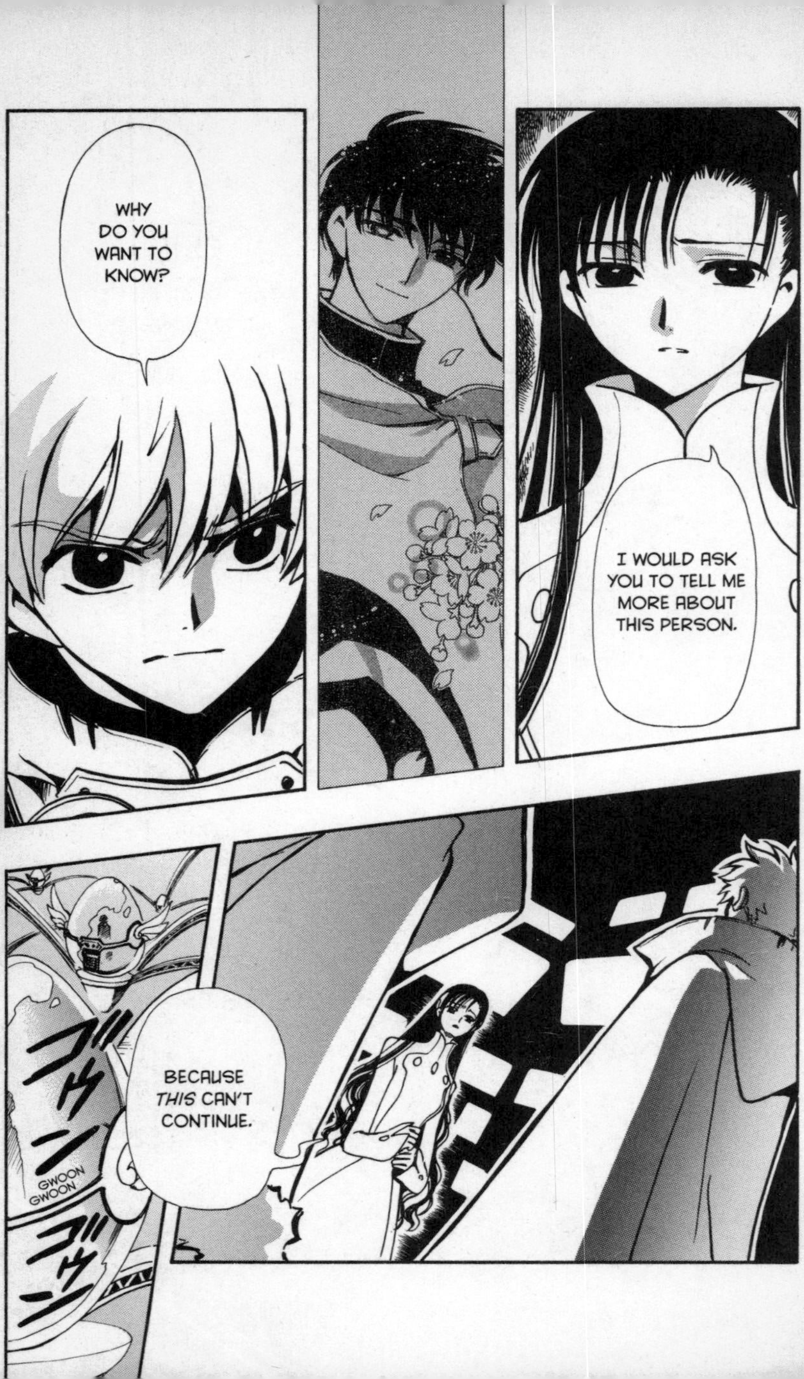
I WOULD ASK YOU TO TELL ME MORE ABOUT THIS PERSON.
WHY DO YOU WANT TO KNOW?
BECAUSE *THIS* CAN'T CONTINUE.
GWOON GWOON

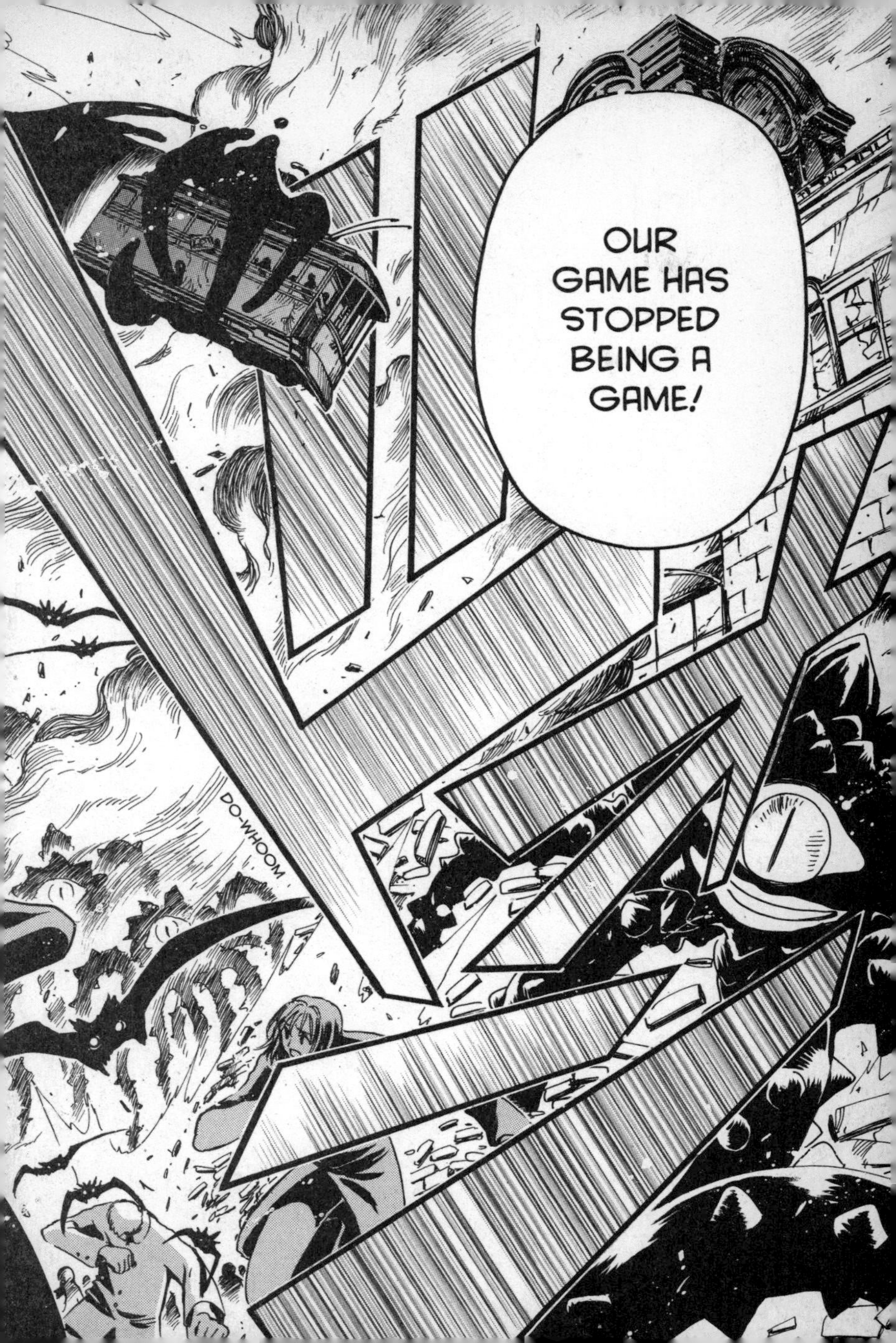
OUR GAME HAS STOPPED BEING A GAME!
DO-WHOOM

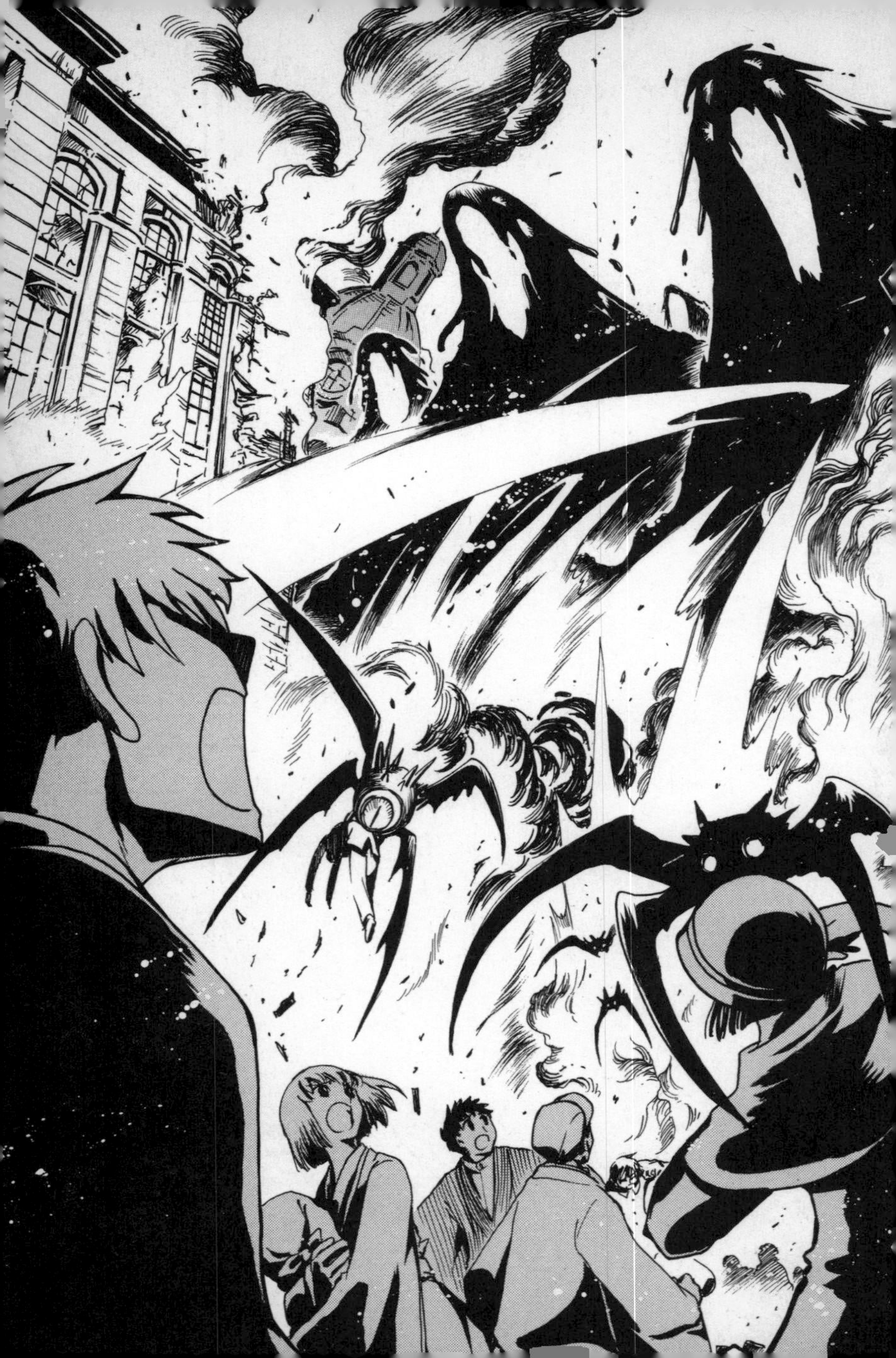

ツバサ

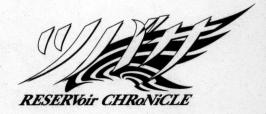

RESERVoir CHRoNiCLE

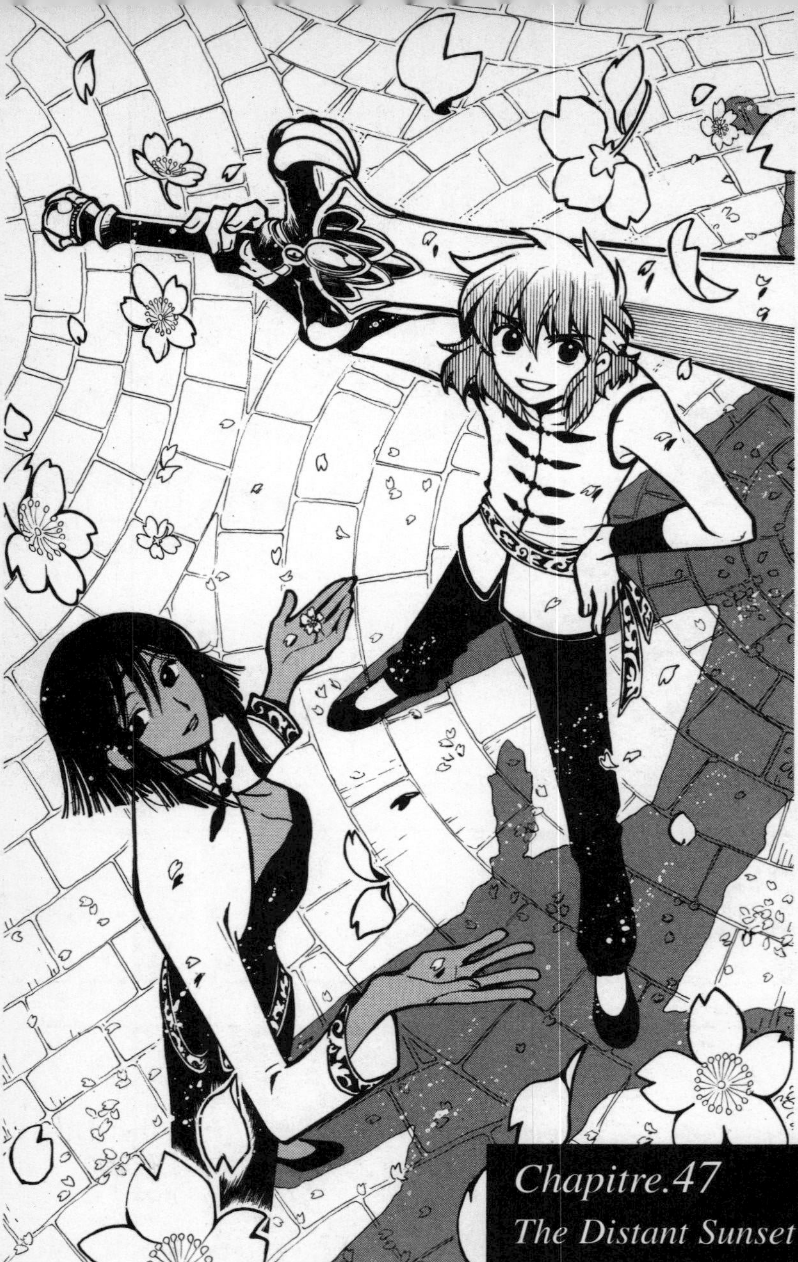

Chapitre.47
The Distant Sunset

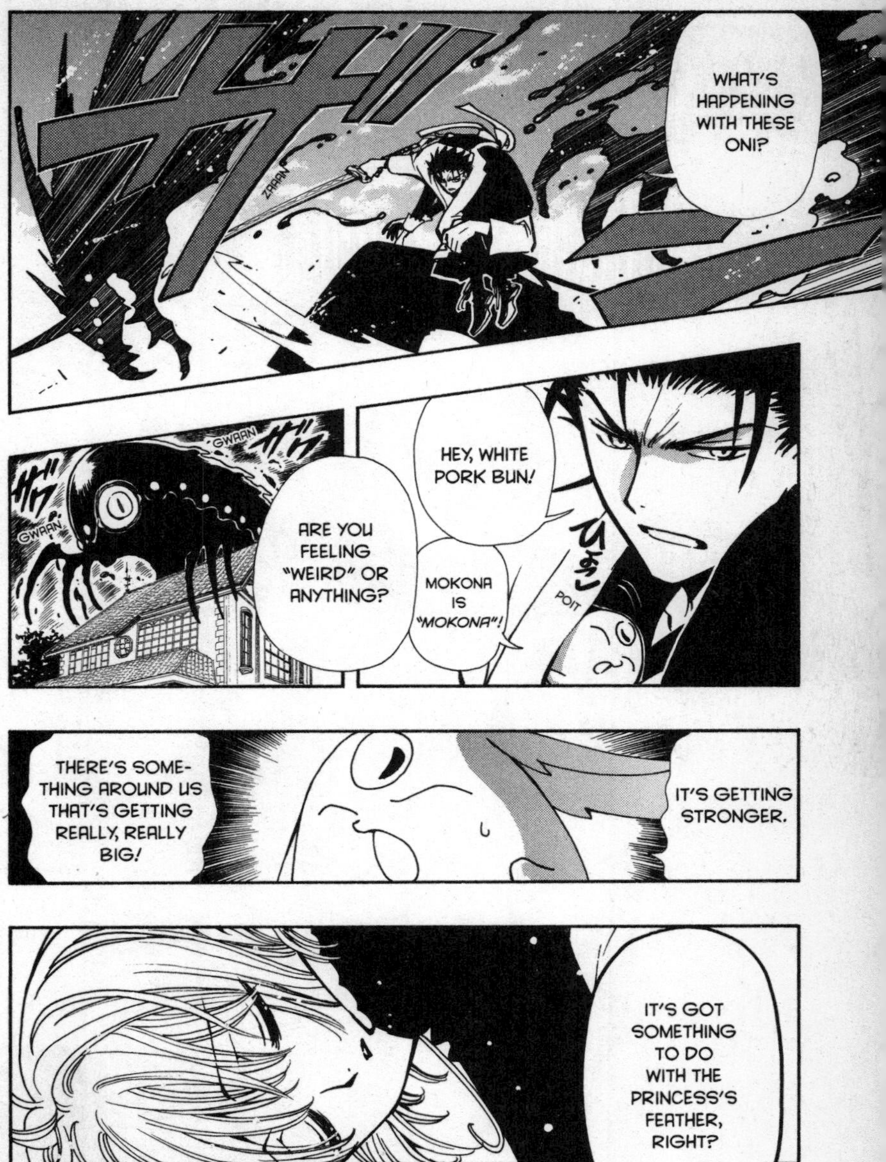
WHAT'S HAPPENING WITH THESE ONI?
HEY, WHITE PORK BUN!
ARE YOU FEELING "WEIRD" OR ANYTHING?
MOKONA IS "MOKONA"!
POIT
GWAAN
GWAAN
IT'S GETTING STRONGER.
THERE'S SOME-THING AROUND US THAT'S GETTING REALLY, REALLY BIG!
IT'S GOT SOMETHING TO DO WITH THE PRINCESS'S FEATHER, RIGHT?

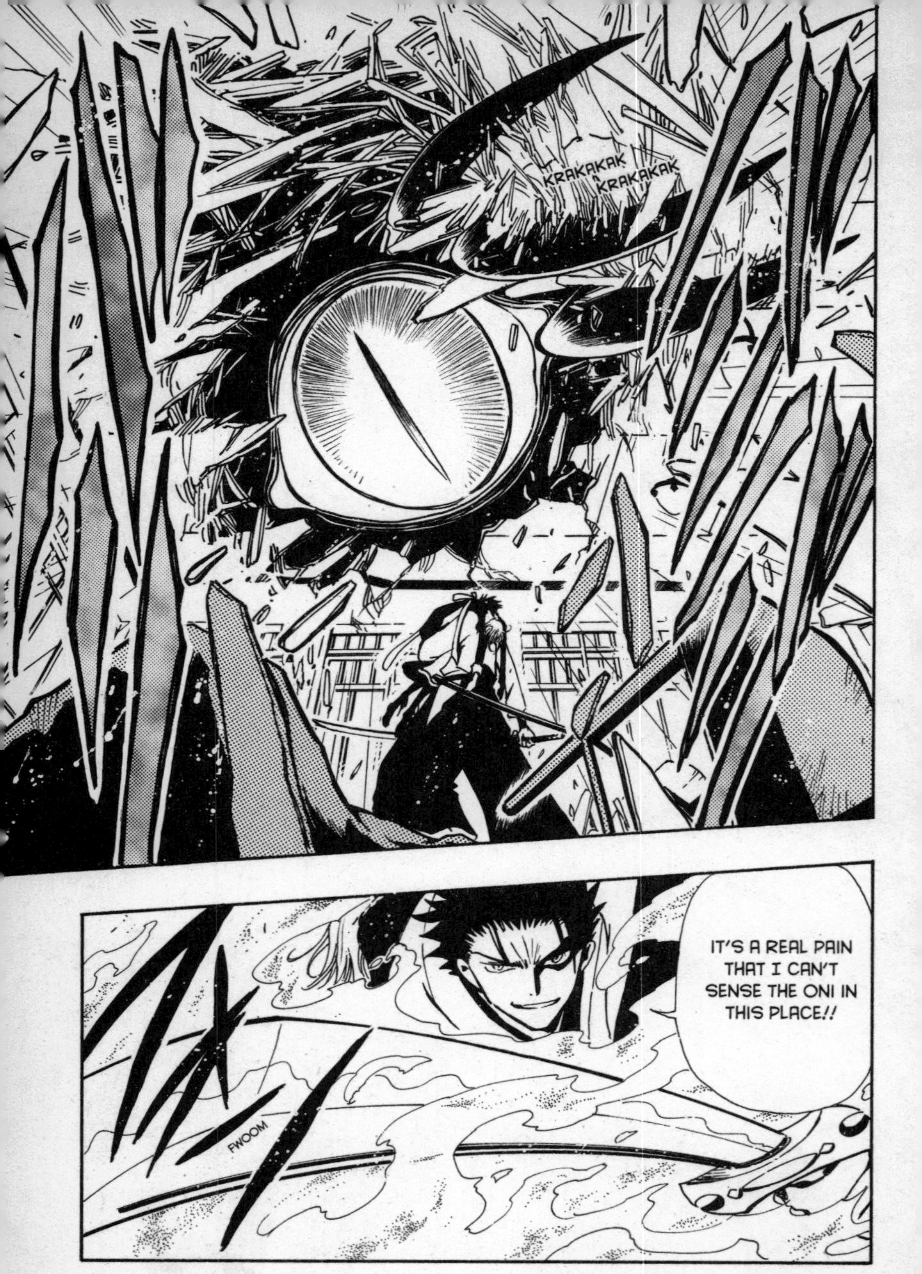
KRAKAKAK
KRAKAKAK
IT'S A REAL PAIN THAT I CAN'T SENSE THE ONI IN THIS PLACE!!
FWOOM

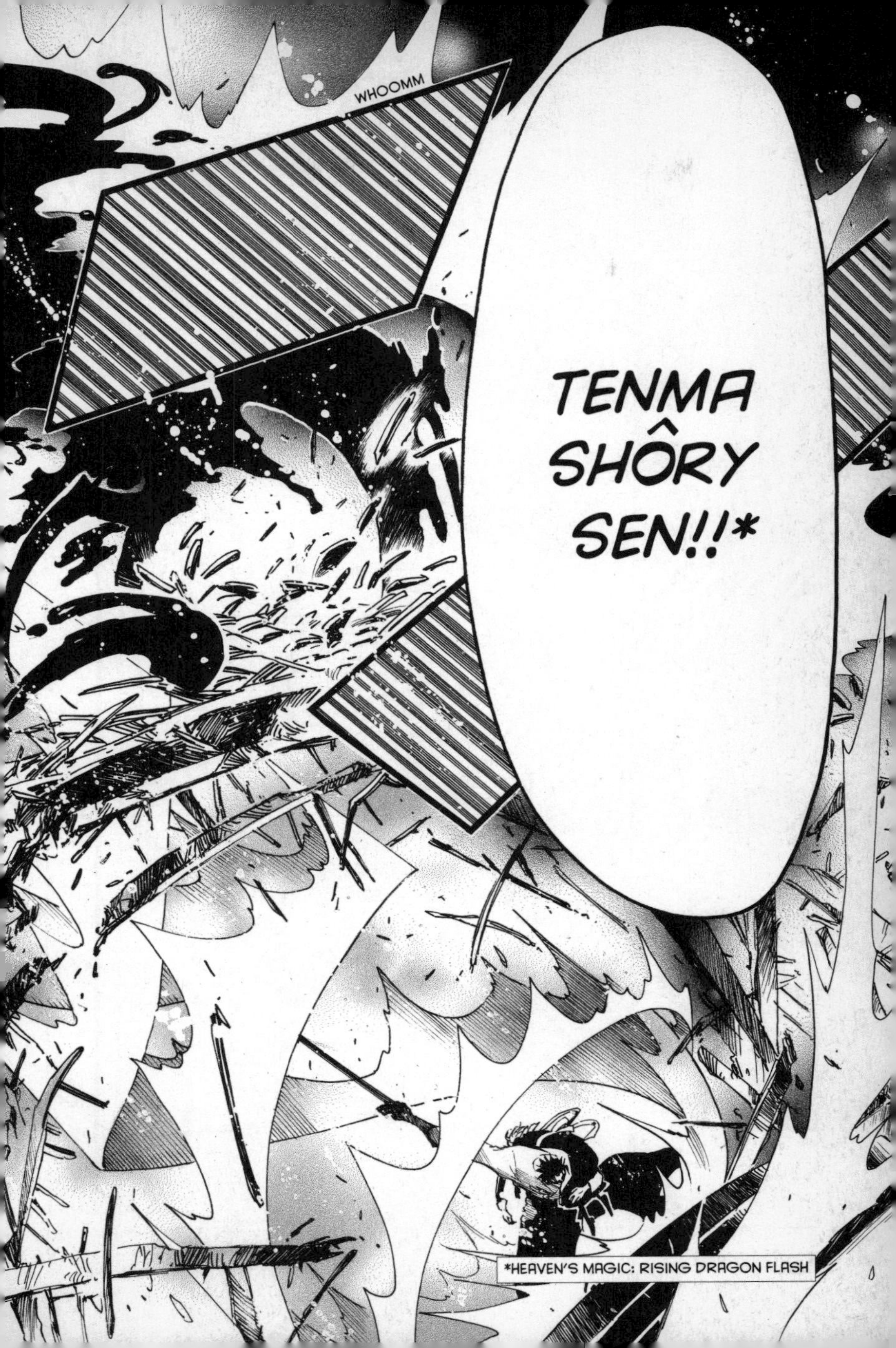
WHOOMM
TENMA SHÔRY SEN!!*
*HEAVEN'S MAGIC: RISING DRAGON FLASH

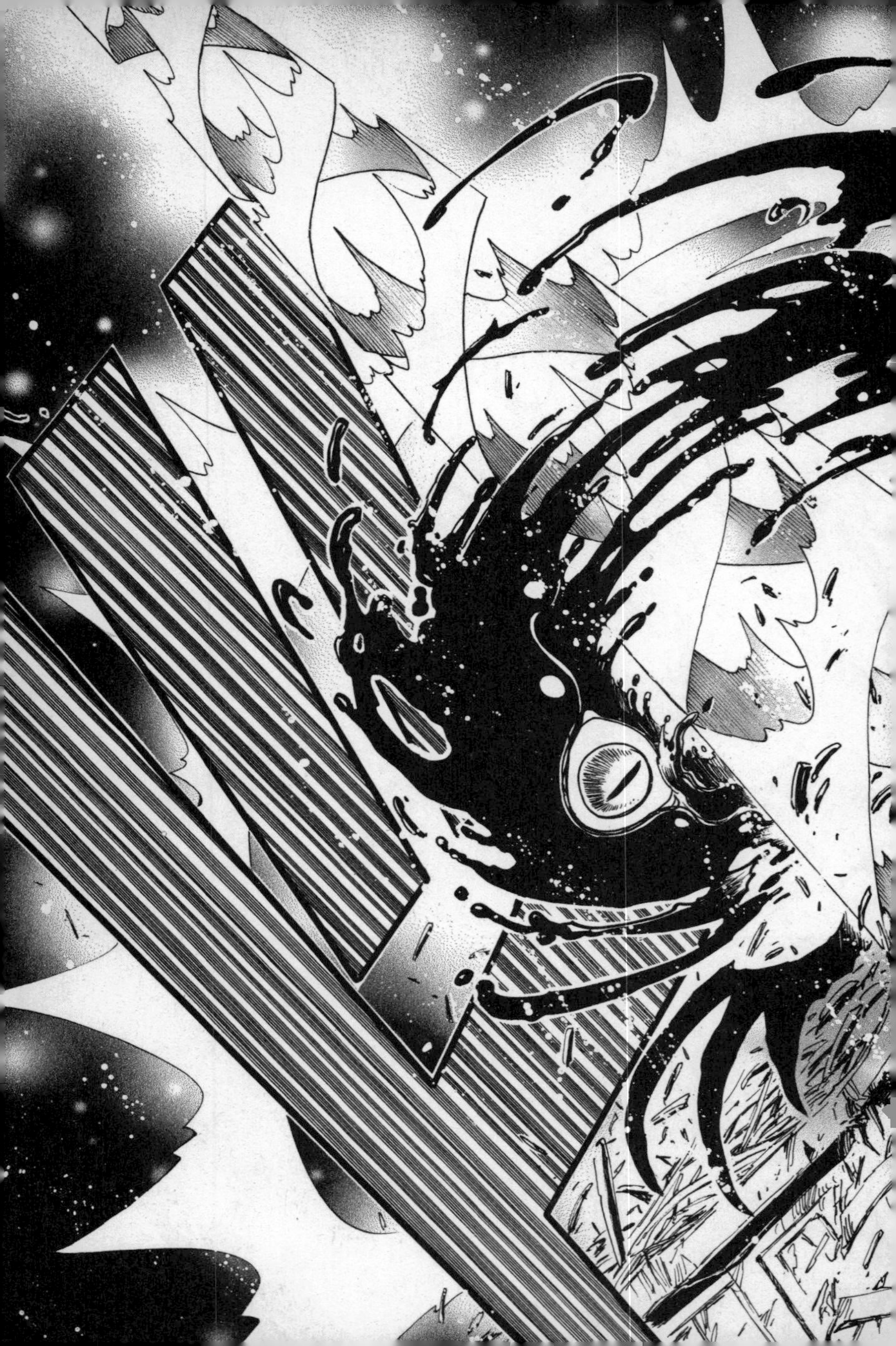

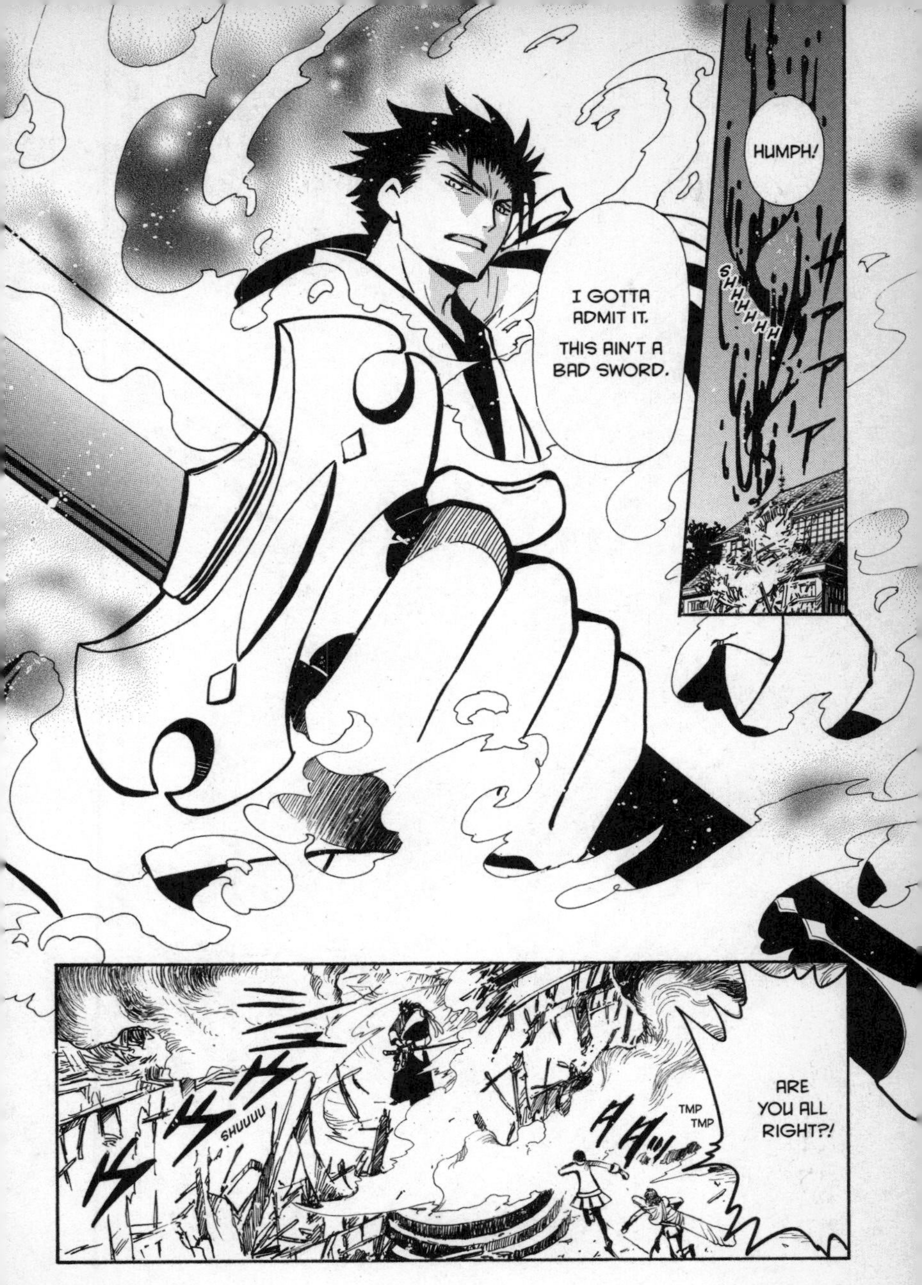
HUMPH!
SHHHHHH
I GOTTA ADMIT IT.
THIS AIN'T A BAD SWORD.
ARE YOU ALL RIGHT?!
TMP TMP
SHUUUU

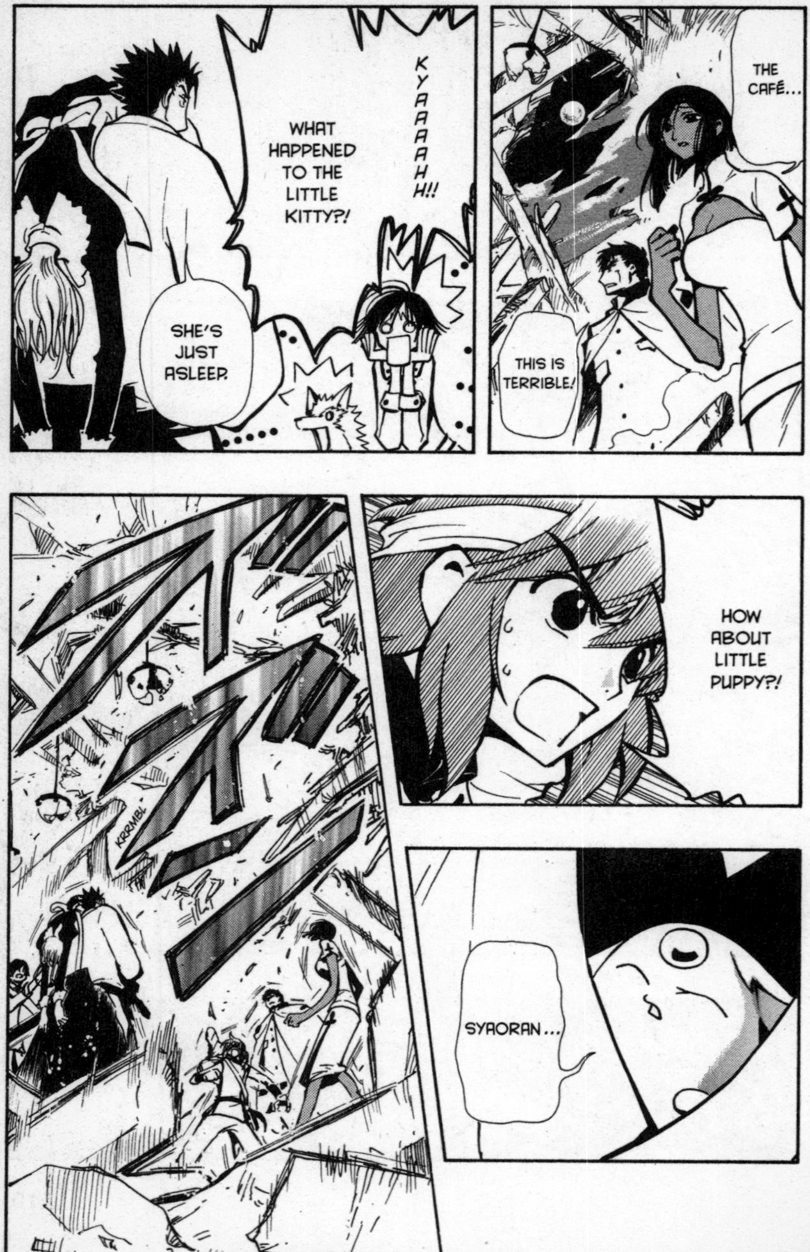
THE CAFÉ...
THIS IS TERRIBLE!
WHAT HAPPENED TO THE LITTLE KITTY?!
KYAAAAAH!!
SHE'S JUST ASLEEP.
HOW ABOUT LITTLE PUPPY?!
SYAORAN...
KRRMBL

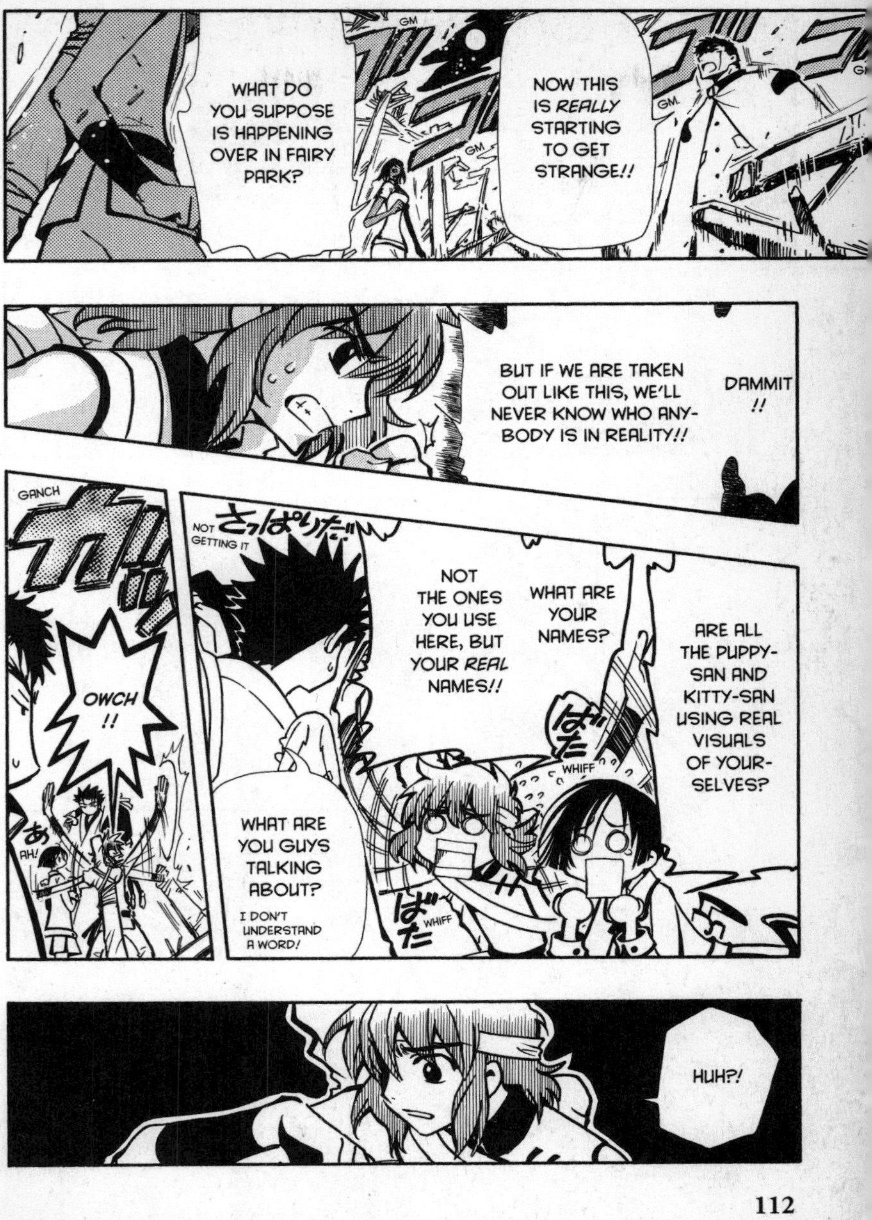
GM
GM.
NOW THIS IS *REALLY* STARTING TO GET STRANGE!!
GM
GM
WHAT DO YOU SUPPOSE IS HAPPENING OVER IN FAIRY PARK?
DAMMIT!!
BUT IF WE ARE TAKEN OUT LIKE THIS, WE'LL NEVER KNOW WHO ANYBODY IS IN REALITY!!
ARE ALL THE PUPPY-SAN AND KITTY-SAN USING REAL VISUALS OF YOURSELVES?
WHAT ARE YOUR NAMES?
NOT THE ONES YOU USE HERE, BUT YOUR *REAL* NAMES!!
ばた
WHIFF
さっぱりだ
NOT GETTING IT
WHAT ARE YOU GUYS TALKING ABOUT?
I DON'T UNDERSTAND A WORD!
ばた
WHIFF
GANCH
OWCH!!
あ
AH!
HUH?!

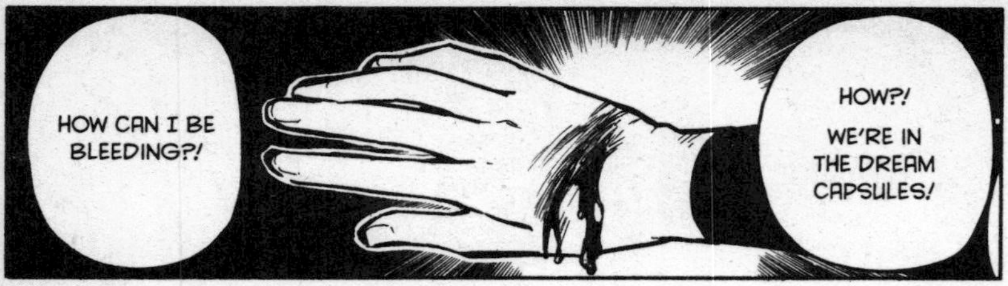
HOW?! WE'RE IN THE DREAM CAPSULES!
HOW CAN I BE BLEEDING?!
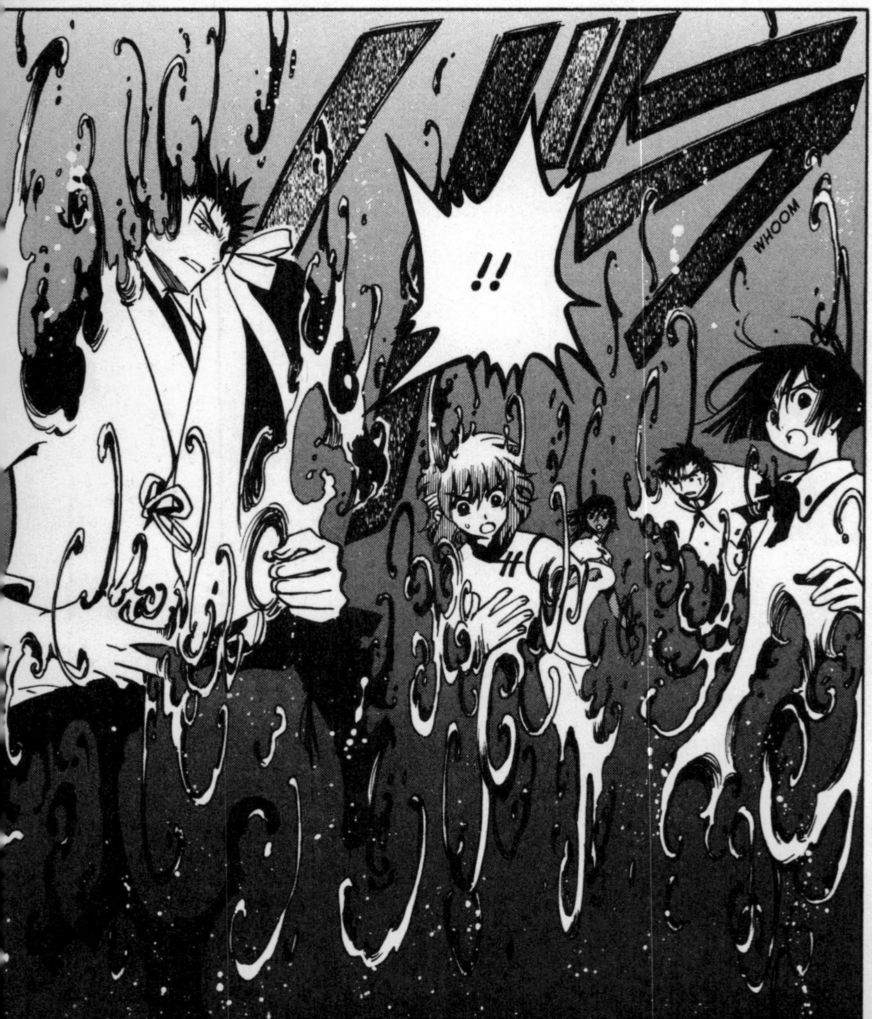
WHOOM
!!

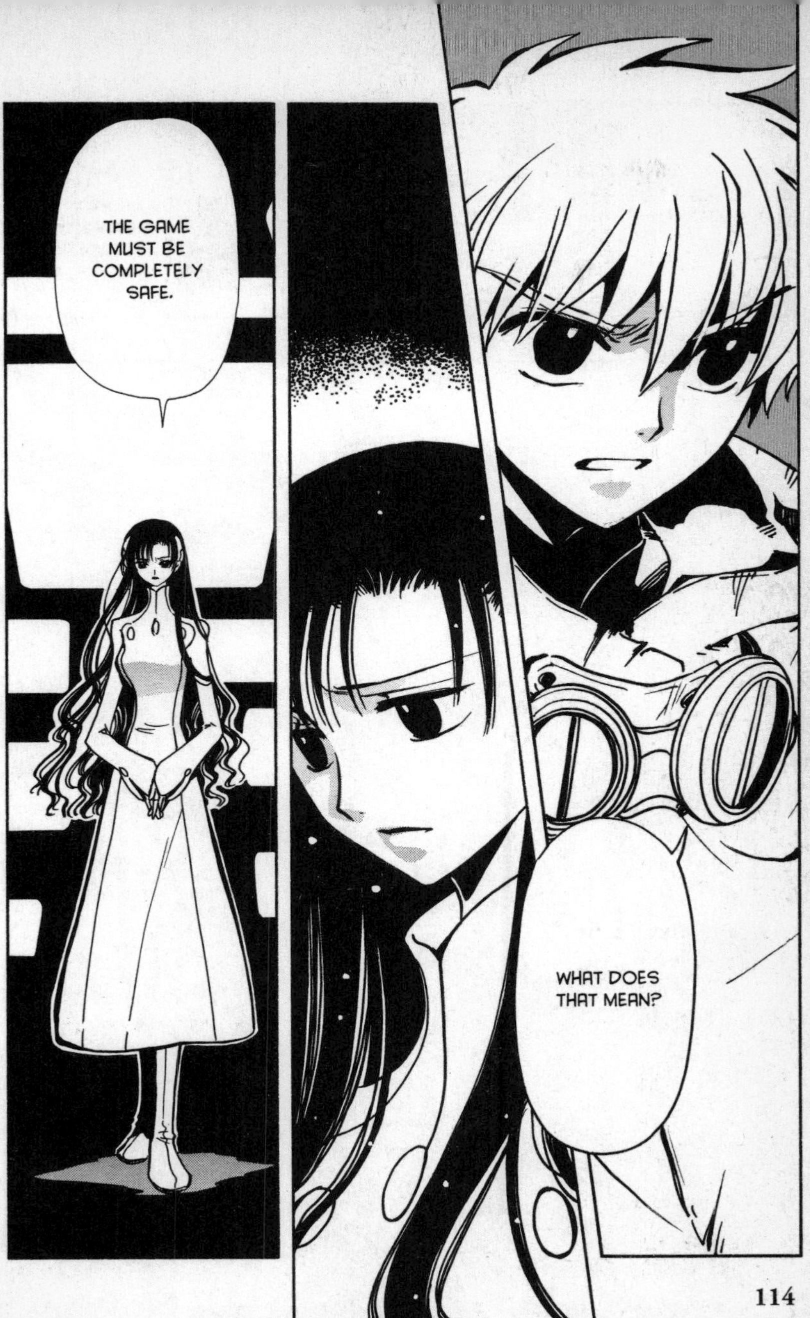
WHAT DOES THAT MEAN?
THE GAME MUST BE COMPLETELY SAFE.

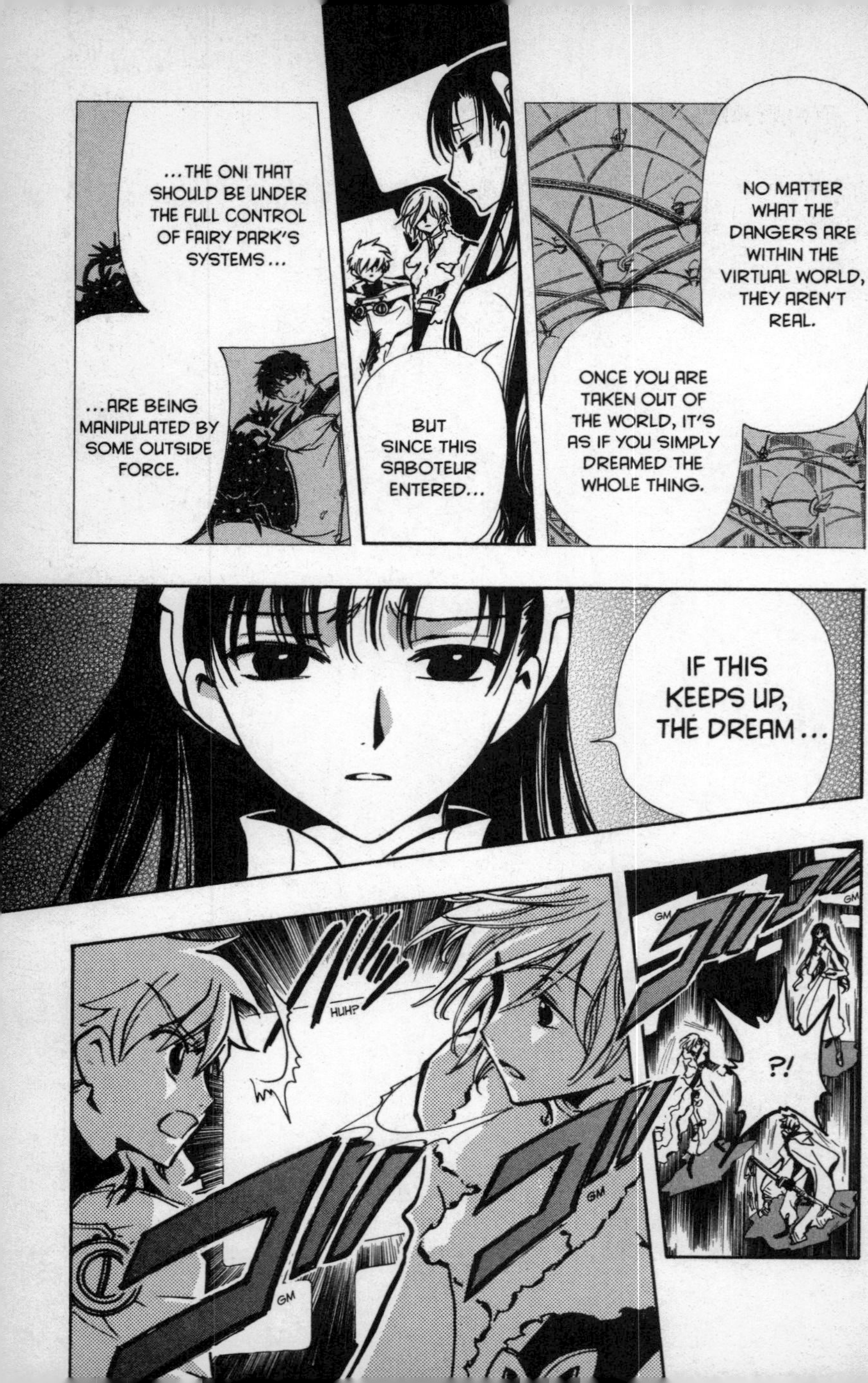
NO MATTER WHAT THE DANGERS ARE WITHIN THE VIRTUAL WORLD, THEY AREN'T REAL.
ONCE YOU ARE TAKEN OUT OF THE WORLD, IT'S AS IF YOU SIMPLY DREAMED THE WHOLE THING.
BUT SINCE THIS SABOTEUR ENTERED...
...THE ONI THAT SHOULD BE UNDER THE FULL CONTROL OF FAIRY PARK'S SYSTEMS...
...ARE BEING MANIPULATED BY SOME OUTSIDE FORCE.
IF THIS KEEPS UP, THE DREAM...
GM
GM
?!
HUH?
GM
GM

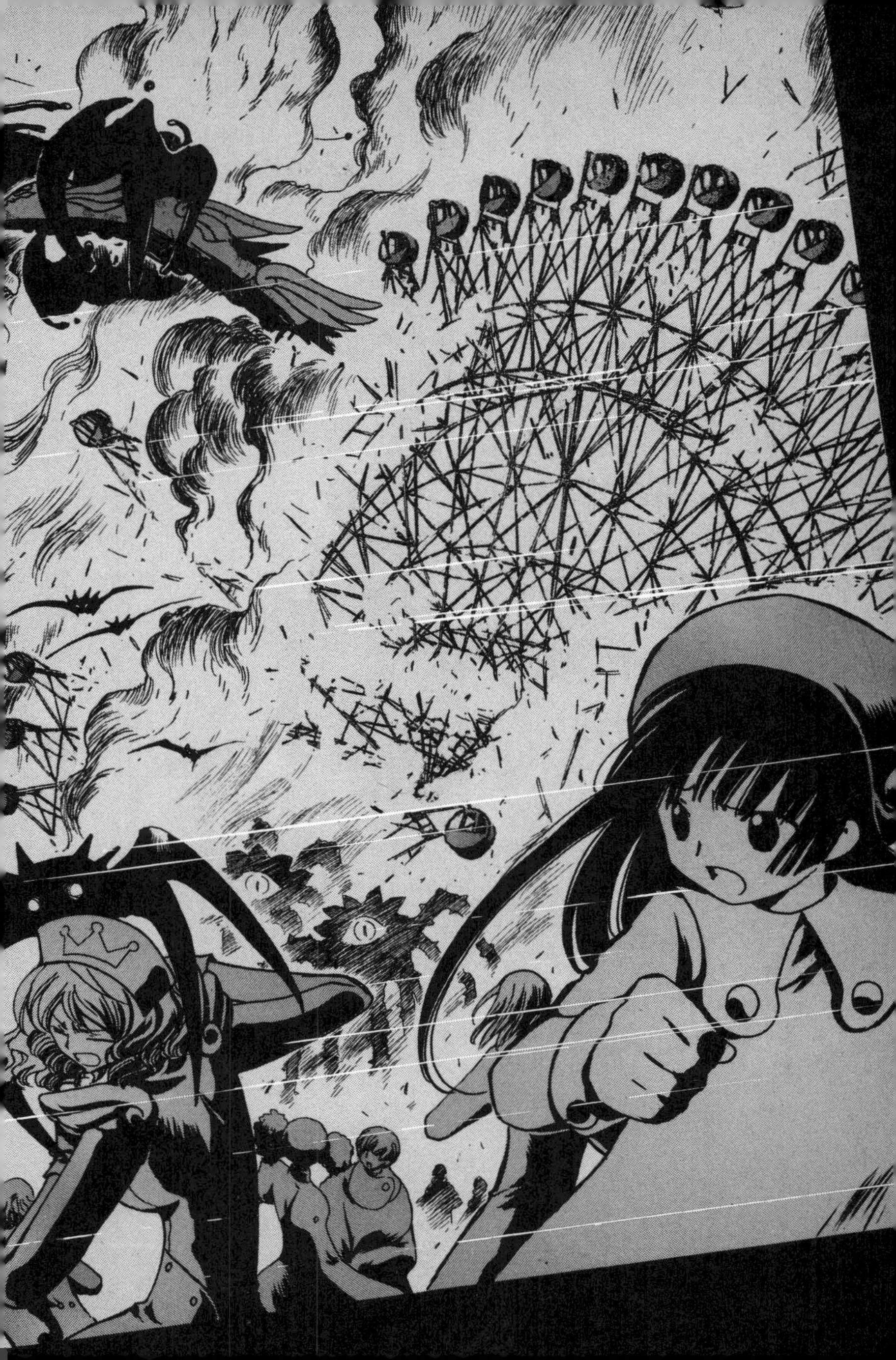

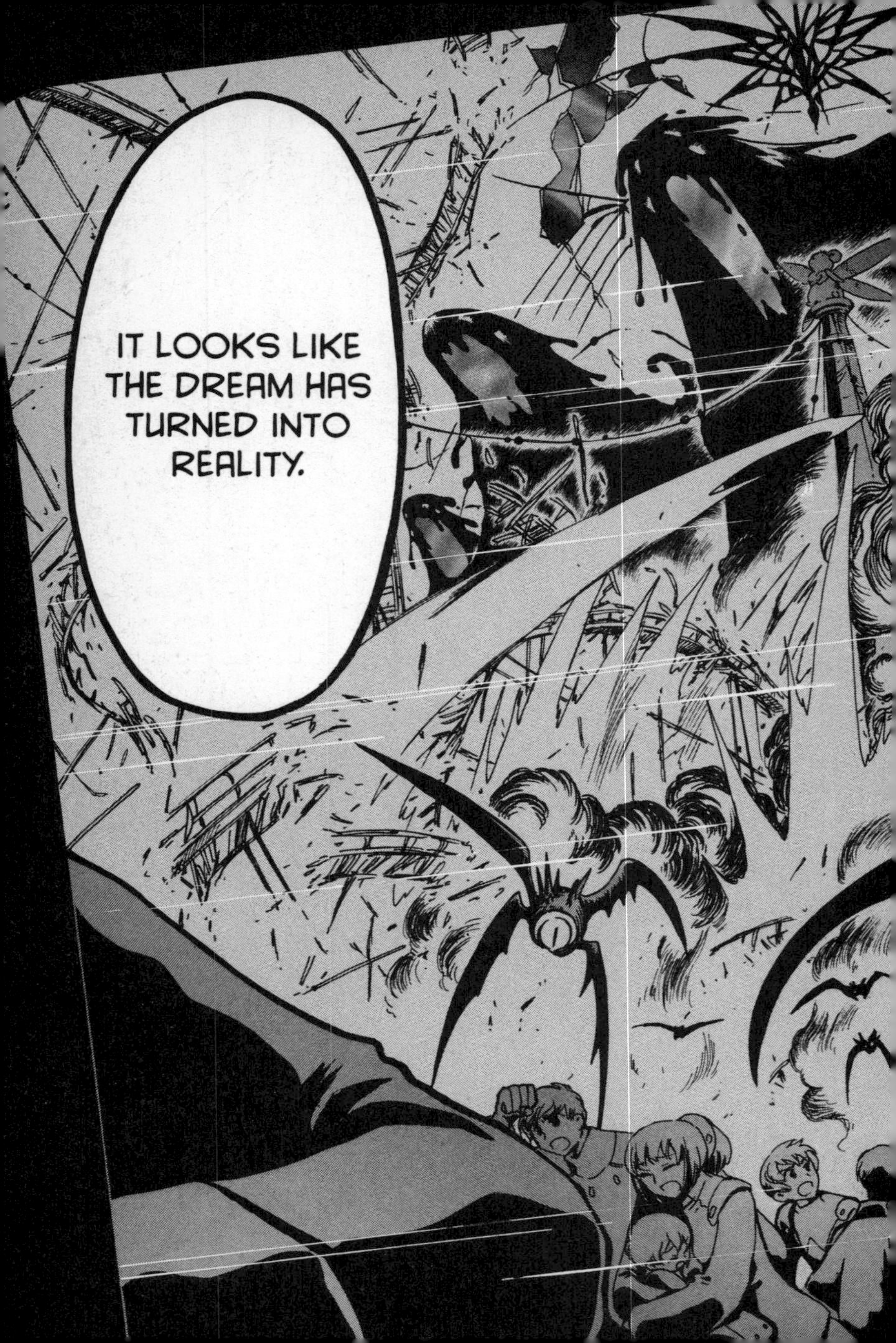
IT LOOKS LIKE THE DREAM HAS TURNED INTO REALITY.

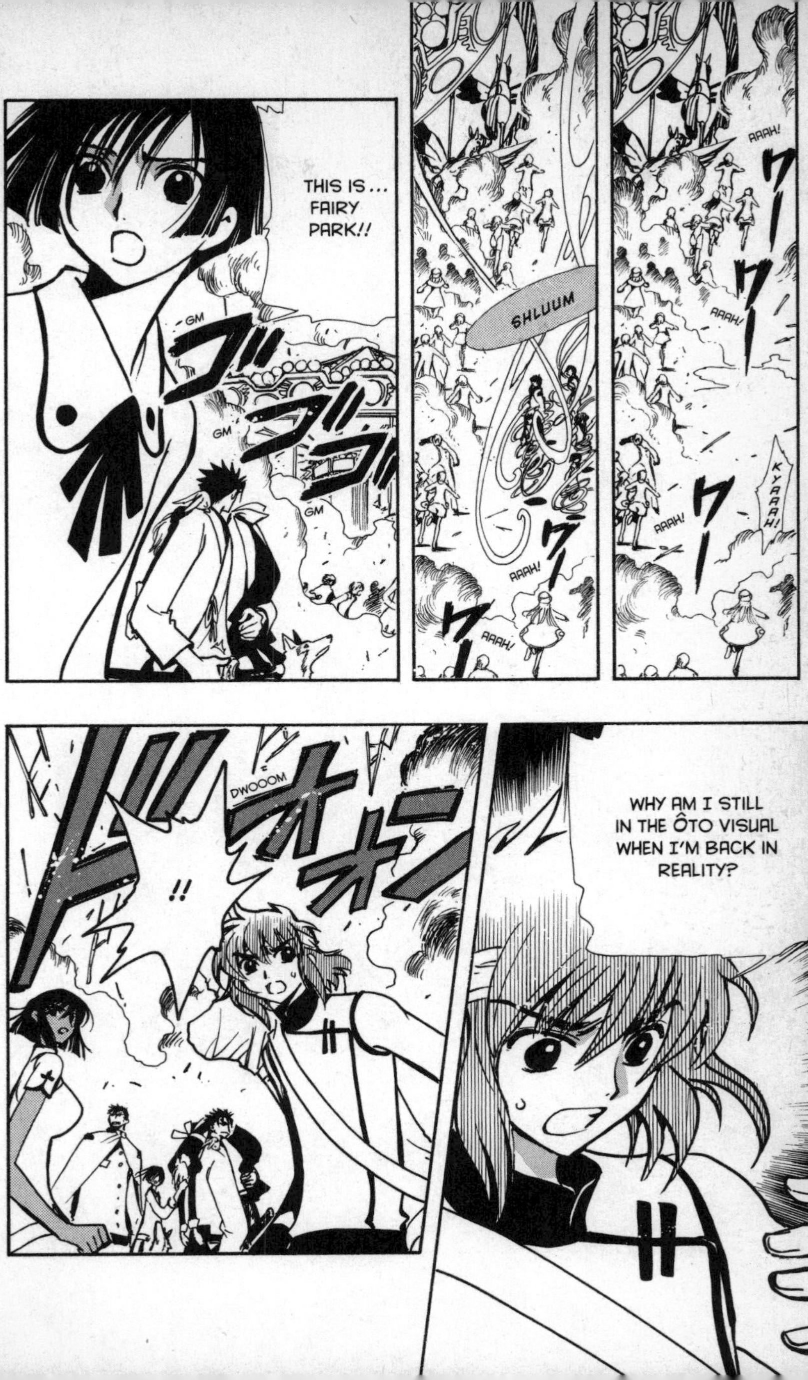

AAAH!
AAAH!
KYAAAAH!
AAAH!
SHLUUM
AAAH!
AAAH!
THIS IS... FAIRY PARK!!
GM
GM
GM
WHY AM I STILL IN THE ÔTO VISUAL WHEN I'M BACK IN REALITY?
DWOOOM
!!

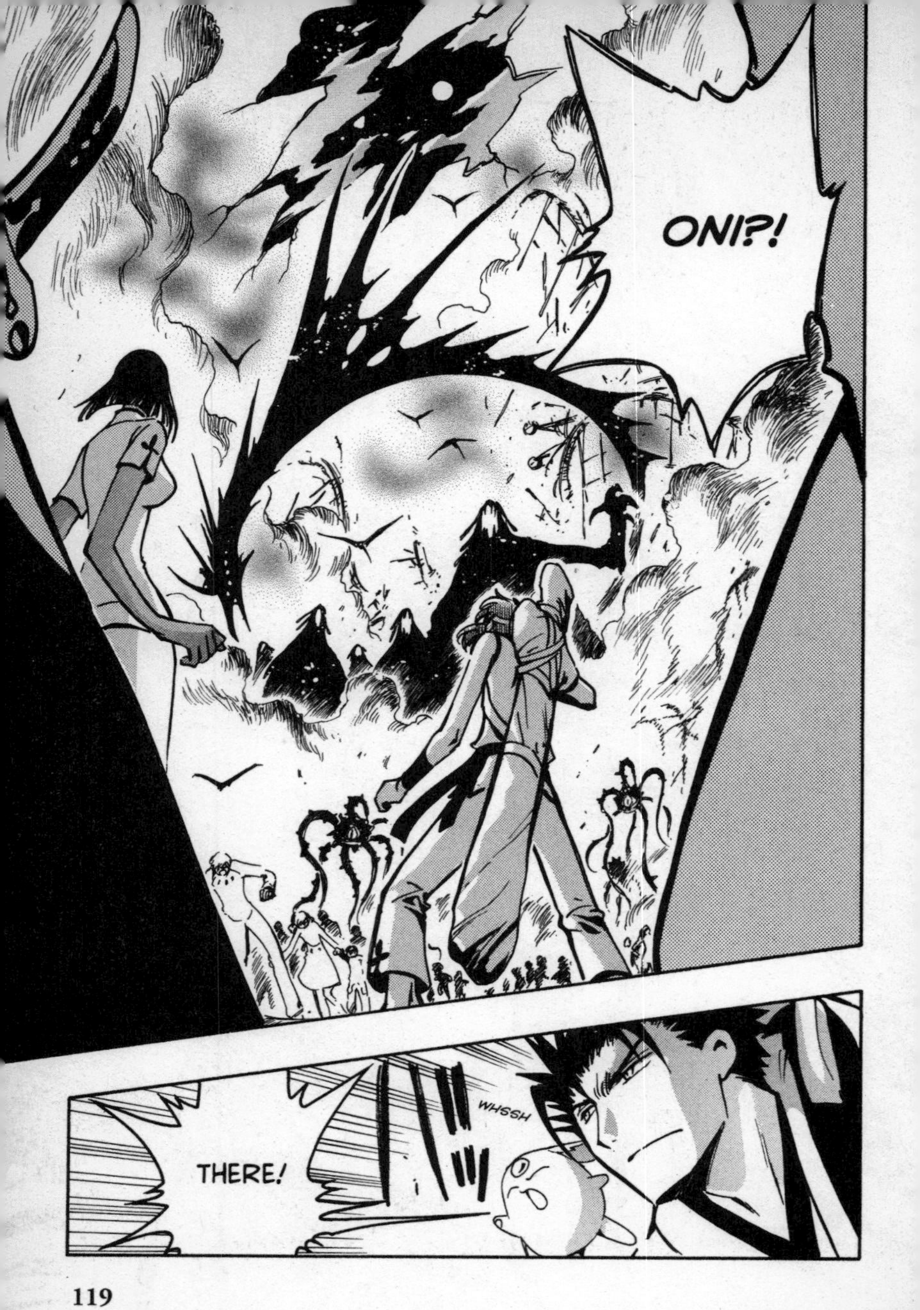
ONI?!
WHSSH
THERE!

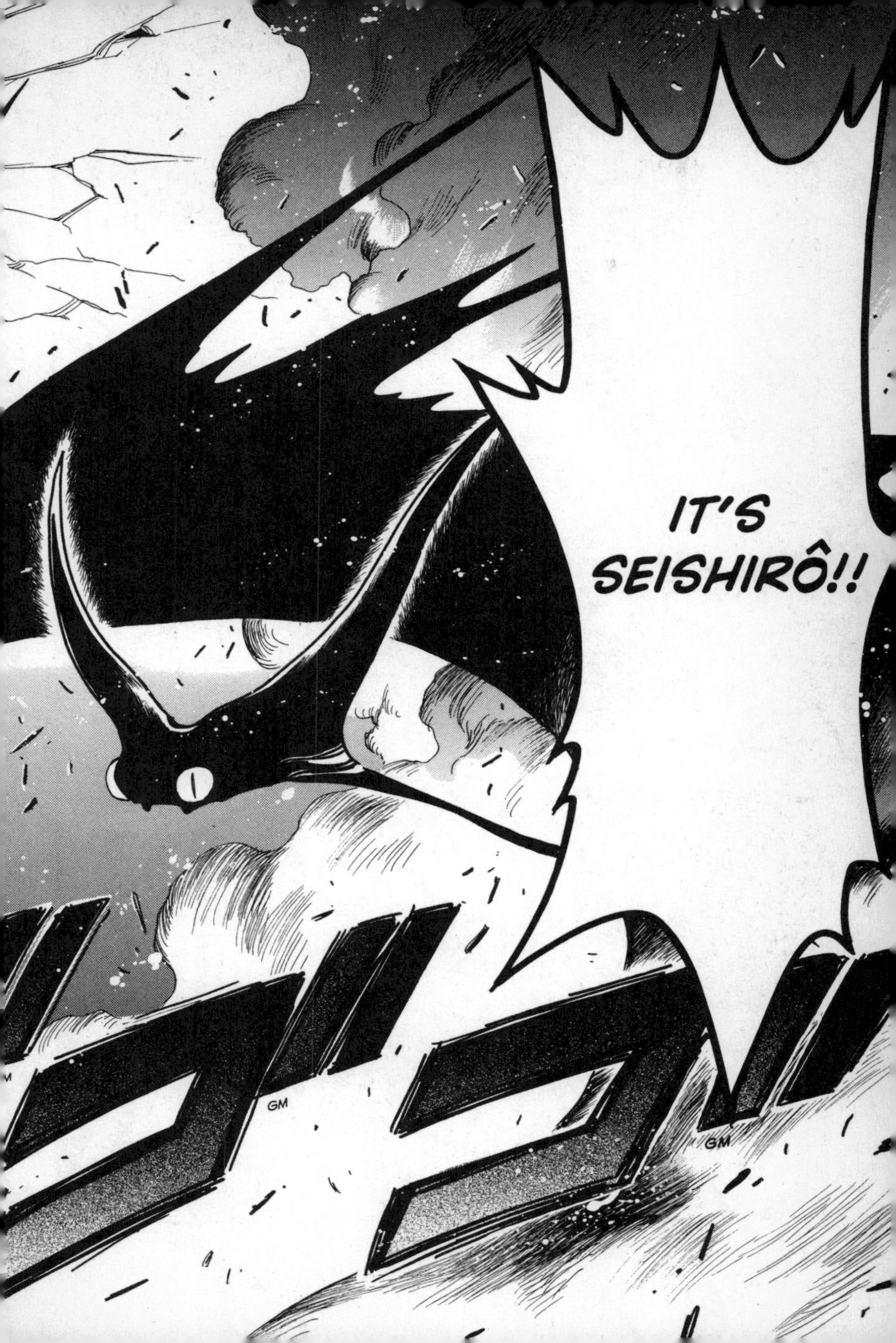
IT'S SEISHIRÔ!!
GM
GM
GM

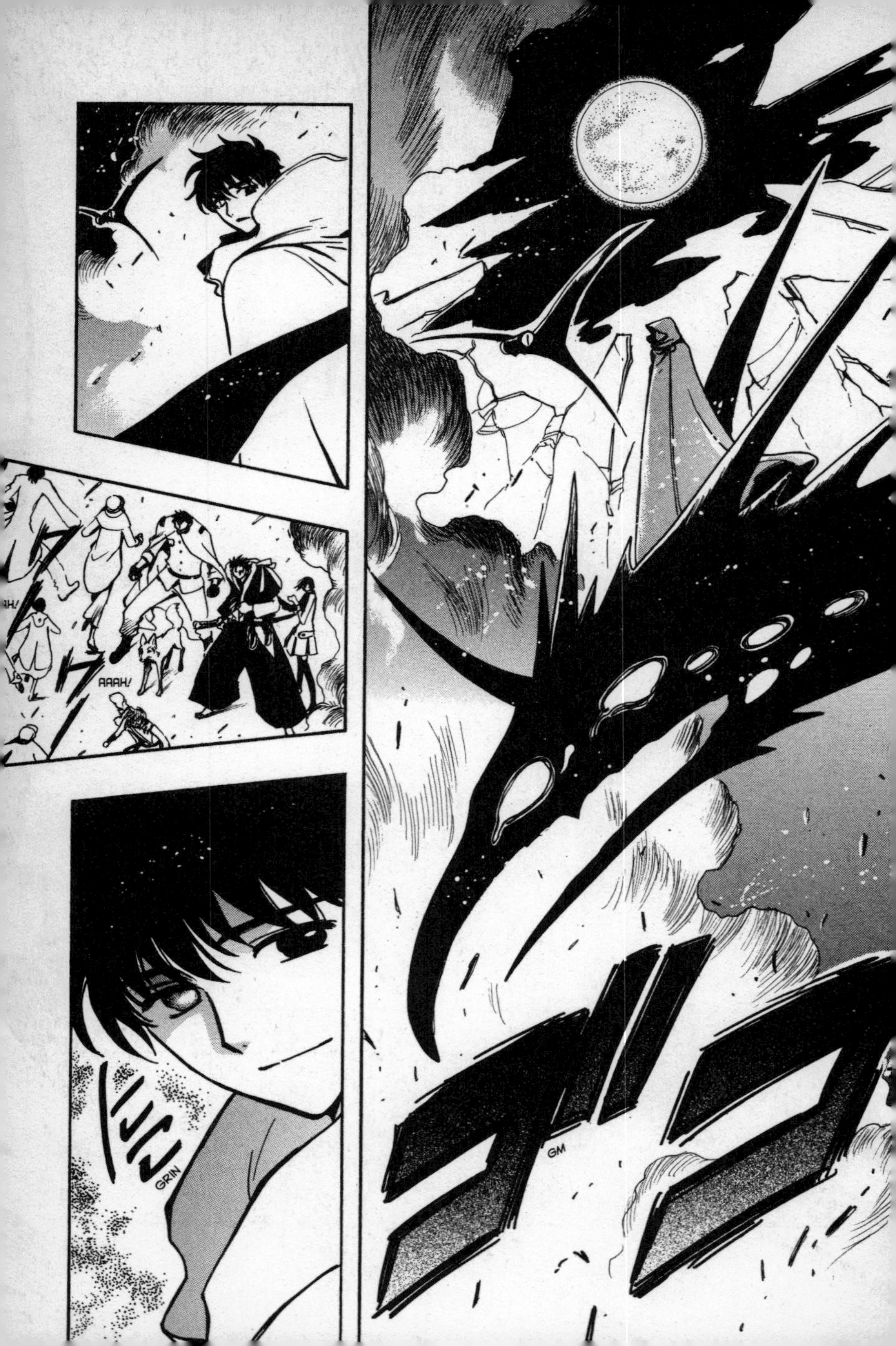
GM
AAAH!
GRIN

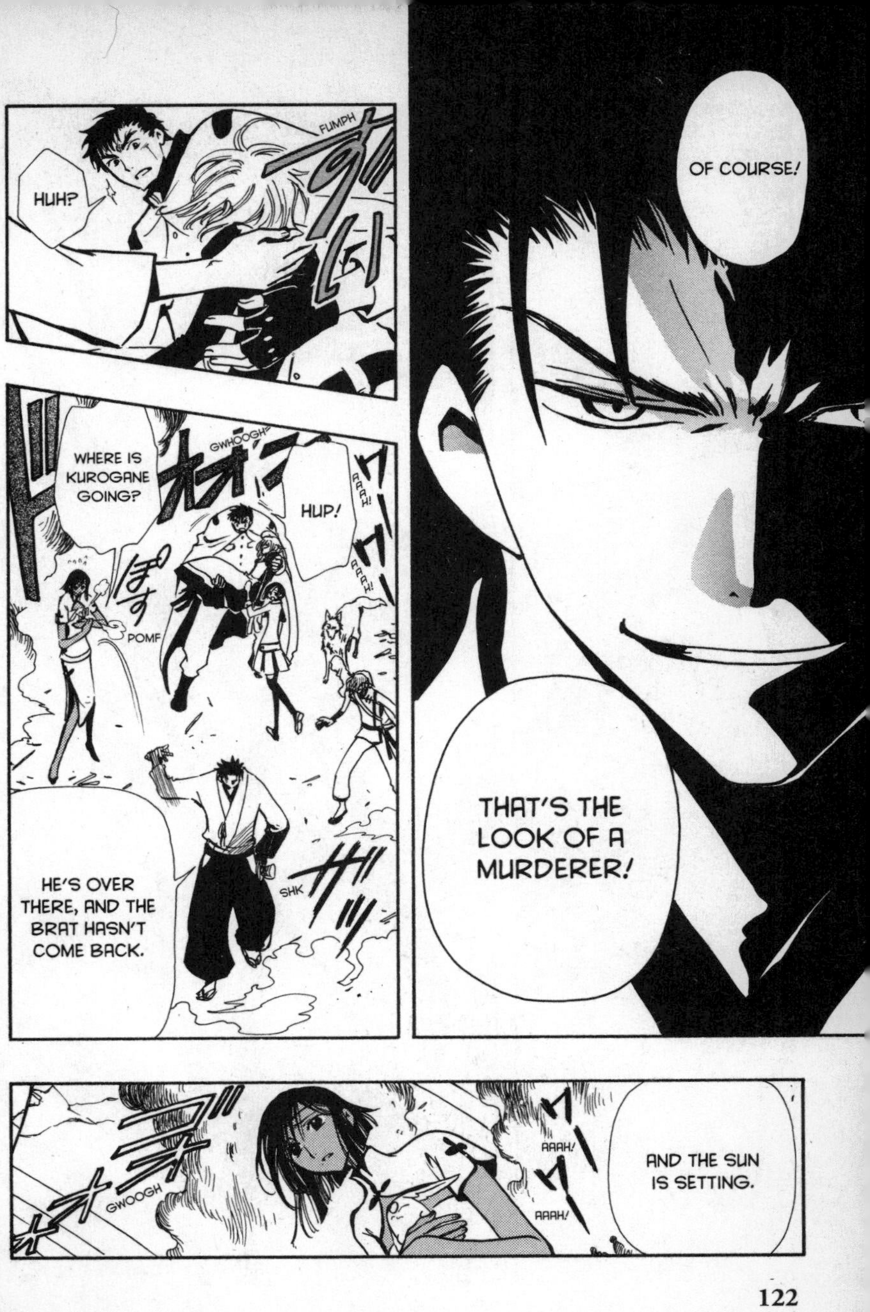
OF COURSE!
THAT'S THE LOOK OF A MURDERER!
FUMPH
HUH?
GWHOOGH
AAAH!
AAAH!
HUP!
WHERE IS KUROGANE GOING?
POMF
SHK
HE'S OVER THERE, AND THE BRAT HASN'T COME BACK.
AND THE SUN IS SETTING.
AAAH!
AAAH!
GWOOGH

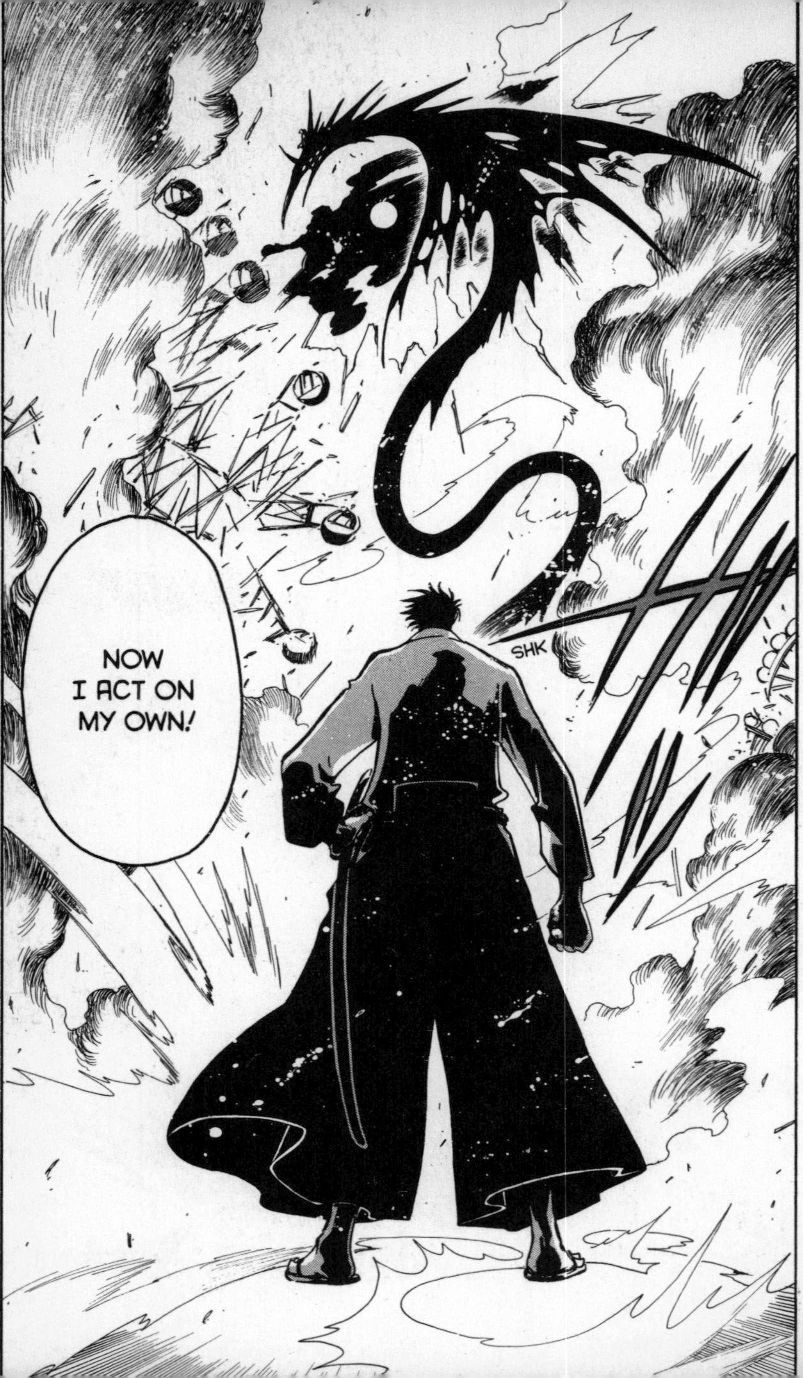
SHK
NOW I ACT ON MY OWN!

ツバサ
RESERVoir CHRoNiCLE

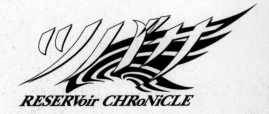

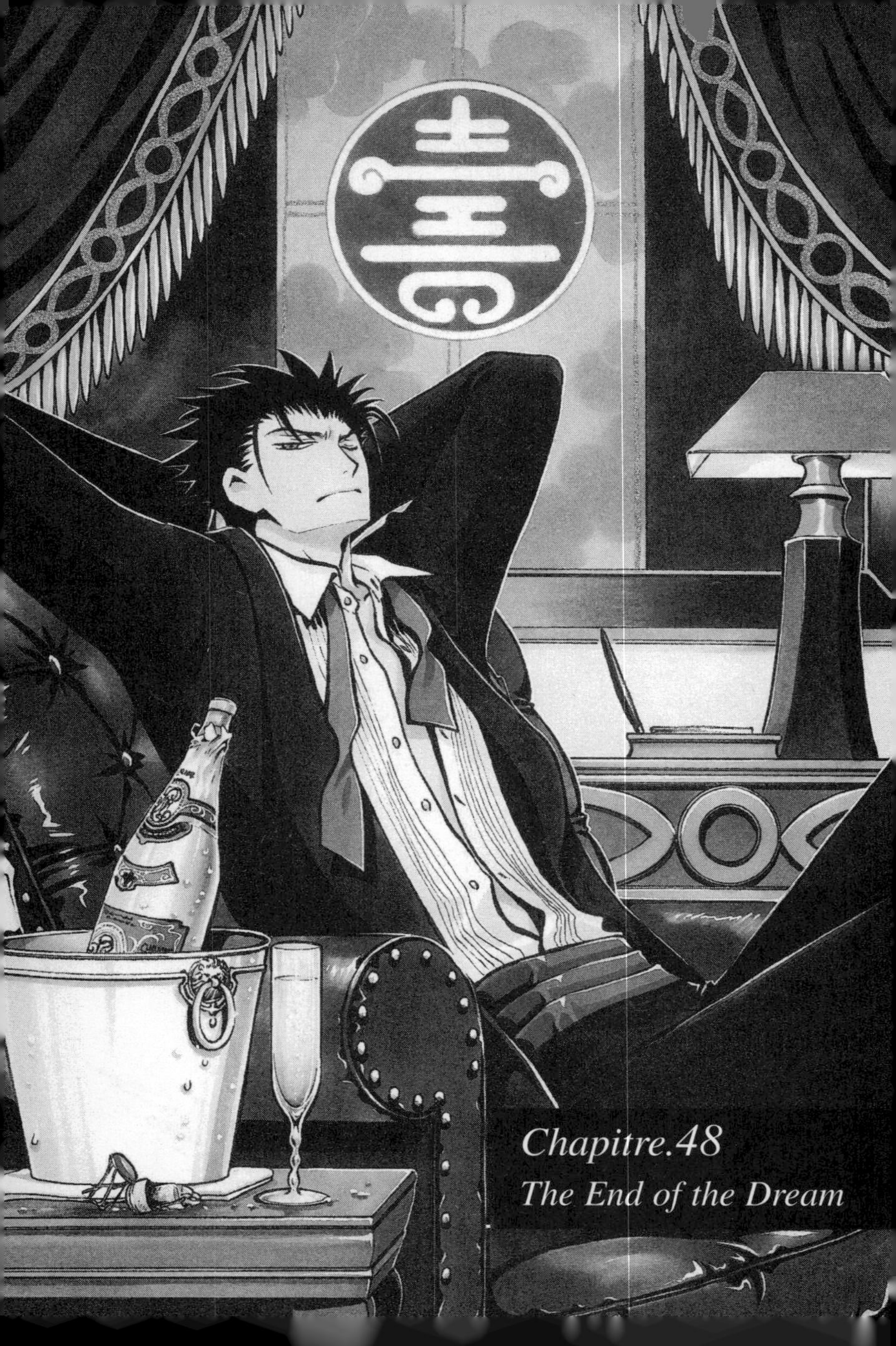
Chapitre.48
The End of the Dream

ツバサ
RESERVoir CHRoNiCLE

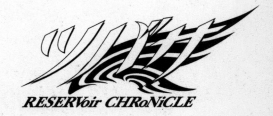

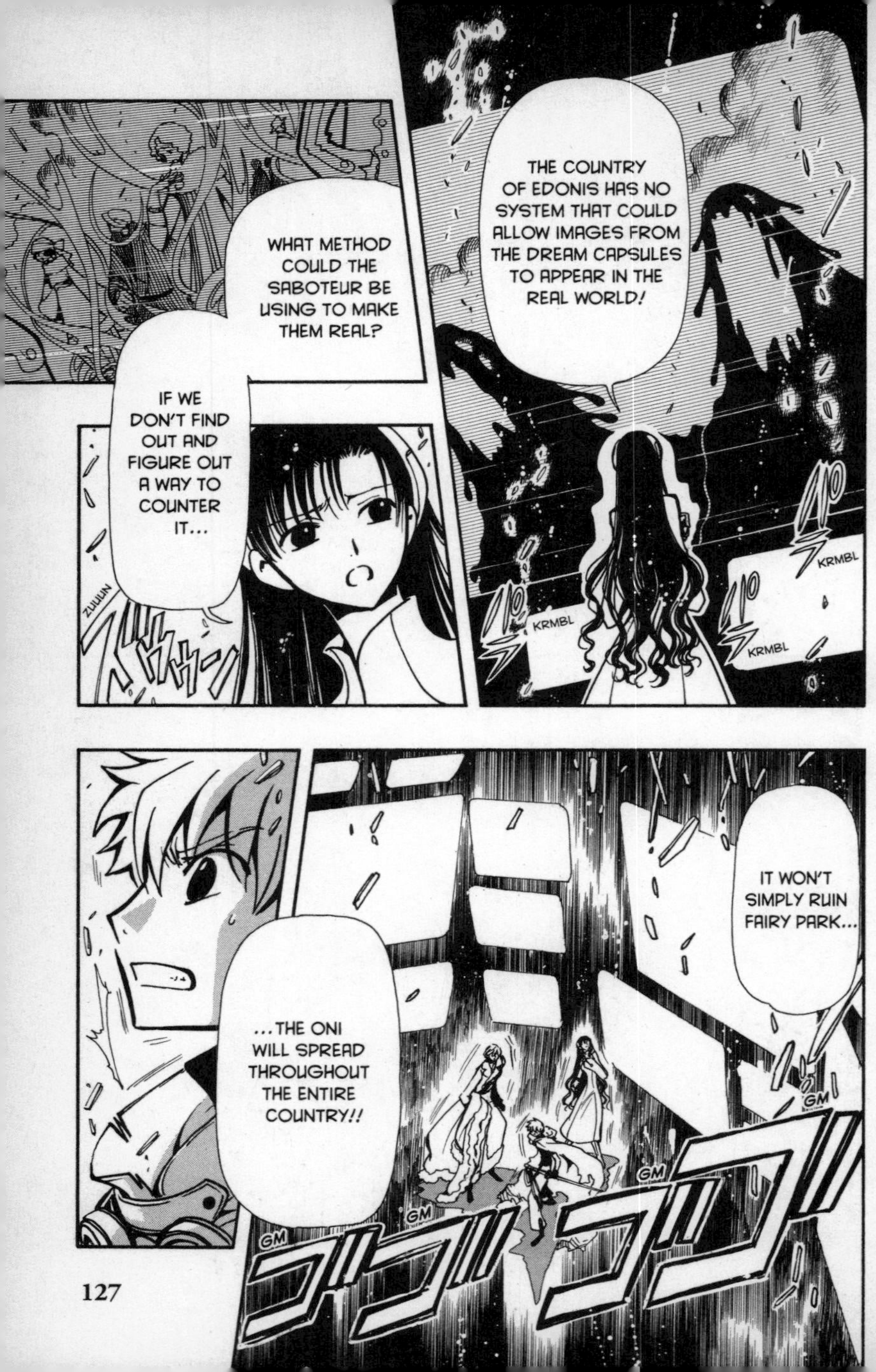
THE COUNTRY OF EDONIS HAS NO SYSTEM THAT COULD ALLOW IMAGES FROM THE DREAM CAPSULES TO APPEAR IN THE REAL WORLD!
KRMBL
KRMBL
KRMBL
WHAT METHOD COULD THE SABOTEUR BE USING TO MAKE THEM REAL?
IF WE DON'T FIND OUT AND FIGURE OUT A WAY TO COUNTER IT...
ZUUUN
IT WON'T SIMPLY RUIN FAIRY PARK...
...THE ONI WILL SPREAD THROUGHOUT THE ENTIRE COUNTRY!!
GM
GM
GM
GM

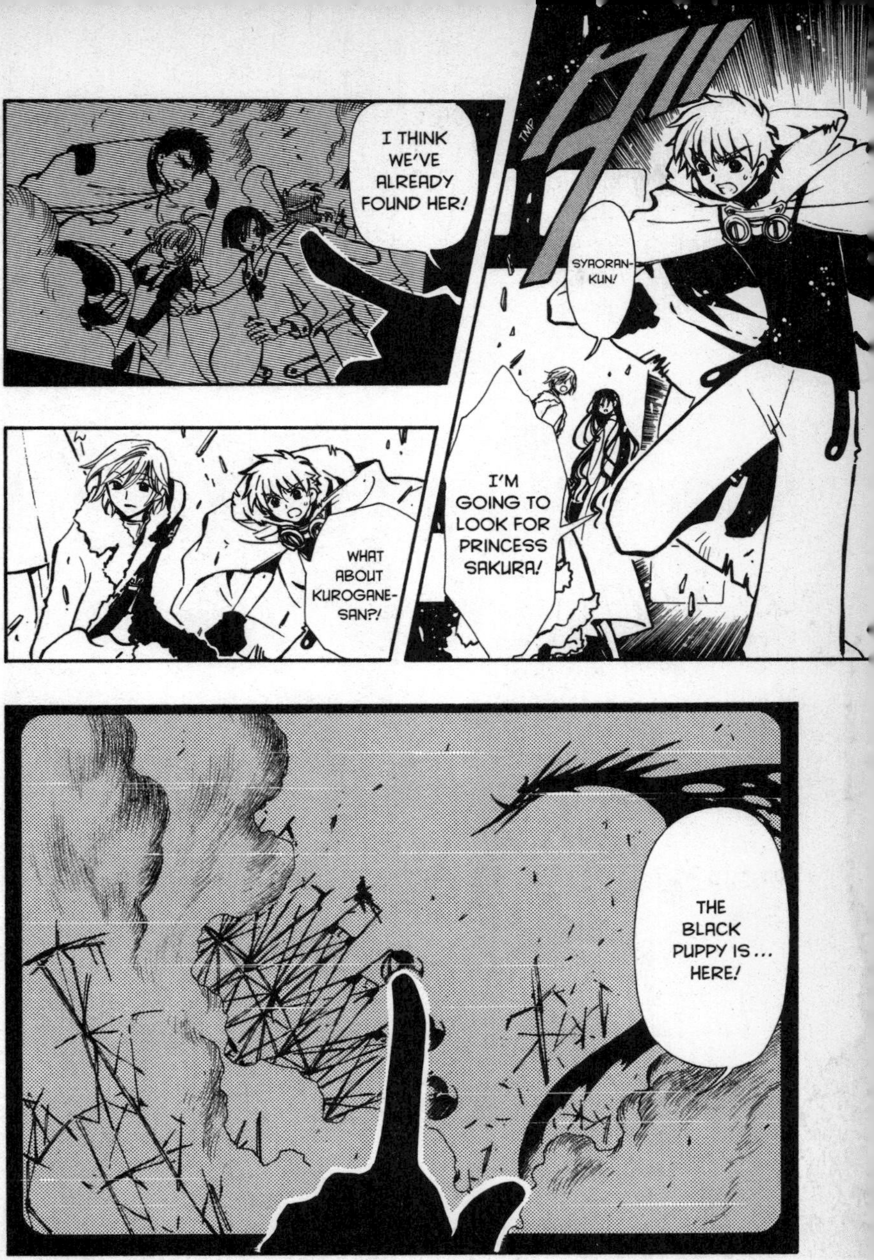
TMP
SYAORAN-KUN!
I'M GOING TO LOOK FOR PRINCESS SAKURA!
I THINK WE'VE ALREADY FOUND HER!
WHAT ABOUT KUROGANE-SAN?!
THE BLACK PUPPY IS... HERE!

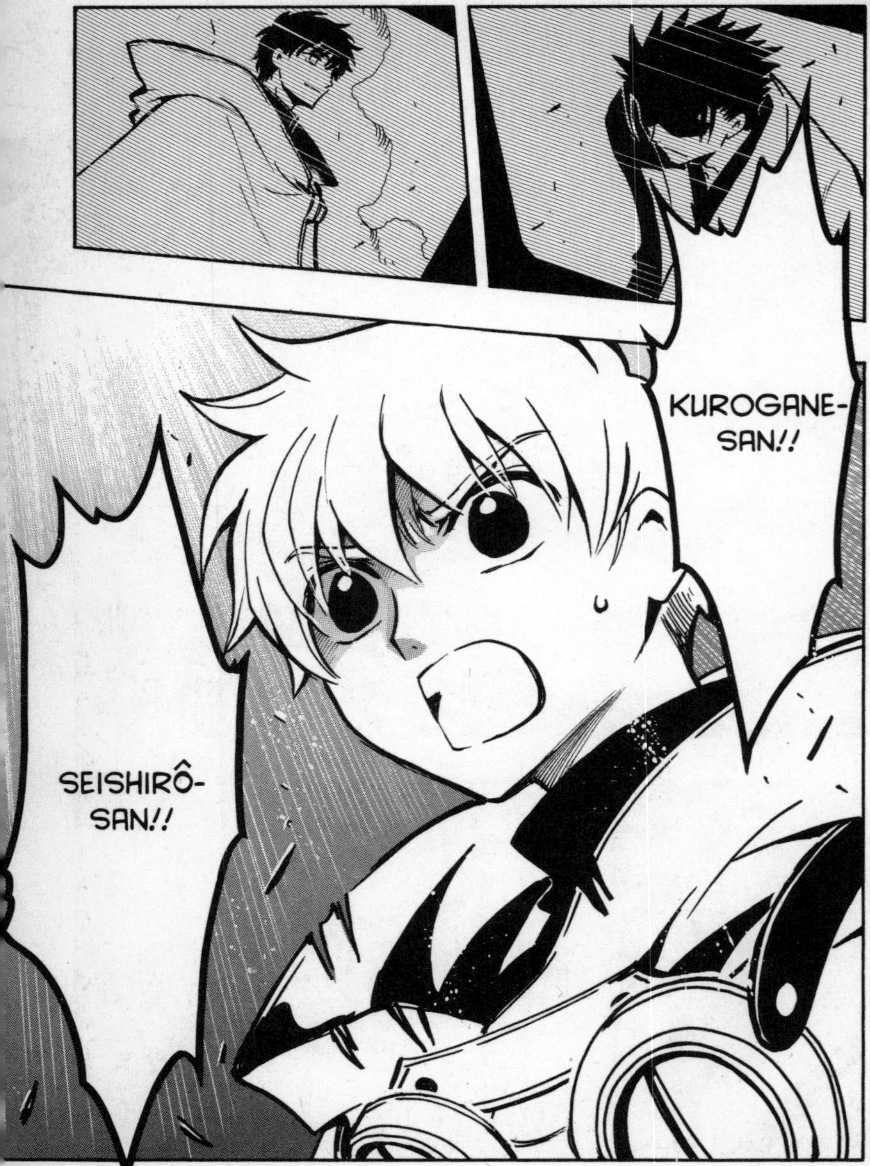
KUROGANE-SAN!!
SEISHIRÔ-SAN!!

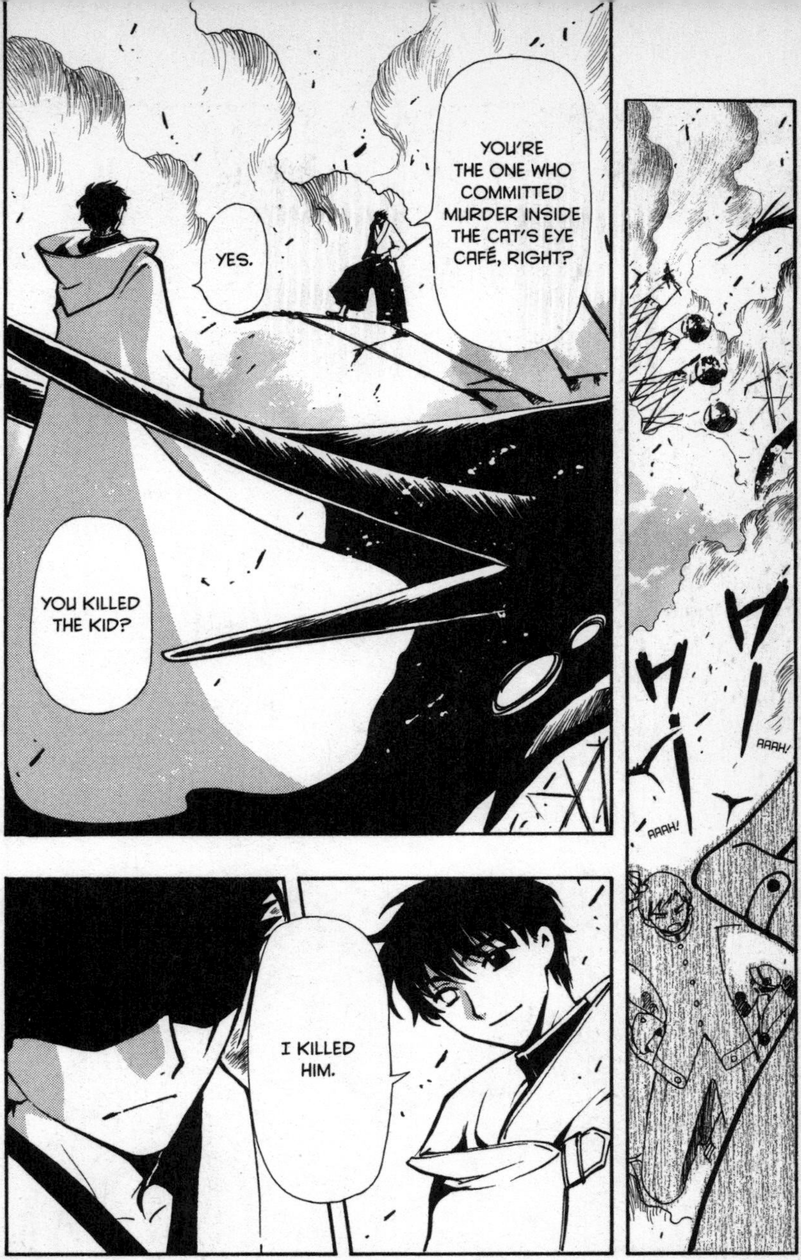
AAAH!
AAAH!
YOU'RE THE ONE WHO COMMITTED MURDER INSIDE THE CAT'S EYE CAFÉ, RIGHT?
YES.
YOU KILLED THE KID?
I KILLED HIM.

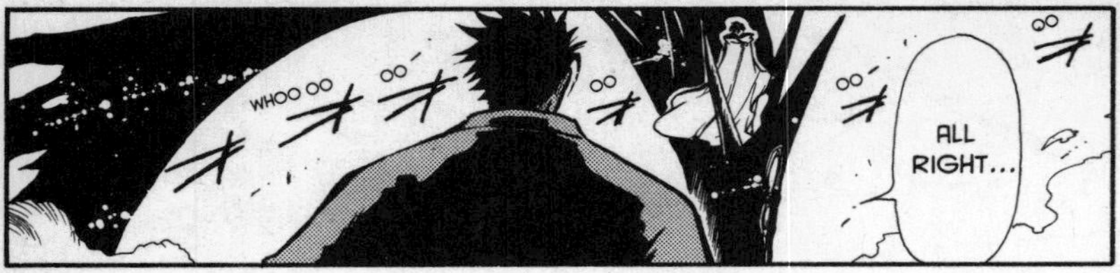
ALL RIGHT...
WHOO OO

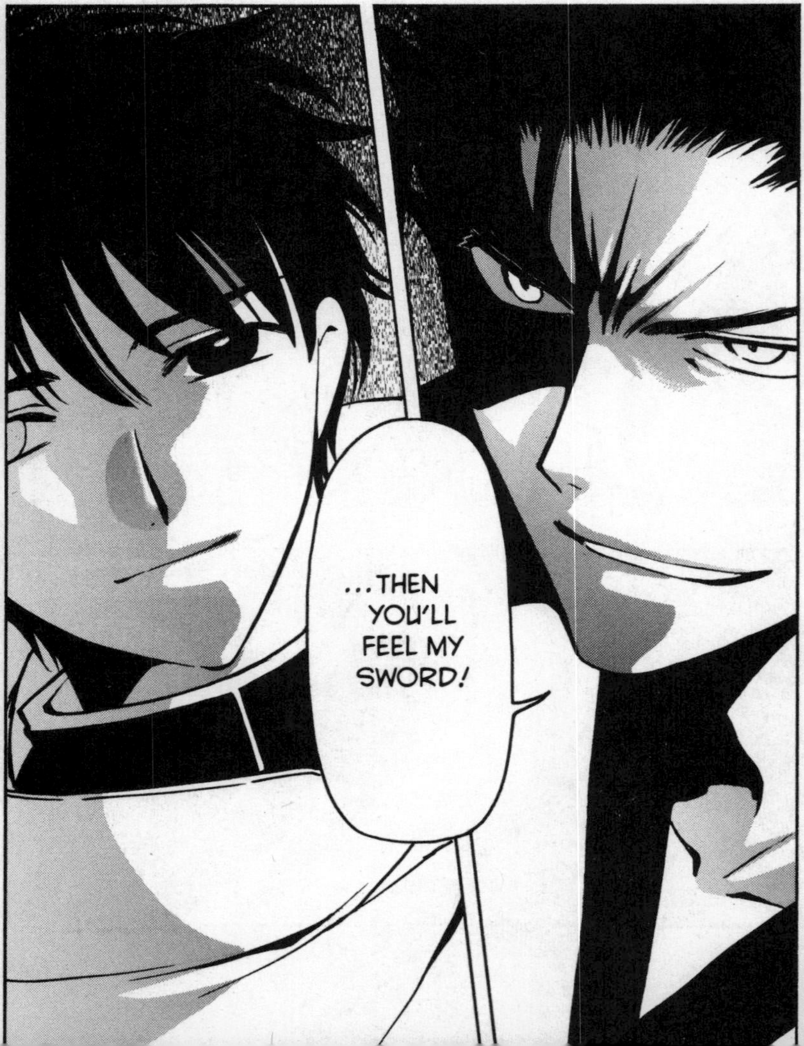
...THEN YOU'LL FEEL MY SWORD!

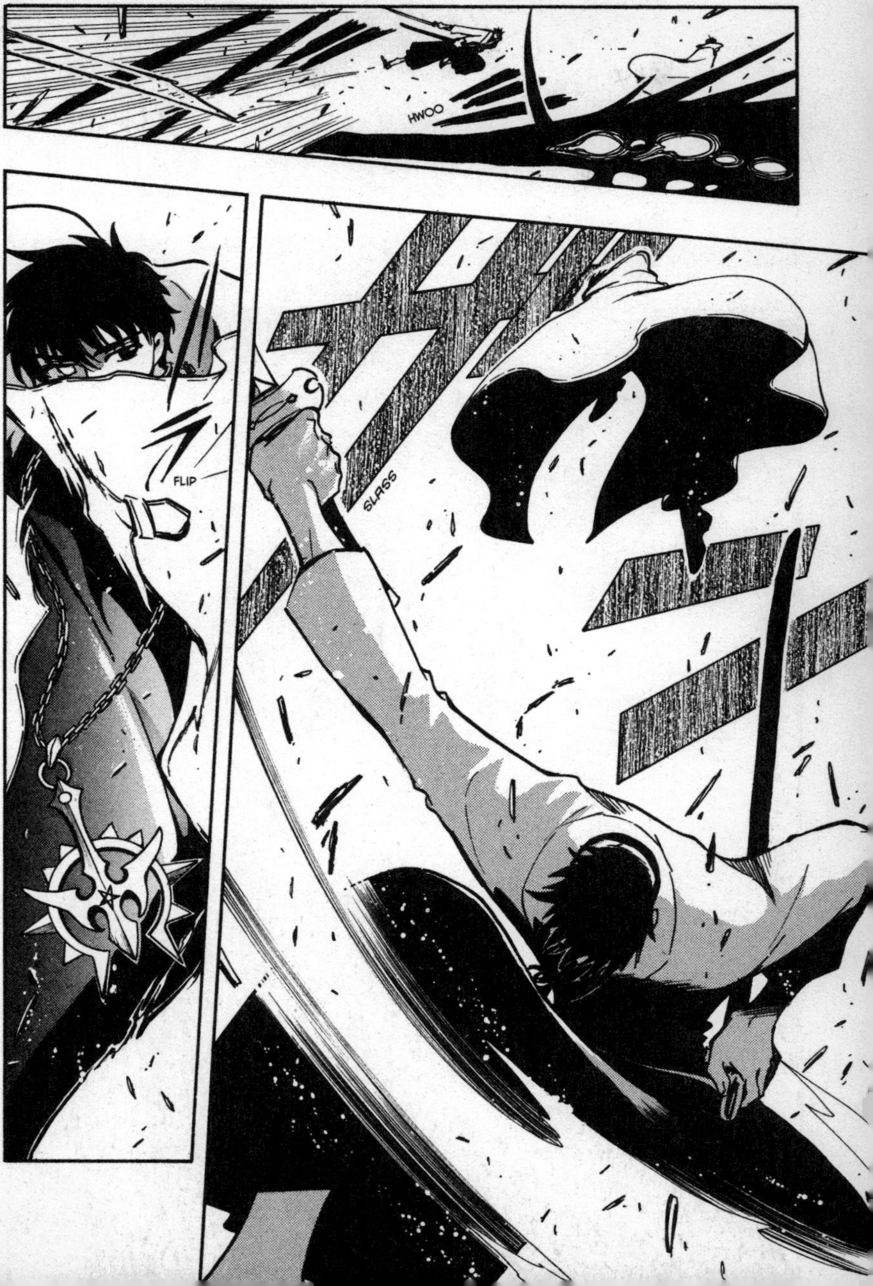
HWOO
SLASS
FLIP

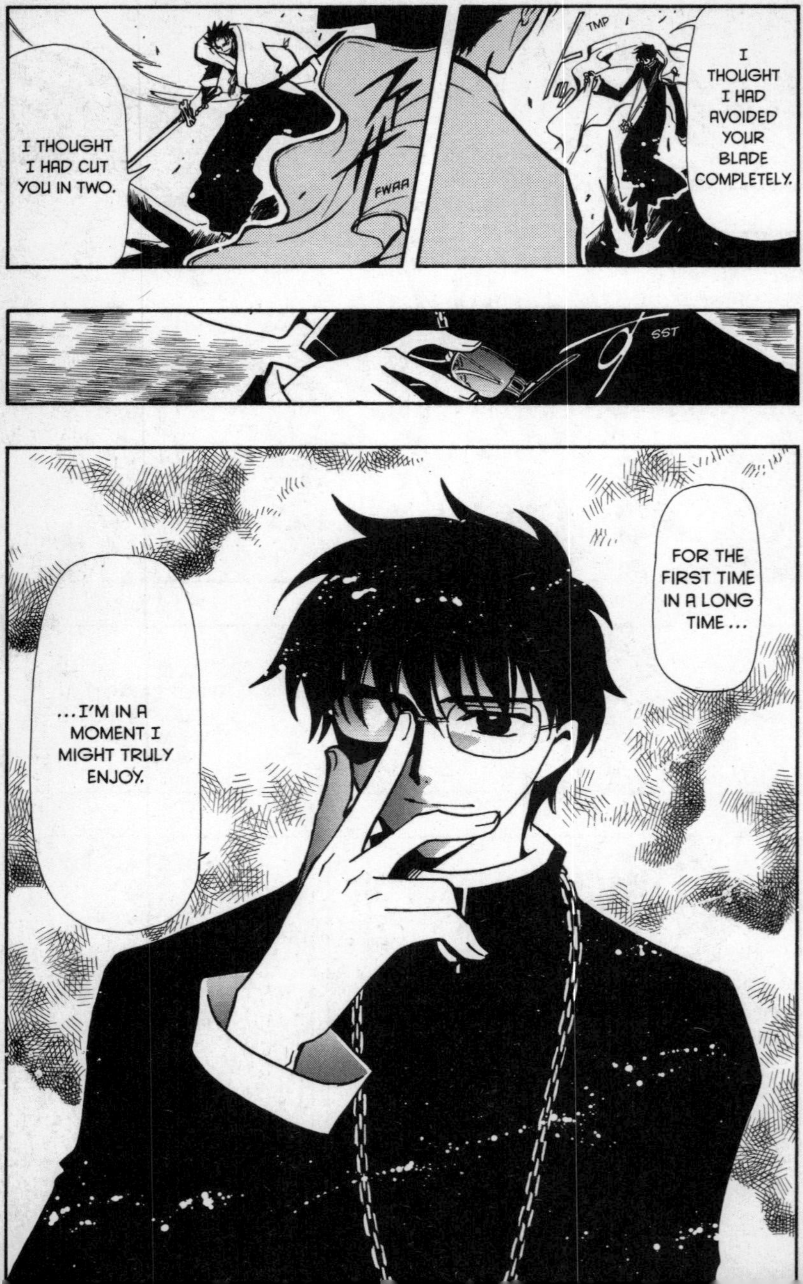
TMP
I THOUGHT I HAD AVOIDED YOUR BLADE COMPLETELY.
FWAA
I THOUGHT I HAD CUT YOU IN TWO.
SST
FOR THE FIRST TIME IN A LONG TIME...
...I'M IN A MOMENT I MIGHT TRULY ENJOY.

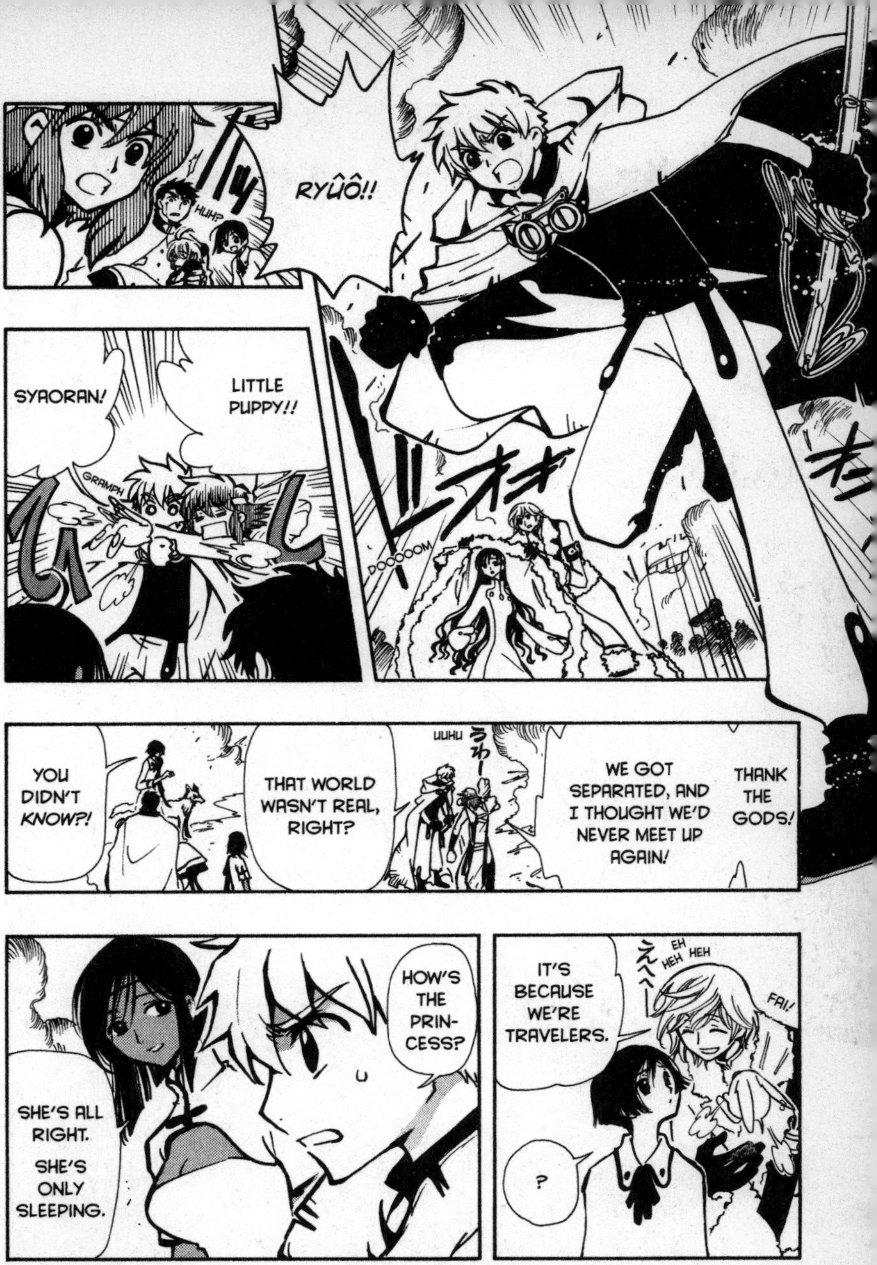
RYÛÔ!!
DOOOOOM
HUH?
LITTLE PUPPY!!
SYAORAN!
GRAMPH
THANK THE GODS!
WE GOT SEPARATED, AND I THOUGHT WE'D NEVER MEET UP AGAIN!
UUHU
THAT WORLD WASN'T REAL, RIGHT?
YOU DIDN'T KNOW?!
FAI!
EH HEH HEH
IT'S BECAUSE WE'RE TRAVELERS.
?
HOW'S THE PRIN-CESS?
SHE'S ALL RIGHT.
SHE'S ONLY SLEEPING.

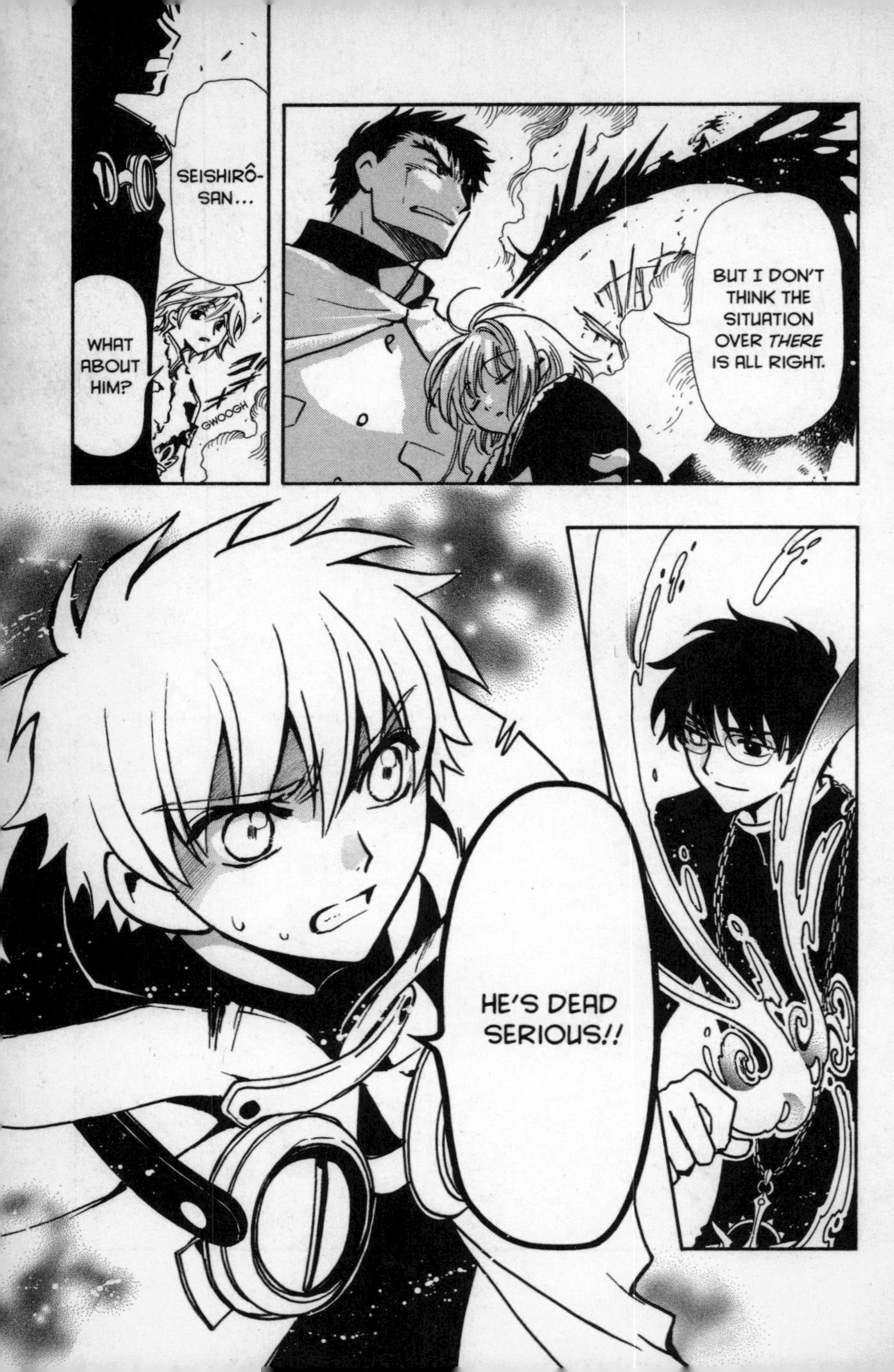
BUT I DON'T THINK THE SITUATION OVER *THERE* IS ALL RIGHT.
SEISHIRÔ-SAN...
WHAT ABOUT HIM?
GWOOGH
HE'S DEAD SERIOUS!!

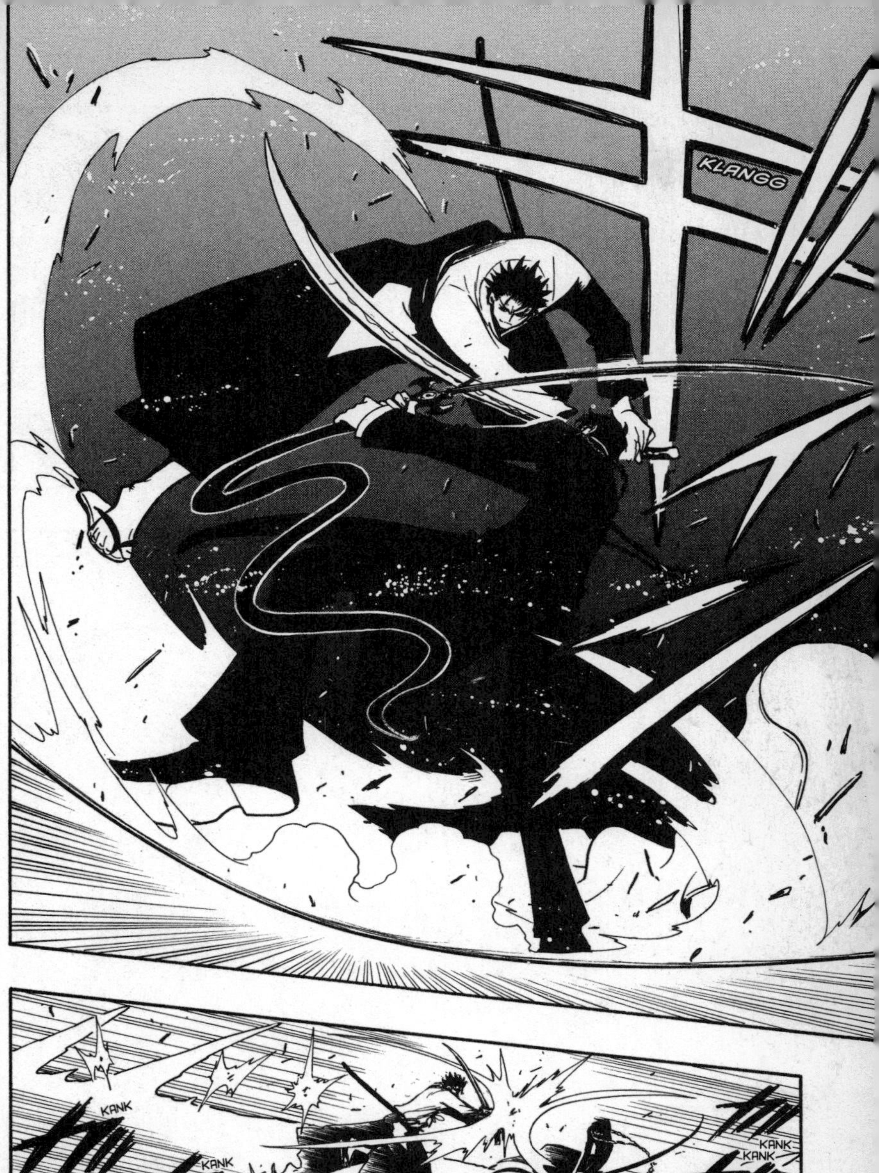
KLANGG
KANK
KANK
KANK
KANK
KANK

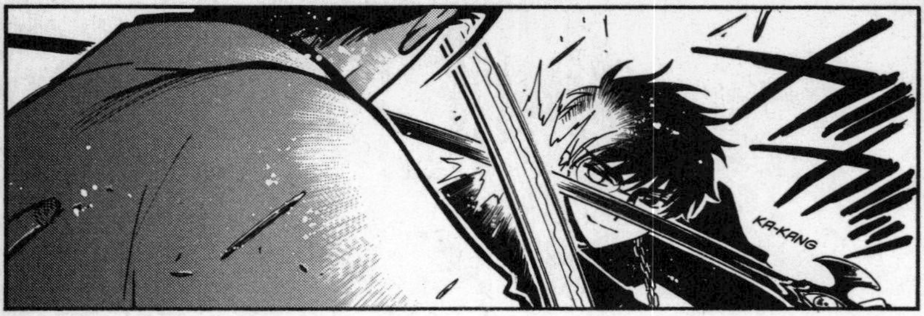
KA-KANG

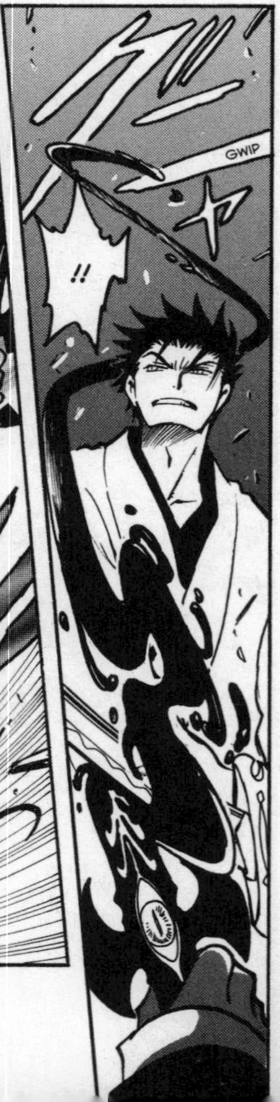
GWIP
!!

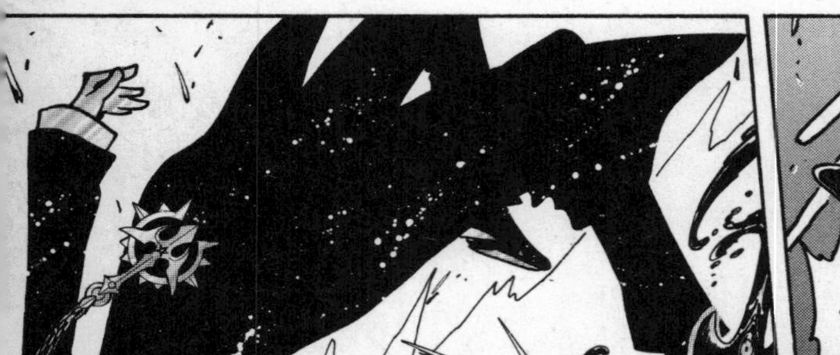
WHOOO

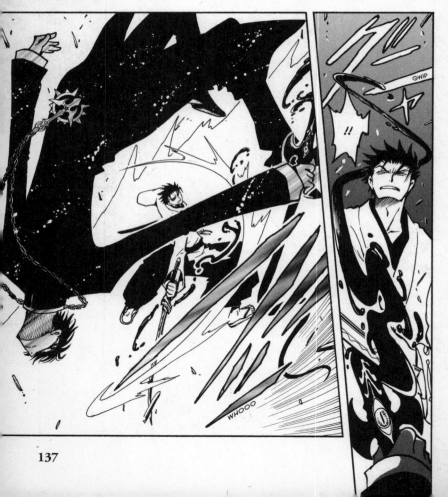

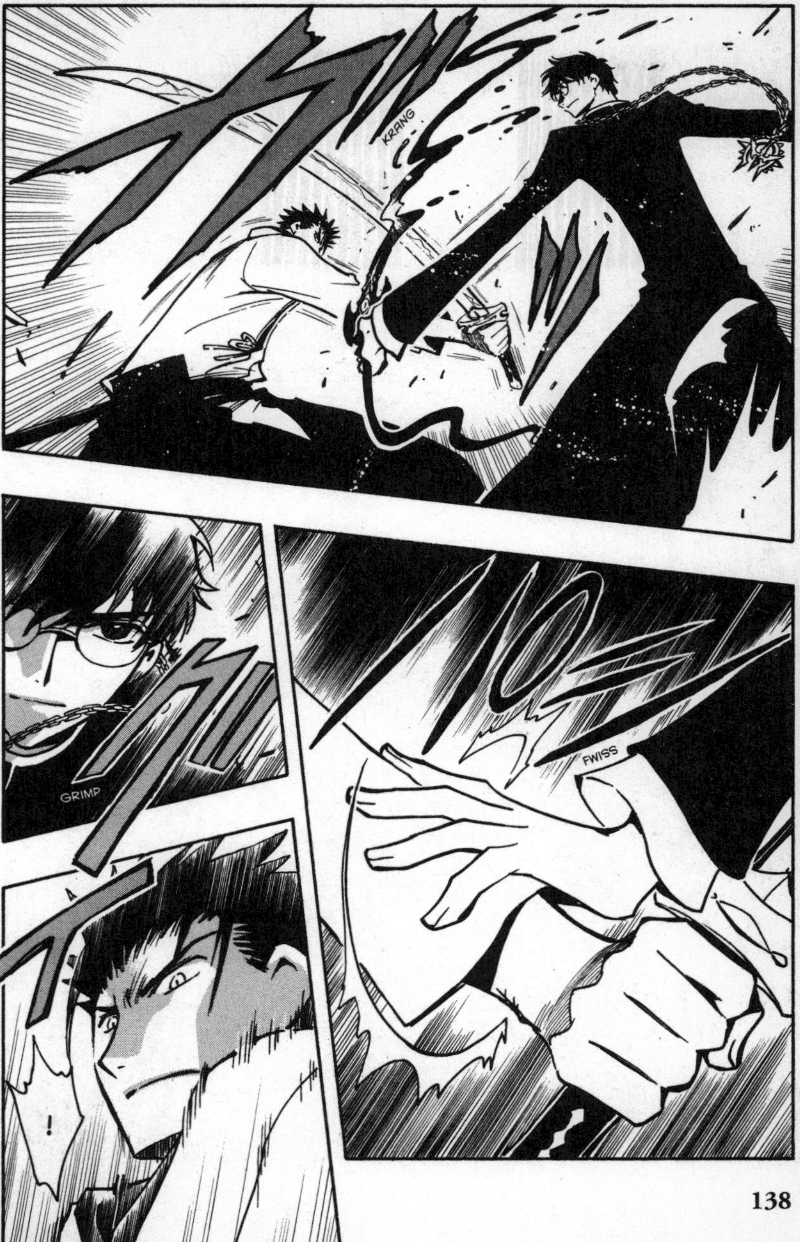
KRANG
FWISS
GRIMP
!

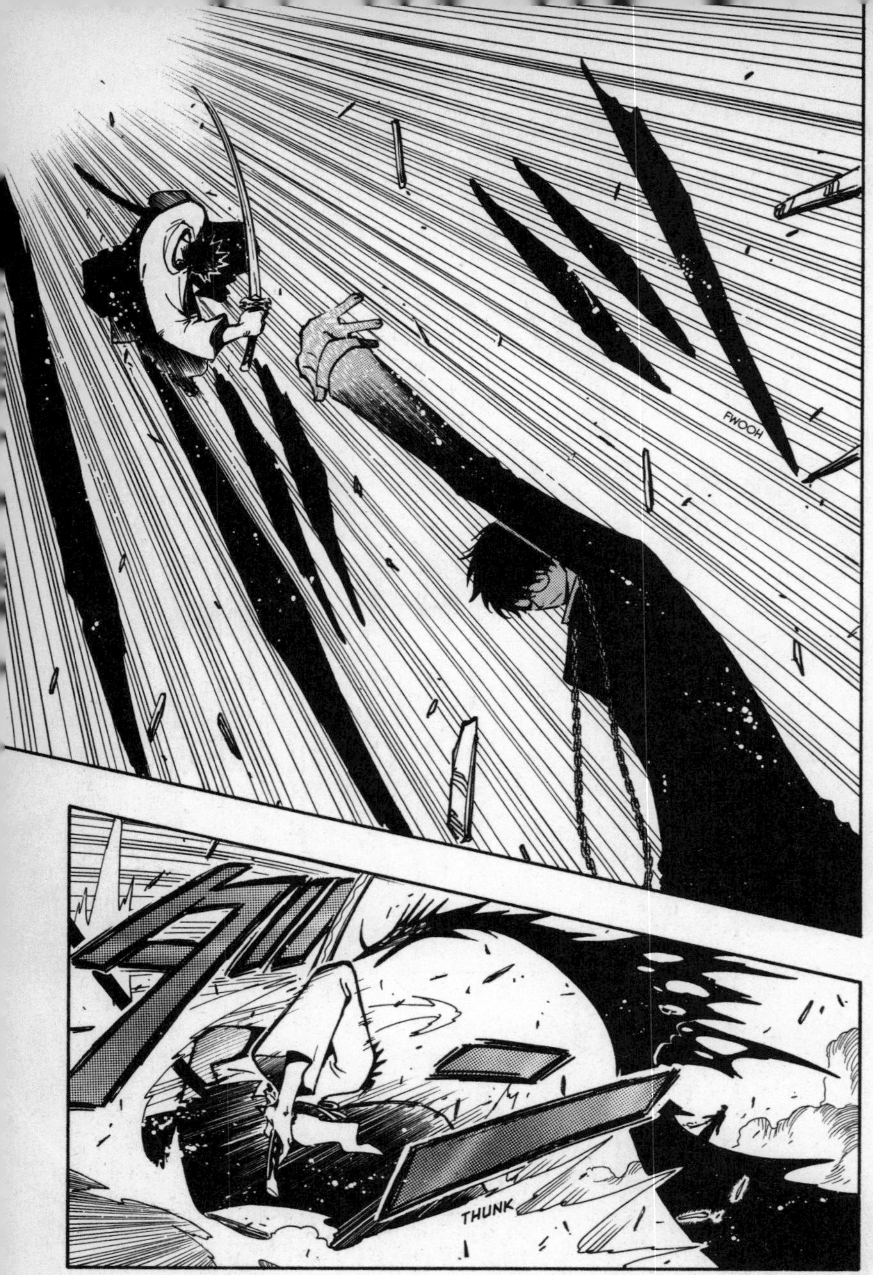
FWOOH
THUNK

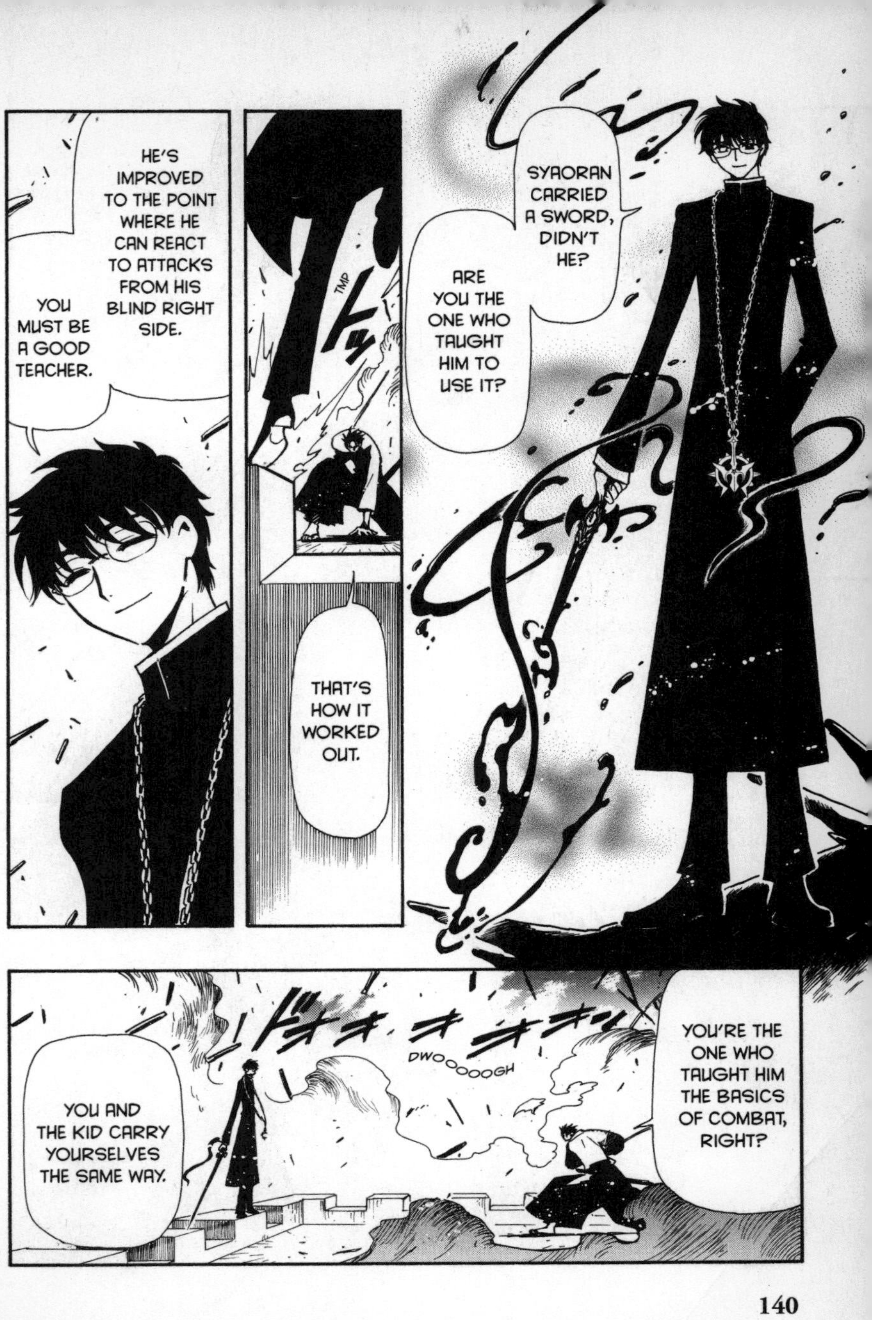
SYAORAN CARRIED A SWORD, DIDN'T HE?
ARE YOU THE ONE WHO TAUGHT HIM TO USE IT?
TMP
THAT'S HOW IT WORKED OUT.
HE'S IMPROVED TO THE POINT WHERE HE CAN REACT TO ATTACKS FROM HIS BLIND RIGHT SIDE.
YOU MUST BE A GOOD TEACHER.
DWOOOOOOGH
YOU'RE THE ONE WHO TAUGHT HIM THE BASICS OF COMBAT, RIGHT?
YOU AND THE KID CARRY YOURSELVES THE SAME WAY.

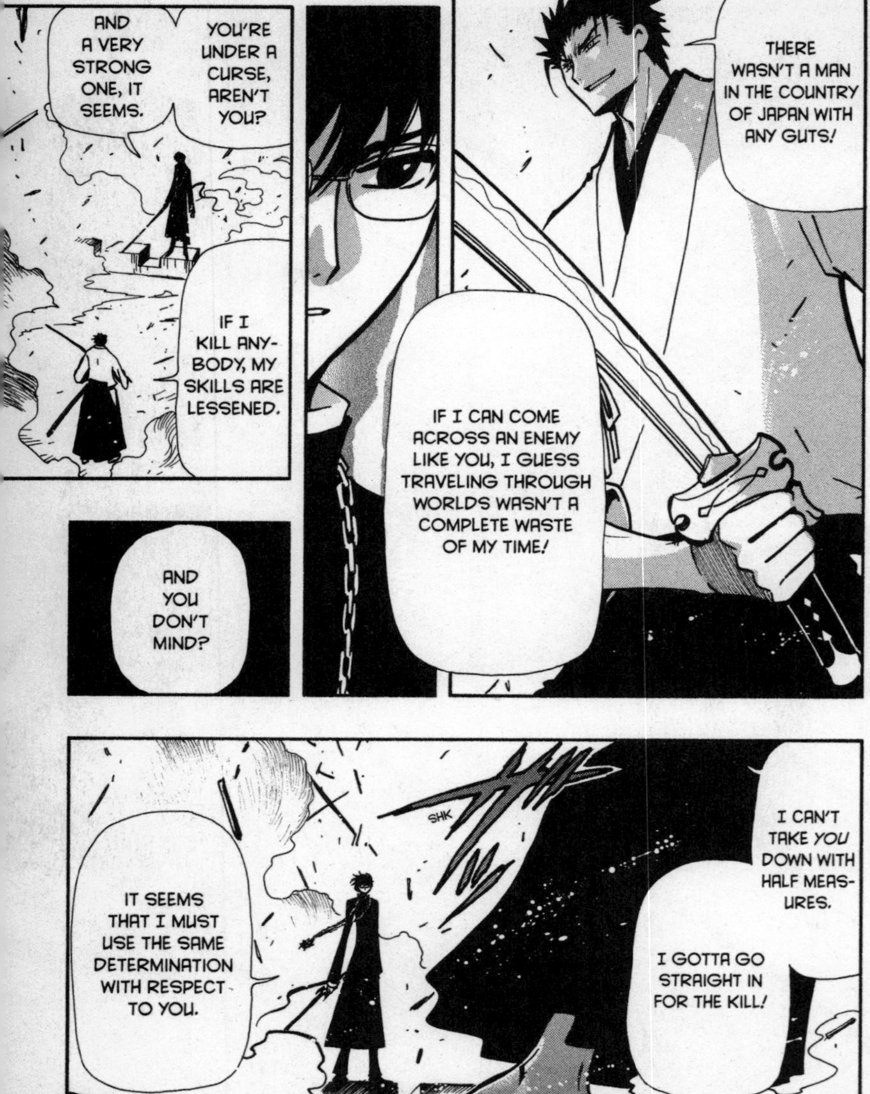
THERE WASN'T A MAN IN THE COUNTRY OF JAPAN WITH ANY GUTS!
IF I CAN COME ACROSS AN ENEMY LIKE YOU, I GUESS TRAVELING THROUGH WORLDS WASN'T A COMPLETE WASTE OF MY TIME!
YOU'RE UNDER A CURSE, AREN'T YOU?
AND A VERY STRONG ONE, IT SEEMS.
IF I KILL ANYBODY, MY SKILLS ARE LESSENED.
AND YOU DON'T MIND?
I CAN'T TAKE *YOU* DOWN WITH HALF MEASURES.
I GOTTA GO STRAIGHT IN FOR THE KILL!
SHK
IT SEEMS THAT I MUST USE THE SAME DETERMINATION WITH RESPECT TO YOU.

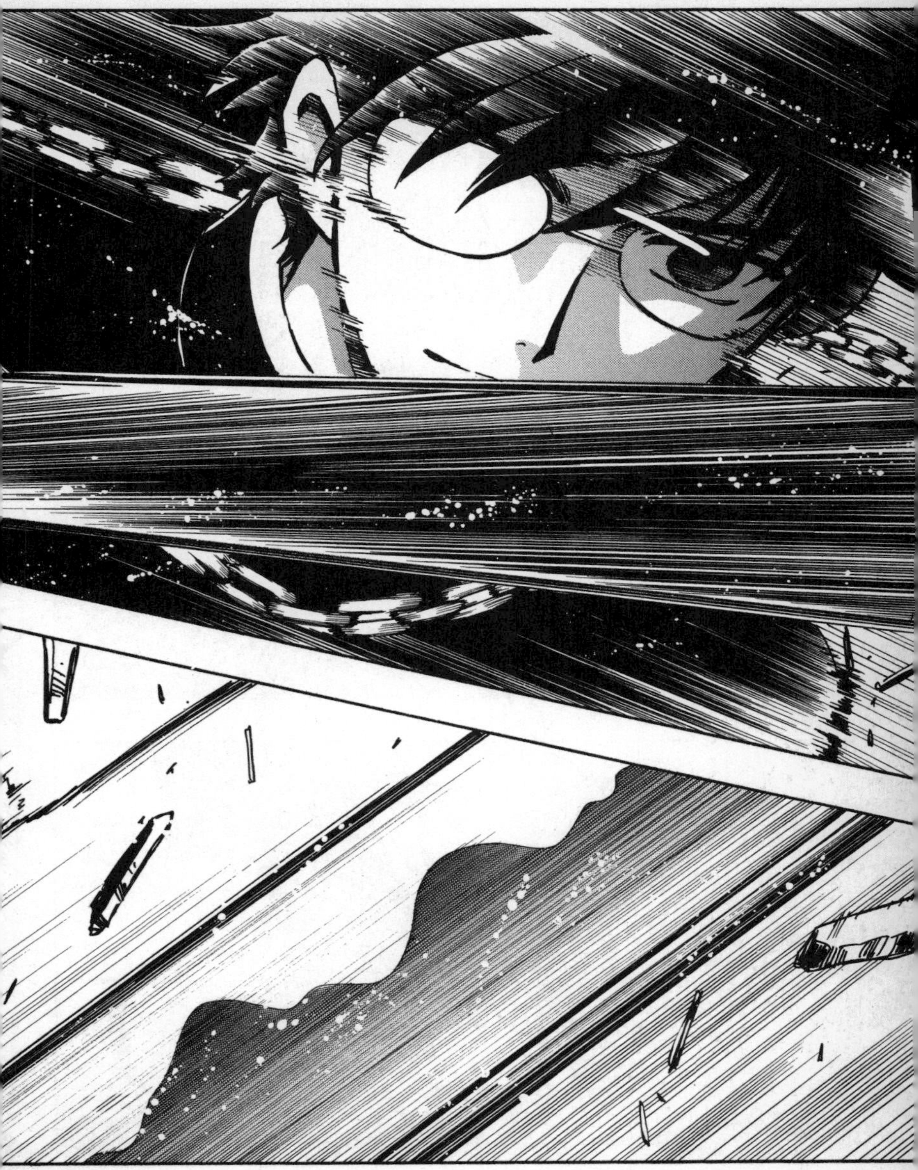

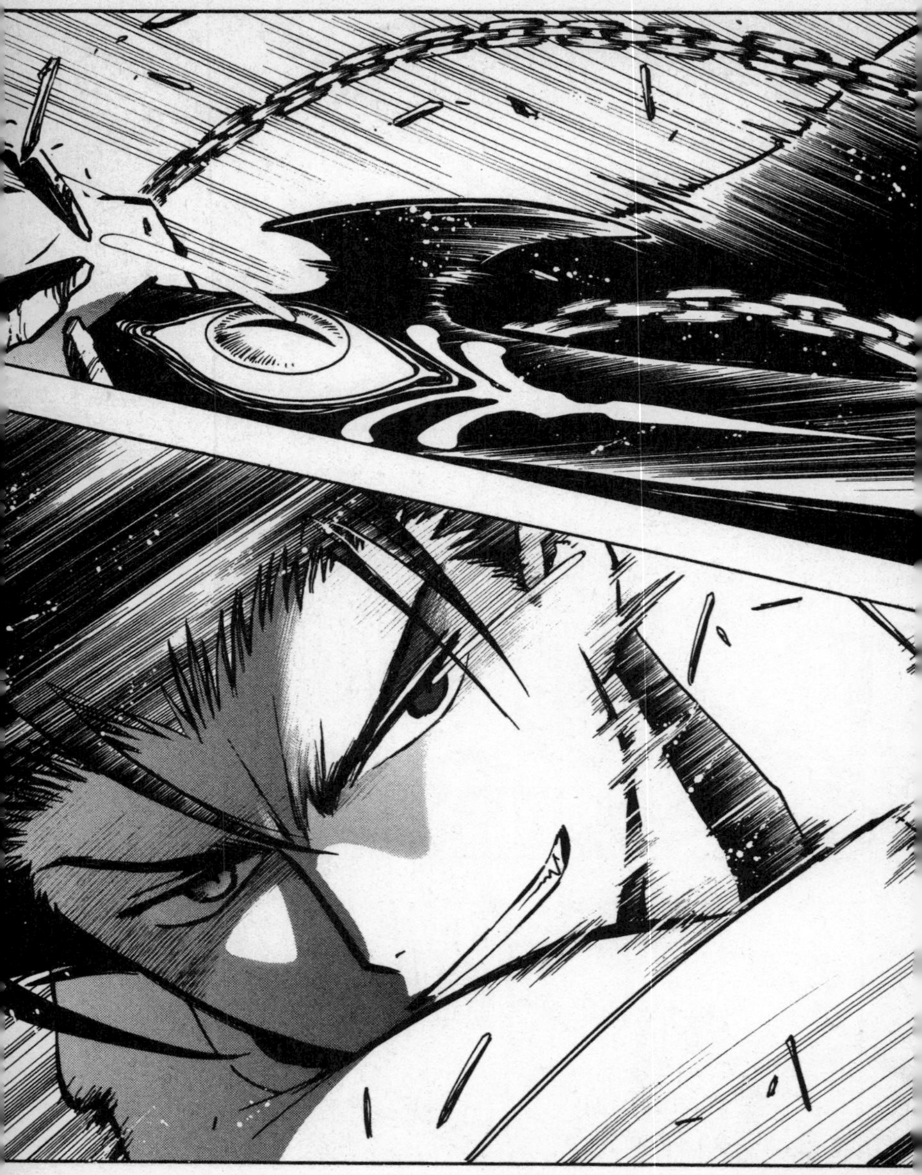

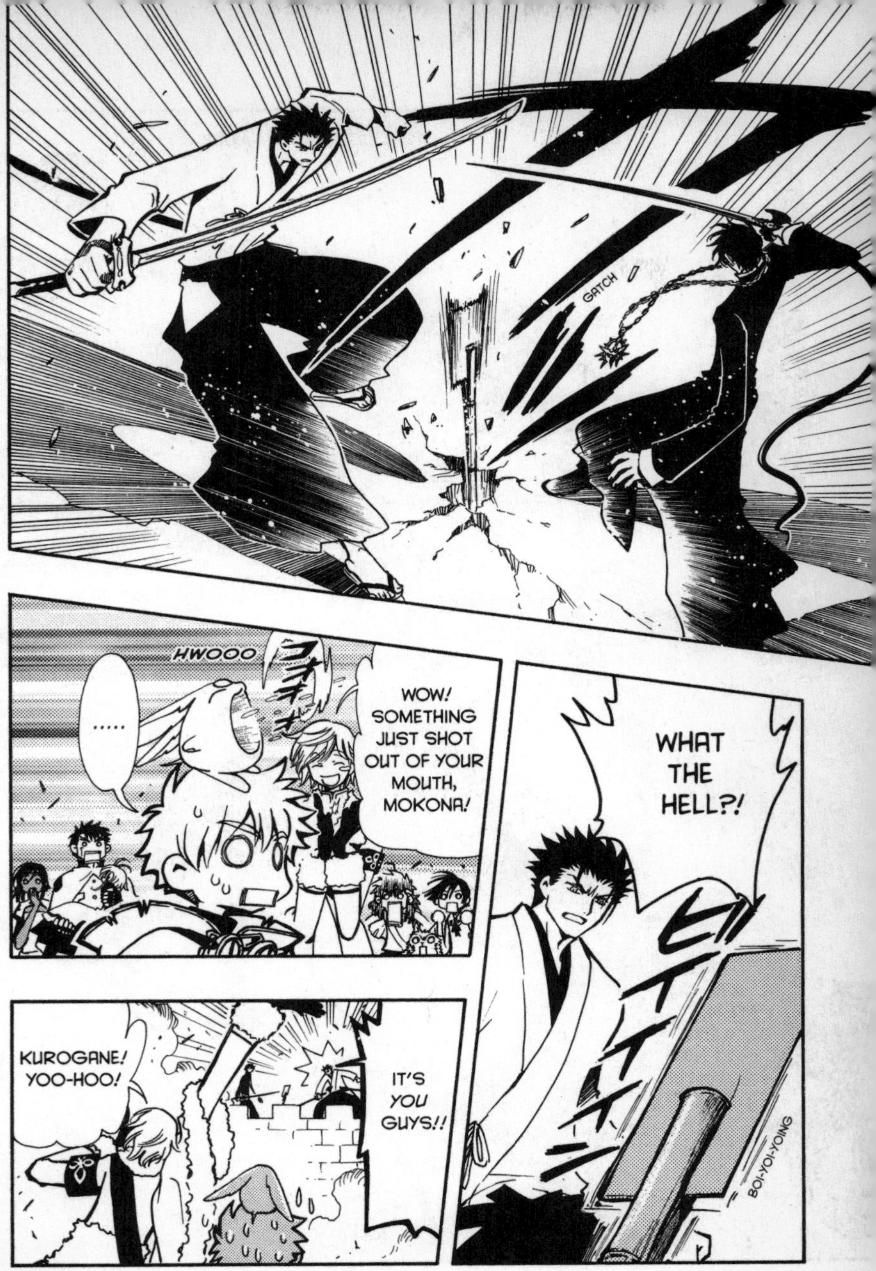
GATCH
WHAT THE HELL?!
BOI-YOI-YOING
WOW! SOMETHING JUST SHOT OUT OF YOUR MOUTH, MOKONA!
HWOOO
.....
IT'S YOU GUYS!!
KUROGANE! YOO-HOO!

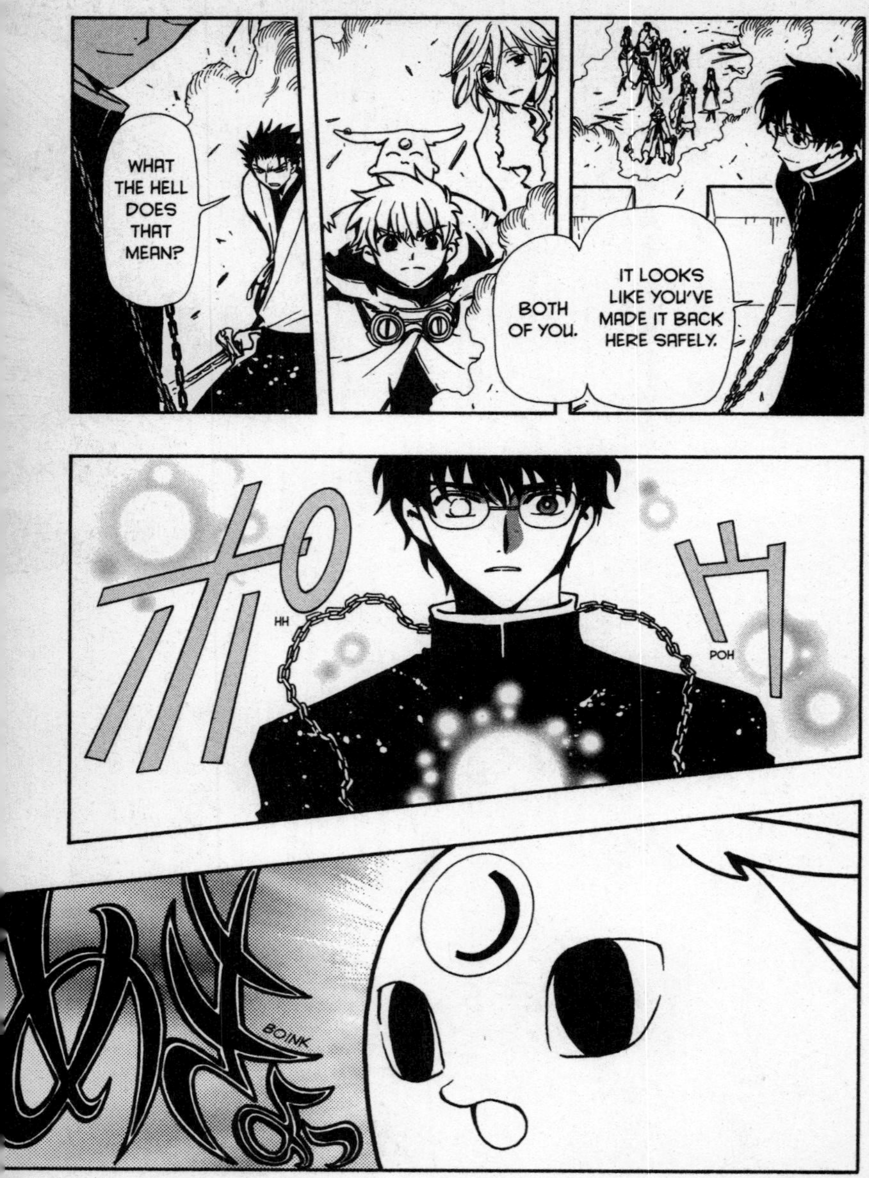

IT LOOKS LIKE YOU'VE MADE IT BACK HERE SAFELY.
BOTH OF YOU.
WHAT THE HELL DOES THAT MEAN?
POH
HH
BOINK

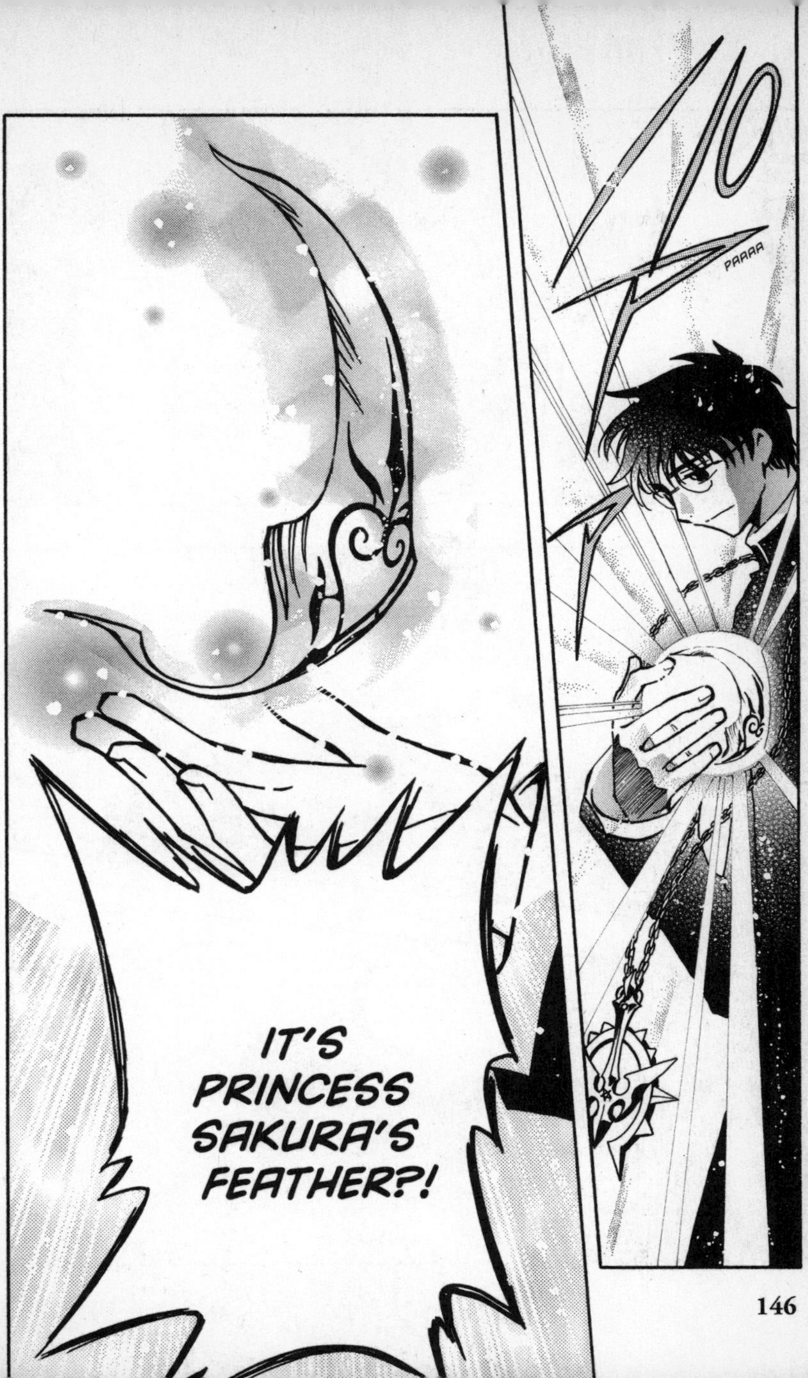
PAAAA
IT'S PRINCESS SAKURA'S FEATHER?!

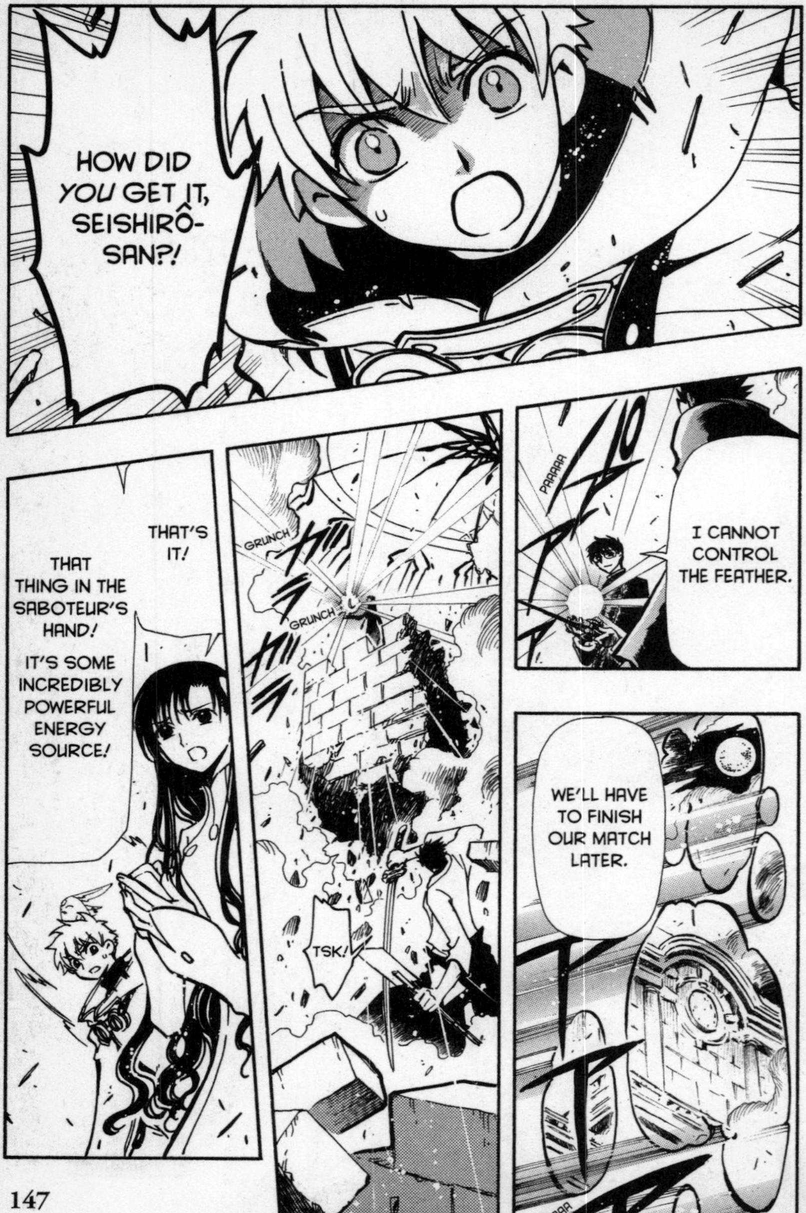
HOW DID YOU GET IT, SEISHIRÔ-SAN?!
PAAAAA
I CANNOT CONTROL THE FEATHER.
WE'LL HAVE TO FINISH OUR MATCH LATER.
AAAAA
GRUNCH
GRUNCH
TSK!
THAT'S IT!
THAT THING IN THE SABOTEUR'S HAND!
IT'S SOME INCREDIBLY POWERFUL ENERGY SOURCE!

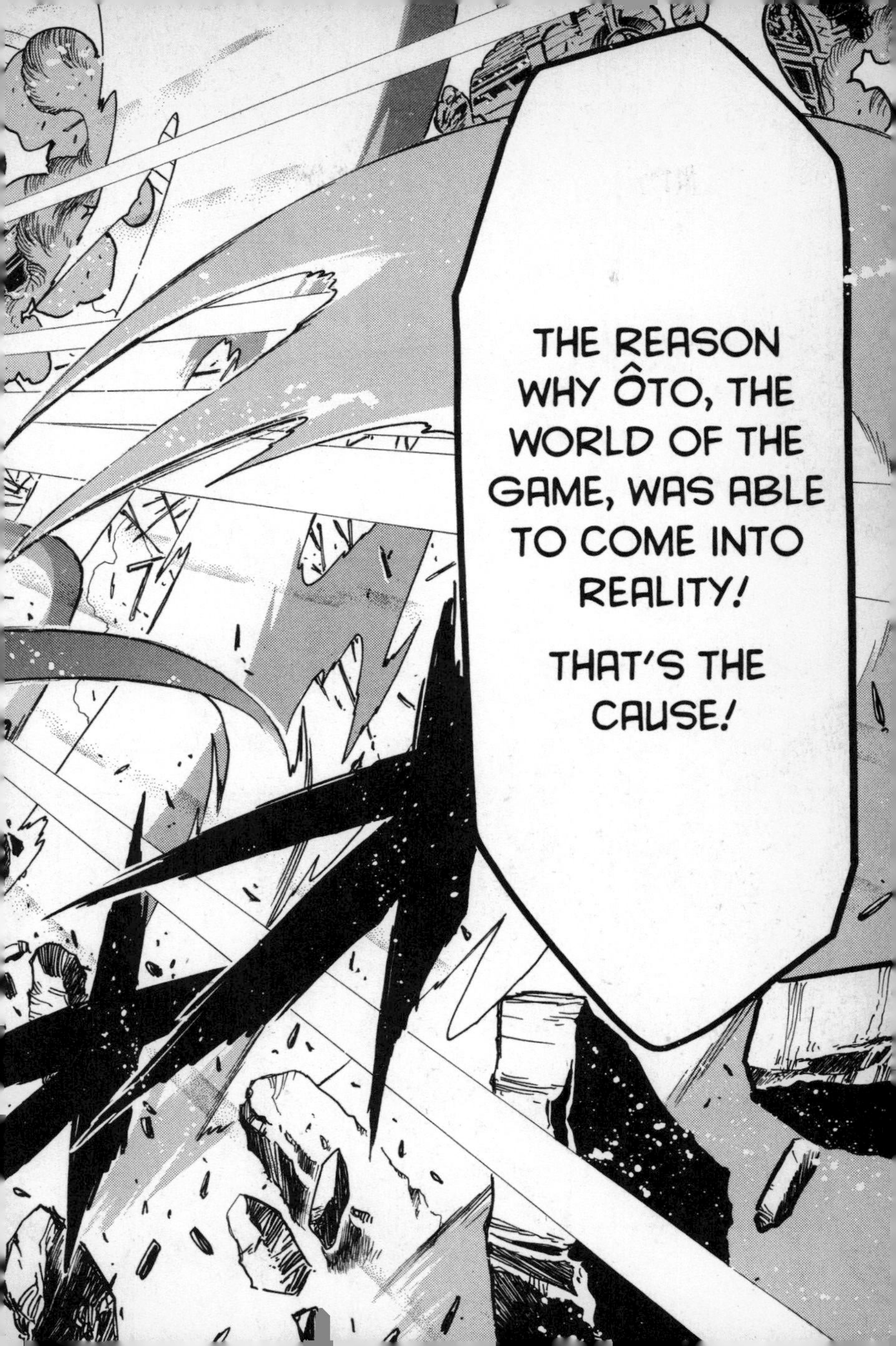
THE REASON WHY ÔTO, THE WORLD OF THE GAME, WAS ABLE TO COME INTO REALITY!
THAT'S THE CAUSE!

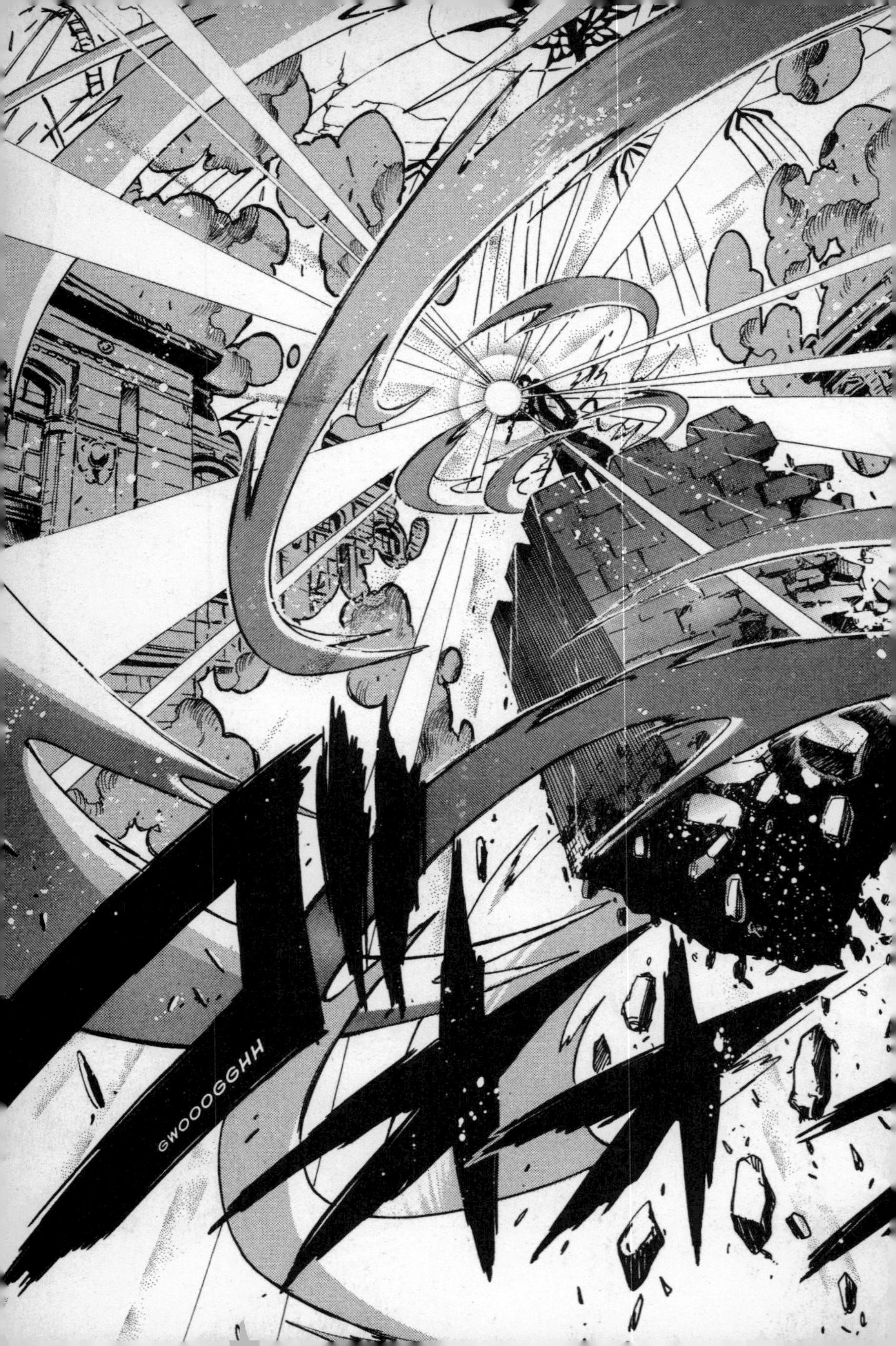
GWOOOGGHH

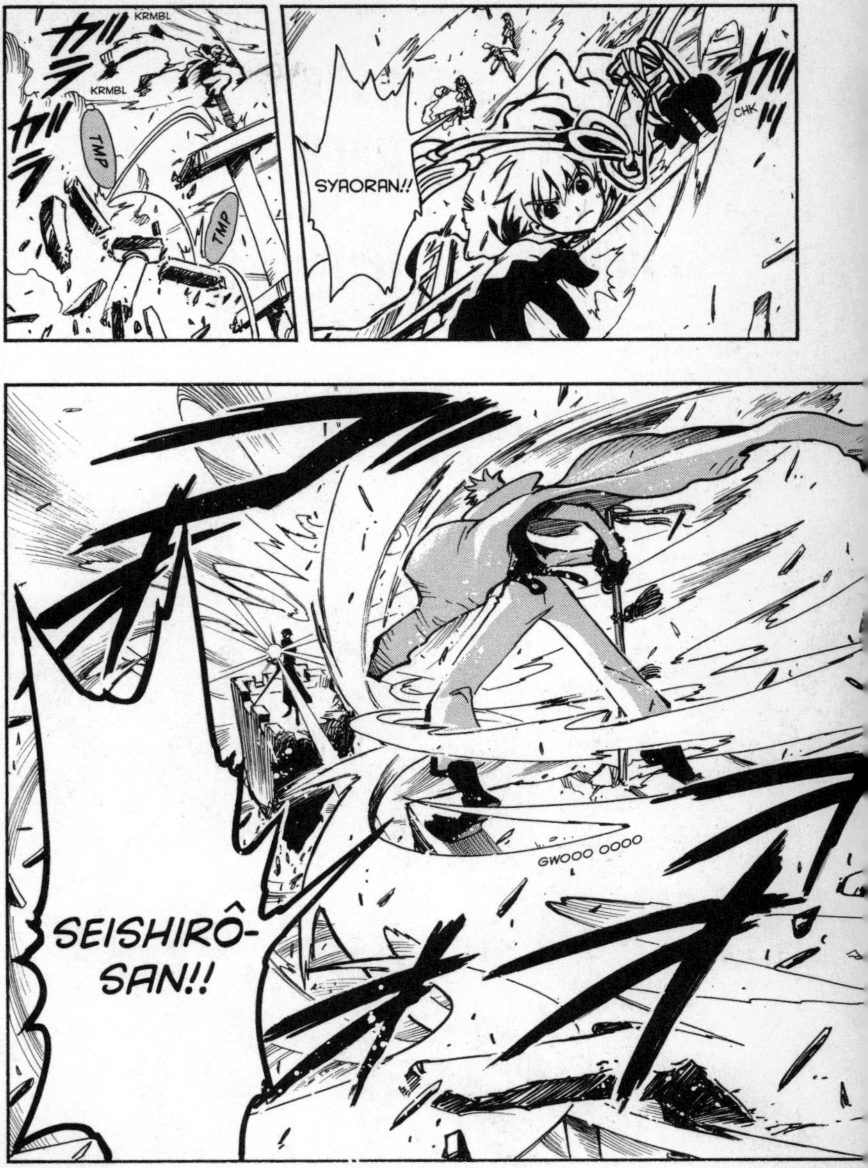
CHK
SYAORAN!!
KRMBL
KRMBL
TMP
TMP
GWOOO OOOO
SEISHIRÔ-
SAN!!

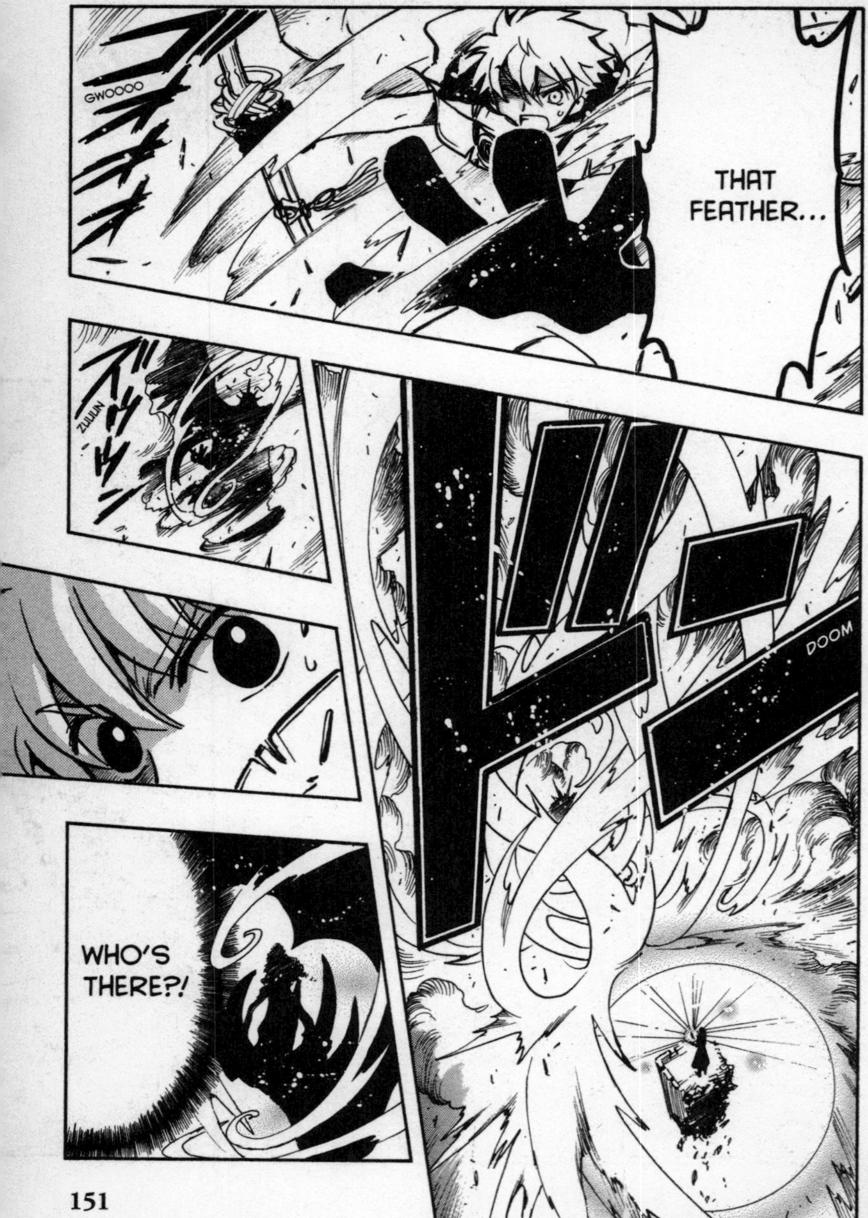
THAT FEATHER...
GWOOOO
DOOM
ZUUUN
WHO'S THERE?!

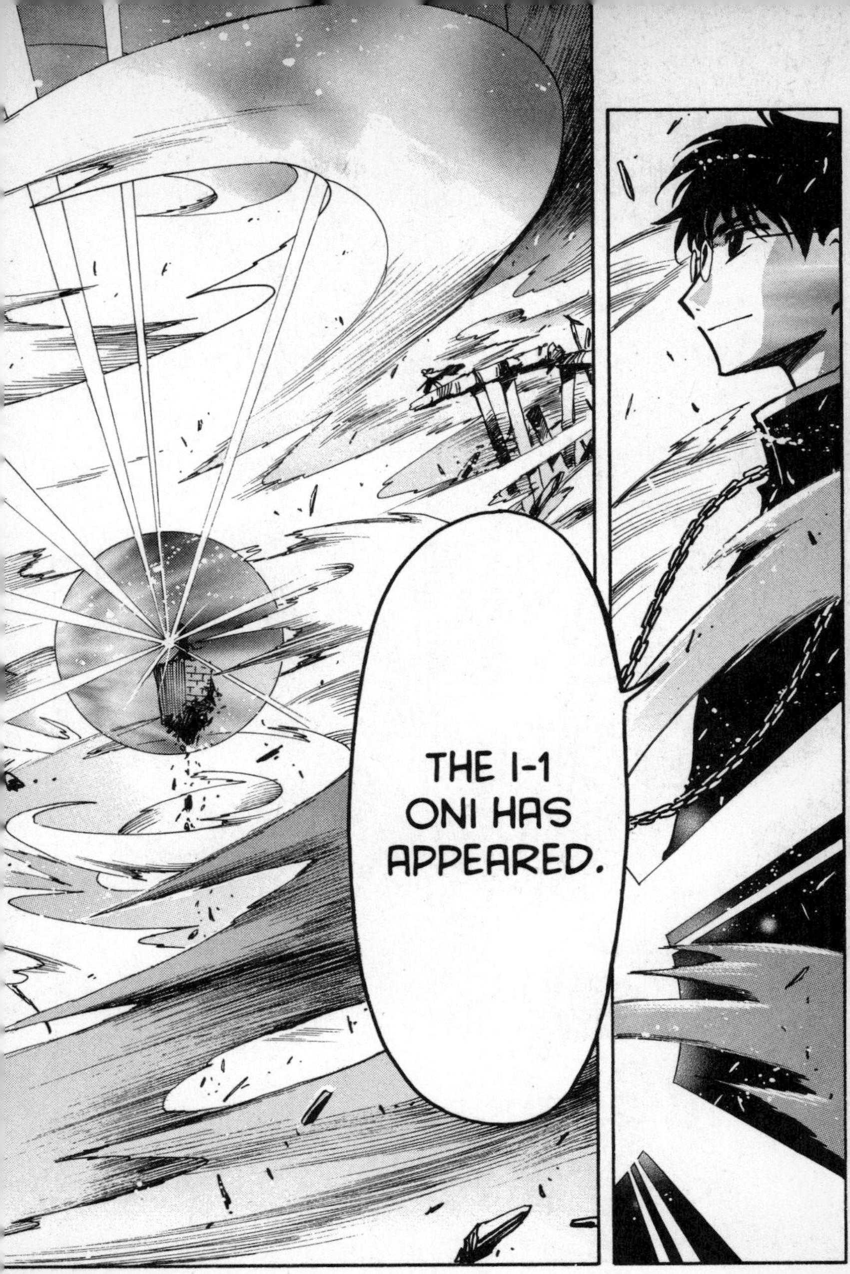
THE 1-1
ONI HAS
APPEARED.

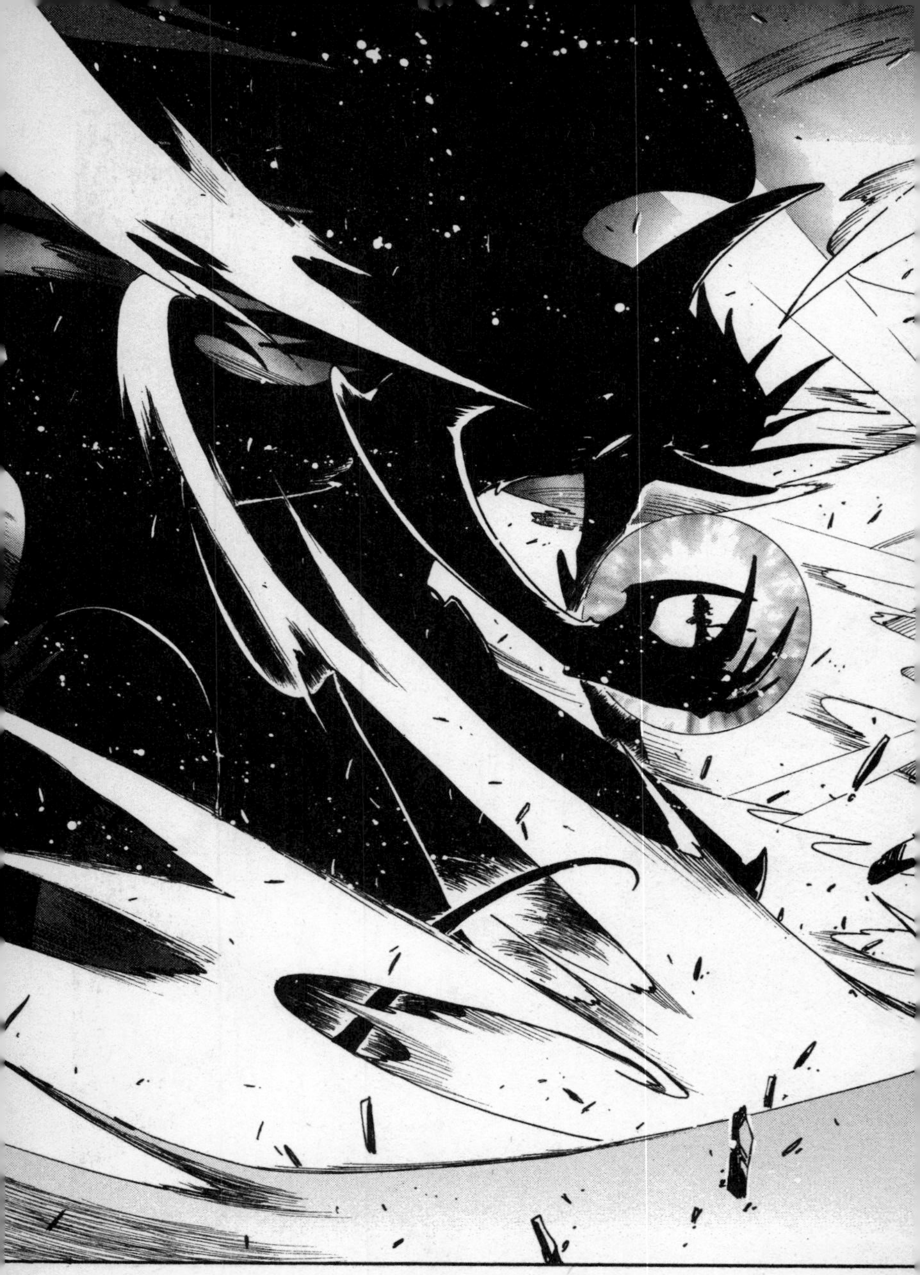

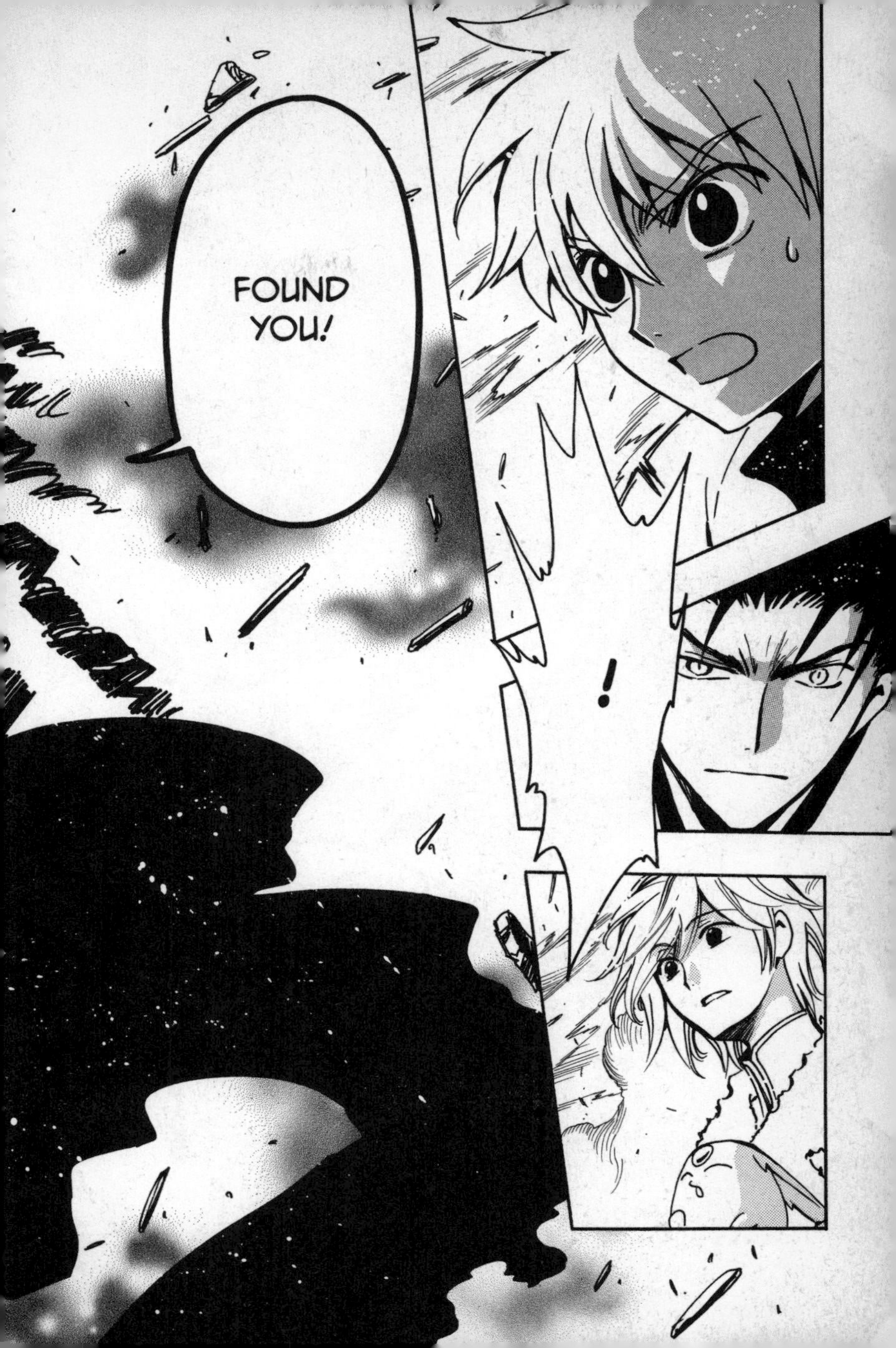

!
FOUND YOU!

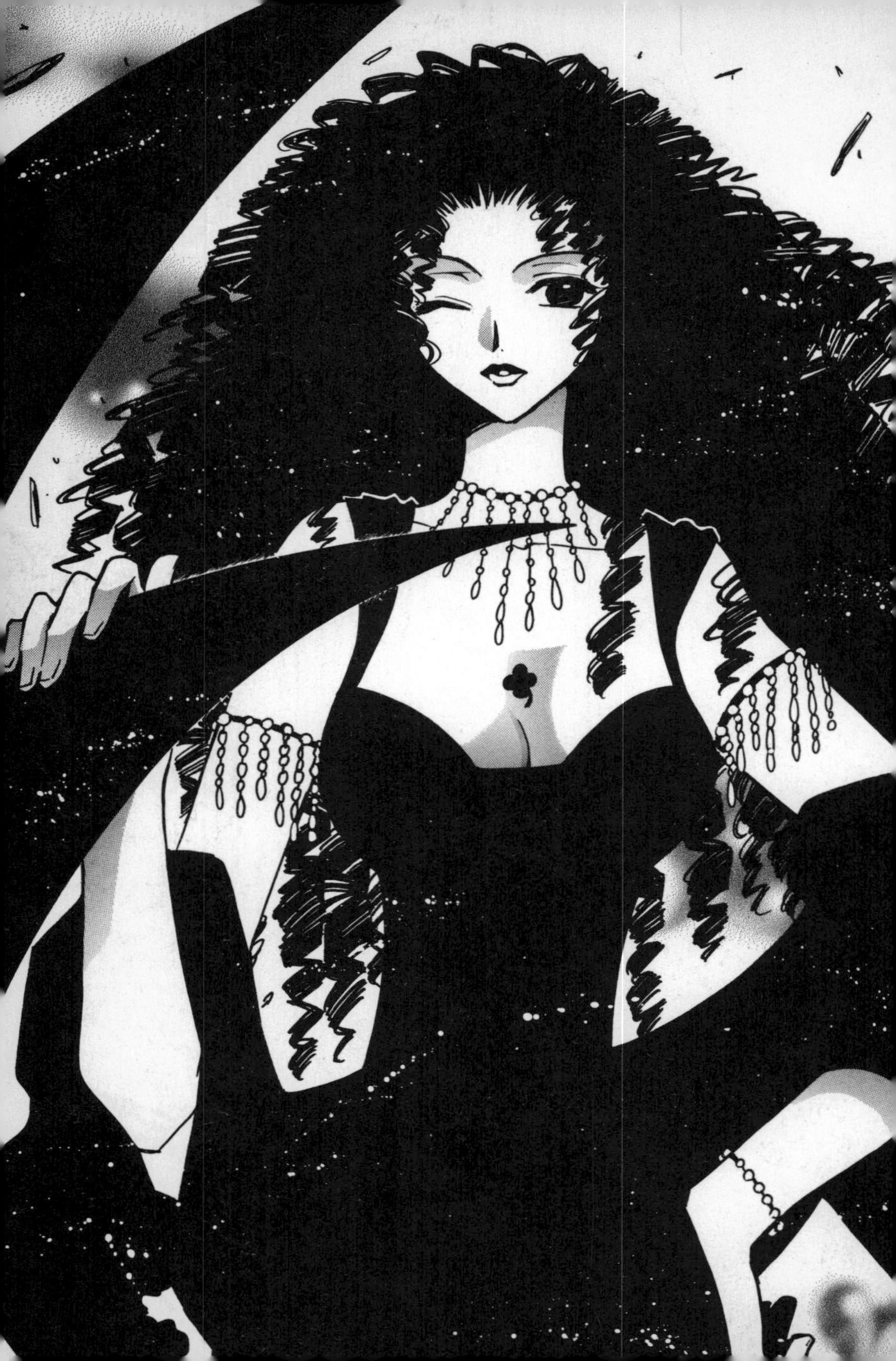

ツバサ

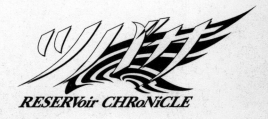

RESERVoir CHRoNiCLE

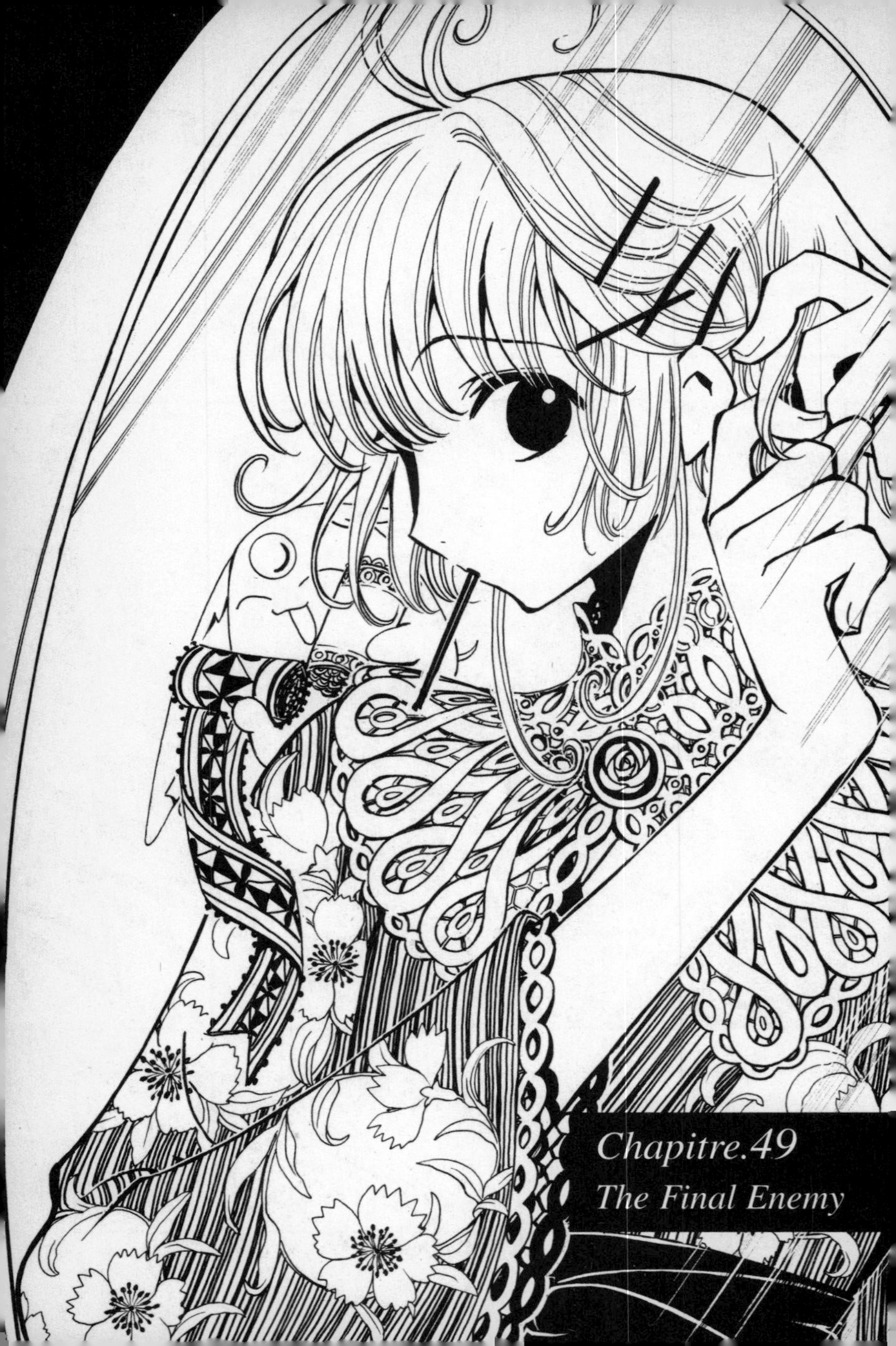

Chapitre.49
The Final Enemy

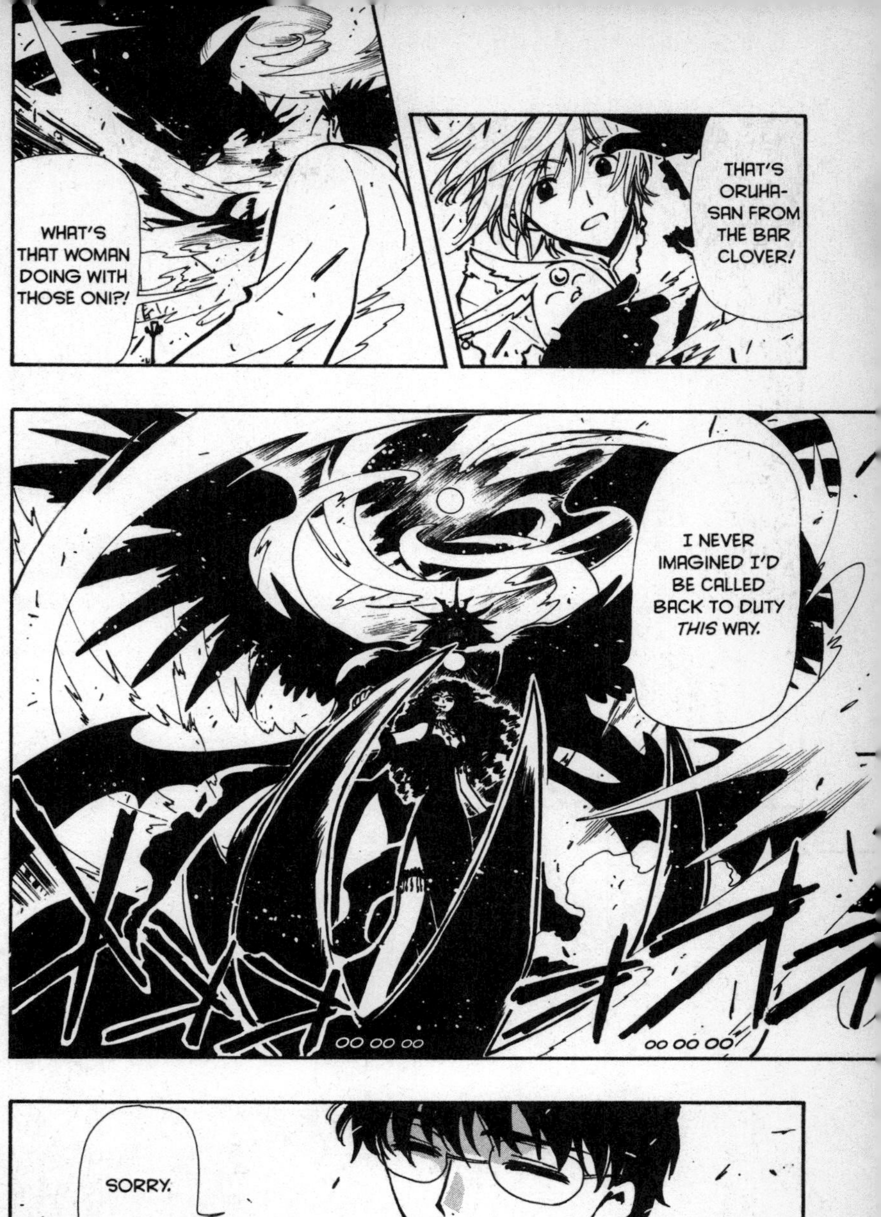
THAT'S ORUHA-SAN FROM THE BAR CLOVER!
WHAT'S THAT WOMAN DOING WITH THOSE ONI?!
I NEVER IMAGINED I'D BE CALLED BACK TO DUTY *THIS* WAY.
oo oo oo
oo oo oo
SORRY.

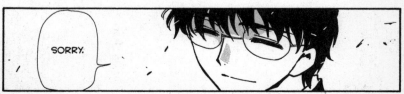

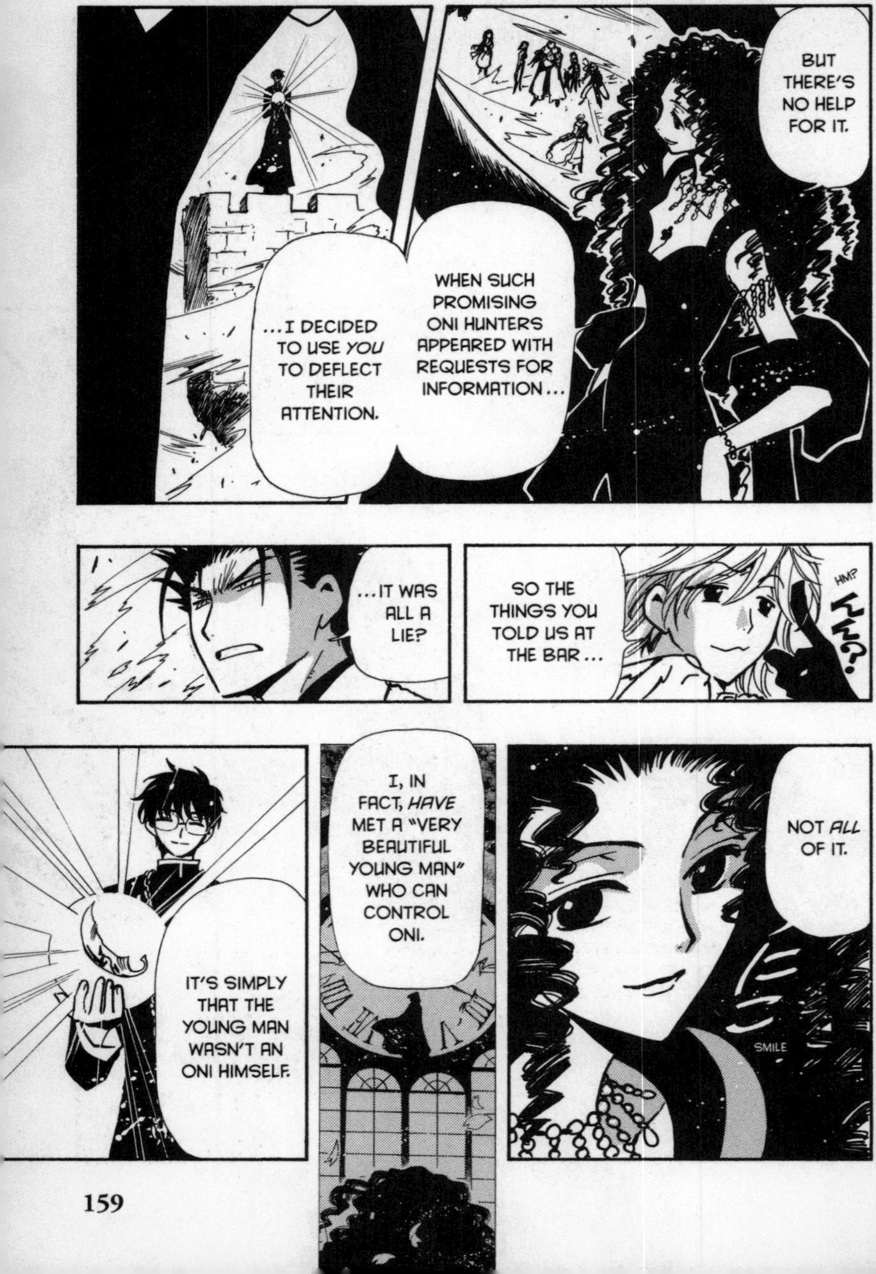
BUT THERE'S NO HELP FOR IT.
WHEN SUCH PROMISING ONI HUNTERS APPEARED WITH REQUESTS FOR INFORMATION...
...I DECIDED TO USE *YOU* TO DEFLECT THEIR ATTENTION.
HM?
SO THE THINGS YOU TOLD US AT THE BAR...
...IT WAS ALL A LIE?
NOT *ALL* OF IT.
SMILE
I, IN FACT, *HAVE* MET A "VERY BEAUTIFUL YOUNG MAN" WHO CAN CONTROL ONI.
IT'S SIMPLY THAT THE YOUNG MAN WASN'T AN ONI HIMSELF.

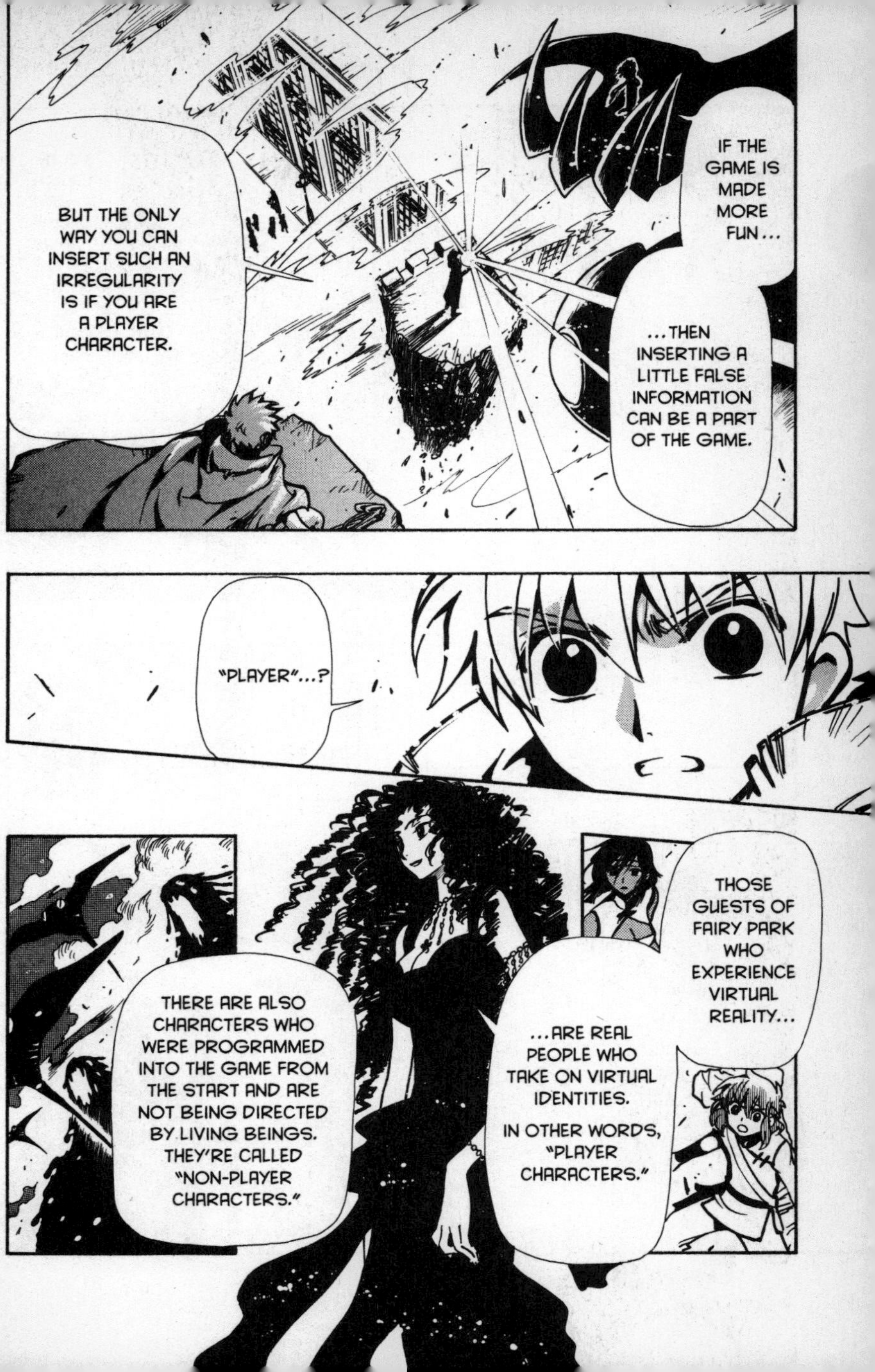
IF THE GAME IS MADE MORE FUN...
...THEN INSERTING A LITTLE FALSE INFORMATION CAN BE A PART OF THE GAME.
BUT THE ONLY WAY YOU CAN INSERT SUCH AN IRREGULARITY IS IF YOU ARE A PLAYER CHARACTER.
"PLAYER"...?
THOSE GUESTS OF FAIRY PARK WHO EXPERIENCE VIRTUAL REALITY...
...ARE REAL PEOPLE WHO TAKE ON VIRTUAL IDENTITIES.
IN OTHER WORDS, "PLAYER CHARACTERS."
THERE ARE ALSO CHARACTERS WHO WERE PROGRAMMED INTO THE GAME FROM THE START AND ARE NOT BEING DIRECTED BY LIVING BEINGS. THEY'RE CALLED "NON-PLAYER CHARACTERS."

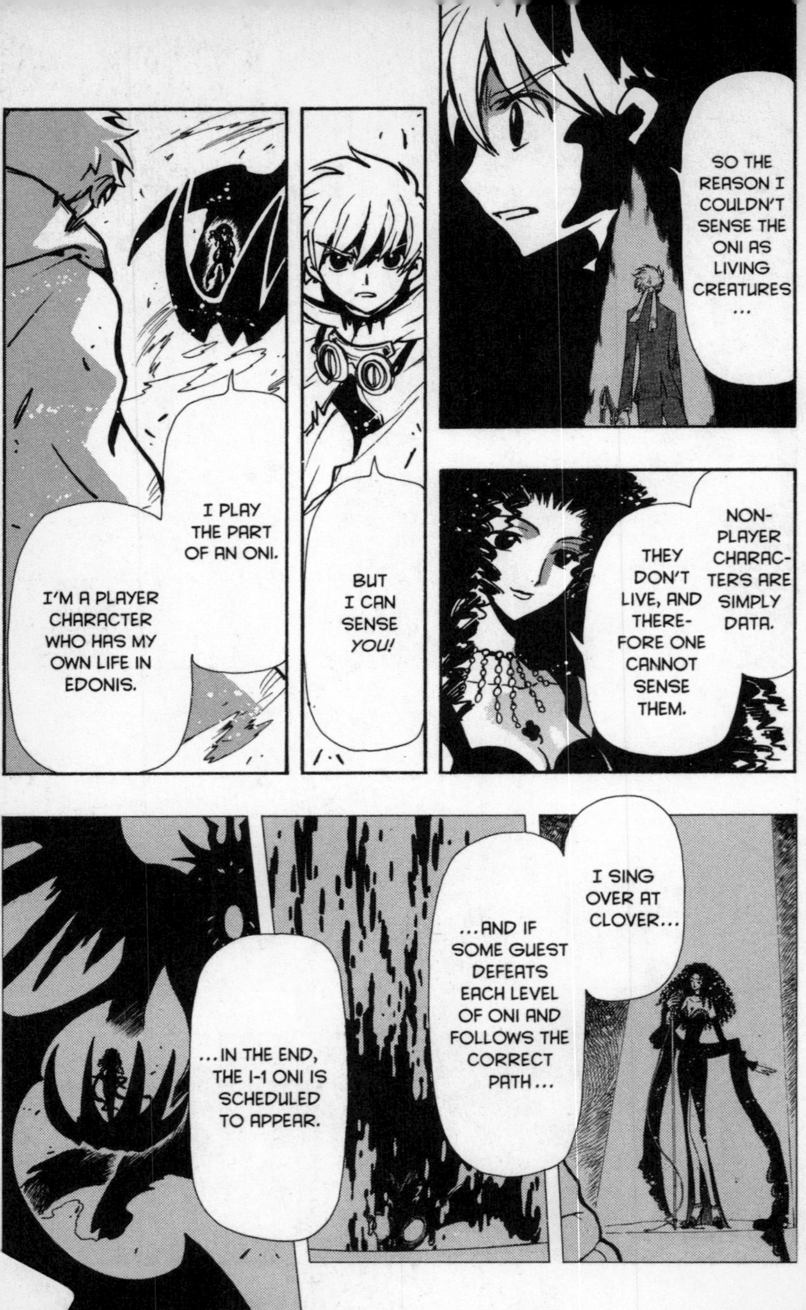
SO THE REASON I COULDN'T SENSE THE ONI AS LIVING CREATURES...
NON-PLAYER CHARACTERS ARE SIMPLY DATA.
THEY DON'T LIVE, AND THEREFORE ONE CANNOT SENSE THEM.
BUT I CAN SENSE *YOU!*
I PLAY THE PART OF AN ONI.
I'M A PLAYER CHARACTER WHO HAS MY OWN LIFE IN EDONIS.
I SING OVER AT CLOVER...
...AND IF SOME GUEST DEFEATS EACH LEVEL OF ONI AND FOLLOWS THE CORRECT PATH...
...IN THE END, THE I-1 ONI IS SCHEDULED TO APPEAR.

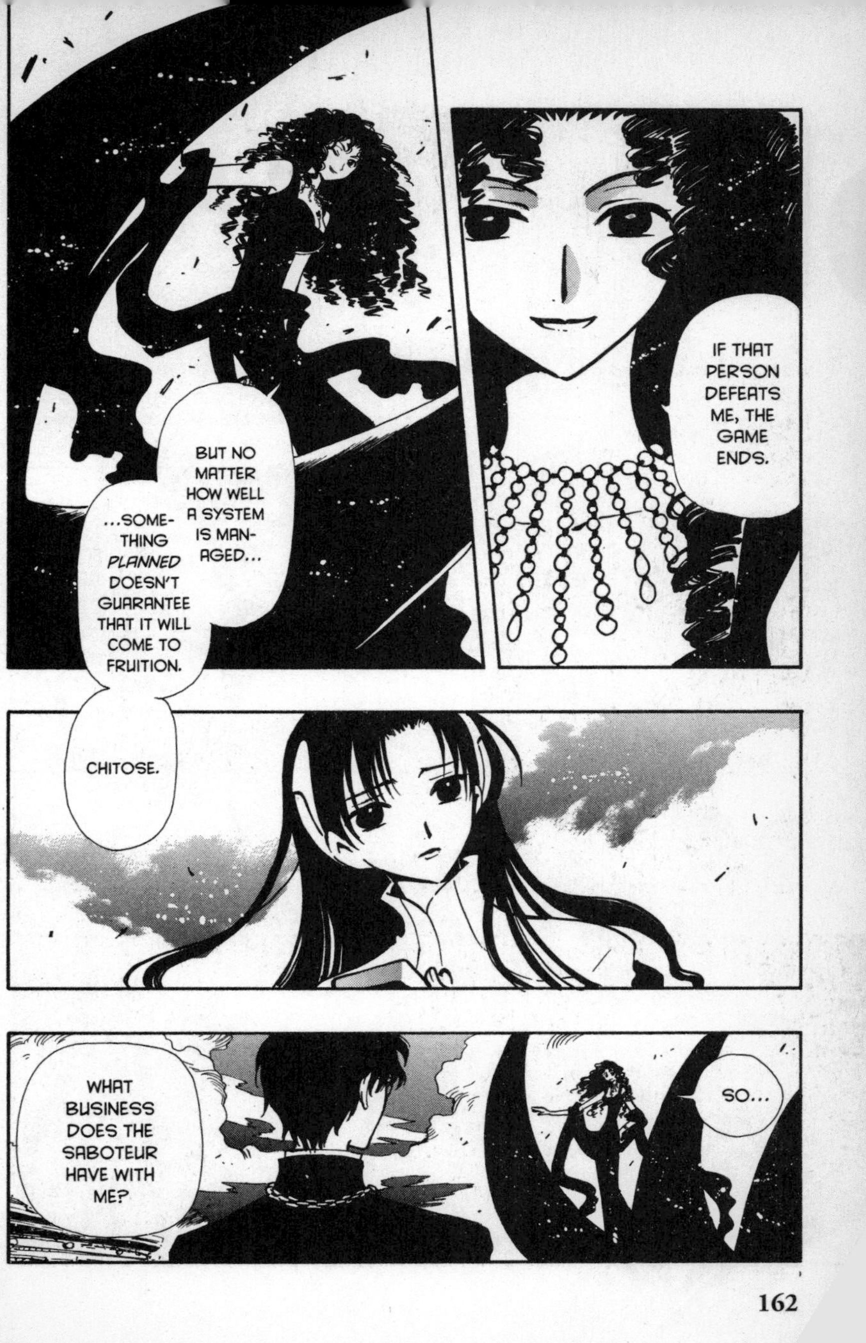
IF THAT PERSON DEFEATS ME, THE GAME ENDS.
BUT NO MATTER HOW WELL A SYSTEM IS MAN-AGED...
...SOME-THING *PLANNED* DOESN'T GUARANTEE THAT IT WILL COME TO FRUITION.
CHITOSE.
SO...
WHAT BUSINESS DOES THE SABOTEUR HAVE WITH ME?

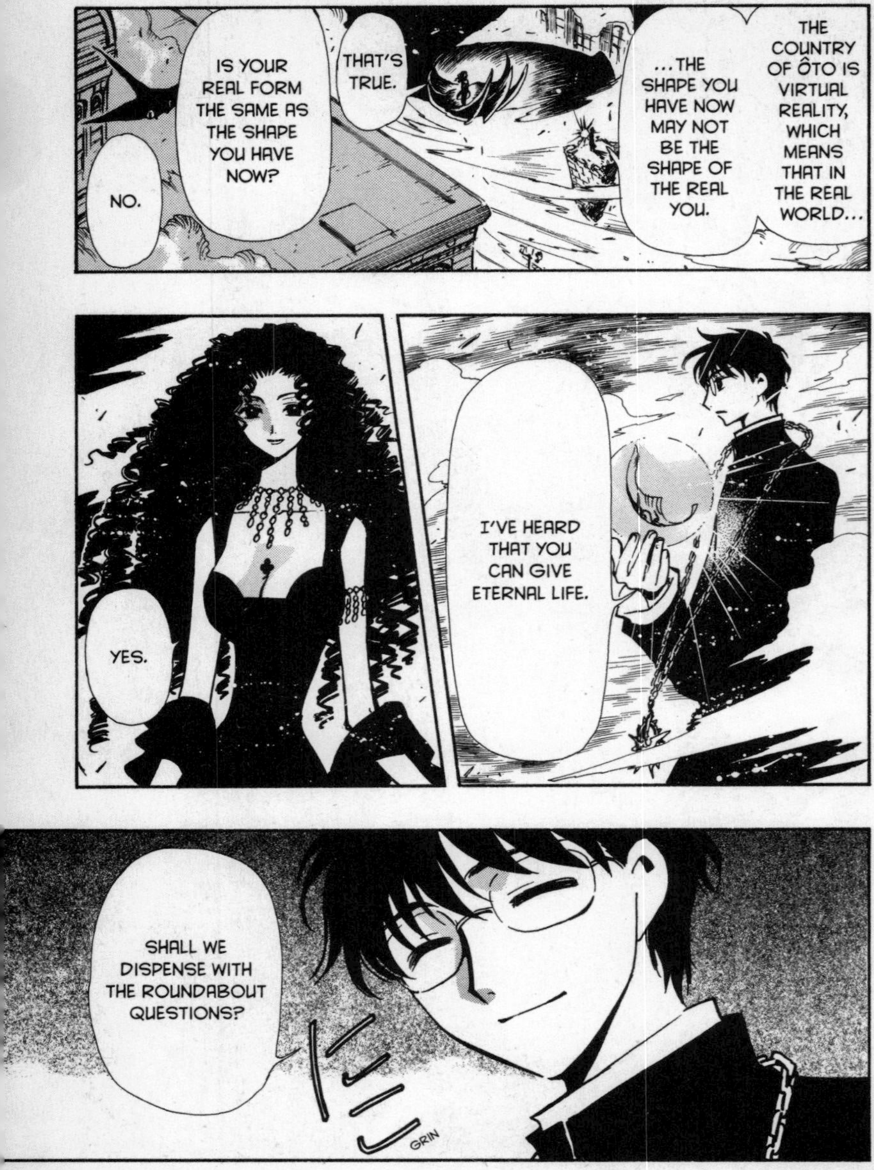
THE COUNTRY OF ÔTO IS VIRTUAL REALITY, WHICH MEANS THAT IN THE REAL WORLD...
...THE SHAPE YOU HAVE NOW MAY NOT BE THE SHAPE OF THE REAL YOU.
THAT'S TRUE.
IS YOUR REAL FORM THE SAME AS THE SHAPE YOU HAVE NOW?
NO.
I'VE HEARD THAT YOU CAN GIVE ETERNAL LIFE.
YES.
SHALL WE DISPENSE WITH THE ROUNDABOUT QUESTIONS?
GRIN

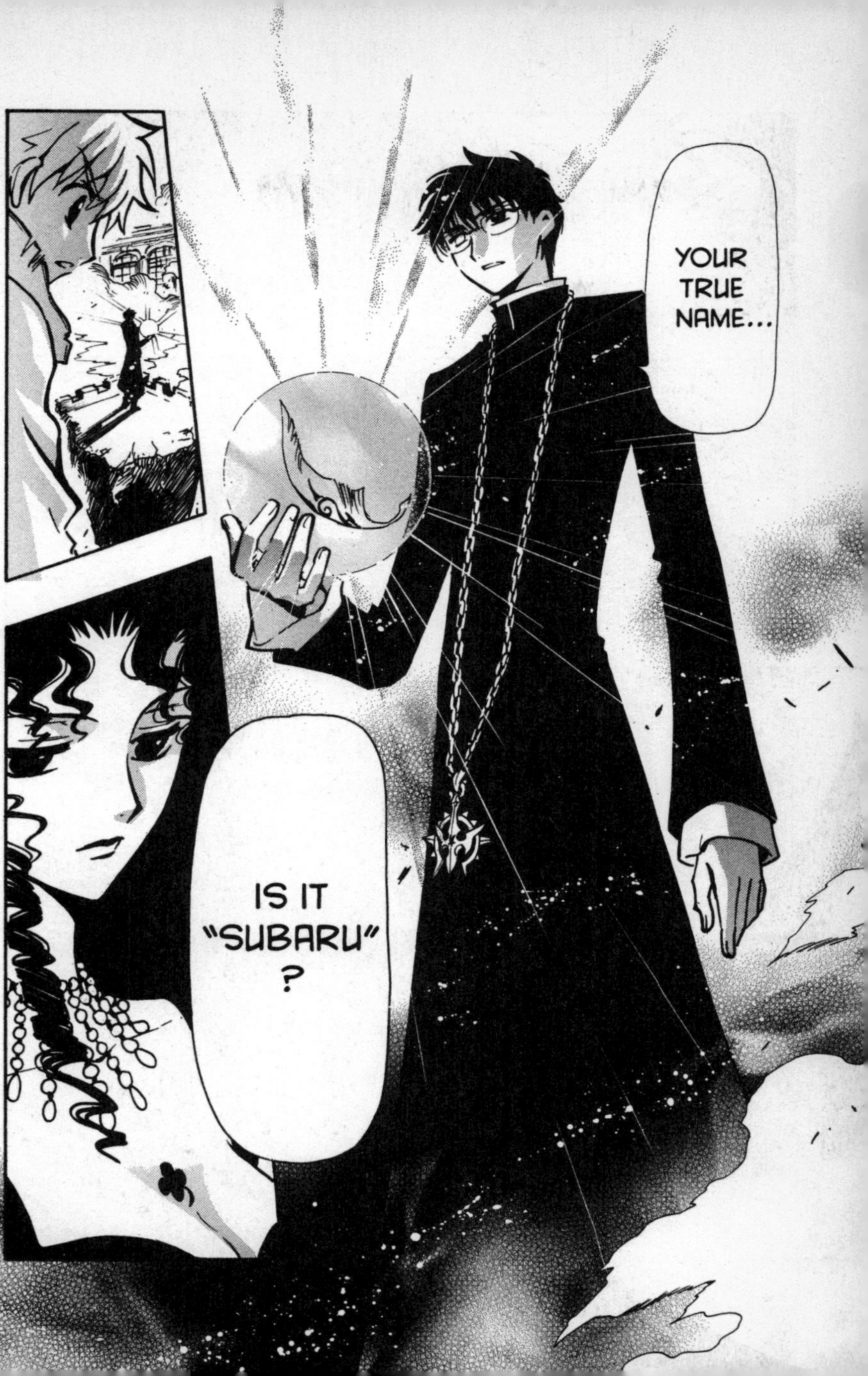
YOUR TRUE NAME...
IS IT "SUBARU"?

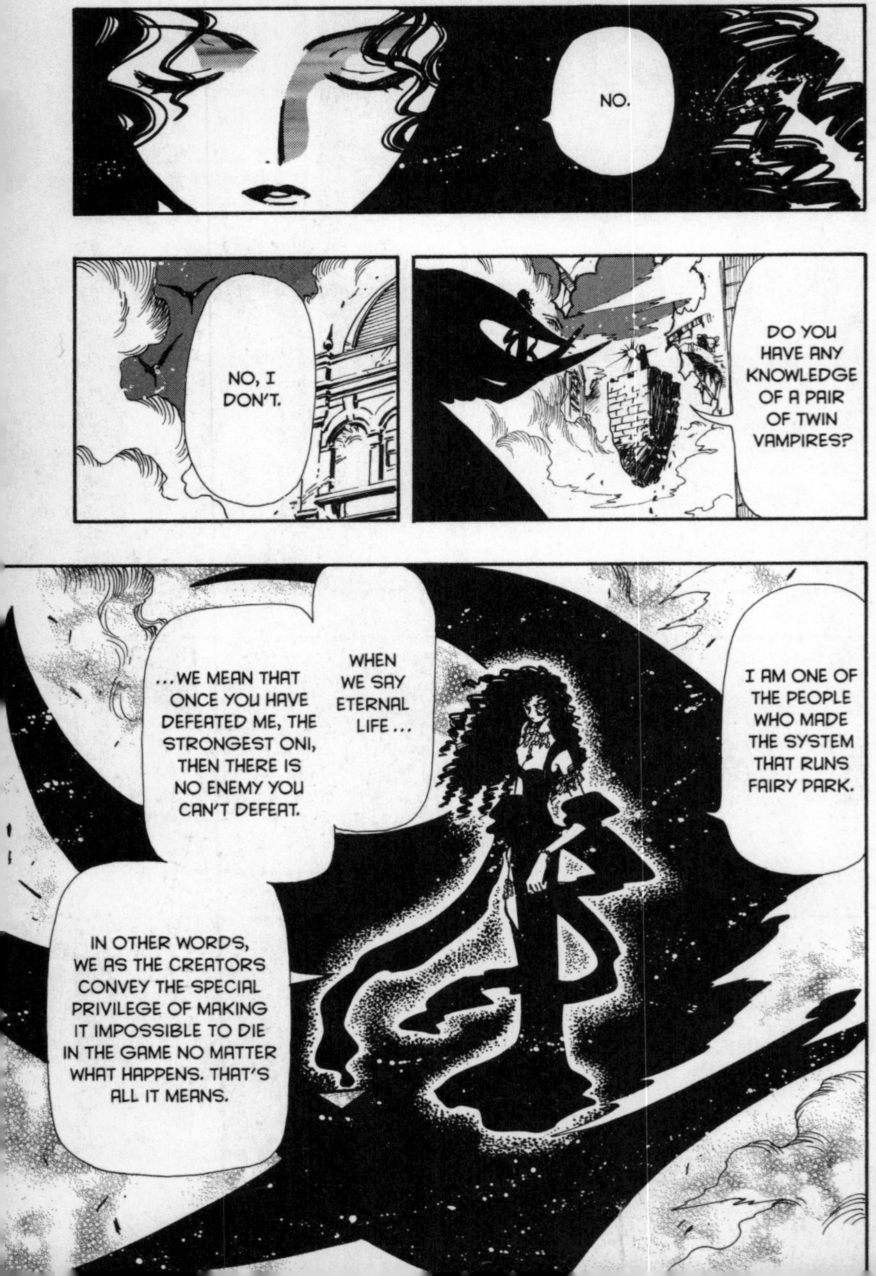
NO.
DO YOU HAVE ANY KNOWLEDGE OF A PAIR OF TWIN VAMPIRES?
NO, I DON'T.
I AM ONE OF THE PEOPLE WHO MADE THE SYSTEM THAT RUNS FAIRY PARK.
WHEN WE SAY ETERNAL LIFE...
...WE MEAN THAT ONCE YOU HAVE DEFEATED ME, THE STRONGEST ONI, THEN THERE IS NO ENEMY YOU CAN'T DEFEAT.
IN OTHER WORDS, WE AS THE CREATORS CONVEY THE SPECIAL PRIVILEGE OF MAKING IT IMPOSSIBLE TO DIE IN THE GAME NO MATTER WHAT HAPPENS. THAT'S ALL IT MEANS.

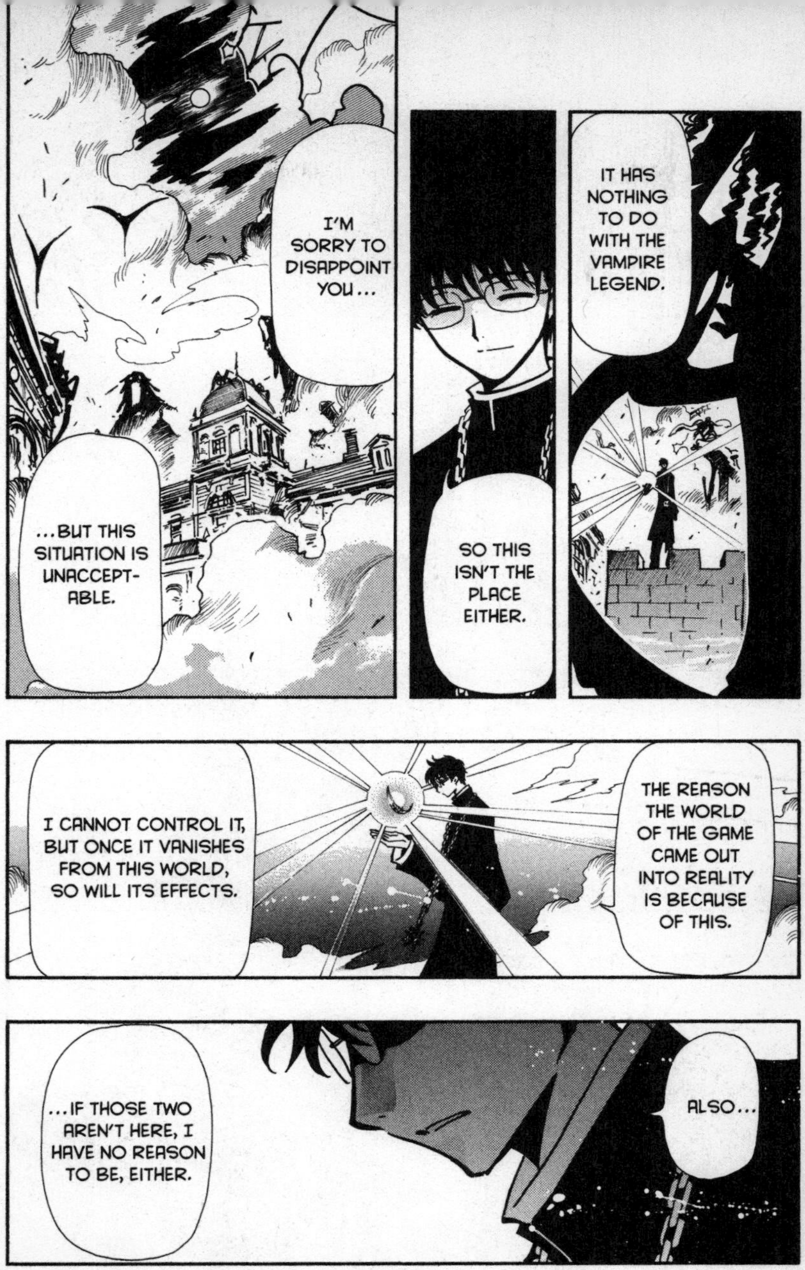
IT HAS NOTHING TO DO WITH THE VAMPIRE LEGEND.
SO THIS ISN'T THE PLACE EITHER.
I'M SORRY TO DISAPPOINT YOU...
...BUT THIS SITUATION IS UNACCEPT-ABLE.
THE REASON THE WORLD OF THE GAME CAME OUT INTO REALITY IS BECAUSE OF THIS.
I CANNOT CONTROL IT, BUT ONCE IT VANISHES FROM THIS WORLD, SO WILL ITS EFFECTS.
ALSO...
...IF THOSE TWO AREN'T HERE, I HAVE NO REASON TO BE, EITHER.

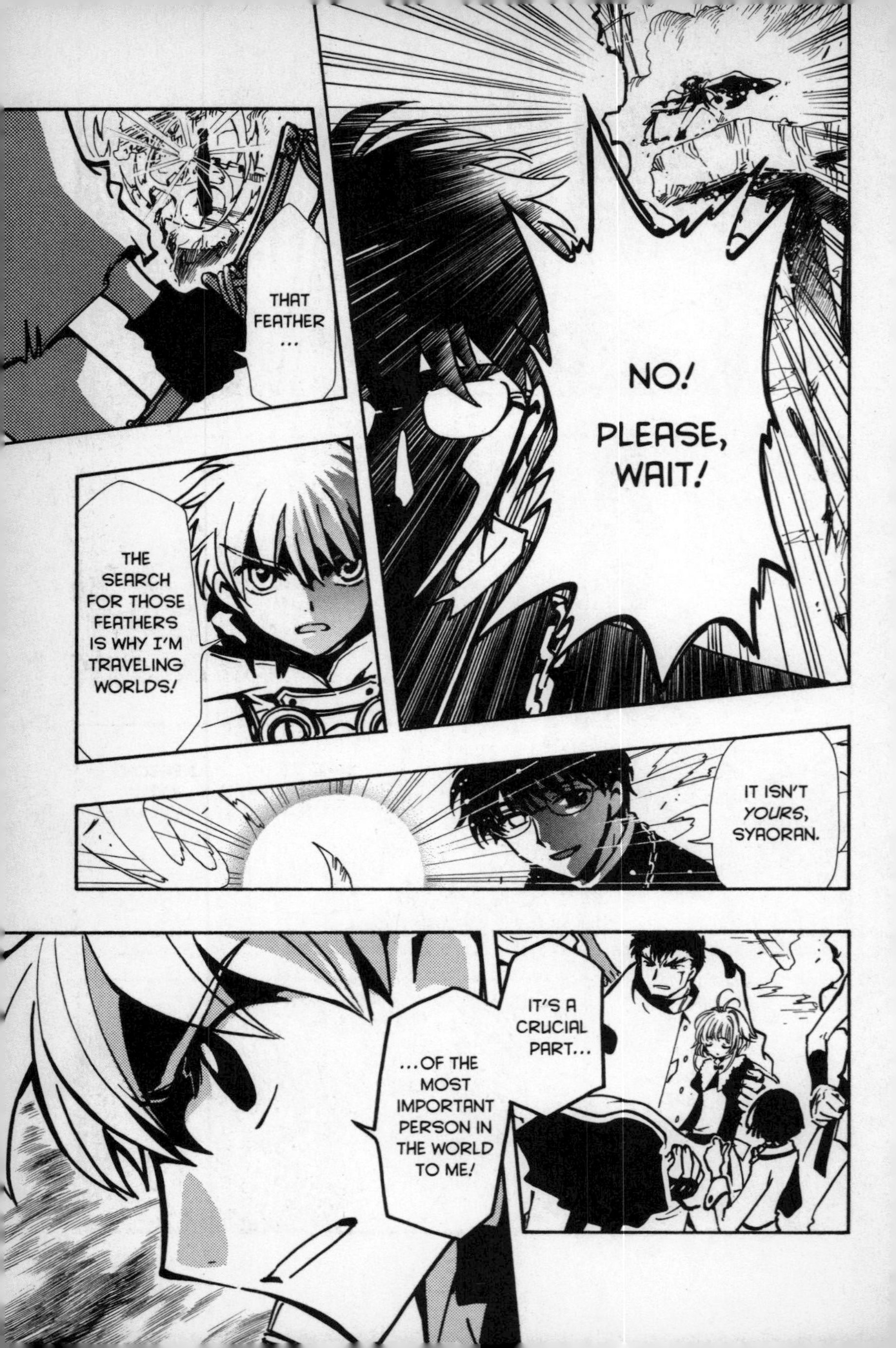
NO!
PLEASE, WAIT!
THAT FEATHER ...
THE SEARCH FOR THOSE FEATHERS IS WHY I'M TRAVELING WORLDS!
IT ISN'T *YOURS*, SYAORAN.
IT'S A CRUCIAL PART...
...OF THE MOST IMPORTANT PERSON IN THE WORLD TO ME!

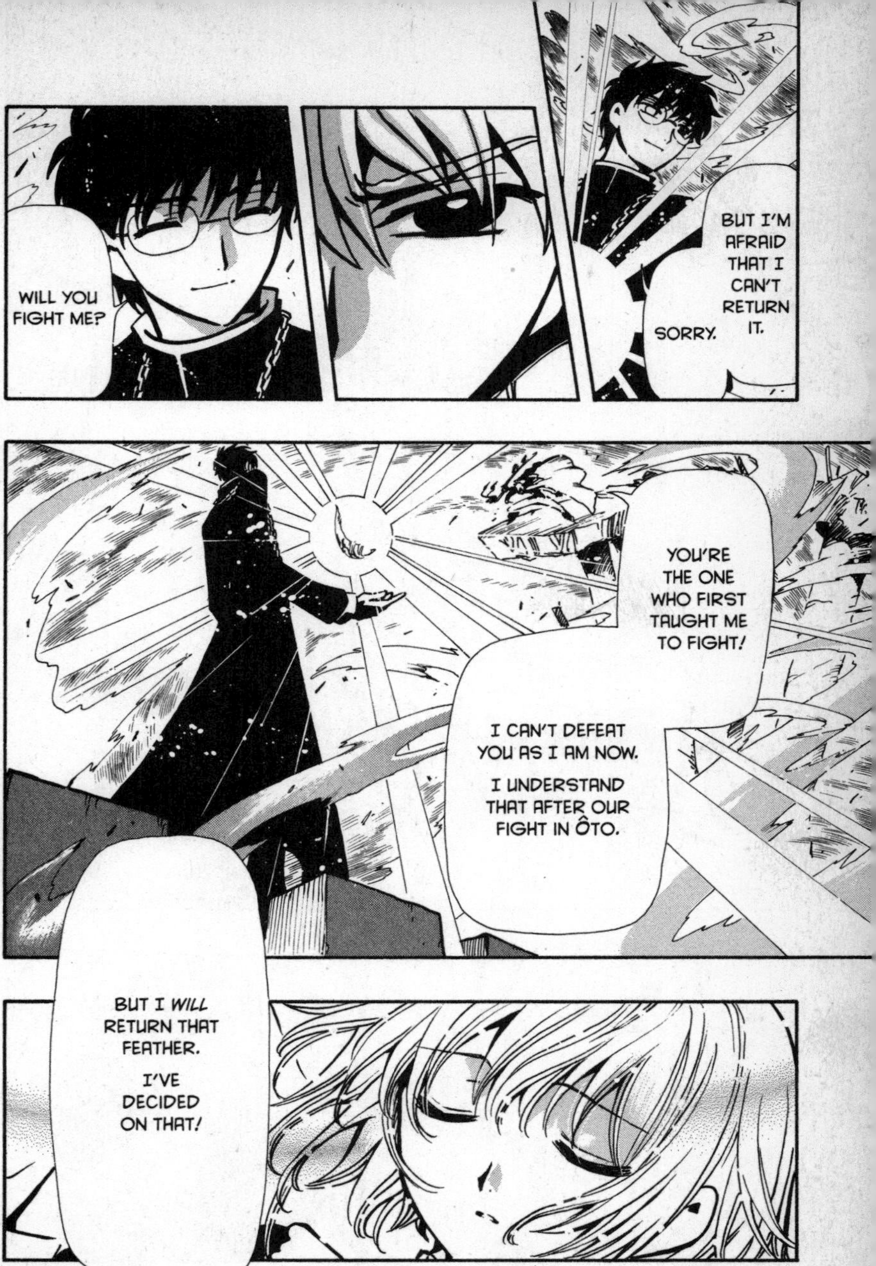
BUT I'M AFRAID THAT I CAN'T RETURN IT.
SORRY.
WILL YOU FIGHT ME?
YOU'RE THE ONE WHO FIRST TAUGHT ME TO FIGHT!
I CAN'T DEFEAT YOU AS I AM NOW.
I UNDERSTAND THAT AFTER OUR FIGHT IN ÔTO.
BUT I *WILL* RETURN THAT FEATHER.
I'VE DECIDED ON THAT!

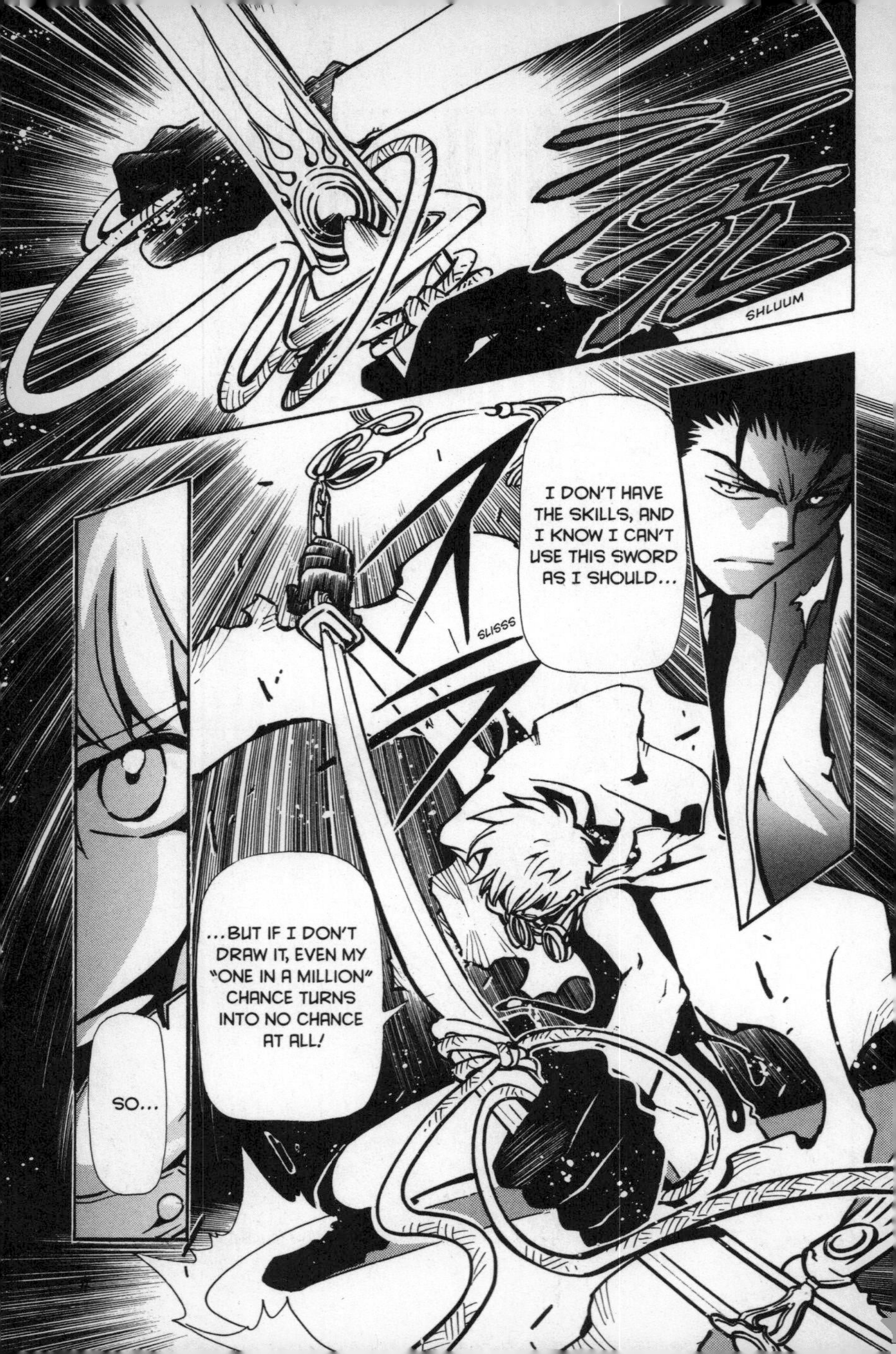
SHLUUM
I DON'T HAVE THE SKILLS, AND I KNOW I CAN'T USE THIS SWORD AS I SHOULD...
SLISSS
...BUT IF I DON'T DRAW IT, EVEN MY "ONE IN A MILLION" CHANCE TURNS INTO NO CHANCE AT ALL!
SO...

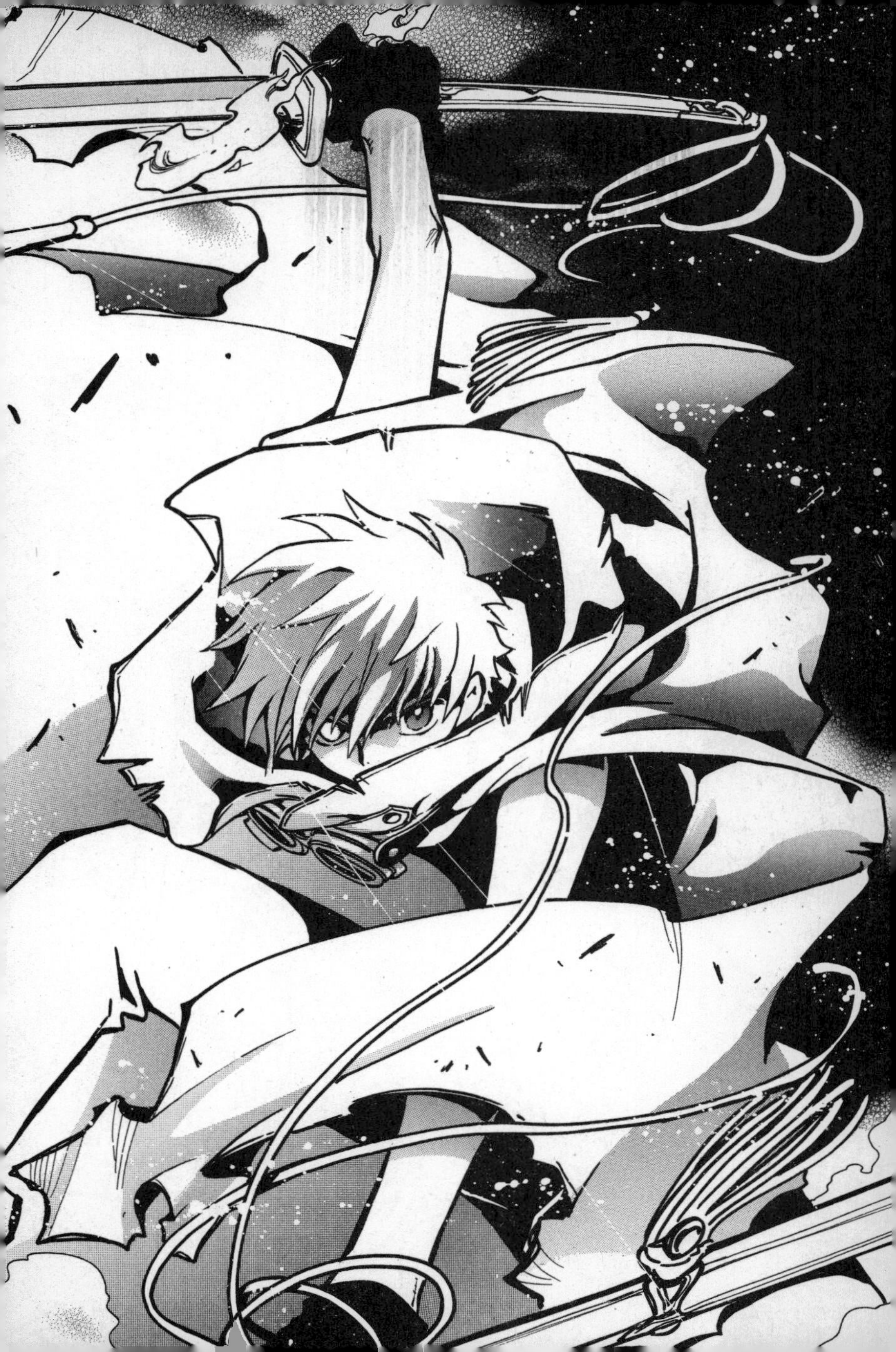

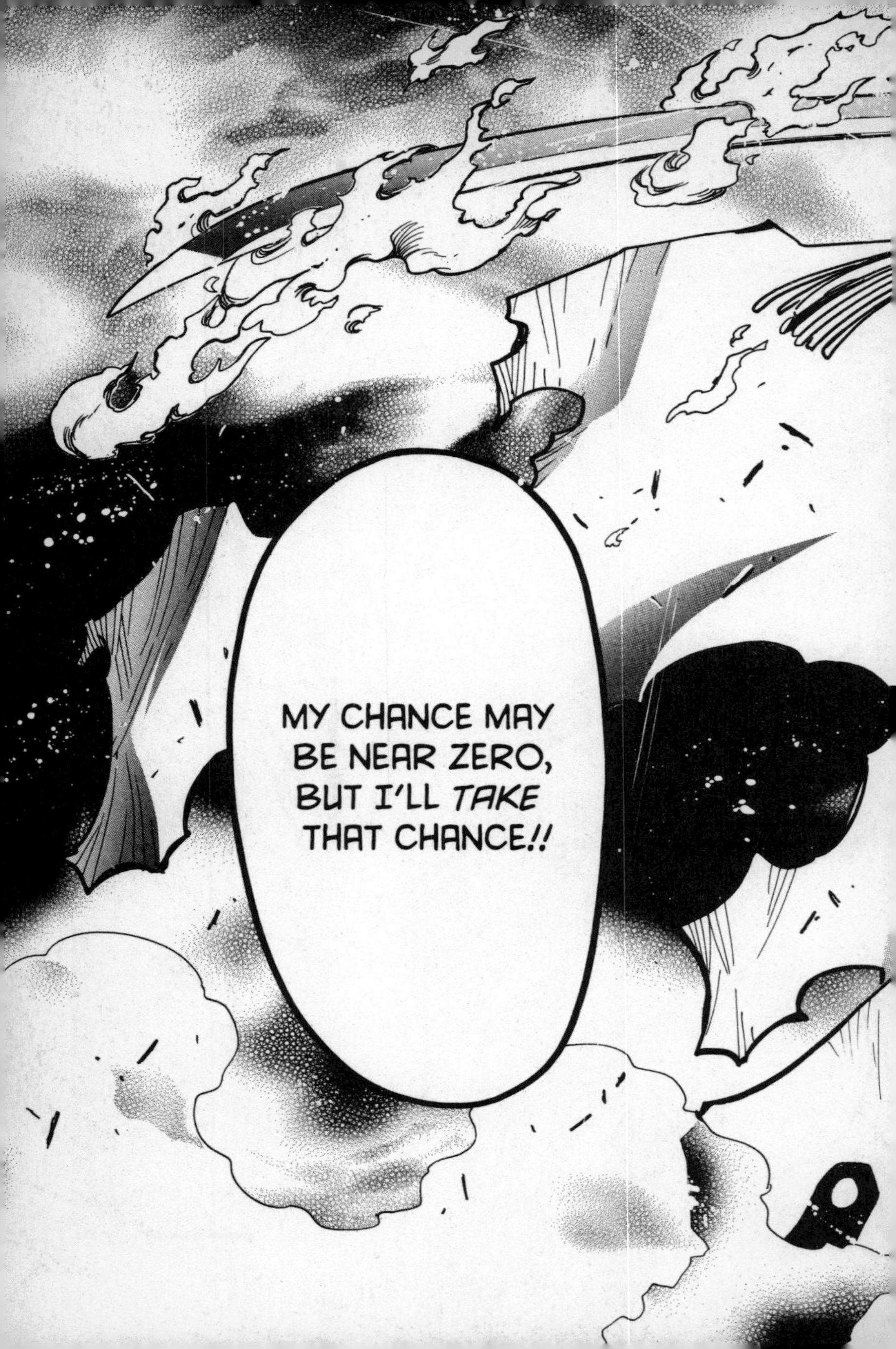
MY CHANCE MAY BE NEAR ZERO, BUT I'LL *TAKE* THAT CHANCE!!

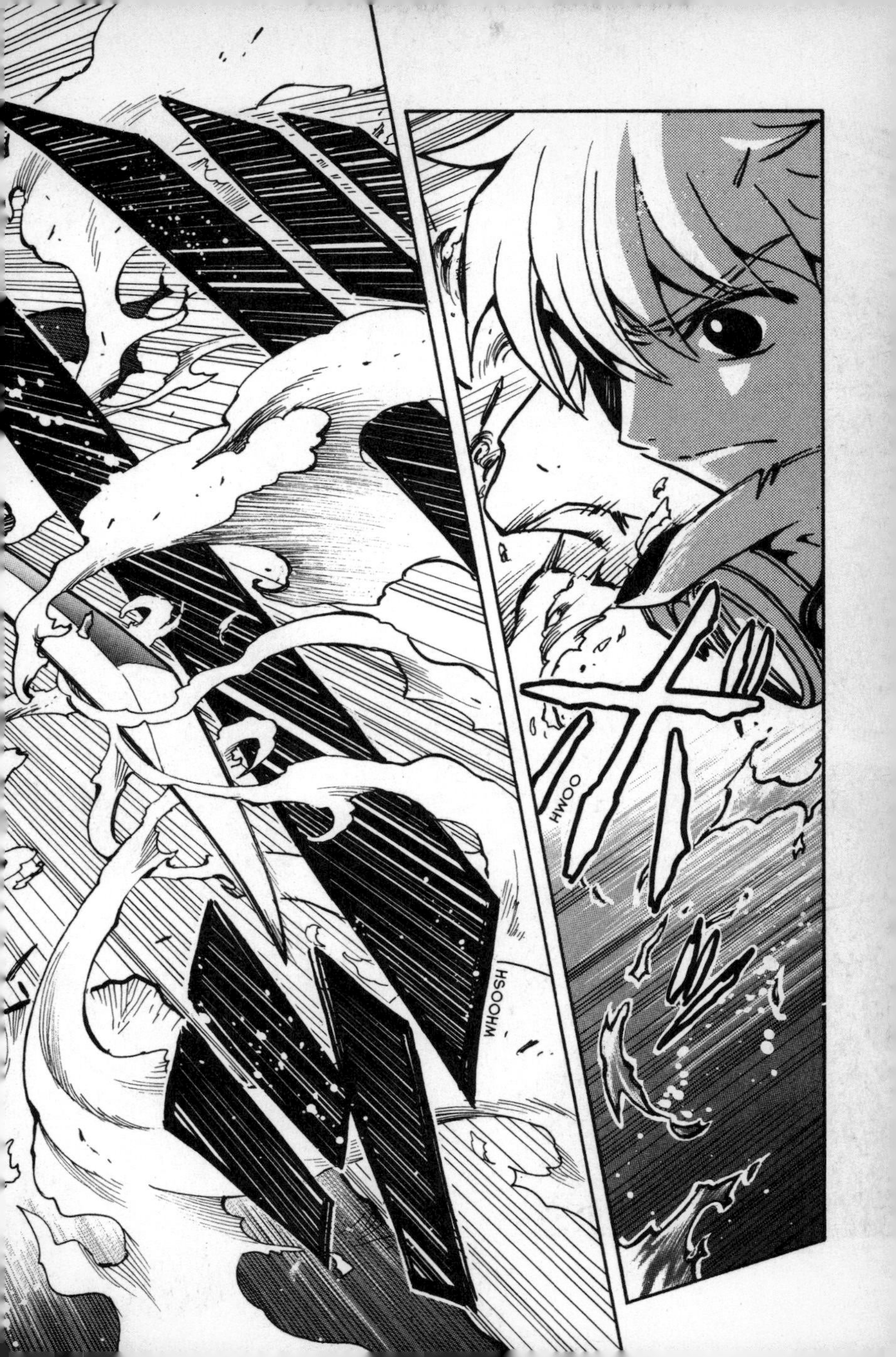
HWOOH
WHOOSH

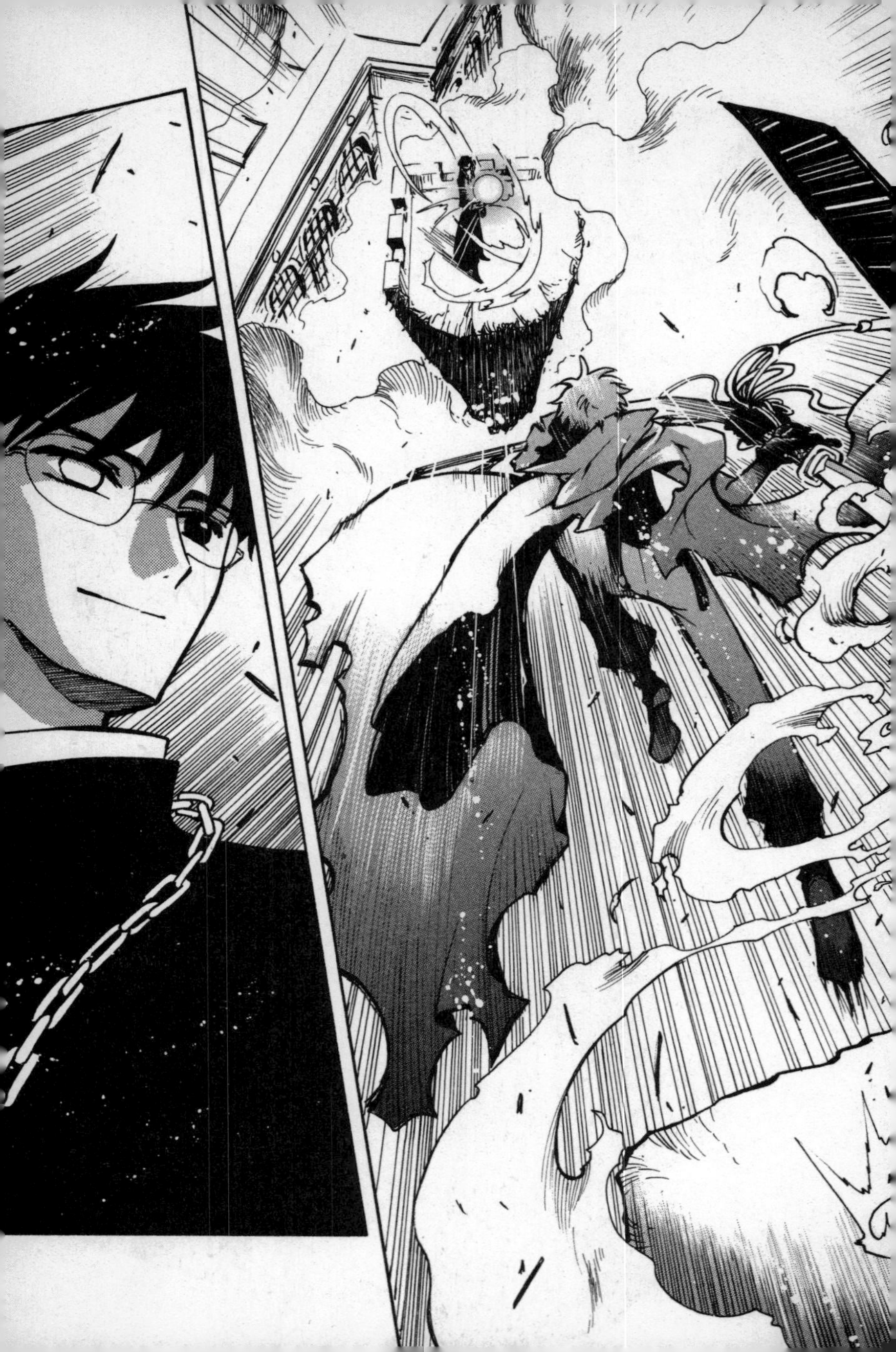

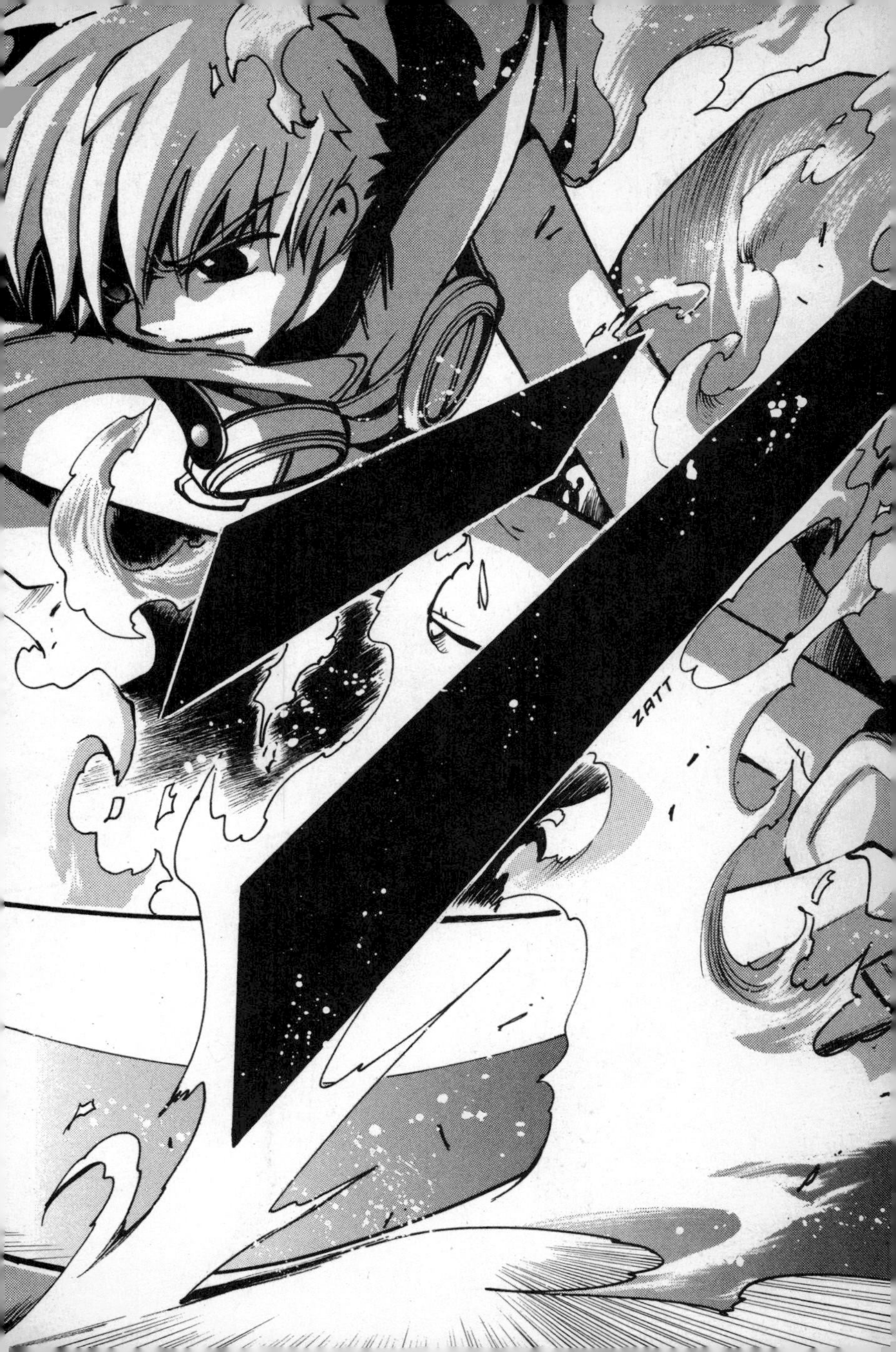
ZATT

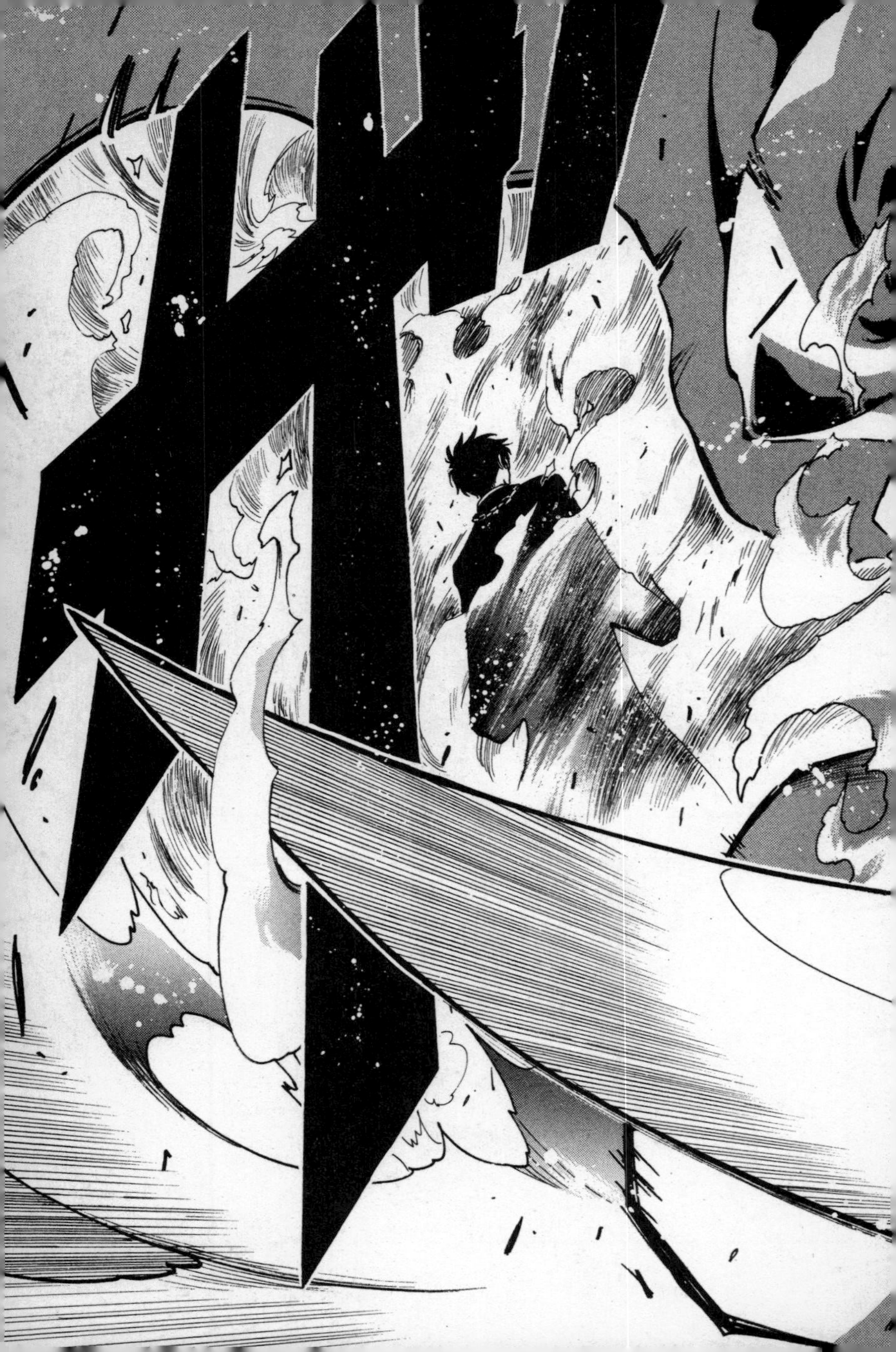

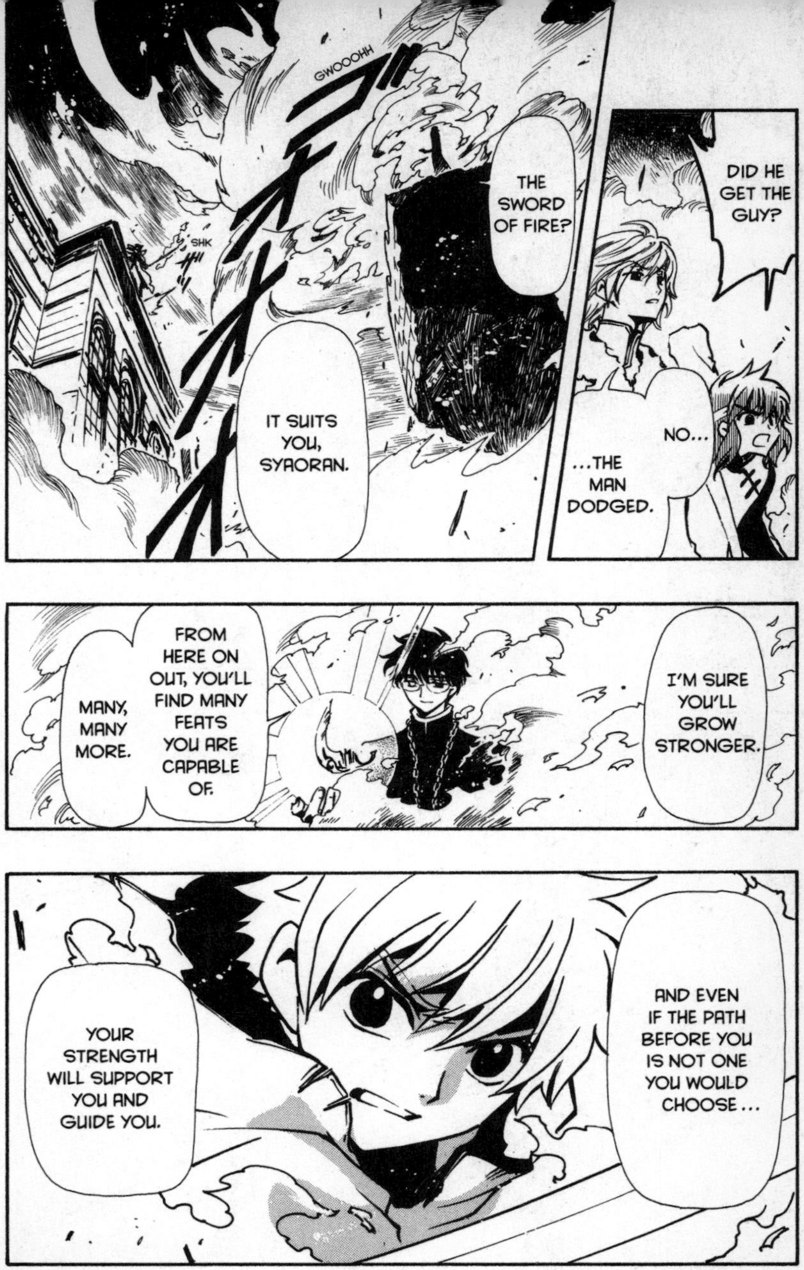
DID HE GET THE GUY?
NO...
...THE MAN DODGED.
GWOOOHH
THE SWORD OF FIRE?
SHK
IT SUITS YOU, SYAORAN.
I'M SURE YOU'LL GROW STRONGER.
FROM HERE ON OUT, YOU'LL FIND MANY FEATS YOU ARE CAPABLE OF.
MANY, MANY MORE.
AND EVEN IF THE PATH BEFORE YOU IS NOT ONE YOU WOULD CHOOSE...
YOUR STRENGTH WILL SUPPORT YOU AND GUIDE YOU.

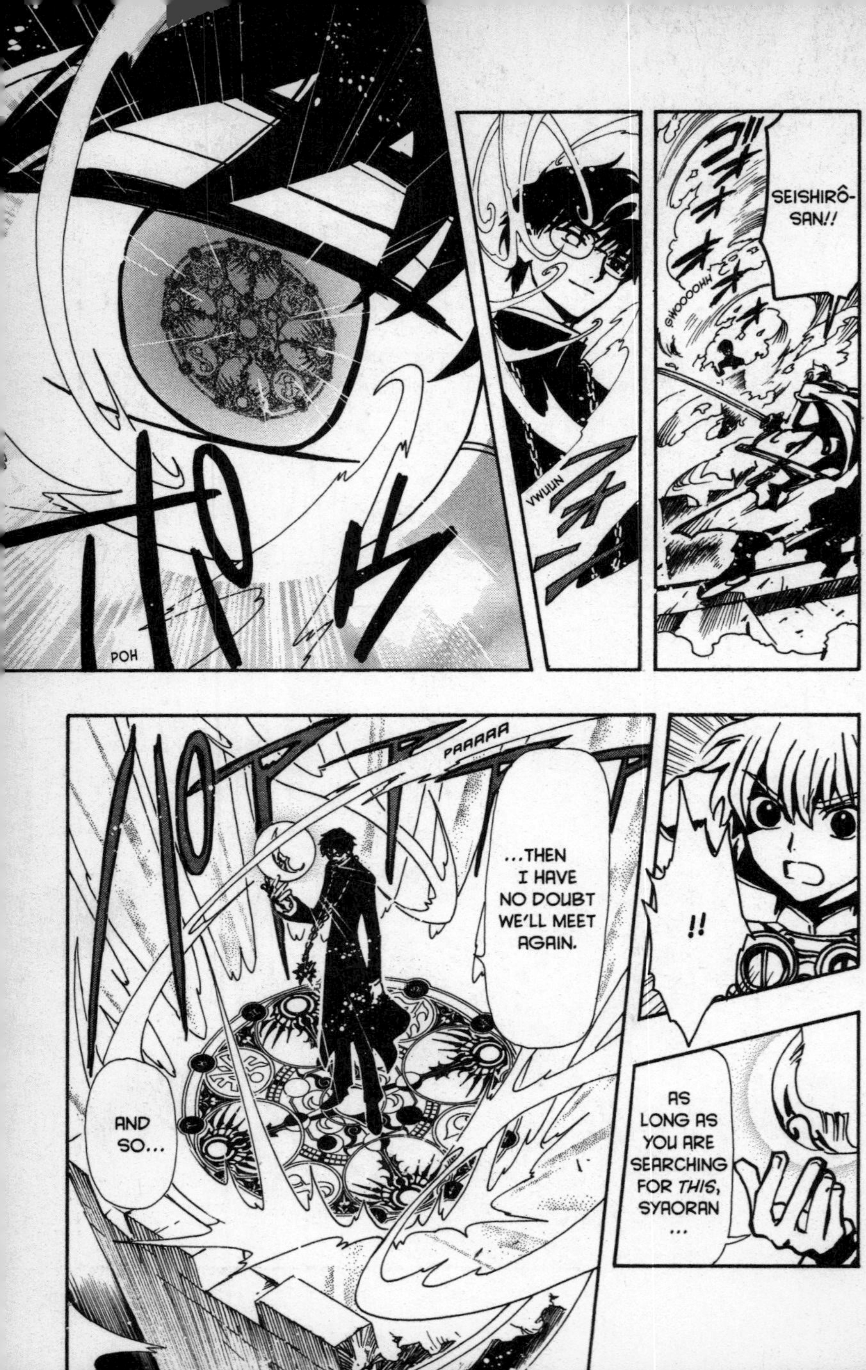
SEISHIRÔ-SAN!!
GWOOOOHH
VWUUN
POH
!!
AS LONG AS YOU ARE SEARCHING FOR *THIS*, SYAORAN ...
PAAAAA
...THEN I HAVE NO DOUBT WE'LL MEET AGAIN.
AND SO...

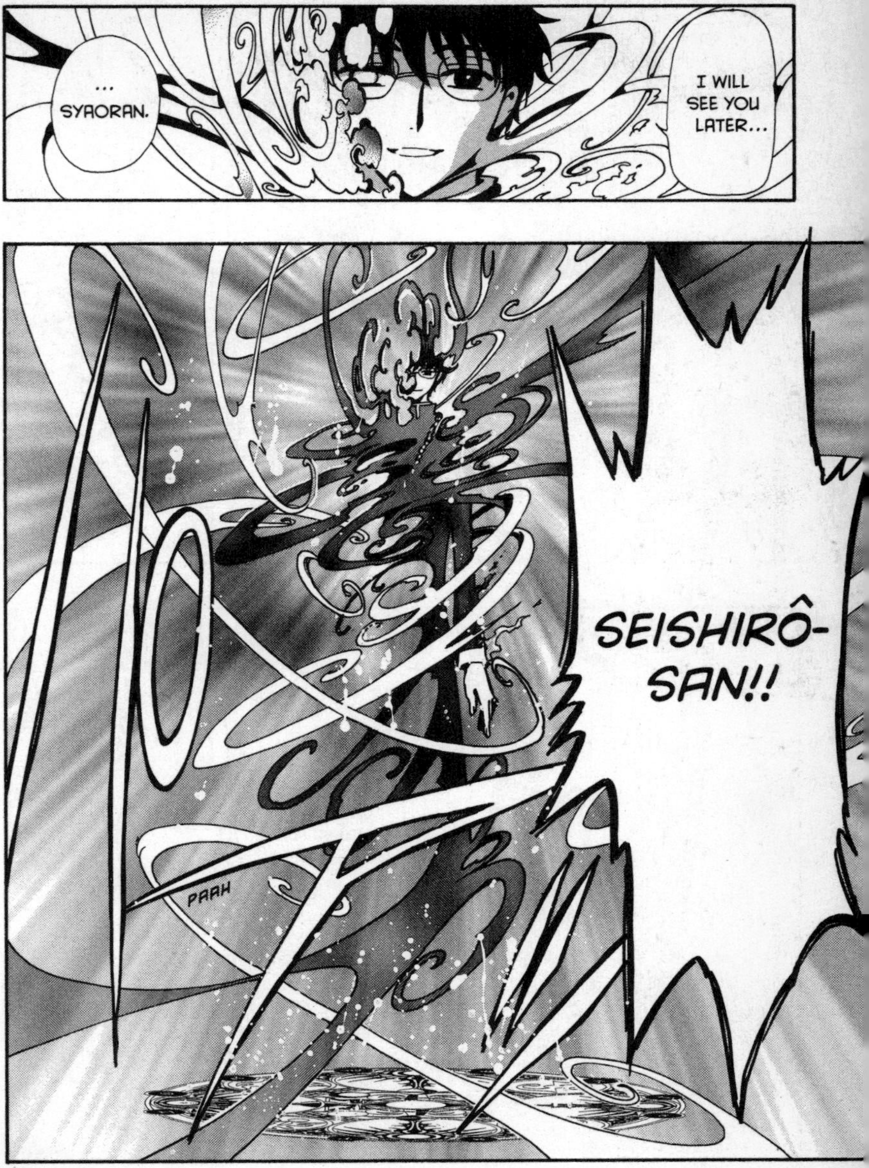
I WILL SEE YOU LATER...
... SYAORAN.
SEISHIRÔ-SAN!!
PAAH

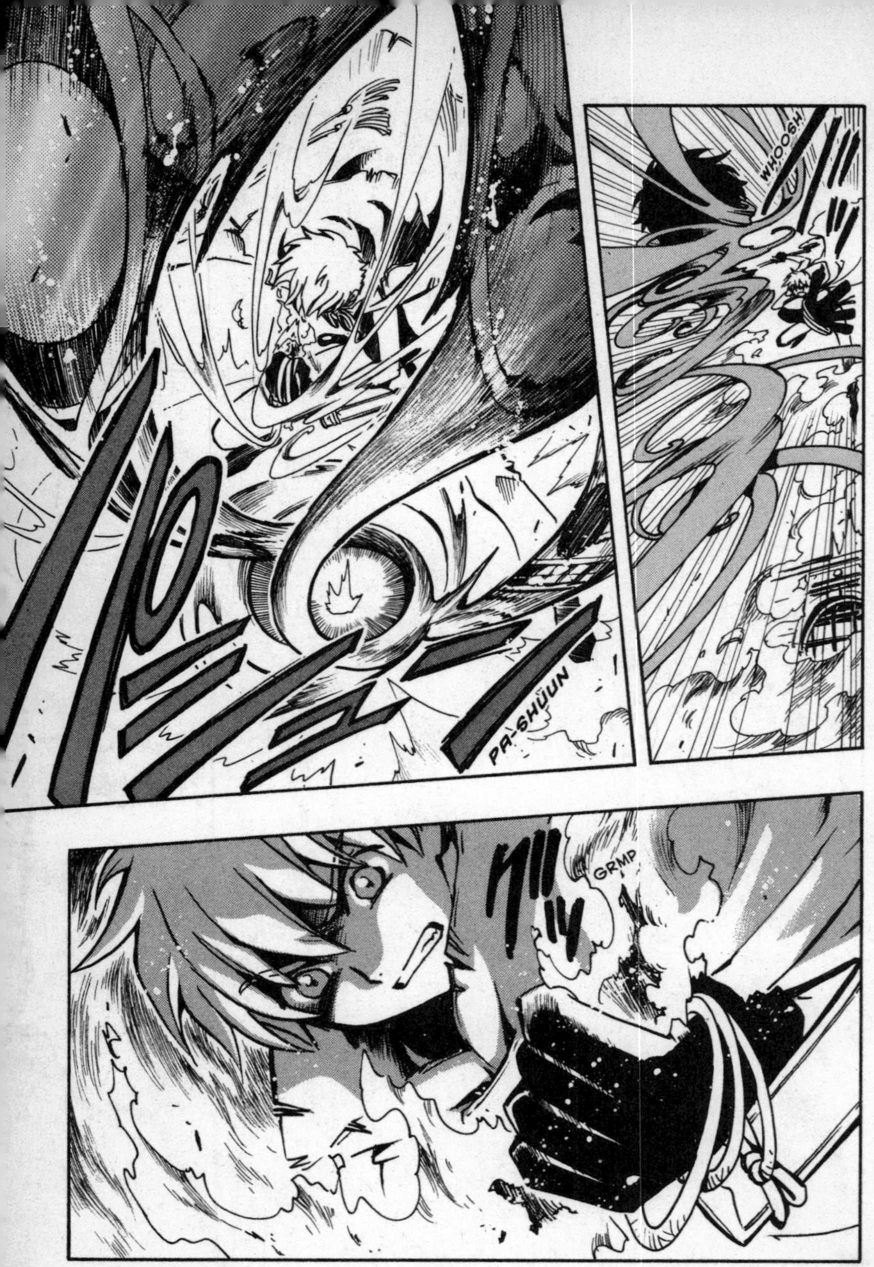
WHOOSH
PA-SHUUN
GRMP

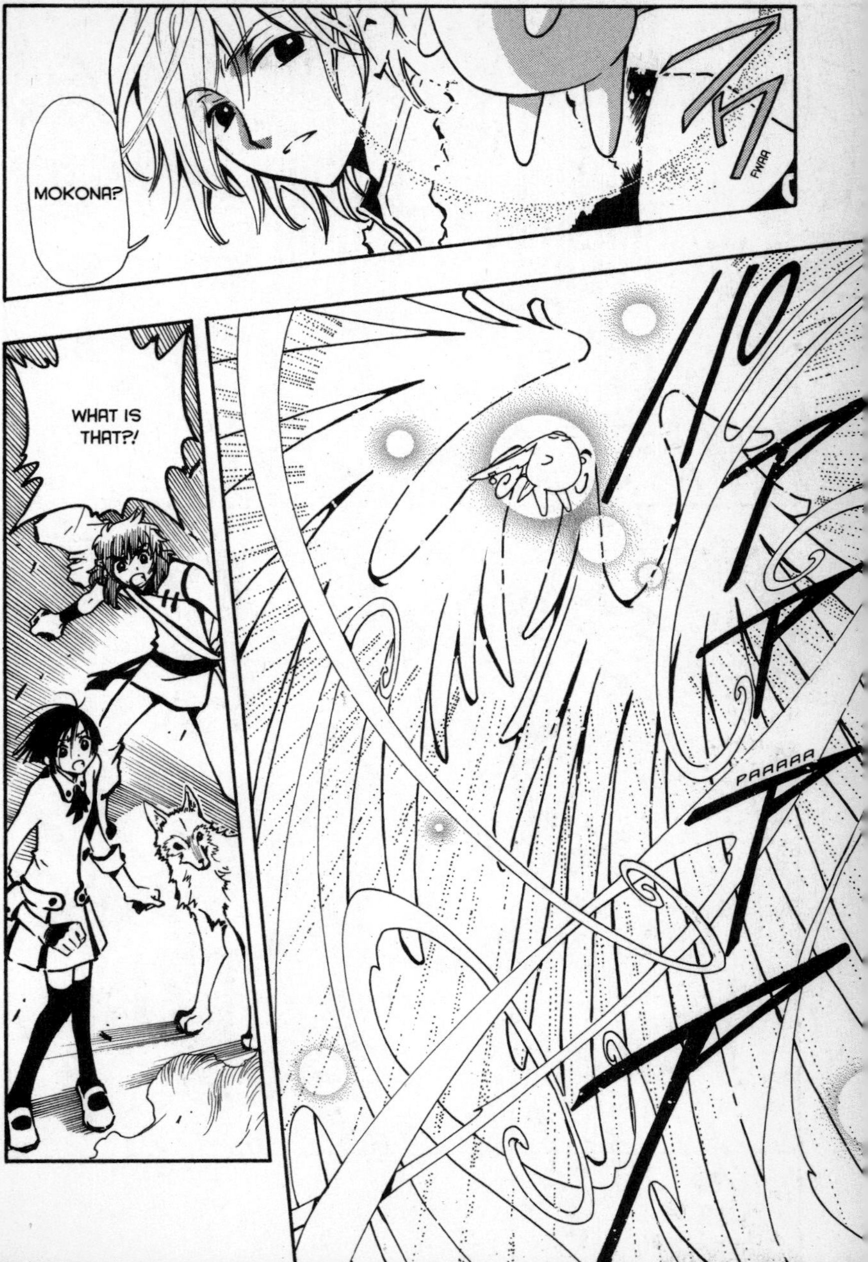
FWAA
MOKONA?
PAAAAA
WHAT IS THAT?!

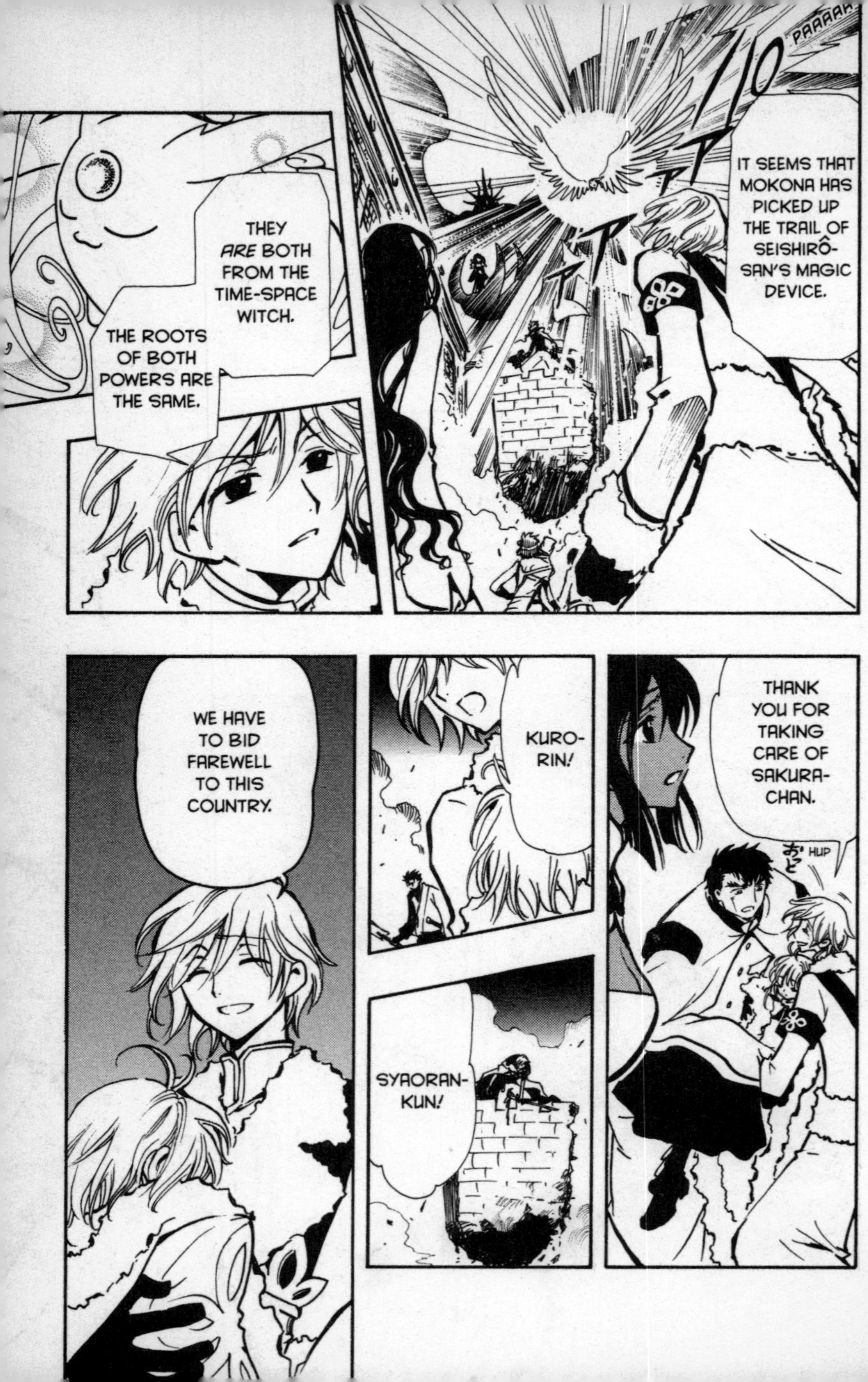
PAAAAH
IT SEEMS THAT MOKONA HAS PICKED UP THE TRAIL OF SEISHIRÔ-SAN'S MAGIC DEVICE.
THEY *ARE* BOTH FROM THE TIME-SPACE WITCH.
THE ROOTS OF BOTH POWERS ARE THE SAME.
THANK YOU FOR TAKING CARE OF SAKURA-CHAN.
HUP
KURO-RIN!
SYAORAN-KUN!
WE HAVE TO BID FAREWELL TO THIS COUNTRY.

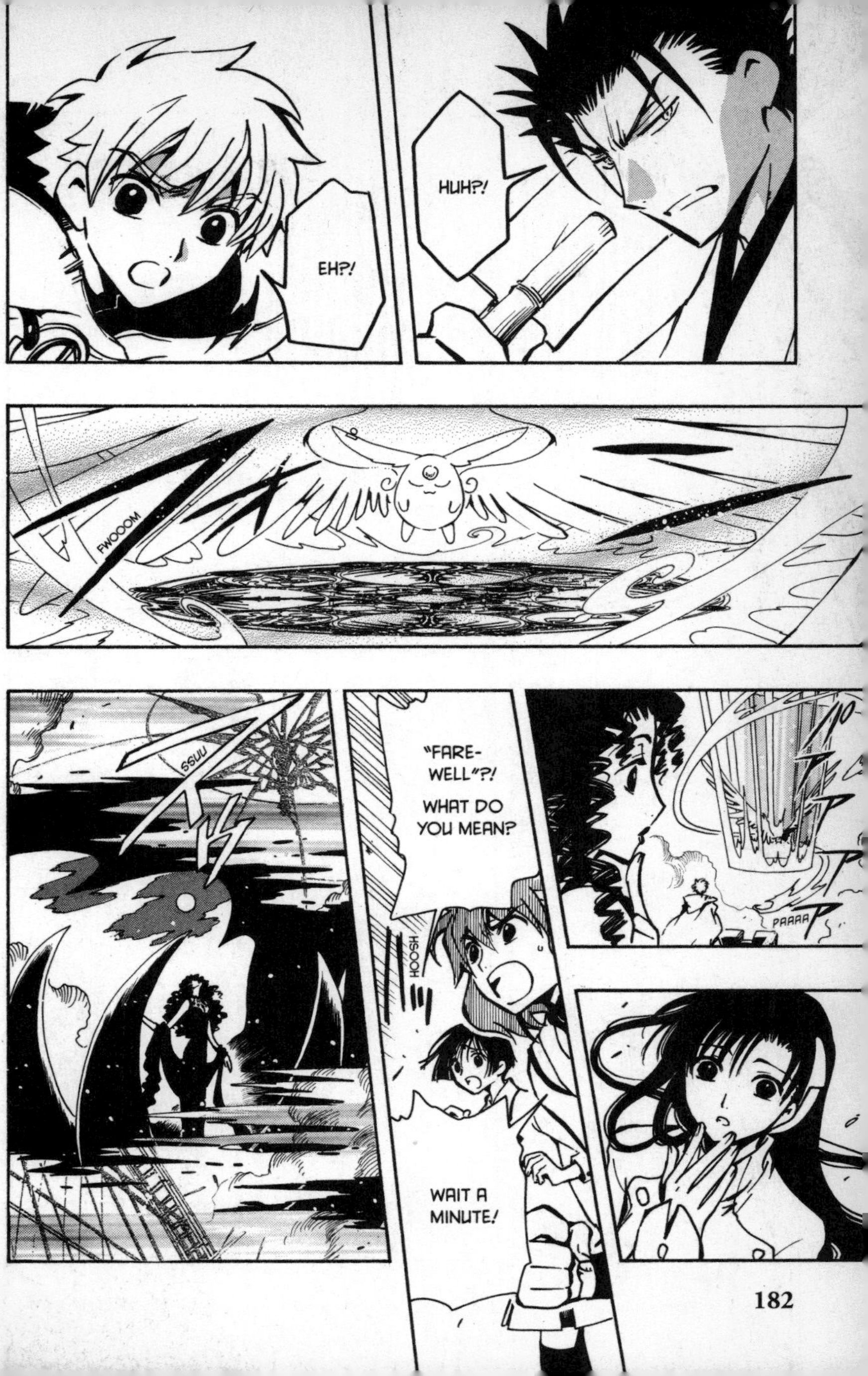
HUH?!
EH?!
FWOOOM
PAAAAP
"FARE-WELL"?!
WHAT DO YOU MEAN?
HOOSH
WAIT A MINUTE!
SSUU

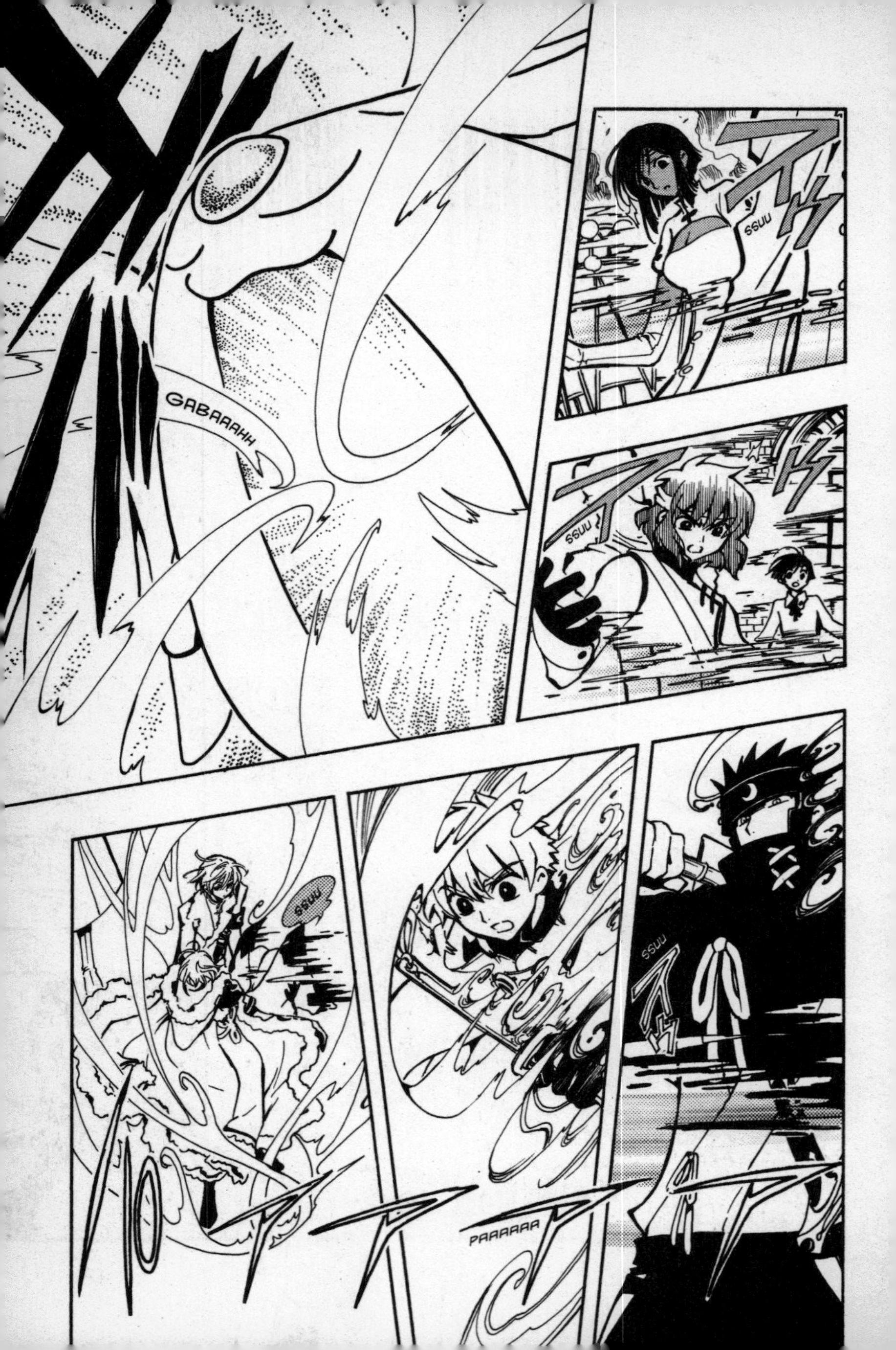
SSUU
SSUU
GABAAAHH
SSUU
SSUU
PRAAAAA

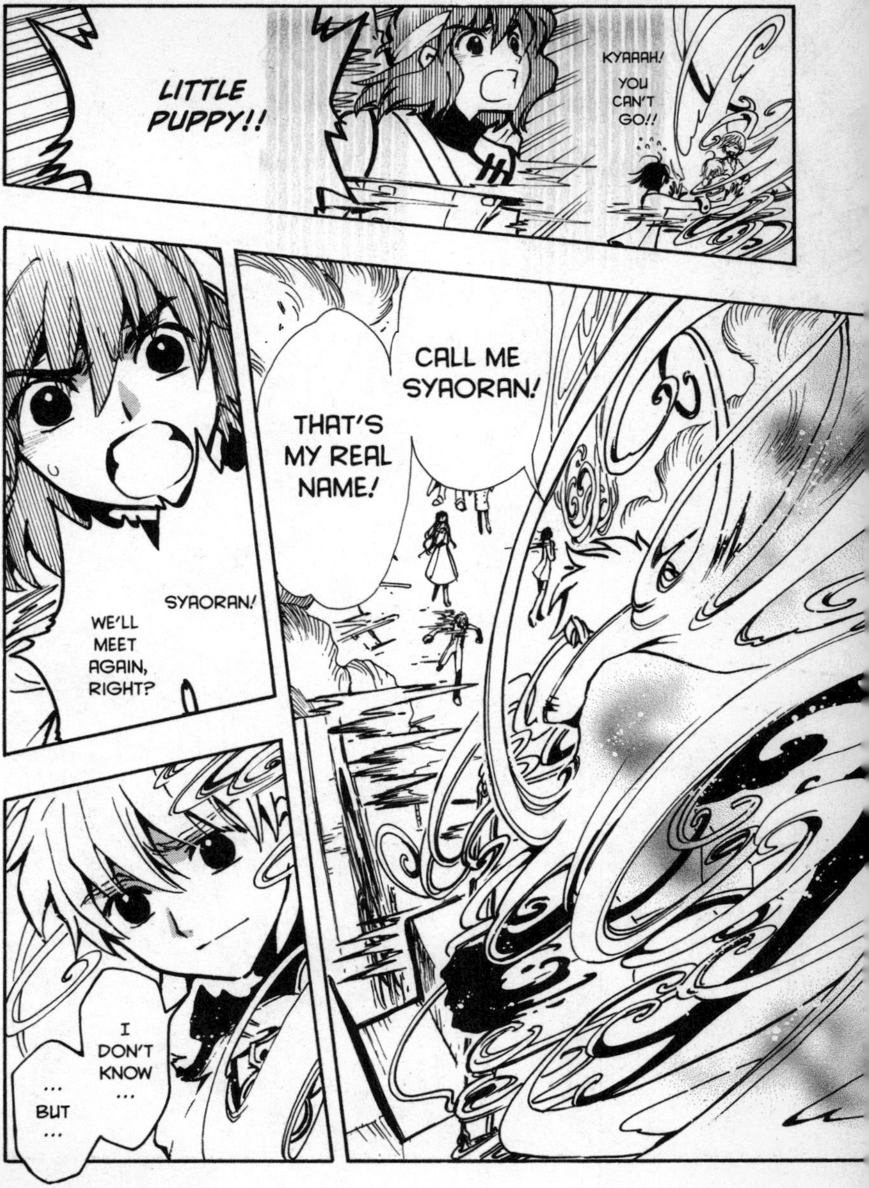
KYAAAH! YOU CAN'T GO!!
LITTLE PUPPY!!
CALL ME SYAORAN!
THAT'S MY REAL NAME!
SYAORAN!
WE'LL MEET AGAIN, RIGHT?
I DON'T KNOW...
...BUT...

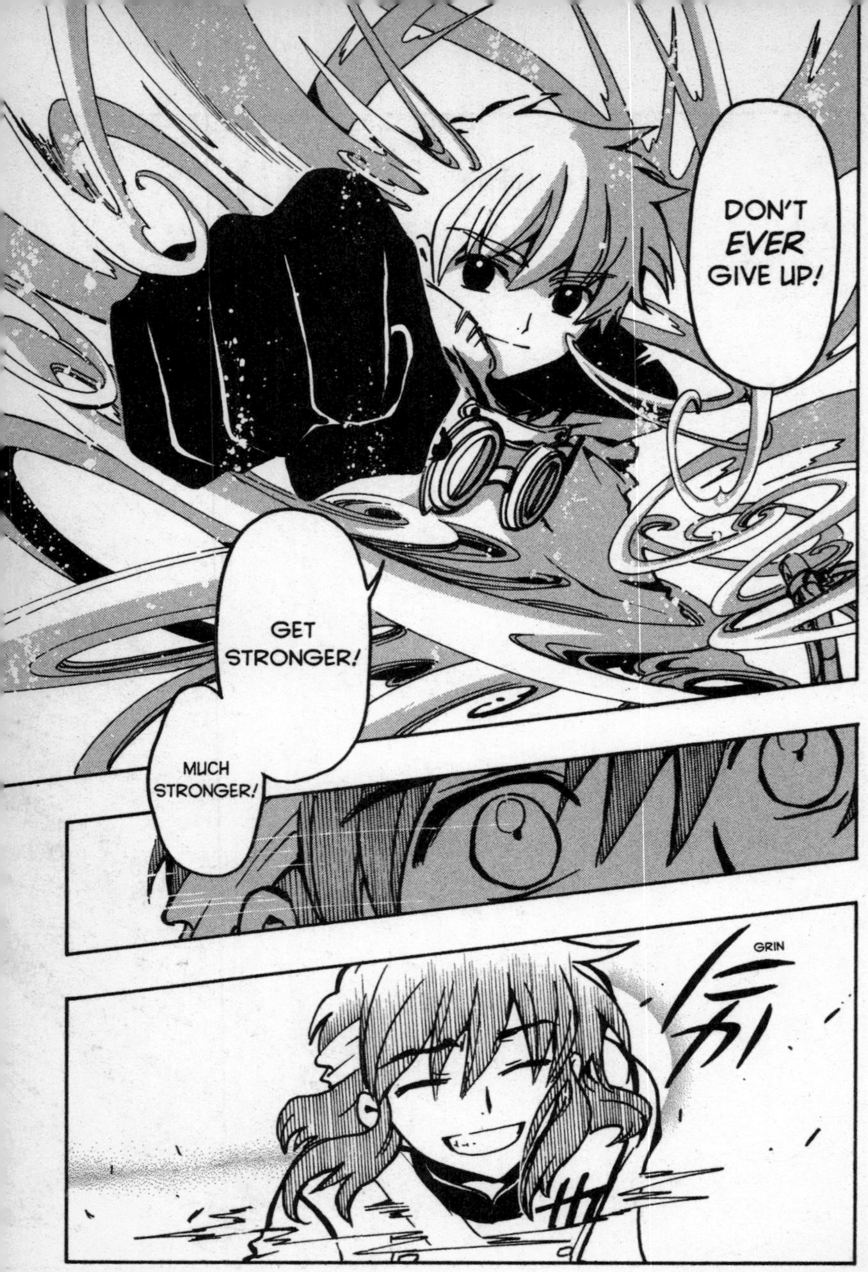
DON'T *EVER* GIVE UP!
GET STRONGER!
MUCH STRONGER!
GRIN

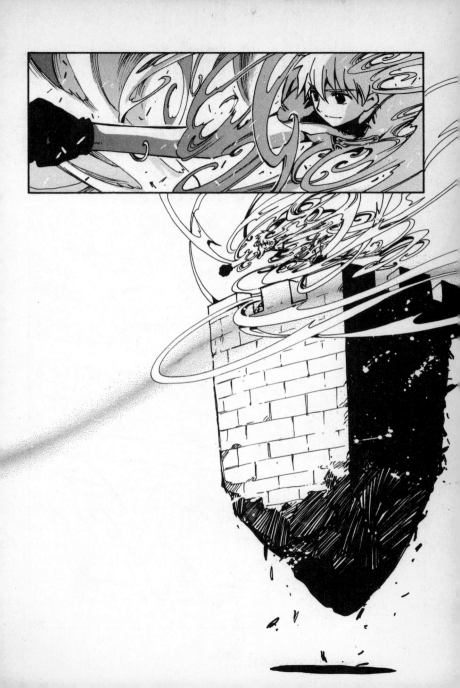

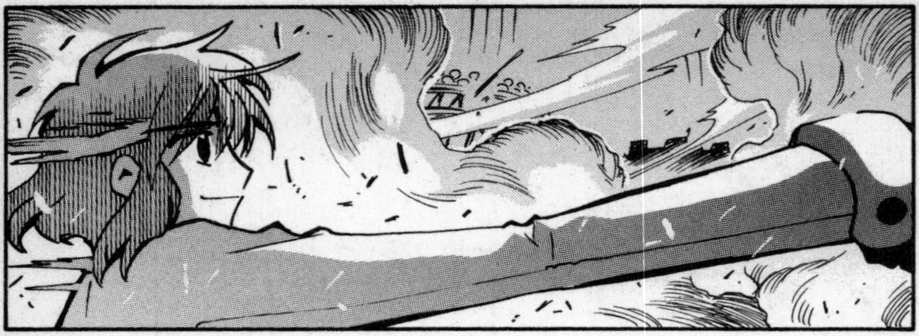

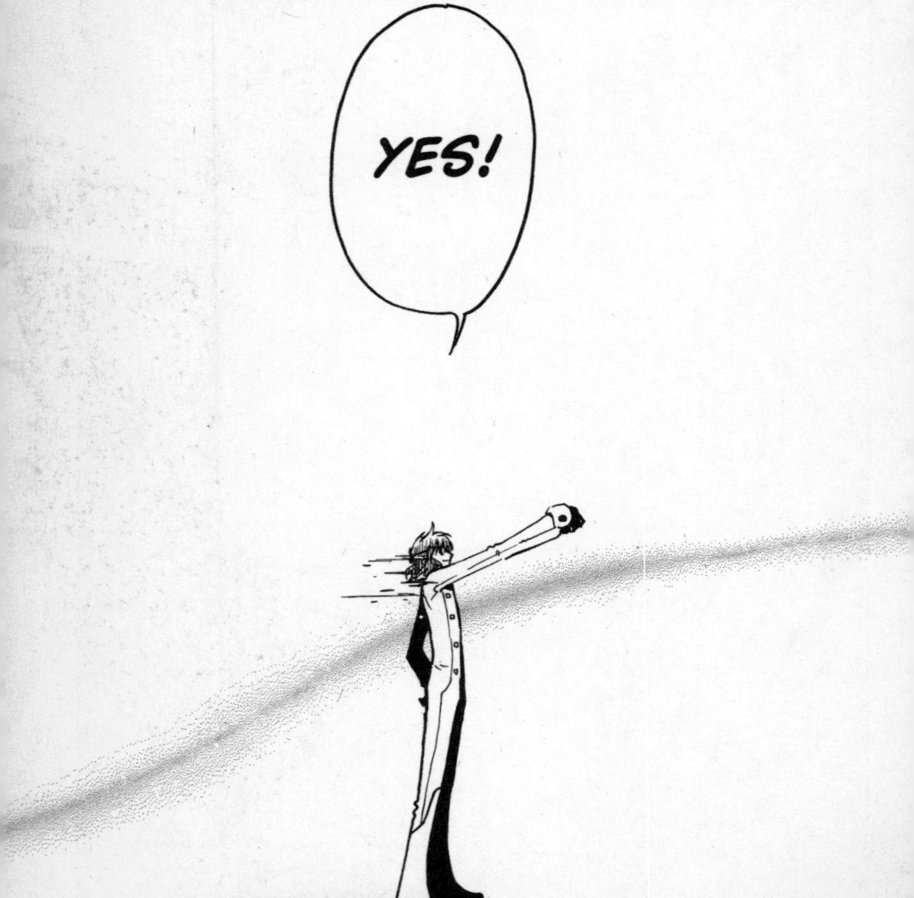
YES!

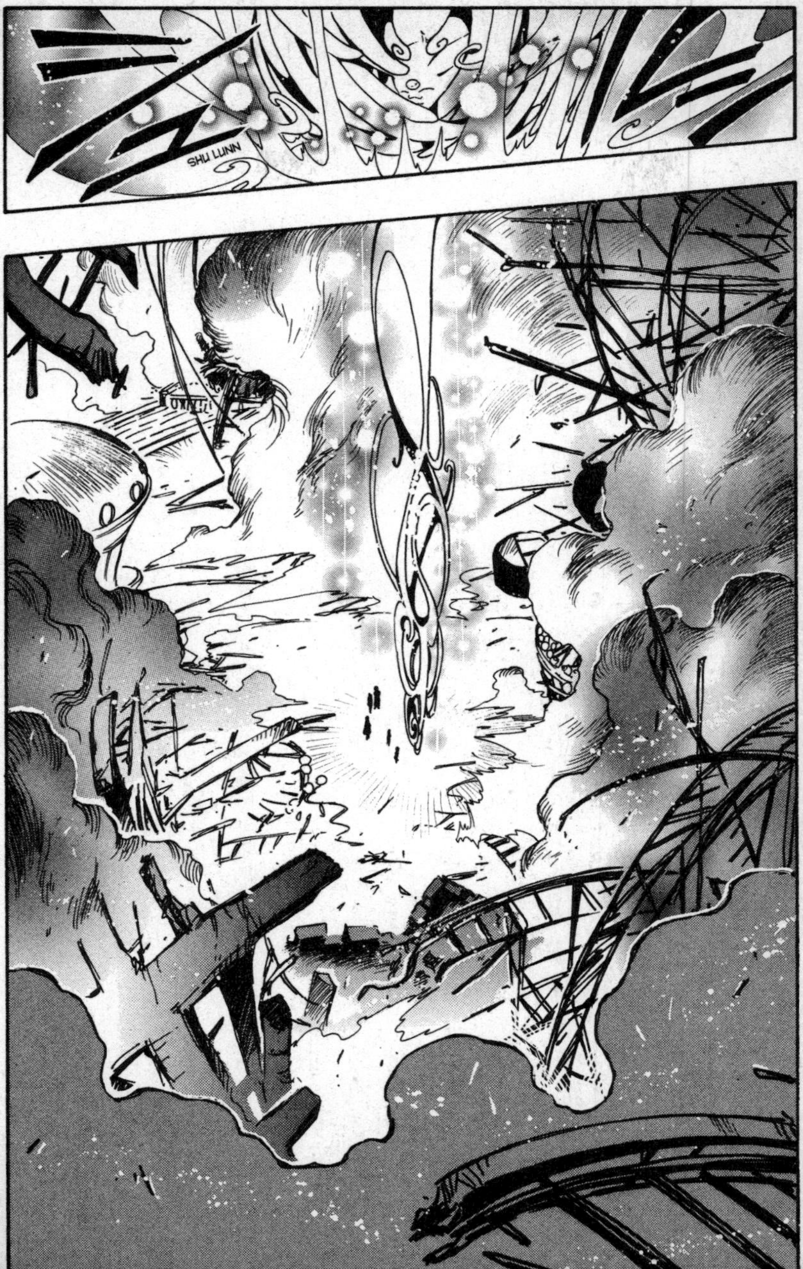
SHU LUNN

To Be Continued

About the Creators

CLAMP is a group of four women who have become the most popular manga artists in America—Ageha Ohkawa, Mokona, Satsuki Igarashi, and Tsubaki Nekoi. They started out as doujinshi (fan comics) creators, but their skill and craft brought them to the attention of publishers very quickly. Their first work from a major publisher was *RG Veda*, but their first mass success was with *Magic Knight Rayearth*. From there, they went on to write many series, including *Cardcaptor Sakura* and *Chobits*, two of the most popular manga in the United States. Like many Japanese manga artists, they prefer to avoid the spotlight, and little is known about them personally.

CLAMP is currently publishing three series in Japan: *Tsubasa* and *xxxHOLiC* with Kodansha and *Gohou Drug* with Kadokawa.

Translation Notes

Japanese is a tricky language for most Westerners, and translation is often more art than science. For your edification and reading pleasure, here are notes on some of the places where we could have gone in a different direction in our translation of the work, or where a Japanese cultural reference is used.

Just to catch you up . . .

The country of Ôto is based on the romantic notion of early twentieth-century Japan, where the traditional feudal Japanese lifestyle still mixed with strong Western influences. The enemies, oni, are ranked in a system known to the Japanese as Iroha, a way of counting that might be compared to counting in English using "Eenie meanie minie moe," but with more historical and poetic relevance (see more on Iroha in the notes from Volume 5). The ranking of oni start with I, which is the highest, down to To, which is the lowest. Each rank has a level with 1 being the highest and 5 being the lowest. Thus we have:

Rank	
I	levels 5 to 1
Ro	levels 5 to 1
Ha	levels 5 to 1
Ni	levels 5 to 1
Ho	levels 5 to 1
He	levels 5 to 1
To	levels 5 to 1

Cyclone Cuts, page 25

The vacuum of a tornado can cause multiple cuts on exposed skin. This in Japanese is called *kamaitachi*, and is an effect that is often duplicated in fictional swordplay in which the swordsman represents the whirlwind and the multiple cuts are caused by the sword.

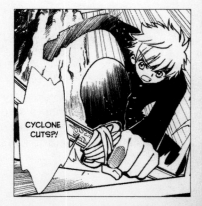

CYCLONE CUTS?!

Auras, page 29

The presence of distinctive life-force auras (usually described as *chi* in Chinese and *ki* in Japanese) is prevalent in the martial arts, but also in healing techniques originally imported from China but developed in Japan. Such familiar concepts as shiatsu massage are methods of channeling *ki* to promote well-being. One less familiar technique is *reiki* (spelled with the characters for spirit and *ki*), of which practitioners are said to be able to see or sense a person's *ki*.

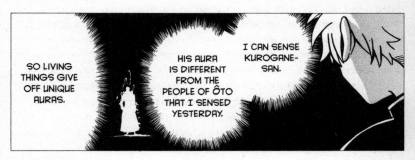

I CAN SENSE KUROGANE-SAN.
HIS AURA IS DIFFERENT FROM THE PEOPLE OF ÔTO THAT I SENSED YESTERDAY.
SO LIVING THINGS GIVE OFF UNIQUE AURAS.

Little People, page 61

Although the Tower of the Little People uses the word *kobito*, it becomes obvious that the little people in question are part of a drawing style that's come to be known as *chibi* (slang for little) or SD (which originally stood for Super Deformed). Both in America and Japan, the height of a drawn character is measured in heads. You

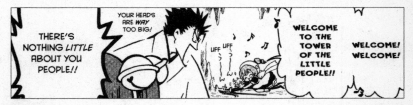

WELCOME! WELCOME!
WELCOME TO THE TOWER OF THE LITTLE PEOPLE!!
UFF UFF
YOUR HEADS ARE *WAY* TOO BIG!
THERE'S NOTHING *LITTLE* ABOUT YOU PEOPLE!!

take the height of the character's head and measure it against the body. In American comics, most characters are around eight heads tall, a trait which emphasizes nobility. Normal humans are seven to seven and a half heads tall. Manga characters can be about five

heads tall. *Chibi* characters range from three and a half heads (like Sumomo and Kotoko) to about two, where the head is as big as the entire body. But as CLAMP emphasizes, *chibi* doesn't necessarily mean tiny these days.

Fairy Park, page 90

Fairy Park may seem inspired by America's amusement parks such as the Disney parks and Six Flags chain, but the inspiration for Fairy Park may be local to Japan. North Asia is second only to North America for the number and attendance of theme parks. Japan has about thirty large amusement parks with attendance of over a million guests per year, and an equal number of medium-sized parks with an annual attendance of 500,000 guests. Overall the industry accounts for 75 million attendees and $1.5 billion in annual revenues—about 30 percent of the U.S. figures in a country that's only as large as California. (figures circa 1998)

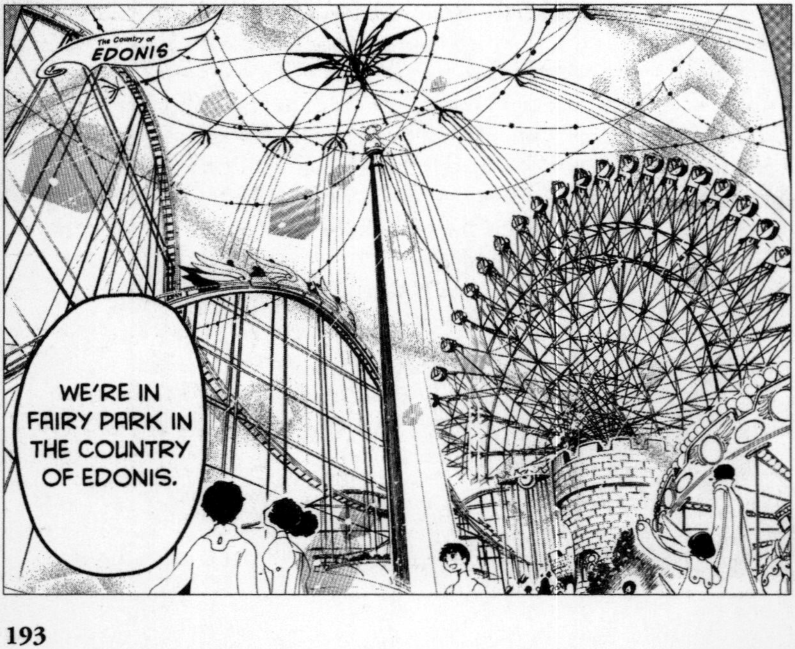
The Country of
EDONIS
WE'RE IN FAIRY PARK IN THE COUNTRY OF EDONIS.

Edonis, page 91

There are several variations of the pronunciations possible for the katakana characters representing the name of the country: e-do-ni-su. Since "do" can represent "do" or "d" and "su" can represent "su" or "s," the possible pronunciations could be, "Edonisu," "Edonis," "Ednisu," or "Ednis." Since the characters are furigana (pronunciation guides) for a Japanese kanji combination for "Cherry Blossom," the first task was to check a bunch of foreign-language dictionaries to see if any language had a word like Edonisu for Cherry Blossom. No luck. (To be fair, we didn't check every language—there are three thousand languages in the world—but we checked many of the major ones.) So the next step was to check what meanings could be found for the possible pronunciations. Ednis is a place in Ireland; the Sindarin (*The Lord of the Rings* elvish) word for gray; an information technology anagram; and a bunch of last names. "Ednisu" turned up basically nothing. "Edonisu" is used on certain Tsubasa fan websites. But "Edonis" produced some results. The closest to "cherry blossom" is Edonis: a small, sweet dessert melon. But the melon is also called "Charentais" which could be confused with "cherry." Could that be where CLAMP got the name? Another thing with the name Edonis is a super-fast Italian car with its name taken from the Greek *adônis*, which means pleasure. Edonis is a location in Macedonia, too. And finally, Edonis is also found on many fan websites of Tsubasa as the name of this country. I went with the majority vote of fan sites, but if anyone has the true etymology of the name of this country, we'd love to hear it!

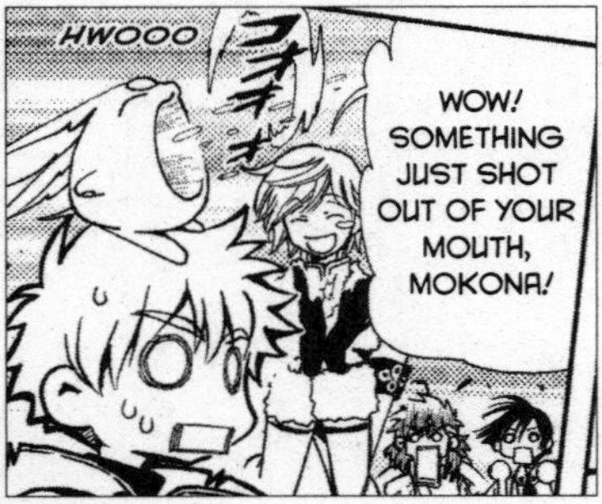
HWOOO
WOW! SOMETHING JUST SHOT OUT OF YOUR MOUTH, MOKONA!

The Arrow, page 144

Readers of *xxxHOLiC* will know that the arrow came from the Time-Space Witch, Yûko Ishihara, to remind our travelers that she expects them to send her a present for White Day, and she's getting very impatient!

Preview of Volume 8

We're pleased to present you a preview from Volume 8. This volume is available in English now.

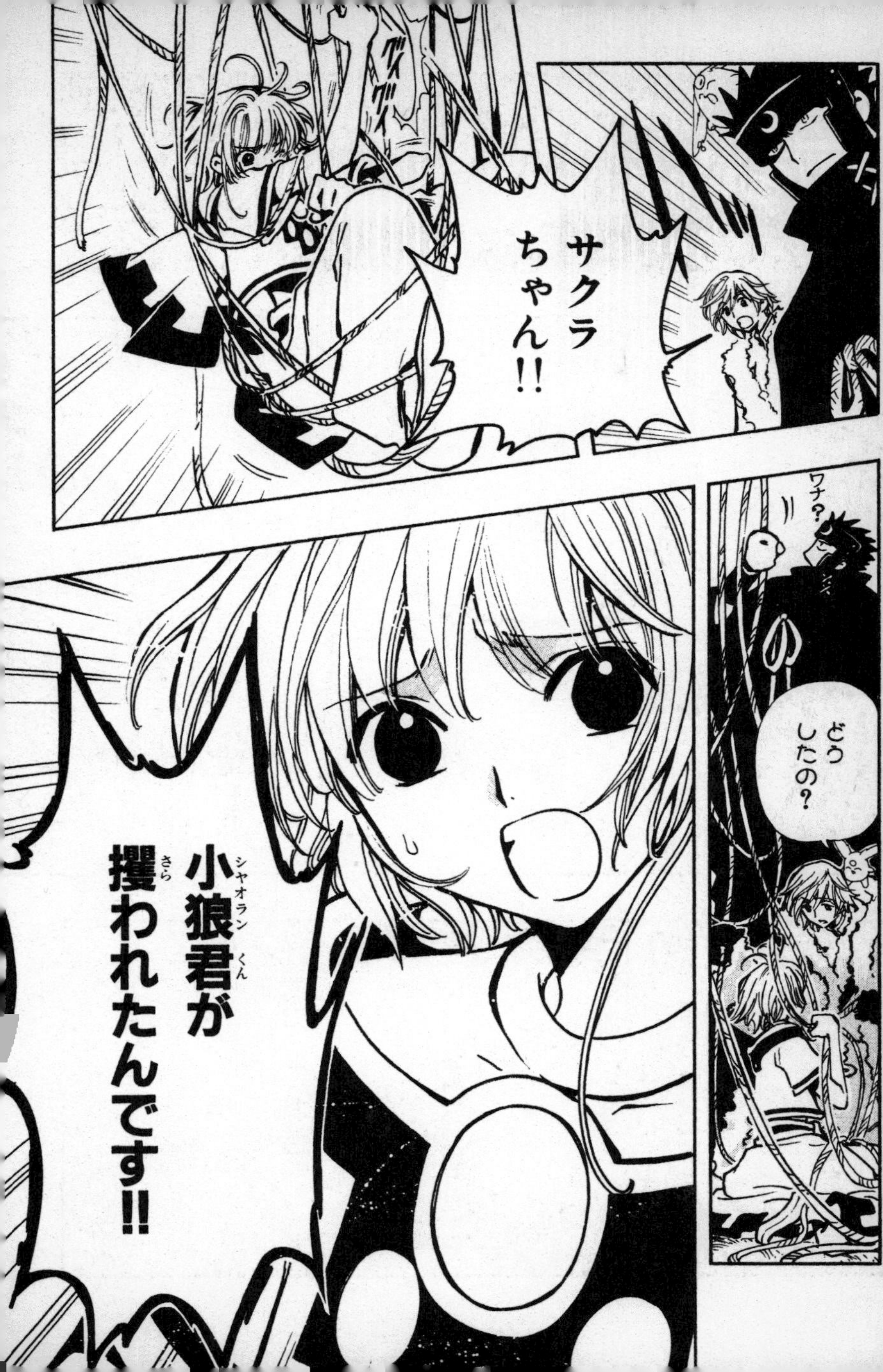
グイグイ
サクラちゃん!!
ワナ?
どうしたの?
小狼君が攫われたんです!!

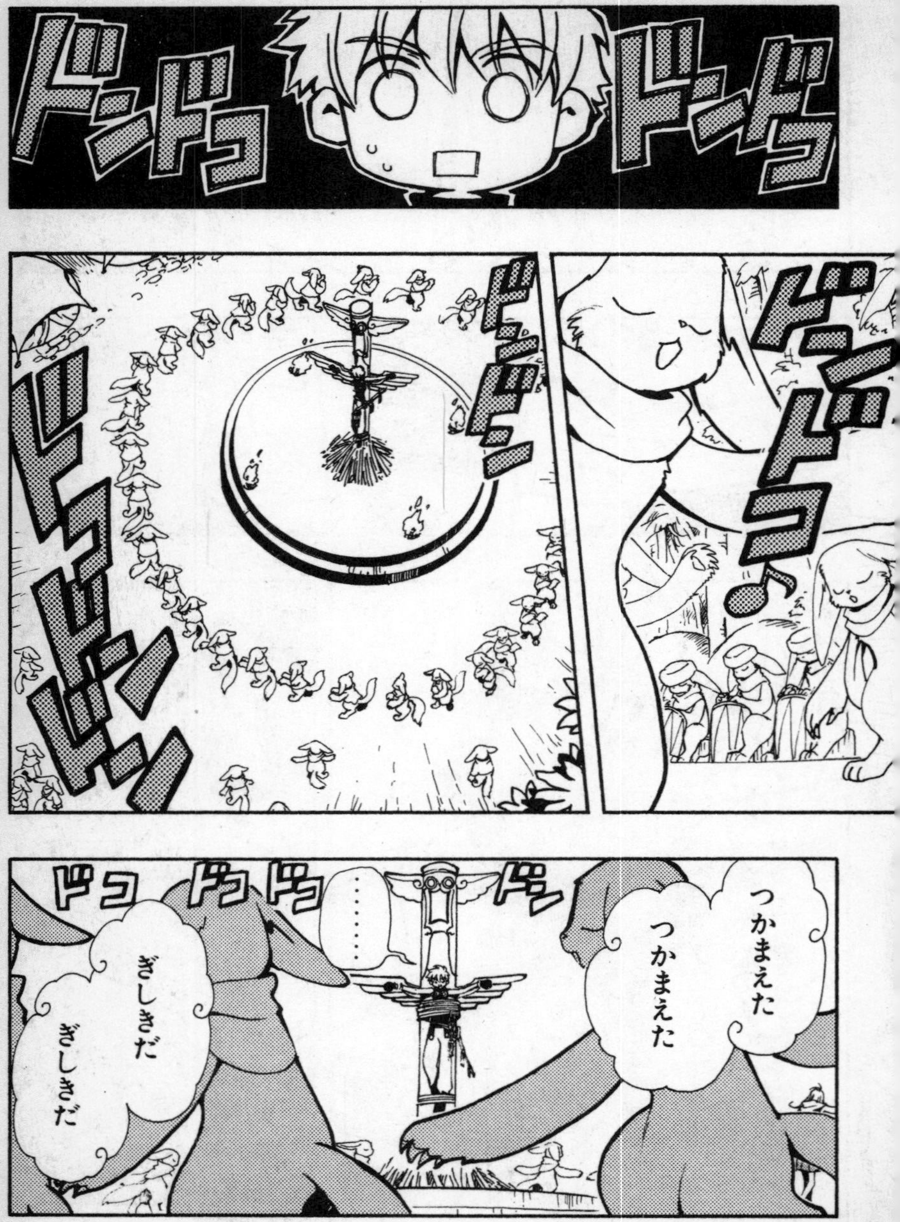

ドンドコ
ドンドコ
ドンドンドコ♪
ドンドン
ドコドンドン
ドン
つかまえた
つかまえた
……
ドコドコ
ドコ
ぎしきだ
ぎしきだ

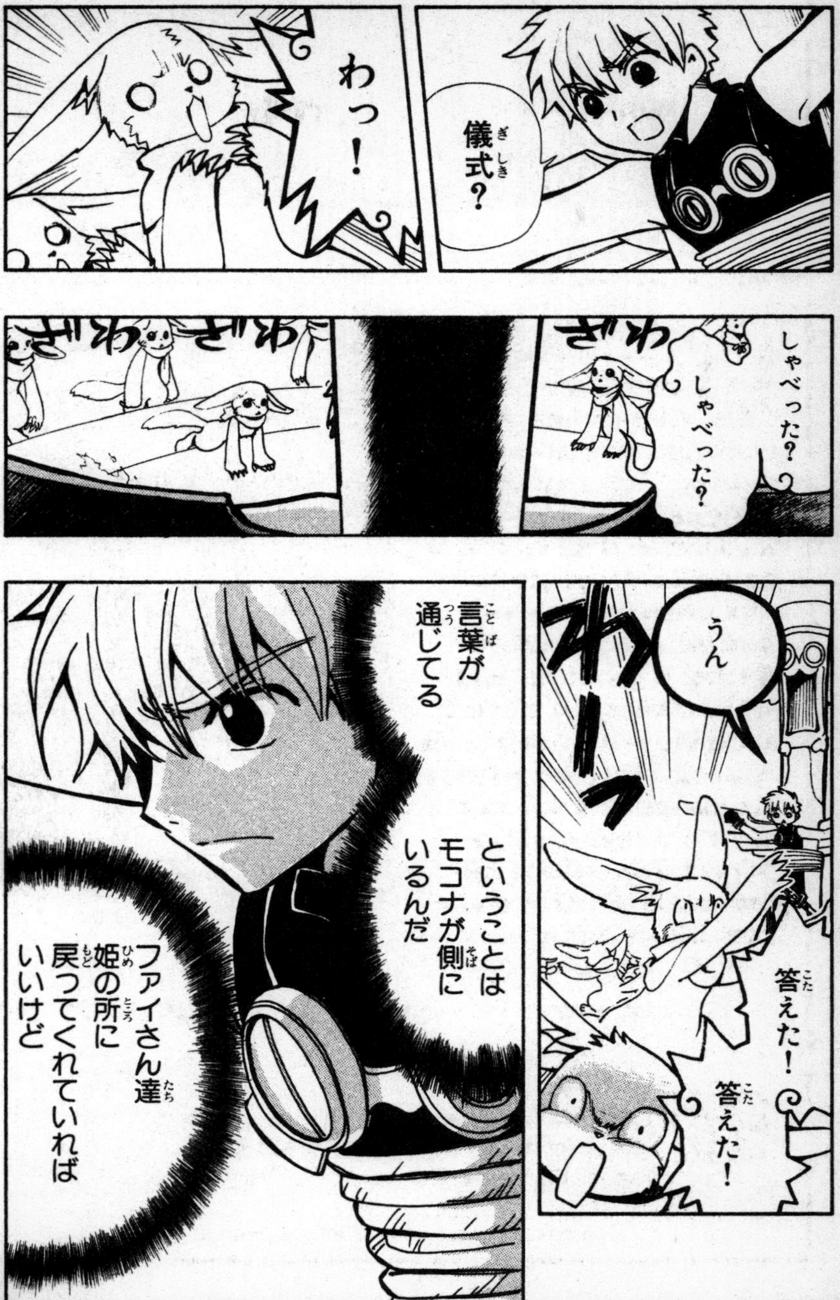
儀式？
わっ！
しゃべった？
しゃべった？
ざわ
ざわ ざわ
うん
わーっ
答えた！
答えた！
言葉が通じてる
ということはモコナが側にいるんだ
ファイさん達姫の所に戻ってくれていればいいけど

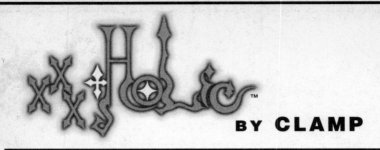

BY CLAMP

Watanuki Kimihiro is haunted by visions. When he finds himself irresistibly drawn into a shop owned by Yûko, a mysterious witch, he is offered the chance to rid himself of the spirits that plague him. He accepts, but soon realizes that he's just been tricked into working for the shop to pay off the cost of Yûko's services! But this isn't any ordinary kind of shop . . . In this shop, Yûko grants wishes to those in need. But they must have the strength of will not only to truly understand their need, but to give up something incredibly precious in return.

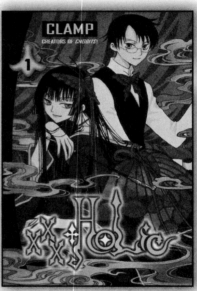

Ages: 13 +

Special extras in each volume! Read them all!

Sugar Sugar Rune

BY MOYOCO ANNO

QUEEN OF HEARTS

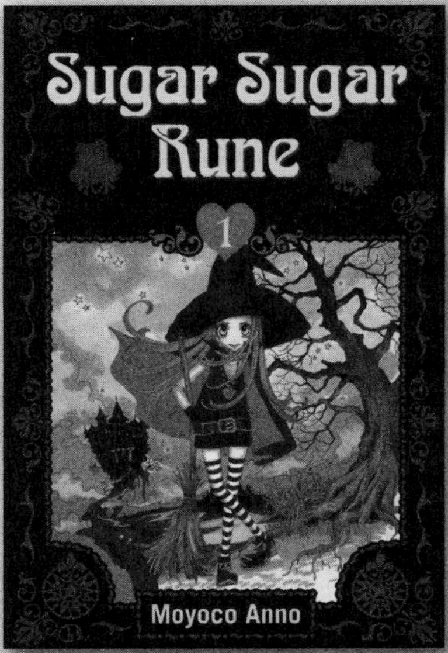
Sugar Sugar Rune
1
Moyoco Anno

Chocolat and Vanilla are young witch princesses from a magical land. They've come to Earth to compete in a contest—whichever girl captures the most hearts will become queen! While living in a boarding school, they must make as many boys fall in love with them as possible if they want to achieve their goal. Standing against them are a pair of rival princes looking to capture their hearts because they want to be king!

There's danger for the witch-girls, though: If they give their hearts to a human, they may never return to the Magical World....

Ages: 10 +

Special extras in each volume! Read them all!

DEL REY

VISIT WWW.DELREYMANGA.COM TO:

- View release date calendars for upcoming volumes
- Sign up for Del Rey's free manga e-newsletter
- Find out the latest about new Del Rey Manga series

Guru Guru Pon-Chan

BY SATOMI IKEZAWA

WINNER OF THE KODANSHA MANGA OF THE YEAR AWARD!

Ponta is a normal Labrador Retriever puppy, the Koizumi family's pet. Full of energy, she is always up to some kind of trouble. However, when Grandpa Koizumi, a passionate amateur inventor, creates the "Guru Guru Bone," which empowers animals with human speech, Ponta turns into a human girl!

Ponta dashes out into the street and is saved by Mirai Iwaki, the most popular boy at school! Her heart pounds and her face flushes. Why does she feel this way? Can there be love between a human and a dog?

The effects of the "Guru Guru Bone" are not permanent, and Ponta turns back and forth between dog and girl.

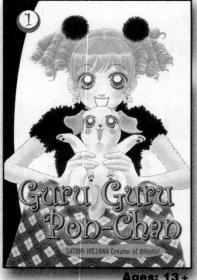

Ages: 13 +

Special extras in each volume! Read them all!

VISIT WWW.DELREYMANGA.COM TO:
- View release date calendars for upcoming volumes
- Sign up for Del Rey's free manga e-newsletter
- Find out the latest about new Del Rey Manga series

TOMARE!

[STOP!]

You're going the wrong way!

Manga is a completely different type of reading experience.

To start at the *beginning*, go to the *end*!

That's right! Authentic manga is read the traditional Japanese way—from right to left. Exactly the *opposite* of how American books are read. It's easy to follow: Just go to the other end of the book, and read each page—and each panel—from right side to left side, starting at the top right. Now you're experiencing manga as it was meant to be.